UNRIDDLING THE EXETER RIDDLES

THE PENNSYLVANIA STATE UNIVERSITY PRESS
UNIVERSITY PARK, PENNSYLVANIA

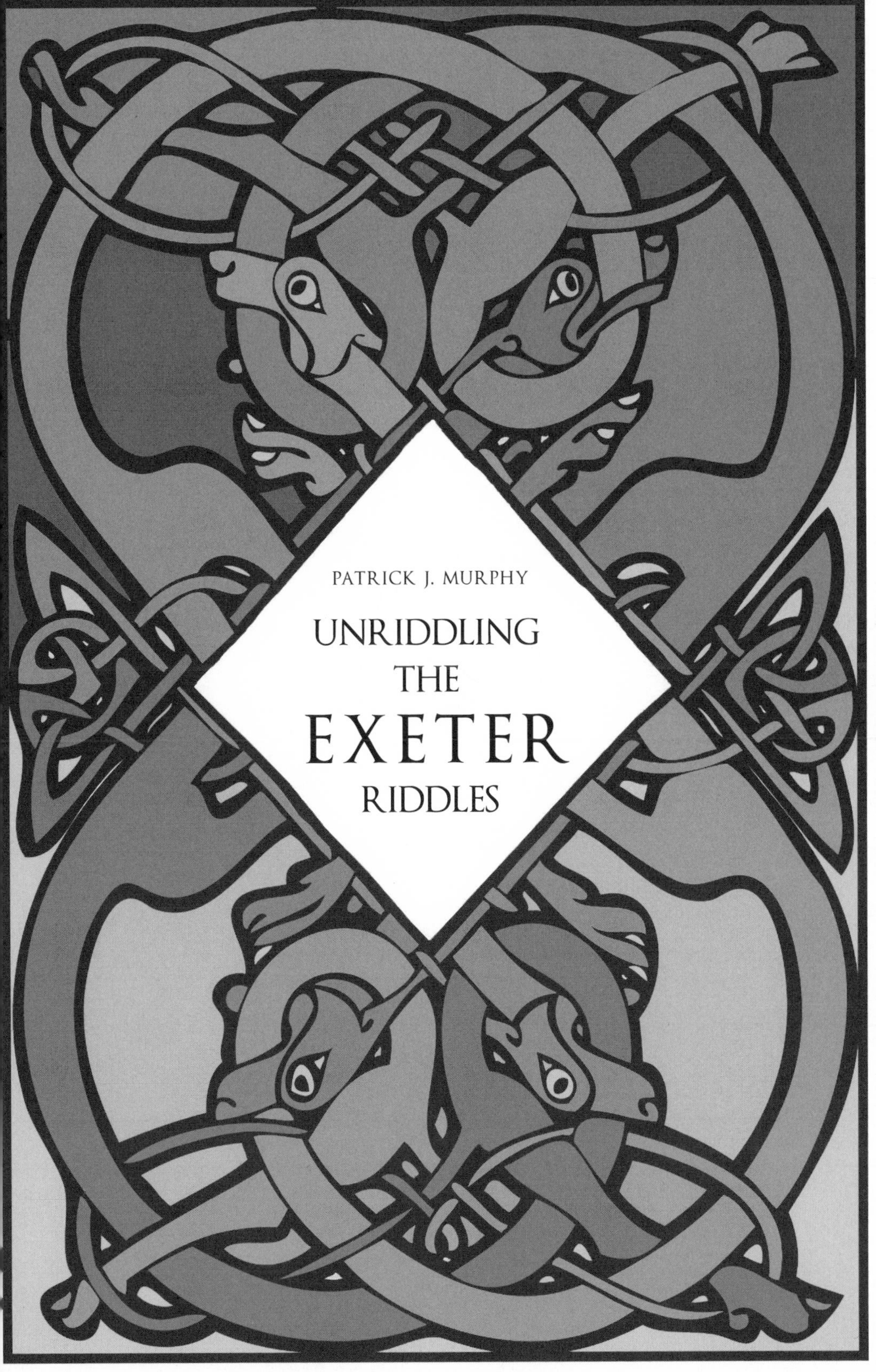
PATRICK J. MURPHY
UNRIDDLING
THE
EXETER
RIDDLES

Portions of this work have appeared in Patrick J. Murphy, "Bocstafas: A Literal Reading of Exeter Book Riddle 57," *Philological Quarterly* 84, no. 2 (2005): 139–60; "The Riders of the Celestial Wain in Exeter Book Riddle 22," *Notes and Queries* 251, no. 4 (2006): 401–7; and "*Leo ond Beo:* Exeter Book Riddle 17 as Samson's Lion," *English Studies* 88, no. 4 (2007): 371–87 (reprinted by permission of the publisher, Taylor & Francis Ltd., http://www.tandf.co.uk/journals).

LIBRARY OF CONGRESS CATALOGING-IN-PUBLICATION DATA

Murphy, Patrick J.
Unriddling the exeter riddles / Patrick J. Murphy.
p. cm.
Summary: "Examines the Old English riddles found in the tenth-century Exeter Book manuscript, with particular attention to their relationship to larger traditions of literary and traditional riddling"—Provided by publisher.
Includes bibliographical references and index.
ISBN 978-0-271-04841-3 (cloth : alk. paper)
1. Exeter book.
2. Riddles, English (Old)—History and criticism.
3. English poetry—Old English, ca. 450–1100—History and criticism.
4. Riddles in literature.
I. Title.

PR1764.M75 2011
829′.109—dc22
2010044080

Printed in the United States of America
Published by The Pennsylvania State University Press,
University Park, PA 16802–1003

It is the policy of The Pennsylvania State University Press to use acid-free paper. Publications on uncoated stock satisfy the minimum requirements of American National Standard for Information Sciences—Permanence of Paper for Printed Library Material, ANSI Z39.48–1992.

This book is printed on Natures Natural, which contains 50% post-consumer waste.

FOR *Nora and Nicole*

CONTENTS

ACKNOWLEDGMENTS

I would like to thank all those who supported and advised me during the writing of this book. I am very grateful to John D. Niles, at the University of Wisconsin, for his guidance at every stage of this project. At Wisconsin I was also fortunate to study under A. N. Doane, whose advice and insight have improved this book. I am likewise grateful to Sherry L. Reames and Carole E. Newlands, who provided me with generous help from my earliest drafts to my latest revisions. Lisa H. Cooper has been a great mentor, and this book would probably not exist were it not for her encouragement. Fred Porcheddu first introduced me to Old English and the Exeter riddles while I was an undergraduate at Denison University. He continues to be a very dear friend.

Countless others have offered me expert advice and useful suggestions as I worked on this project. In particular, I would like to thank Andrea Benton, Kristin Funk-Neubauer, Katharine Gillespie, Britton Harwood, Matthew T. Hussey, Garrett Jacobsen, Katherine Lynch, and Brian O'Camb. I would also like to thank Eleanor H. Goodman and the rest of those at Penn State University Press who helped bring this book into print. My fine copyeditor, Suzanne Wolk, saved me from many errors. All the rest are my own.

Finally, I would like to thank my family for their support. I am lucky to have such a wonderful mother, father, and sister. Writing a book takes time, and some of that time was taken away from my wife, Nicole, and my daughter, Nora. So this book is for them, with love.

INTRODUCTION

This book is about the ninety-odd literary riddles, all but one composed in Old English, included in Exeter, Cathedral Library MS. 3501 ("the Exeter Book"), a neatly written poetic miscellany that has been dated by its most recent editor to circa AD 965–975.[1] The dialect is predominantly West Saxon, and the manuscript may have been produced in a West Saxon center of learning such as Crediton, Glastonbury, or possibly Exeter itself.[2] The book has resided in Exeter at least from the death in 1072 of Leofric, Bishop of Exeter, in whose list of donations to the cathedral library we find mentioned "an mycel Englisc

1. Bernard J. Muir, ed., *The Exeter Anthology of Old English Poetry,* vols. 1–2 (Exeter: University of Exeter Press, 2000), 1:1. Patrick W. Conner, *Anglo-Saxon Exeter: A Tenth-Century Cultural History* (Woodbridge, Suffolk, UK: Boydell Press, 1993), 48–94, dates the Exeter Book somewhat earlier on paleographical grounds: "A close analysis of its script suggests that the 'Exeter Book' began to be written probably after 950 and before 968" (94).

2. For the case for Exeter, see Conner, *Anglo-Saxon Exeter.* Richard Gameson, "The Origin of the Exeter Book of Old English Poetry," *Anglo-Saxon England* 25 (1996): 135–85, offers a critique of Conner's conclusions and suggests Glastonbury or Canterbury as likely places of origin. Muir, *Exeter Anthology,* 1:3, judges Exeter or Crediton (Leofric moved the episcopal see from Crediton to Exeter in 1050) the most likely candidates. More recently, Robert M. Butler, "Glastonbury and the Early History of the Exeter Book," in *Old English Literature in Its Manuscript Context,* ed. Joyce Tally Lionarons (Morgantown: West Virginia University Press, 2004), 173–215, argues for Glastonbury.

boc be gehwilcum þingum on leoðwisan geworht" (one large English book on various subjects composed in verse).[3] The Exeter riddles take up more than one section of this manuscript. Riddles 1–29, 30a, and 31–59 are found on folios 101r–115r, while Riddles 61–95 are found on 124v–130v, the final section of the book. In between these two groups of riddles are a number of miscellaneous texts, including the poems known as *The Wife's Lament, Judgment Day I, Resignation, The Descent into Hell, Alms-Giving, Pharaoh, The Lord's Prayer I,* and *Homiletic Fragment II, The Husband's Message,* and *The Ruin,* as well as Riddles 30b and 60. Riddles 30a and 30b are variations of the same basic text, with a few notable differences in diction and morphology.[4]

As the titles of Riddle 30a and Riddle 30b suggest, the numbering of the Exeter riddles can be a bit confusing. In various editions and translations, several systems have been employed. Throughout this study I use the numbers of Krapp and Dobbie's ASPR edition of the Exeter Book simply for clarity, since most recent criticism employs them.[5] For the most part, however, I take my texts from Craig Williamson's excellent 1977 edition of the riddles, which numbers the collection differently.[6] Objections could be raised against any numbering system, not only because of damage to the Exeter Book and ambiguous textual divisions within the manuscript, but

3. Max Förster, "The Donations of Leofric to Exeter," in *The Exeter Book of Old English* (London: Percy Lund, Humphries, 1933), 10.

4. For Riddles 30a–b, see Roy Michael Liuzza, "The Texts of the Old English *Riddle 30*," *Journal of English and Germanic Philology* 87 (1988): 1–15; A. N. Doane, "Spacing, Placing, and Effacing: Scribal Textuality and Exeter Riddle 30a/b," in *New Approaches to Editing Old English Verse,* ed. Sarah Larratt Keefer and Katherine O'Brien O'Keeffe (Cambridge: D. S. Brewer, 1998), 45–65.

5. George Philip Krapp and Elliott van Kirk Dobbie, eds., *The Exeter Book,* ASPR 3 (New York: Columbia University Press, 1936).

6. Unless otherwise indicated, all quotations of the Exeter riddles are from Craig Williamson, ed., *The Old English Riddles of the Exeter Book* (Chapel Hill: University of North Carolina Press, 1977). In many instances important to this study, Williamson preserves manuscript readings where Krapp and Dobbie choose to emend (e.g., Riddle 13, line 6a; Riddle 22, line 16b; Riddle 25, line 10b). Moreover, Williamson's explanatory notes remain the most detailed and authoritative available for the complete Exeter riddles. Muir's 2000 edition is of course more up to date in terms of taking into account recent scholarship, but his commentary is limited: "The processes by which individual solutions have been arrived at are not discussed below, since this would involve unwarranted duplication of the work of Williamson and others" (*Exeter Anthology,* 735). Since I often have occasion to discuss such processes of solving, it seems best to use the same text as Williamson, which is nevertheless not markedly different from Muir's edition. Frederick Tupper Jr., ed., *The Riddles of the Exeter Book* (Boston: Ginn and Co., 1910), though in some ways dated, remains an invaluable resource for the study of Old English riddling. Other editions of the Exeter riddles I have consulted include Thorpe (1842), Wyatt (1912), Trautmann (1915), Mackie (1934), and Pinsker and Ziegler (1985).

also because questions remain as to which of the Exeter texts are properly to be called "riddles." Poems such as *The Husband's Message, The Wife's Lament,* and *Wulf and Eadwacer* have sometimes been interpreted as riddles, while the generic status of Riddle 60 has at times been called into question.[7] Whatever the exact number of riddles, it was probably quite close to a hundred, and many have speculated that the compiler of the Exeter Book (or the compiler of its exemplar) would have been aiming at something near a so-called century of riddles, a hundred being the traditional number of enigmas in Latin collections.[8]

The medieval paradigm for a century of literary riddles was established by the collection of Symphosius, an author who may have written his Latin enigmas sometime between the late fourth and early sixth centuries AD. Although we know virtually nothing about Symphosius's personal history, his riddles were a popular text in Anglo-Saxon England from at least the late seventh century on.[9] Even more influential were the hundred riddles written by the English scholar Aldhelm (c. 639–709), whose *Enigmata* became a favorite text both in Anglo-Saxon England and on the Continent.[10] Two of the Exeter riddles (numbers 35 and 40) are translations from Aldhelm, while others show his influence.[11] A contemporary of Aldhelm, Tatwine (d. 734),

7. For a discussion of these issues, see John D. Niles, *Old English Enigmatic Poems and the Play of the Texts* (Turnhout: Brepols, 2006), 46–48.

8. See, for instance, Andy Orchard, "Enigma Variations: The Anglo-Saxon Riddle-Tradition," in *Latin Learning and English Lore: Studies in Anglo-Saxon Literature for Michael Lapidge,* ed. Katherine O'Brien O'Keeffe and Andy Orchard, 2 vols. (Toronto: University of Toronto Press, 2005), 1:286.

9. Michael Lapidge, *The Anglo-Saxon Library* (Oxford: Oxford University Press, 2006), 334, lists four extant copies of Symphosius's *Aenigmata* from Anglo-Saxon England. For more on Symphosius, see Zoja Pavlovskis, "The Riddler's Microcosm: From Symphosius to St. Boniface," *Classica et Mediaevalia* 39 (1988): 219–51. For texts and translations, see Raymond Theodore Ohl, ed. and trans., *The Enigmas of Symphosius* (PhD diss., University of Pennsylvania, 1928).

10. For an introduction to and translation of Aldhelm's *enigmata,* see Michael Lapidge and James L. Rosier, trans., *Aldhelm: The Poetic Works* (Cambridge: D. S. Brewer, 1985), 59–94. For the text of the *enigmata* (with English translations by James Hall Pitman), see Frans Glorie, ed., *Variae collectiones aenigmatum Merovingicae aetatis* (Turnhout: Brepols, 1968), 359–540. See also Rudolf Ehwald, *Aldhelmi opera,* Monumenta Germaniae Historica: Auctores Antiquisimi 15 (Berlin: Weidmann, 1919); Nicholas Howe, "Aldhelm's Enigmata and Isidorian Etymology," *Anglo-Saxon England* 14 (1985): 37–59; Nancy Porter Stork, ed., *Through a Gloss Darkly: Aldhelm's Riddles in the British Library MS Royal 12.C.xxiii* (Toronto: Pontifical Institute of Mediaeval Studies, 1990); and Andy Orchard, *The Poetic Art of Aldhelm* (Cambridge: Cambridge University Press, 1994).

11. For more on Riddle 40, see Katherine O'Brien O'Keeffe, "The Text of Aldhelm's *Enigma* no. c in Oxford, Bodleian Library, Rawlinson C. 697 and Exeter Riddle 40," *Anglo-*

composed a group of forty Latin enigmas, while another eighth-century author known as Eusebius seems to have sought to "complete" Tatwine's collection by writing sixty more to form the century.[12] Boniface (c. 675–754) composed twenty enigmas on Christian virtues and vices (ten on each).[13] Other early medieval collections of Latin riddles are suspected to have their origin in Anglo-Saxon England, including the sixty-three "Bern Riddles" (also referred to as the *Enigmata Tullii*) and the "Lorsch Riddles," a collection of twelve riddles preserved in a single surviving manuscript.[14] Latin riddles also show up gathered together with catechism-type puzzlers and proverbs in collections such as the *Flores,* once attributed to Bede, and the *Disputatio Pippini,* a riddlic dialogue of questions and answers framed as a conversation between Alcuin (735–804) and Charlemagne's son Pippin.[15] Stray riddles are also found here and there in the manuscript record, including a text known as the Leiden Riddle (like Riddle 35, an Old English version of Aldhelm's *Lorica* "corselet" enigma, but written in an early Northumbrian dialect) and at least one Old English prose riddle.[16] Yet despite such a robust tradition of

---

Saxon England 14 (1985): 61–73. For Riddle 35, see Thomas Klein, "The Old English Translation of Aldhelm's Riddle *Lorica,*" *Review of English Studies,* n.s., 48 (1997): 345–49.

12. For texts of the enigmas of Tatwine and Eusebius (as well as an English translation by Erika von Erhardt-Siebold), see Glorie, *Variae collectiones aenigmatum,* 165–271. See also F. H. Whitman, "Aenigmata Tatwini," *Neuphilologische Mitteilungen* 88 (1987): 8–17.

13. Glorie, *Variae collectiones aenigmatum,* 273–343.

14. For the text of the Lorsch Riddles (as well as a German translation by K. J. Minst), see ibid., 345–58. For the text of the Bern Riddles (as well as a German translation by K. J. Minst), see ibid., 542–610. See also Chauncey E. Finch, "The Bern Riddles in Codex Vat. Reg. Lat. 1553," *Transactions and Proceedings of the American Philological Association* 92 (1961): 145–55.

15. See Frederick Tupper Jr., "Riddles of the Bede Tradition: The 'Flores' of Pseudo-Bede," *Modern Philology* 2 (1904): 561–72; Martha Bayless and Michael Lapidge, ed. and trans., *Collectanea Pseudo-Bedae* (Dublin: School of Celtic Studies, Dublin Institute of Advanced Studies, 1998); Thomas D. Hill, "A Riddle on the Three Orders in the *Collectanea Pseudo-Bedae*?" *Philological Quarterly* 80 (2001): 205–12; Martha Bayless, "Alcuin's *Disputatio Pippini* and the Early Medieval Riddle Tradition," in *Humour, History, and Politics in Late Antiquity and the Early Middle Ages,* ed. Guy Halsall (Cambridge: Cambridge University Press, 2001), 157–78; and James E. Cross and Thomas D. Hill, eds., *The Prose Solomon and Saturn and Adrian and Ritheus* (Toronto: University of Toronto Press, 1982).

16. For the Leiden Riddle and its relationship to Riddle 35, see Williamson, *Old English Riddles,* 243–48. See also M. B. Parkes, "The Manuscript of the Leiden Riddle," *Anglo-Saxon England* 1 (1972): 207–17; Rolf H. Bremmer Jr. and Kees Dekker, "Leiden, Universiteitsbibliotheek, Vossianus Lat. Q. 106," in *Anglo-Saxon Manuscripts in Microfiche Facsimile,* vol. 13, ed. A. N. Doane (Tempe: Arizona Center for Medieval and Renaissance Studies, 2006), 107. For the Old English prose riddle, see Max Förster, "Ein altenglisches Prosa-Rätsel," *Archive für das Studium der Neueren Sprachen und Literaturen* 115 (1905): 392–93. For stray Latin riddles in Anglo-Saxon manuscripts, see Tony Perrello, "An Undiscovered Riddle in Brussels, Bibliothèque

literary riddling in Anglo-Saxon England, the Exeter riddles are unique as an early medieval riddle collection in the vernacular.

In addition to this strong textual tradition, it is a safe guess that the Anglo-Saxons shared riddles by word of mouth. As Michael Lapidge notes, "We may be sure that popular, oral riddles were in circulation in Aldhelm's England, as they are in circulation everywhere in the world."[17] Indeed, it has often been remarked that riddling is a profoundly ancient, widespread practice and that its conventional motifs are amazingly durable in oral transmission, with numerous identical riddling conceits found in collected materials spanning centuries and crossing multiple linguistic boundaries.[18] In fact, the riddle's ubiquity and concision have made it a favorite study of folklorists, who have devoted considerable energy to analyzing its structure and social

---

Royale MS 1828–1830," *English Language Notes* 43, no. 2 (2005): 8–14; David W. Porter, "A Double Solution to the Latin Riddle in MS. Antwerp, Plantin-Moretus Museum M16.2," *American Notes and Queries* 9 (1996): 3–9; David W. Porter, "Aethelwold's Bowl and the *Chronicle of Abingdon*," *Neuphilologische Mitteilungen* 97 (1996): 163–67; and Paul Sorrell, "Alcuin's 'Comb' Riddle," *Neophilologus* 80 (1996): 311–18.

17. Lapidge and Rosier, *Aldhelm: The Poetic Works*, 62. Williamson expresses skepticism on this question: "Of course it is impossible to prove or disprove the contention that the *Riddles* in the *Exeter Book* were based on earlier speech genres, but if the tradition of riddling were widespread in England, one might expect some mention of it in the poetry and prose" (*Old English Riddles*, 23). In general, Williamson's edition stresses the originality of the Exeter riddles as poems written by "lovers of nature and of men and careful observers of the world about them" (12). This may be true, but the existence of oral traditional riddling in Anglo-Saxon England is not to be seriously doubted. Archer Taylor, "The Riddle," *California Folklore Quarterly* 2 (1943): 141, notes that "riddling is virtually universal. Orthodox anthropologists declare that American Indians do not ask riddles, but Jetté's excellent collection of Ten'a riddles seems to contradict them." Andrew Welsh, "Riddle," in *Medieval Folklore: An Encyclopedia of Myths, Legends, Tales, Beliefs, and Customs*, vol. 2, ed. Carl Lindahl, John McNamara, and John Lindow (Santa Barbara: ABC-CLIO, 2000), 824, writes: "Riddles appear in the oral traditions of nearly all human societies and are found among the oldest written records." Savely Senderovich, *The Riddle of the Riddle: A Study of the Folk Riddle's Figurative Nature* (London: Kegan Paul, 2005), surveying the enomous bibliography on the subject, notes that "the folk riddle, one of the most ancient verbal genres, is also one of the elementary types of traditional oral culture" (12).

18. Senderovich writes: "The remarkable thing is [riddling's] ubiquitousness. Even more remarkable are the affinities that have been displayed by folk riddles recorded in various cultures on different continents, notwithstanding significant differences. Collections of riddles with parallels from various languages have been known for a long time, and the second half of the 19th century witnessed the rise of comparative thought" (*Riddle of the Riddle*, 12). Barre Toelken, in *Morning Dew and Roses* (Urbana: University of Illinois Press, 1995), speculates on the durability of riddles compared to other more disposable "question-and-answer jokes": "Riddles, by contrast, are far less tied to immediate historical matrices for their content and are instead responsive to broader ongoing themes in the culture, especially those that mark liminal processes and events like maturation, marriage, and death" (105).

contexts, as well as to gathering vast collections of folk riddles for comparative study.[19] Collections such as Archer Taylor's monumental *English Riddles from Oral Tradition* draw on both the fieldwork of folklorists as well as early riddle books with roots in oral tradition to demonstrate the richness of the riddling genre.[20] Today, however, the conventional metaphors, common motifs, and patterns of traditional riddling are unknown to most English speakers, who are more likely to be familiar with the genre from the playful conundrums of children's literature or, in many cases perhaps, from reading the widely admired Exeter riddles in translation.[21]

In fact, the popularity of these poems for modern anthologies of medieval poetry means that many readers today have at least an introductory understanding of the prominent features and formulas of Old English riddling. A

19. Charles T. Scott, "On Defining the Riddle: The Problem of a Structural Unit," *Genre* 2 (1969): 129–42, notes that "the texts of riddles are characteristically short enough to investigate with a certain degree of ease and efficiency" (129). Important studies of folk riddling include numerous articles by Archer Taylor as well as Robert A. Georges and Alan Dundes, "Toward a Structural Definition of the Riddle," *Journal of American Folklore* 76 (1963): 111–18; Charles T. Scott, *Persian and Arabic Riddles: A Language-Centered Approach to Genre Definition* (Bloomington: Indiana University Press, 1965); Ian Hamnett, "Ambiguity, Classification, and Change: The Function of Riddles," *Man,* n.s., 2 (1967): 379–92; Charles T. Scott, "Some Approaches to the Study of the Riddle," in *Studies in Language, Literature, and Culture of the Middle Ages and Later,* ed. E. Bagby Atwood and Archibald A. Hill (Austin: University of Texas Press, 1969), 111–27; Dan Ben-Amos, "Solutions to Riddles," *Journal of American Folklore* 89 (1976): 249–54; Elli Köngäs Maranda, "Riddles and Riddling: An Introduction," *Journal of American Folklore* 89 (1976): 127–37; and Senderovich, *Riddle of the Riddle.*

20. Archer Taylor, *English Riddles from Oral Tradition* (Berkeley and Los Angeles: University of California Press, 1951). A glance at Taylor's bibliography reveals how vast the resources for comparative study of the riddle were even in 1951. They have only expanded since. Other major collections of folk riddles include Vernam E. Hull and Archer Taylor, *A Collection of Irish Riddles* (Berkeley and Los Angeles: University of California Press, 1955); Vernam E. Hull and Archer Taylor, *A Collection of Welsh Riddles* (Berkeley and Los Angeles: University of California Press, 1942); Eugéne Rolland, *Devinettes ou énigmes populaires de la France* (Paris: F. Vieweg, 1877); Ilhan Basgöz and Andreas Tietze, eds., *Bilmece: A Corpus of Turkish Riddles* (Berkeley and Los Angeles: University of California Press, 1973); and D. Sadovnikov, *Riddles of the Russian People,* trans. Ann C. Bigelow (Ann Arbor: Ardis, 1986). Numerous other smaller collections of folk riddles appear as journal articles. Online access to dozens of printed early modern riddle books can now be had through Early English Books Online (EEBO), while many late medieval and early modern manuscript collections of riddles are available in editions. See, for instance, Frederic Peachy, ed., *Clareti Enigmata: The Latin Riddles of Claret* (Berkeley and Los Angeles: University of California Press, 1957), and Frederick Tupper Jr., ed., "The Holme Riddles (MS. Harl. 1960)," *PMLA* 18 (1903): 211–72.

21. Senderovich, *Riddle of the Riddle,* remarks, "The true folk riddle of oral traditions that have been rapidly disappearing from the face of the earth in the last hundred years is one of the most ancient threads of culture" (1). Leea Virtanen, "The Function of Riddles," in *Nordic Folklore: Recent Studies,* eds. Reimund Kvideland and Henning K. Sehmsdorf (Bloomington: Indiana University Press, 1989), 221–31, provides a fascinating account of how "this once-common Finnish genre disappeared" in the twentieth century.

few short, thematically related examples may nevertheless prove useful to introduce the collection, as well as some of the basic questions and concerns of this study. The very shortest text of the Exeter Book, Riddle 69, is a mere one-liner.[22] It reads:

> Wundor wearð on wege—wæter wearð to bane![23]
>
> [There was a wonder along the way—water became bone!]

What is the answer? No one can say with certainty, for the Exeter riddles, unlike most of their Latin counterparts, come to us without supplied solutions.[24] This circumstance has shaped their reception, for scholars have been racking their wits to solve these texts for nearly two hundred years, rarely agreeing on anything. Let us agree in this case, however, that the answer to Riddle 69 must involve ice. We might then ask what this solution *does.* Among other things, the solution snaps the text into sudden focus and reveals the great wonder of a commonplace thing. This sense of the miraculous in the mundane is at the heart of Old English riddling. Many Exeter riddles begin with the formulaic observation that "Is þes middangeard missenlicum / wisum gewlitegad, wrættum gefrætwad" (This middle earth is beautified in a variety of ways, decked out with ornaments), a lavish preface for texts describing the features of a common rake, bell, well, or book. Often animated or lent a voice to speak its own story—in accordance with long-standing conventions of riddling—each of these uninspiring items is defined as a "wunderlicu wiht," a wondrous creature, something rich and strange.

22. Initial capitalization and end punctuation in the manuscript indicate that Exeter Riddle 69 is a discrete text, set apart from the riddles around it. Williamson, *Old English Riddles,* however, takes Riddles 68–69 as a single riddle "on the basis of formal evidence within the text" (335). Orchard, "Enigma Variations," 291, agrees. Most recently, Niles, *Old English Enigmatic Poems,* 112–13, interprets Riddle 69 as a separate text. A good case can be made either way, but I tend to agree with Krapp and Dobbie that "Riddle 69 is complete in itself, with the obvious solution 'ice'" (*Exeter Book,* 369).

23. In this instance I repunctuate the text of Krapp and Dobbie, *Exeter Book,* 231.

24. I mean here only that the solutions to most Latin *enigmata* are known from medieval sources, while the answers we have for the Exeter riddles come in the main from scholarly sleuthing, comparative analysis, and simple guesswork. Orchard provides ample evidence to show that "the notion that Latin *enigmata* always circulate with their solutions, while the Old English *riddles* never do is easily dismissed." "Enigma Variations," 285–86.

As if disappointed with such simple solutions, though, modern solvers of the Exeter riddles have sometimes offered dramatic answers to match the outlandish descriptions. Past guesses for Riddle 69, for instance, include literally petrified objects from a "Dripping Well" and "Christ walking on the sea."[25] Although somewhat less miraculous, the current favorite solution, "iceberg," seems unnecessarily spectacular, given the genre's penchant for defamiliarizing common objects. The form of ice in question is a small matter, but it seems strange that no one has yet suggested a simple icicle (OE *gicel*) as the answer.[26] The *Dictionary of Old English*—making a rather bold excursus into riddle explication—tells us that the solution is "iceberg" and explains that the use of *ban* in Riddle 69 is "figurative, referring to ice as a hard material."[27] The solution "icicle," though, extends that figurative sense to the elongated, rodlike forms of ice that would most readily activate the image of ossification: *wæter wearð to bane* 'water became bone'.[28] The same image applies to folk riddles in which ice is described in terms of bone: "I have a riddle! You have a riddle! / What is the meaning of the three rods? / What is the splinter that Brigid put in her cloak? / It is not a figure, it is not a bone, and it is not a stone.—An icicle."[29] Other icicle riddles from oral

25. A. J. Wyatt, ed., *Old English Riddles* (Boston: D. C. Heath, 1912), 113, dismisses the answer ice as "feeble and inaccurate" and suggests we consider "something in the nature of petrifaction, recalling to mind various objects that I once possessed that had been petrified in the Dripping Well at Knaresborough [a tourist destination where everyday objects may be coated in limestone by dripping waters that can 'turn them to stone' in a matter of months]." Norman E. Eliason, "Riddle 68 of the Exeter Book," in *Philologica: The Malone Anniversary Studies,* ed. Thomas A. Kirby and Henry Bosley Woolf (Baltimore: Johns Hopkins University Press, 1949), 18–19, argues for the solution "Christ walking on the sea."

26. For "iceberg," see Williamson, *Old English Riddles,* 335–36. For "pack-ice," see Santha Bhattacharji, "An Approach to Christian Aspects of *The Wanderer* and *The Seafarer,*" in *The Christian Tradition in Anglo-Saxon England,* ed. Paul Cavill (Cambridge: D. S. Brewer, 2004), 158. For *is-mere* 'frozen pool', see Niles, *Old English Enigmatic Poems,* 113.

27. *Dictionary of Old English: A–G on CD-ROM,* ed. Angus Cameron, Ashley Crandell Amos, Antonette de Paolo Healey, et al. (Toronto: Pontifical Institute of Mediaeval Studies, for the Dictionary of Old English Project, 2008), s.v. "bān," B.1.

28. The most famous instance of a *gicel* in the Old English corpus must be in *Beowulf,* lines 1605b–1611a, where the monsters' blood dissolves Beowulf's sword: "Þa þæt sweord ongan / æfter heaþoswate hildegicelum, / wigbil wanian; þæt wæs wundra sum, / þæt hit eal gemealt ise gelicost, / ðonne forstes bend Fæder onlæteð, / onwindeð wælrapas se geweald hafað / sæla ond mæla" (Then that sword, that war blade, began to diminish after the battle blood into battle icicles. That was a wondrous thing how it all melted away just the way ice does when the Lord Father releases the bonds of frost, unwinds the death ropes—He who holds sway over times and seasons). Here, as well as in Riddle 69, the visual rope- or rodlike shape of the icicles is emphasized.

29. Hull and Taylor, *Collection of Irish Riddles,* no. 359b.

tradition describe similar formations: "a silver stick," for example, or "a bayonet hang[ing] from the eaves."[30] Reading these traditional texts alongside Riddle 69 underlines riddling's sharp sense of wonder for the ordinary slice of life.

More convincing as an iceberg, though, is the speaking creature of Riddle 33:

> Wiht cwom æfter wege   wrætlicu liþan;
> cymlic from ceole   cleopode to londe,
> hlinsade hlude—   hleahtor wæs gryrelic,
> egesful on earde.   Ecge wæron scearpe;
> wæs hio hetegrim,   hilde to sæne,
> biter beadoweorca.   Bordweallas grof
> heardhiþende.   Heterune bond!
> Sægde searocræftig   ymb hyre sylfre gesceaft:
> "Is min modor   mægða cynnes
> þæs deorestan   þæt is dohtor min
> eacen uploden;   swa þæt is ældum cuþ,
> firum on folce,   þæt seo on foldan sceal
> on ealra londa gehwam   lissum stondan."[31]

> [A marvelous creature came moving along the way. The beautiful thing called to the land from its ship, loudly resounded—its laughter was horrid, terrifying on earth. Its edges were sharp; the cruel one was slow to battle, fierce in its fighting. The hard-plundering one delved into the shield wall. It bound up a terrible secret! Said the cunning one concerning her own creation: "My mother is of the most precious of the race of women: she is my daughter, grown up pregnant. Likewise, it is known to men, to people among the folk, that it is her custom to stand gracefully on earth."][32]

30. Basgöz and Tietze, *Bilmece,* 398 (nos. 386.6–7).

31. In line 2a, I leave MS *ceole* unemended and follow the common meaning of the word listed in the *Dictionary of Old English,* s.v. "cēol." The rest of the text is Williamson's. The perceived need to emend here seems mostly motivated by a conviction that the solution is "iceberg," a questionable assumption. Williamson, *Old English Riddles,* writes: "Does the creature cry out *from the ship?* Metaphorically, the iceberg as a wave-traveler is equated with a ship; it does not ride one" (240). If the solution is a more general sense of "ice," however, "its ship" may simply refer to the floating form of the creature in question. From a riddling point of view, this is no problem at all.

32. All translations of the Exeter riddles and other Old English sources are my own unless otherwise noted.

If only in terms of line count, Riddle 33 is more representative of the Exeter riddles than Riddle 69.[33] It also combines the two most characteristic riddling frames in the collection: the third-person description of a "marvelous creature" and the first-person monologue of an object or animal that "feels and speaks likes a person."[34] Most Exeter riddles are either one or the other, but by interjecting her voice into the description, the creature of Riddle 33 expresses an explicit paradox, another hallmark of riddling: in this case, the contradiction of a mother as her own daughter. Such paradoxes have sometimes been labeled "block elements," the idea being that impossibilities of this kind bind the riddle solver's mind in a hopeless knot.[35] In fact, though, set paradoxes and other conventional motifs are often the clearest clues we have to unriddling the Exeter riddles and would no doubt be readily recognizable by Anglo-Saxon readers of the collection. Simply put, in traditional riddling *ice* is the daughter of water and the mother of water as well. The idea is a standard conceit, well known both in English oral tradition and as a default example of *aenigma* in many medieval texts.[36]

The opening of the riddle, too, is a variation on conventional riddle formulas: "Wiht cwom æfter wege wrætlicu liþan" (A marvelous creature came moving along the way). Formulaic openings (e.g., *ic eom wundorlicu wiht* 'I am a wonderful creature') and closings (e.g., *saga hwæt ic hatte* 'say what I am called') seem to have been recognizable markers of vernacular riddling to an Anglo-Saxon audience. Note the similarities we see in a lone Old English prose riddle found in BL Cotton Vitellius E. xviii.[37] Here we find language reminiscent of the Exeter riddles, including the opening assertion, "Nys þis fregen syllic þinc to rædenne" (Nor is this question a strange thing to unriddle), which echoes standard Exeter formulas such as *ic seah sellic þing* 'I saw a

33. Without taking into consideration any of the many possible complications to such a calculation (such as ambiguous textual divisions and damaged sections in the manuscript), the average number of lines per Exeter riddle is roughly fourteen (as edited by Krapp and Dobbie).

34. To borrow Margaret Schlauch's definition of prosopopoeia in her classic article "The 'Dream of the Rood' as Prosopopoeia," in *Essays and Studies in Honour of Carleton Brown,* ed. P. W. Long (New York: New York University Press, 1940), 30.

35. See, for instance, Thomas A. Green and W. J. Pepicello, "Wit in Riddling: A Linguistic Perspective," *Genre* 11 (1978): "It seems that the basic problem in the consideration of riddles is that the riddlee is (or should be) incapable of solving the riddles posed by the riddler. That is, there is a block element, or an irresolvable opposition, contained in the composition of the riddle" (5).

36. Tupper, "Holme Riddles," 246, provides numerous references to this extremely widespread motif.

37. Edited in Förster, "Ein altenglisches Prosa-Rätsel," 392–93.

strange thing' and *ræd hwæt ic mæne* 'unriddle what I mean'. A related observation is that the scribe of the Exeter Book seems at least once to have mistakenly divided one of the texts through a misapplication of a known riddling formula. On folio 107v, punctuation signaling the conclusion of Riddle 27 has been inserted after the formulaic half-line *frige hwæt ic hatte* 'ask what I am called', although the text continues with the qualifying clause "ðe on eorþan swa esnas binde / dole æfter dyntum be dæges leohte" (who on earth binds as slaves the foolish after fighting, in the light of day). As Patrick W. Conner observes, "The error suggests a scribe whose attention was not completely on his texts, but who also understood Old English riddles well enough to react to a riddling formula."[38]

The Exeter riddles presuppose readers familiar with such riddling formulas and conceits, as well as with the conventions of Old English poetry more generally. Anita R. Riedinger has convincingly argued that Riddle 33's obfuscating language is set against the expectations of heroic action so that, for instance, when the fearsome creature is said to be "hilde to sæne / biter beadoweorca" (slow to battle, fierce in its fighting), the paradoxical details clash with the convention of warriors described as *nalas hild-lata* 'not at all a laggard in battle'.[39] As Riedinger stresses, details like this are meant to be "misleadingly accurate" in their ironic relationship with the solution, and indeed ice, quite unlike a fierce warrior, is slow to battle in its powerful erosive action, whether "erratic icebergs" or a less titanic form of ice is imagined.[40] In fact, a more general solution (*is* 'ice') would suffice, for the riddle reflects the creature's existence both raging on water (as floes breaking up on a river or lake?) and in a more placid state: "seo on foldan sceal / on ealra londa gehwam lissum stondan" (it is her custom to stand gracefully on

38. Conner, *Anglo-Saxon Exeter,* 142. Conner continues, "The mistake seems to have come from familiarity, not only with riddles, but specifically with Old English riddles, and not at all from ignorance of the riddling tradition. To apply a concept borrowed from modern linguistics, this is an error in performance, not an error in competence."

39. Anita R. Riedinger, "The Formulaic Style in the Old English Riddles," *Studia Neophilologica* 75 (2003): 34.

40. Riedinger explains that "most icebergs move slowly" (ibid., 39), but the sluggish force of ice satisfies the obfuscation quite well, without appealing to the possible rare sighting of "icebergs from east Greenland" by an Anglo-Saxon riddler (as discussed by Williamson, *Old English Riddles,* 238). River ice would be a commoner sight, even farther north, as reflected in the bizarre solution to a riddle posed in an Old Norse saga: "a dead horse on an icefloe, and on the horse a dead snake, and they all floated together down the river"; see Christopher Tolkien, ed. and trans., *The Saga of King Heidrek the Wise* (New York: Thomas Nelson and Sons, 1960), 37. Riedinger borrows the phrase "misleadingly accurate" from Wyatt, *Old English Riddles,* xxviii.

earth). In the Old English dialogue poem *Solomon and Saturn II,* a riddle on *yldo* 'old age' portrays the destructive actions of the abstraction:

> Ac hwæt is ðæt wundor ðe geond ðas worold færeð,
> styrnenga gæð, staðolas beateð,
> aweceð wopdropan, winneð oft hider?
>
> [But what is that strange thing that travels throughout this world, sternly goes, beats the foundations, arouses tears, often forces its way here?][41]

Solomon's explication of this riddle elaborates further on the subtle violence of *yldo* as it *bebriceð* 'shatters' tree branches and *abiteð* 'bites' into iron.[42] Saturn responds by inquiring into the erosive action of snow and ice:

> Full oft gecostað eac
> wildeora worn, wætum he oferbricgeð,
> gebriceð burga geat, baldlice fereð
> reafað ***
>
> [Very often it distresses many wild animals too, makes a bridge over water, breaches the gate of the citadel, boldly proceeds, robs ***][43]

Such passages are reminiscent of the destructive ice of Riddle 33, another bold creature who is *hilde to sæne* 'slow to battle' in doing her damage. No berg is necessary for ice to work its will, and a less dramatic solution again better reflects the genre's tendency to dramatize more commonplace, if no less powerful, forces in the world.

At any rate, Riddle 33 counts on the reader's familiarity with both Old English poetry and the particular quirks of the genre in question. These riddles are not posed out of thin air but are often allusive variations on standard themes. In fact, one might see the traditional conceit of ice as the eternal mother of its own water as shaping Riddle 33 throughout. The paradox stresses the creature's transformation from a solid to a liquid state and

41. Daniel Anlezark, ed. and trans., *The Old English Dialogues of Solomon and Saturn* (Cambridge: D. S. Brewer, 2009), 84–85 (lines 104–6).

42. Ibid., 84 (lines 118, 123).

43. Ibid., 84–85 (lines 127–30).

back again. Around this core conceit, the Old English riddle builds an extended image of ice in the dynamic, sluggishly violent, and above all loud process of thawing, cracking up (*hleahtor wæs gryrelic* 'the laughter was terrible') and fragmenting (*ecge wæron scearp* 'the edges were sharp'). It is possible, too, that the riddle's conclusion reflects the opposite process of freezing, as the daughter comes again to "stand" on the land. Echoing the shift from crystal daughter to mother water (and vice versa), ice in a state of transformation forms the riddle's basic theme.

Lively variation on such themes is often the name of the game for the Exeter riddles, though modern solvers may find themselves in the dark when it comes to the traditional patterns of riddling behind these texts. A particularly murky example is Riddle 74, a text that has been solved and re-solved again and again in the critical literature:

> Ic wæs fæmne geong,   feaxhar cwene,
> ond ænlic rinc   on ane tid;
> fleah mid fuglum   ond on flode swom,
> deaf under yþe   dead mid fiscum,
> ond on foldan stop—   hæfde ferð cwicu.

> [I was a young woman, a gray-haired lady, and a beautiful warrior at one time; I flew with the birds and swam in the sea, dove under the wave, dead with the fishes, and stepped onto the earth—I had a living spirit.]

A strong spirit would be needed to inventory and evaluate all the ingenious guesses for Riddle 74. These five spare lines have yielded cuttlefish, shadows, quill pens, the sun, sirens, sea eagles, swans, barnacle geese, and, in Williamson's edition, the figurehead of a ship. Each of these solutions makes elegant sense of many details in the riddle, and each at times strains to explain a clue or two.[44] With so many good options, it seems impossible to choose among them. One of the most attractive answers, in fact, is once again "water in its various forms," offered by Moritz Trautmann about a hundred years ago.[45] The basic idea is that the young woman is a stream, the gray-haired lady an

44. For a discussion of the solving history of Riddle 74, see Niles, *Old English Enigmatic Poems,* 18–23.

45. Moritz Trautmann, "Alte und neue Antworten auf altenglische Rätsel," *Bonner Beiträge zur Anglistik* 19 (1905): 201–3.

iceberg (!), and the beautiful warrior a blanket of snow. The last three lines make good sense in terms of a hydrologic cycle from rain, to flowing water, to frost, while the shifting character of the speaker in lines 1–2 may be attributed to grammatical gender: the young woman, for instance, may be a *burne* 'stream' (a feminine noun), while the masculine warrior may be *snaw* 'snow' (a masculine noun).

No doubt other possibilities could be named, whether we choose to include in this group a gray-haired *ēa* 'river' (a feminine noun), the peerless figure of *forst* 'frost' (a masculine noun), or another princely *is-gicel* 'icicle' (another masculine noun). The embarrassment of possibilities illustrates both the potential and the problems of using grammatical gender as a clue to solving these Exeter riddles.[46] It is nevertheless probably the best way to account for the opening lines of Riddle 74 and comes into play in what I consider the text's best solution, one recently proposed by John D. Niles. That solution is a ship of some kind, but the exact wording of the solution is what counts most in making sense of the first two lines. Niles's answer is to offer a doublet, *āc* 'oak tree' (a feminine noun) and *bāt* 'boat' (a masculine noun). As Niles himself notes, this solution solves one problem but raises another. How can the speaker be an oak tree and a boat *on ane tid* 'at one time'? Niles offers two alternative ways out of this difficulty. The first is to repunctuate the poem so that the phrase *on ane tid* applies not to the first statement in the riddle but the second: "At a single time I flew among birds and swam in the sea." Niles's other suggestion is that a single *tid* may be taken as a long stretch of time: "It is nothing magical, then, for a sapling to become a tree and a tree to be turned into a ship in a single *tid*."[47] Recently, however, Mark Griffith has contested both of these arguments on philological grounds, while at the same time acknowledging the attraction of Niles's basic solution. What is needed, he claims, is "an Old English word meaning both 'tree' and 'ship' which is at once both feminine and masculine in gender." That solution, Griffith tells us, is simply *āc,* a single word that can have either feminine or masculine gender and mean either "oak tree" or "ship of oak."[48]

For both Niles and Griffith, the chief concern, understandably, is to account for the puzzling gender of the speaker's opening statement, and indeed

46. For more on grammatical gender and Old English riddling, see ibid., 181; Tupper, *Riddles of the Exeter Book,* lxxxix–xc; Niles, *Old English Enigmatic Poems,* 36–37.

47. Niles, *Old English Enigmatic Poems,* 36, 38, 39.

48. Mark Griffith, "Exeter Book Riddle 74 *Ac* 'Oak' and *Bat* 'Boat,'" *Notes and Queries* 55 (2008): 393–96.

the solution *āc* as oak tree and ship of oak fits the bill brilliantly. But why should we accept it more than Trautmann's water? Arguments could be launched (and have been) for any number of answers that satisfy the clues coherently. Rather than simply satisfying clues, then, the real trick is to situate this Old English poem within known traditions of riddling. Niles, in fact, begins to do just this by directing our attention to a riddle type found in Archer Taylor's *English Riddles from Oral Tradition:* "Folk riddles of Taylor type 828 are usually put into the voice of an imagined speaker, who declares one or another variation on the theme 'When I was alive, I fattened the living. Dead, I carried the living.' "[49] As Niles provides only a couple of examples, it is worth tracing the tradition more fully to understand how this riddle type has played out over time.[50] As is the case with many distinct riddling patterns, the riddle of the oak ship is quite old and widespread. The earliest known examples date from the medieval period. Paul Sorrell, in fact, has drawn a clear connection between this motif and the Old English *Rune Poem:*

ᚪ (āc) byþ on eorþan   elda bearnum
flæsces fodor,   fereþ gelome
ofer ganotes bæþ;   garsecg fandaþ
hwæþer ac hæbbe   æþele treowe.

[The oak on the earth is food for flesh for the children of men. It often travels over the gannet's bath; the ocean tests whether the oak has a noble faith.][51]

The food provided by the oak is acorn mast consumed by swine, whose flesh in turn is consumed by the children of men. This passage confirms the amazing durability of riddle motifs over time, for an early modern manuscript of popular riddles (the so-called Holme Riddles) includes the following:

49. Niles, *Old English Enigmatic Poems,* 41–42.

50. For many medieval and early modern analogues, see Paul Sorrell, "Oaks, Ships, Riddles and the Old English *Rune Poem,*" *Anglo-Saxon England* 19 (1990): 103–16. Sorrell's work demonstrates the influence of these traditional oak riddles on the Old English *Rune Poem.*

51. Elliott van Kirk Dobbie, ed., *The Anglo-Saxon Minor Poems* (New York: Columbia University Press, 1942), 30; Sorrell, "Oaks, Ships, Riddles," 106n16. Sorrell, 103–5, offers an extensive range of analogues for the oak-ship riddle motif, including vernacular versions and Latin parallels dating back to the early eighth century. He does not, however, connect this motif with Riddle 74. Niles, *Old English Enigmatic Poems,* 40–41, was the first to notice this relationship.

Q. W[n] j lived j fed the liveing now j am dead j beare the live[in]g & with swift speed j walk ou[r] the liveing

A. a ship mad[e] of oake groweing feeds hogs with acorns now b[e]ars men & swims ou[r] fishes.[52]

In other words, the oak ship is *dead mid fiscum* 'dead with the fishes'. Other early modern variations are solved specifically as a "ship built of oak," or "An Oak now a ship."[53] The latter solution is provided in an illustrated book of riddles, which includes two variations on the theme in a row, along with the striking image of an oak tree positioned above the woodcut of a ship. Such analogues suggest that *āc* 'oak' or 'ship of oak' is indeed the likely solution to Riddle 74.

It could be objected that Riddle 74 includes no reference to the acorn mast, unlike all the examples cited above. It is in the nature of riddling traditions, however, that such motifs take on a protean range of forms, with a cluster of recognizable elements recombined in endless variation. Some versions of the ship riddle, for instance, focus primarily on the paradox of the dead bearing the living, as in the opening lines of this eighth-century riddle from the Bern collection:

Mortua maiorem uiuens quam porto laborem.
Dum iaceo, multos seruo; si stetero, paucos.

[Dead, I bear a greater labour than when living. When I lie dead I preserve many; if I remain standing, few.][54]

In riddle after riddle the quick and the dead play out in multiform fashion: "A dead man bears a living man to take the living (pl.) to make the living (pl.) live.—Boat, fisher, fish."[55] Other variations stress the tall mast and sail of the oak ship: "I spread my Wings to forreign Regions fly, / Over the Living [fish] pass, and yet have I / the Living in the Womb."[56] In this strand of ship riddling, the creature is often journeying forth on a liminal path, alive

52. Tupper, "Holme Riddles," 222.

53. Ibid., 239; *A New Booke of Merry Riddles* (London, 1665), no. 10; *Delights for young Men and Maids* (London, 1725), nos. 4–5.

54. Enigma 11, lines 1–3 (Glorie, *Variae collectiones aenigmatum,* 557; translation from Sorrell, "Oaks, Ships, Riddles," 105n12).

55. Taylor, *English Riddles from Oral Tradition,* 310.

56. *Aristotle's legacy: or, his golden cabinet of secrets opened* (London, 1699), no. xx.

and yet dead, flying with the birds yet swimming with the fish: "I am dead but there is life in me, the living go under me, and the living hover above me, the living walk in me, and the living have regard for me."[57] Dead with the fishes, swimming in the water, flying with the birds, and formerly possessing a living spirit, the creature of Riddle 74 is a snug fit within this tradition. The Old English poem, then, is best read as an elegant variation on this venerable riddling theme, paired with an opening paradox of *āc*'s variable grammatical gender. Needless to say, we can never be certain, but without due attention to this sturdy but fluid tradition, Riddle 74's answer would be anyone's arbitrary guess.

Surprisingly, however, very little weight has been placed on such comparative evidence in the study of the Exeter riddles outside of the examination of Latin literary analogues, which have received considerable attention. Recently, for instance, a full-length study of the Old English riddles by Dieter Bitterli "argues for a vigorous, common tradition of Old English and Anglo-Latin enigmatography."[58] Bitterli's book begins to answer Andy Orchard's challenge that we study Old English riddling and Anglo-Latin *enigmata* as "connected parts of the same literary tradition."[59] The importance of such an approach is beyond question. Much less attention, however, has been paid to the relevance of oral traditional riddles or early modern vernacular analogues in the study of the collection, which, as Orchard stresses, is apparently quite eclectic.[60] The notable exception is the work of Frederick Tupper Jr., whose 1910 edition of the riddles made frequent and useful reference to folk analogues in the introduction and notes. In the century since, however, very little work in this area has appeared, despite the availability of many new resources for comparative study. There are no doubt complicated reasons for this neglect, but Craig Williamson's position may have played a role in discouraging such research. In the introduction to his influential edition of the Old English riddles, he writes, "As I have indicated elsewhere in the notes and commentary to several riddles, the relevance of late medieval, renaissance, or early modern English folklore to Old English riddles (which are, incidentally, literary creations) is doubtful at best."[61] As the small example of Riddle 74 shows, there is little reason for such doubt. The boundaries

57. Taylor, *English Riddles from Oral Tradition,* 309.

58. Dieter Bitterli, *Say What I Am Called: The Old English Riddles of the Exeter Book and the Anglo-Latin Riddle Tradition* (Toronto: University of Toronto Press, 2009), 4.

59. Orchard, "Enigma Variations," 300.

60. Ibid., 286.

61. Williamson, *Old English Riddles,* 22.

between medieval literary enigmas and riddles circulating in oral tradition were probably quite fluid, each often the mother and the daughter of the other.

One of the aims of the present study, then, is to take advantage of this missed opportunity and to read the Exeter riddles as artful and allusive responses to traditional forms of riddling, as well as to Latin enigmatography. The significance of this approach does not lie only in an appeal to conventional motifs and conceits, however. In fact, as the simple presence of "double-entendre" riddles in the collection suggests, the very *modes* of riddling in the Exeter Book are likely to be influenced by popular, as well as learned, enigmatic kinds. In particular, this study focuses on the importance in the collection of metaphorical riddling, a form favored in oral traditional riddling but much less prominent in Latin collections of enigmas. The simple idea is that an Old English riddle's proposition (the "question" or description posed) may at times relate not only to an unnamed solution but also to what I call its "focus," an underlying metaphor that lends coherence to the text's strategy of obfuscation. Scholars have long recognized that the Exeter riddles must sometimes be read as metaphorical, but in practice this has mostly meant that a few scattered individual words and images are taken as figurative. There is thought to be, in other words, no underlying pattern in the riddle's description, beyond what can be accounted for by the literal solution (or the needs of generating a pun, a paradox, or a fairly simple sense of animation or "heroic" personification). On the surface, this assumption makes good sense, especially because so many known literary riddles do in fact work this way. As Archer Taylor explains, "In order to accumulate details enough to permit the listener to guess the answer, the riddler often sacrifices the unity of his conception. The first assertion and its denial are almost certain to conflict with the next pair. Yet the author goes on and on, while his conception becomes more and more incoherent."[62] By contrast, I argue that the dark clues of Old English riddles often add up to something quite coherent, shaped as they are by extended implicit metaphors. Reading many of the riddles in this way, I contend, allows us to resolve some of the most puzzling problems in the collection as well as to revise our understanding of texts that have already received convincing solutions.

One final opening example may help clarify what I mean by referring to a riddle's underlying metaphor as its focus. Riddle 85 reads:

62. Archer Taylor, *The Literary Riddle Before 1600* (Berkeley and Los Angeles: University of California Press, 1948), 3.

Nis min sele swige, ne ic sylfa hlud
ymb * * *; unc dryhten scop
siþ ætsomne. Ic eom swiftre þonne he,
þragum strengra; he þreohtigra.
Hwilum ic me reste; he sceal rinnan forð.
Ic him in wunige a þenden ic lifge;
gif wit unc gedælað, me bið deað witod.

[My hall is not silent, nor am I myself loud; about. . . . The Lord shaped a journey for us two together. I am swifter than he, at times stronger; he is more relentless. At times I rest; he must run on. I dwell in him always while I live; if we two are parted, death is appointed to me.]

The solution to this riddle is fairly certain, grounded as it is in the famous Symphosian conceit of a fish in a river as a silent guest in a noisy house:

Est domus in terris clara quae voce resultat.
Ipsa domus resonat, tacitus sed non sonat hospes.
Ambo tamen currunt hospes simul et domus una.

[There is a home in the earth that resounds with a clear voice. The house itself makes sound, but the silent guest does not. Nevertheless, together the two run, the guest and house at once.][63]

As Williamson notes, the parallels between these poems are largely limited to the first two lines of Riddle 85 and the motifs of a common journey and the silent guest in a resounding house.[64] The Old English text, however, extends the riddling in a series of additional observations that can be explicated in terms of a fish speaker. The fish is swifter than the river, its strength can fight the current, but the river is more relentless in the long run. The fish at times rests, but the river is unrelenting. The fish dwells in the river always while he lives, but if the river and fish are separated, the fish will perish. While Symphosius's enigma is preoccupied by simple paradoxes (how can a house speak? how can a dweller travel in his house?), the emphasis in Riddle 85 is on exploring the contrasting relationship of guest with

63. Enigma 12 (Ohl, *Enigmas of Symphosius,* 44; my translation).
64. Williamson, *Old English Riddles,* 374.

hall. In fact, there is a familiar ring to this discussion, as Andy Orchard observes: "Without the existence of the *enigmata* by Alcuin and Symphosius, one might well conjecture that the Old English riddle is not about a riverfish at all, but rather another 'soul and body' riddle like others in the Exeter Book."[65]

Orchard is right. While the *solution* must be a fish in the river, the riddle's descriptive proposition is shaped by something more—the unspoken metaphor of the soul and body. This "focus" selects and filters out the details of the proposition, lending it an underlying coherence beyond the literal answer. It would be easy, in fact, to rescan the riddle in terms of its focus. The speaker is the silent soul, which dwells inside the hall of the body. The Lord shaped them both for a journey together. The soul is swifter and at times stronger than the body, but not always, since the demands of the flesh are unflagging. But if the body gives up the ghost, the soul experiences death. There is a clear coherence to this description of Riddle 85 not found in Symphosius and one that is compelling to consider beyond the riddle's general employment of paradox, personification, and poetic elaboration.[66] In *Soul and Body II,* a text only a few items away from the riddles in the Exeter Book, the soul upbraids his body:

> Eardode ic þe in innan.   No ic þe of meahte,
> flæsce bifongen,   ond me firenlustas
> þine geþrungon.
>
> [I dwelled within you. Nor could I ever get out of you, encircled with flesh, and your wicked desires pressed in on me.][67]

The language of this poem strongly echoes the second half of Riddle 85 both in diction and in the use of dual grammatical number. The speaker of Riddle 85 declares that "unc dryhten scop / siþ ætsomne" (The Lord shaped

65. Orchard, "Enigma Variations," 294. In a note (p. 304), Orchard credits Irina Dumitrescu for this observation. In his book of translations, Gregory K. Jember, *The Old English Riddles* (Denver: Society for New Language Study, 1976), 56, lists "Body and Soul" as a proposed solution to Riddle 85. One does not know how seriously to take this suggestion, however, as "Body and Soul," "Soul," "Trial of the Soul," "Souls of the Damned," and "Spirit/Revenant" are listed as Jember's solution to no fewer than fourteen of the Exeter riddles. At any rate, "Body and Soul" is not the solution to Riddle 85 but its metaphorical focus.

66. For which, see Williamson, *Old English Riddles,* 374–75; Bitterli, *Say What I Am Called,* 16.

67. Lines 30–32 (Krapp and Dobbie, *Exeter Book,* 175; my translation).

a journey for us two together), while the soul speaker of *Soul and Body II* demands, "Ac hwæt do wit unc, / þonne he unc hafað geedbyrded oþre siþe?" (And what are we two going to do for ourselves, when he has regenerated us two for another journey?)[68] The same language appears in Riddle 43, a text universally solved as "soul and body":

Gif him arlice
esne þenað se þe agan sceal
on þam siðfate, hy gesunde æt ham
findað witode him wiste ond blisse

[If the servant honorably serves him who must rule on that journey, they safely at home will find sustenance and bliss appointed for them.][69]

The body and soul will be united on the day of judgment, while for the fish the situation is more permanent: "gif wit unc gedælað, me bið deað witod" (if we two are parted, death is appointed to me). For Riddle 85, then, the soul and body duo is not the riddle's solution (as it seems to be in Riddle 43) but represents rather an unspoken metaphor governing the selection and form of the riddle's proposition. It shapes the obfuscation.[70] The product of this strategy is at once a lively "fish and river" riddle and a poem that plays artfully against the implied solver's knowledge of the body-soul dynamic.

My chief argument in this book is not that all of the Exeter riddles engage in metaphorical riddling of this kind, but simply that it plays a much more significant role in the collection than has previously been noticed. The riddling strategies of the Exeter Book, after all, are not likely to be straightforward, unenigmatic, or even consistent across the anthology. The collection seems if nothing else eclectic, offering a mixed bag of riddling kinds. Some are loose translations of Aldhelmian *enigmata*—whether on the expansive paradox of the created world or on the unwoven fabric of a coat of mail. Many describe the cunning mechanisms of medieval technologies: well sweeps, weaving looms, and weapon racks have all been detected in the

68. Riddle 85, lines 2b–3a; *Soul and Body II,* lines 93b–94 (Krapp and Dobbie, *Exeter Book,* 177; my translation).

69. Lines 4b–7. In my translation I follow Williamson, *Old English Riddles,* 279.

70. My reading of Riddle 85 may be contrasted with that of Bitterli, *Say What I Am Called,* 16–18, which focuses not on an underlying metaphor but rather on various rhetorical features of the poem.

collection. Others focus on the marvelous qualities of birds and beasts, from bull-calves to barnacle geese, their curious customs, qualities, and calls. Still others describe the elegant transformation of raw materials into crafted books, swords, inkhorns, and ships. Quite a few are preoccupied by the wonders of the written word and silent speech, whether inscribed in metal or ingested by bookworms. Some require a meticulous counting of stars, letters, body parts, or even the offspring of biblical incest. Several rely on runic anagrams, substitution codes, or etymological puzzles. A handful or two deal in double entendre. Many, I argue, are at their core metaphorical.

In recent years there has been a resurgence of interest in the Exeter riddles, with new studies that synthesize and extend our understanding of many of the riddling categories listed above. For instance, John D. Niles's *Old English Enigmatic Poems and the Play of the Texts,* while not dedicated exclusively to the Exeter riddles, devotes several chapters to them, with particular attention to how runes, verbal wit, and the texture of medieval material culture play out in the collection. By contrast, Dieter Bitterli's recent book, *Say What I Am Called,* explores the relationship between the Anglo-Latin tradition of enigmatography and the Exeter Book riddles, though his work is also very interested in runic codes, wordplay, and etymology. With some exceptions, the present study focuses on different aspects of riddling in the Exeter anthology, and so it is probably no accident that there is relatively little overlap in the examples I choose to discuss in detail. Any study of the Exeter riddles, of course, is indebted to the monumental efforts of past scholars, editors, and solvers such as Dietrich, Trautmann, Tupper, Wyatt, and Williamson. Innumerable others have added key contributions to the effort to unriddle these elegant poems. I hope that the following chapters are a useful contribution to this lively, ongoing conversation.

In chapter 1 ("Unriddling the Riddles"), I examine some of the common critical assumptions made in past interpretations of the Exeter riddles and propose a new approach to their study and solution. Rather than classifying or defining the riddles in terms of common features, formulas, or the imagined position of an implied solver, I stress the importance of the two sides of a riddle's binary structure: a descriptive proposition and its named solution. While we should not assume that the relationship between these two elements is the same across the entire eclectic Exeter collection, there are traditional patterns of riddling we can usefully consider in their interpretation. The mystery of the Old English riddles is not best explained by a vague sense of obscurity, a literal accounting of straightforward clues, or an elaborate inside story. Convincing interpretations of these texts must involve rather a coherent account of their obfuscation. In particular, I contend that the propositions of many of the Exeter riddles are shaped not only by their hidden solutions but also by an unnamed metaphor in a way similar to the so-called obscene riddles of the Exeter Book—texts that are often explained as having "double solutions." Such riddles, however, do not feature two solutions, but rather simply show evidence of metaphorical obfuscation similar to what is commonly found in folk riddling. The Exeter riddles are certainly not folk riddles, of course, but they are artfully crafted literary responses to a complex and varied mix of enigmatic forms that were probably available to Anglo-Saxon riddlers.

In chapter 2 ("A Literal Reading of Riddle 57"), I examine one of the most difficult texts in the Exeter collection as a test case for reading the Old English riddles in a more metaphorical mode. Riddle 57 is a short, spare text describing the birdlike sounds and movements of small, dark creatures. In a century and more of solving, these flocks have been variously identified by learned birders as swallows, swifts, starlings, house martins, jackdaws, crows, blackbirds, midges, gnats, and bees. With close attention to a wide range of analogues from oral and textual tradition, I argue that such readings are far too literal in their approach and that a better answer is *bocstafas* 'letters', a solution that resonates with the early medieval conception of *littera* as both written mark and the smallest indivisible unit of speech. In fact, I show that Riddle 57's enigmatic flocks reflect the three key properties of letters—name, shape, and sound value—as commonly defined by grammarian authorities well known in the early Middle Ages. This small riddle, therefore, represents a bookish response to a popular mode of metaphorical riddling, a pattern that appears to be favored in the Exeter anthology.

Chapter 3 ("Transformation and Textual Culture") takes up this theme, not by offering new solutions but by examining the underlying metaphors that shape the propositions of the Exeter riddles almost as much as their hidden answers. The three main readings in this chapter are designed to demonstrate the elegance with which the Exeter riddles transform the traditional forms of metaphorical riddling in the light of Anglo-Saxon textual culture. Perhaps more than any other text in the Exeter Book, Riddle 22 invites a metaphorical reading of its sixty enigmatic riders and fifteen bright horses crossing a deep sea in a mysterious wagon. This wagon, as scholars have long recognized, must be Ursa Major, or *carles wæn* 'Charles's Wain' in the Anglo-Saxon tongue. What modern solvers have not figured out is how to understand the numbers problem posed in the poem's opening lines, and so I offer here a new account of these celestial riders in the context of the particular forms of astronomical learning available to an Anglo-Saxon star-gazer. By unriddling this puzzle, moreover, a clearer picture emerges of the bookish aspect of many of the Exeter riddles, even in those most clearly informed by popular forms of metaphorical riddling. Next I consider a second celestial enigma, Riddle 29, one of the most famous texts of the Exeter Book. Although this riddle is widely admired, modern readers may have overlooked an unspoken metaphorical focus shaping its dramatic depiction of the moon striving against the sun, and in particular its enigmatic ending. Once again, the metaphorical riddle is reshaped by the preoccupations of Christian literate culture, in this case the drama and imagery of a key moment of salvation history. In the final reading of the chapter, I shift from the heavens to the earthy speaker of Riddle 83, a text informed, I argue, by the unspoken pull of the biblical account of Tubalcain and the origins of ore. Here the traditional "transformation riddle" is itself transformed and extended into new territory, an emblematic text for the Exeter collection.

If chapter 3 concerns the literary transformation of metaphorical riddling, chapter 4 ("Riddle 17 as Samson's Lion") explores the possible reworking in the Exeter Book of the most famous moment of biblical riddling. I argue that Riddle 17, one of the most baffling poems in the collection, is best read as an Old English response to the solution of Samson's riddle, "de comedente exivit cibus et de forte est egressa dulcedo" (out of the eater came forth food and, from the strong one, sweetness).[71] That solution, of course, is a lion's carcass colonized by bees, and my analysis of the poem demonstrates not only the aptness of this answer but also the ways in which patristic exegesis shapes Riddle 17's response to its classic exemplar. What is more, this reading accounts for two marginal runic marks in the Exeter Book (an "L" and a "B") that have long proved elusive: the simple rhyming answer *leo ond beo* 'the lion and the bee', I propose, makes instructive sense of both runes and riddle.

In chapter 5 ("Innuendo and Oral Tradition"), I turn to a set of Exeter poems that appear to revise not scriptural riddles but instead the venerable innuendo of oral tradition. Although long suspected of having roots in popular riddling, these "sex riddles" have not to date been studied in relation to

71. Judges 14:14 (*Biblia sacra iuxta vulgatam versionem,* 3d ed., ed. Robert Weber, 2 vols. [Stuttgart: Deutsche Bibelgesellschaft, 1983], 345).

the extensive body of folk riddling analogues available. A comparative study of these texts reveals, however, that the artfully allusive Exeter sex riddles are far from "obscene" and far from simple jokes in their sophisticated response to traditional images and conceits. Beyond the value of these analogues for comparing riddling motifs, however, they may also reveal questionable expectations modern readers of the Exeter Book bring to the interpretation of the double-entendre subgenre. In particular, we should question the current critical trend of naming for these texts explicit "double solutions." The sex riddles, in fact, do not have two solutions any more than do other metaphorical riddles in the Exeter Book. What they have is a proposition shaped at once by a solution and by an unspoken (at times perhaps unspeakable) metaphor. In this crucial respect, the Exeter sex riddles can be said to stand at the center of the collection.

For a final instance of reading the Exeter riddles in context, chapter 6 ("The Roots of Riddle 25") attempts to unravel one of the most deceptively simple texts in the Exeter anthology. In fact, I argue that Riddle 25 might itself be called an anthology of suggestive riddling, relying for its more subtle effects on the reader's recognition of its component parts. Those layers are skillfully combined, yet to be functional they must remain visible to the knowing eye. Close attention to related strains of riddling raises the strong possibility that our very construal of Riddle 25's grammar may be incomplete if read without attention to the traditional motifs informing the text. Indeed, this Old English onion riddle is a surprisingly complex aggregate of some of the oldest jokes in the book, and we can only guess how its readers may have relished the text's comic deflation of sexual pride and the mischief of a played-out riddle serving a new master.

Ræd hwæt ic mæne, demands one of these sex riddles, "unriddle what I mean." There is no easy response to this challenge, whether asked of a single text or of the collection at large. If nothing else, though, we might begin by saying that the Exeter Book provides a variety show of riddling modes, in which runic puzzles, Christian mysteries, and sex riddles all make an appearance. It has often been remarked that the collection offers an expansive and inclusive vision of the created world, from the mysterious visions of the celestial enigmas to the earthy bed of the Exeter sex riddles. In between, these poems catalogue an abundant reality, crawling with strange creatures and adorned with the artifice of daily life. If the arguments of this book are accepted, we might see this sense of abundance as extending beyond the list of solutions to the very metaphorical core of Old English riddling. That is, the Exeter riddles do not simply gather for us a miscellaneous selection of bookworms, glass beakers, and barnacle geese; they also reveal an abundance of metaphorical connections within the riddler's reach. They not only list items in the world, they attempt to uncover unlooked-for patterns in its fabric. They draw intricate links between disparate things, as birds become letters, bright riders shift into suns and stars, and onions strip away layers of allusion and mordant metaphor. To characterize the enigmatic Exeter collection is no easy problem, with no single solution. But at least for the metaphorical riddles, one illuminating answer might be the grammarian Donatus's definition of riddling as revealing the *occultum similitudinem rerum,* 'the hidden similarity of things'.[72]

72. Donatus, *Ars grammatica,* ed. Heinrich Keil (Leipzig: Teubner, 1864), 402 (3.6).

1

UNRIDDLING THE RIDDLES

It is commonplace to point out that the titles we have for Old English poems are provided by modern editors and that such titles may shape later interpretation. The earliest studies of the Exeter Book refer to "ænigmata" and "riddles of the olden time," but the title "riddles" really took root with the publication of Benjamin Thorpe's 1842 *editio princeps* of the Exeter Book, *Codex Exoniensis*.[1] Thorpe's calling of these texts "riddles" both emphasizes their Englishness and lends a sense of unity to what we have come to see as a single "collection" of riddles, despite their placement in more than one section of the Exeter Book manuscript. The process of unifying the collection, however, remains incomplete in Thorpe's edition: it is interesting to note, for instance, that Thorpe begins the numbering of the texts anew for each of the three manuscript sections. For this reason, Thorpe has three different texts designated "Riddle I." In the century and a half since, several other numbering systems have been employed, no two exactly alike, and even today the defined boundaries of the collection remain somewhat in flux.

Along with a title, Thorpe provides a short description of the riddle genre, which he gives in the course of a tangled apology for his translations:

1. L. C. Müller, *Collectanea Anglo-Saxonica* (Copenhagen: Libraria Wahliana, 1835); Benjamin Thorpe, ed., *Codex Exoniensis* (London: William Pickering, 1842).

"Of the 'Riddles' I regret to say that, from the obscurity naturally to be looked for in such compositions, arising partly from inadequate knowledge of the tongue, and partly from the manifest inaccuracies of the text, my translations, or rather my attempts at translation, though the best I can offer, are frequently almost, and sometimes, I fear, quite, as unintelligible as the originals."[2] This knotted statement is perhaps a bit of a riddle itself, but Thorpe's language in fact closely echoes an earlier source. In his *Illustrations of Anglo-Saxon Poetry,* published posthumously in 1826, John Josias Conybeare cites the strangeness of the sole Latin riddle of the collection (Riddle 90) as an exemplum for the difficulty of the riddles as a group: "The obscurity attaching itself to much of this part of the MS. will be rendered most conspicuous by the following specimen of corrupt Latinity, which appears absolutely unintelligible."[3] This basic pattern—a statement of the "obscurity" of the riddles followed by the suggestion of possible textual corruption and unintelligibility—shows up too in Thomas Wright's 1842 *Biographia Britannica Literaria:* "From their intentional obscurity, and from the uncommon words with which they abound, many of these riddles are at present altogether unintelligible."[4] In his 1862 *Anglo-Saxon Home: A History of the Domestic Institutions and Customs of England,* John Thrupp weighs in with his version of this pattern: "A very large number of their riddles have been preserved, but partly owing to their original obscurity, and partly from their having been copied and re-copied by persons evidently ignorant of the Anglo-Saxon language, and from our imperfect knowledge of it, the bulk of them are unintelligible to the best scholars."[5]

I offer these citations to illustrate just how easily our notion of the Exeter riddles' "unintelligible" obscurity can shift from one sense to another. It is easy enough, after all, to say that the riddles are "enigmatic," and this is certainly true in more than one sense. But too often in the scholarship on these texts, terms such as "enigmatic" and "riddling" are used to mean so many different things as to become almost meaningless. Indeed, one of the

2. Thorpe, *Codex Exoniensis,* x.

3. John Josias Conybeare, *Illustrations of Anglo-Saxon Poetry* (London: Harding and Lepard, 1826), 213.

4. Thomas Wright, *Biographia Britannica Literaria* (London: John W. Parker, 1842), 79.

5. John Thrupp, *Anglo-Saxon Home: A History of the Domestic Institutions and Customs of England* (London: Longman, Green, Longman, and Roberts, 1862), 386–87.

basic temptations of any researcher of the Old English riddles is to use such labels as an excuse to offer arbitrary interpretations: if a reading does not make perfect sense, it only confirms the "riddling" nature of the text. Incoherence can seem like a virtue if there are no rules to answering the challenge.

Are there any rules, though? Just what is "enigmatic" or "riddling" about the Exeter riddles? Such questions are seldom addressed in the rush to propose new solutions. In particular, the relationship between the Exeter riddles and their absent answers has largely been supposed a matter resolvable through scholarly intuition and wit. But the Exeter riddles stand at the intersection of several rather idiosyncratic genres that may operate according to rules that do not strike the modern solver as intuitive. Moreover, we are unlikely to find a completely consistent model of riddling underlying every text in the anthology. Even the innocent label of "riddles" implies an apparently unified and transparent generic identity that may not be reflected in the collection—a compilation potentially plundered from a varied and vast field of enigmatic forms. The often obscure relationship between a given Exeter riddle and its solution must be evaluated one case at a time, but our readings should also be intelligible in terms of the particular traditions that inform them.

One common way to define the Old English riddles as a genre has been to list their characteristic features. In analyzing a passage from *Solomon and Saturn,* for instance, John Miles Foley sums up many of the major hallmarks of Old English riddling: "This brief passage has all the characteristics of the riddle genre: a seemingly impenetrable group of clues, a description that turns (like so many of the Exeter Book riddles) on an axis of animate versus inanimate, multifold contradictions (a voiceless beast with great wisdom, for example), and not least a version of the canonical closing formula that issues the challenge."[6] Foley's list is a good starting point, but we could easily add to it. Frequent use of prosopopoeia, occasional wordplay and runic clues, a fondness for unusual compounds, and the *topoi* of craft, transformation, and wondrous creatures are all notable features of many of the Exeter riddles. One problem with any such list is that, given the collection's diversity, none of these characteristics applies to all of the texts. Even the closing formulaic

6. John Miles Foley, "How Genres Leak in Traditional Verse," in *Unlocking the Wordhord: Anglo-Saxon Studies in Memory of Edward B. Irving, Jr.,* ed. Mark C. Amodio and Katherine O'Brien O'Keeffe (Toronto: University of Toronto Press, 2003), 96.

challenges are not found in many of the riddles (although one might argue that they are always implied).

Another approach might be to forgo field marks in favor of classification. This is the common strategy adopted by several editors of the collection. Earlier editions tend to focus on the surmised origins of different riddles, with Frederick Tupper (1910) and A. J. Wyatt (1912) choosing to stress the distinction (in Tupper's words) "between the *Kunsträtsel* and the *Volkrätsel,* between literary and popular problems." This division tends to be made according to length, subject matter, and perceived literary quality.[7] Williamson, on the other hand, rejects such a distinction. Instead, he stresses the difference between first- and third-person riddles and the implications of these shifts in the speaker's position.[8] But Williamson's choice to divide the collection along these lines seems rather arbitrary, and in any case such categories do little to help us understand what makes these riddles recognizably "riddles."

Nor has the frequent appeal to metaphor gone very far to clarify the question, although the authority of Aristotle is often invoked in discussing this aspect of the collection.[9] Indeed, in the *Rhetoric* we learn that "good riddles do, in general, provide us with satisfactory metaphors: for metaphors imply riddles, and therefore a good riddle can furnish a good metaphor," while in the *Poetics* we read, "The very nature indeed of a riddle is this, to describe a fact in an impossible combination of words (which cannot be done with the real names for things, but can be with their metaphorical substitutes)."[10] Another oft-quoted statement is Gaston Paris's definition of the riddle as an unusual and unknown metaphor: "L'énigme est une métaphore ou un groupe de métaphores dont l'emploi n'a point passé dans l'usage commun et dont l'explication n'est pas évidente" (The riddle is a metaphor

7. Tupper, *Riddles of the Exeter Book,* xvi; Wyatt, *Old English Riddles,* xxviii–xxxi.

8. Williamson, *Old English Riddles,* 25.

9. See, for instance, Tupper, *Riddles of the Exeter Book,* xiii. H. H. Abbott, trans., *The Riddles of the Exeter Book* (Cambridge: Golden Head Press, 1968), ii, also mentions Aristotle on the riddle, and in fact lifts his discussion almost verbatim from Tupper. See also Nigel F. Barley, "Structural Aspects of the Anglo-Saxon Riddle," *Semiotica* 10 (1974): 143; Craig Williamson, trans. *A Feast of Creatures: Anglo-Saxon Riddle-Songs* (Philadelphia: University of Pennsylvania Press, 1982), 26; Rafal Boryslawski, "The Elements of Anglo-Saxon Wisdom Poetry in the *Exeter Book* Riddles," *Studia Anglica Posnaniensia* 38 (2002): 43; and Michelle Igarashi, "Riddles," in *A Companion to Old and Middle English Literature,* ed. Laura Cooner Lambdin and Robert Thomas Lambdin (Westport, Conn.: Greenwood Press, 2002), 337.

10. *The Rhetoric and Poetics of Aristotle,* trans. Ingram Bywater (New York: Random House, 1984), 170, 253.

or a group of metaphors, the employment of which has not passed into common use, and the explanation of which is not self-evident).[11] These and other authorities are often cited, but further discussions of the Exeter riddles' metaphorical nature tend to disappoint. Williamson, for instance, declares that "riddles are a form of literary game; they are also a metaphoric disguise." He goes on to discuss the nature of these disguises and concludes that they are nearly always anthropomorphic.[12] For most who address this question, in fact, the Exeter riddles are metaphorical largely insofar as they often employ a first-person speaker or describe an inanimate object as if it were alive. At times a particular personality or social role is detected in the creature or speaker. Most often this involves something like the heroic code of an anchor or sword, the martyrdom of a manufactured object, or simply the general monstrosity of a creature with too many teeth, limbs, heads, or eyes.[13] Beyond such disguises, metaphors may also be noted on a smaller scale, as individual figurative details that do not add up to a larger pattern. Tupper, for instance, declares that "hardly a riddle is without its element of metaphor," but he restricts his discussion of the Exeter riddles to three rather weak examples: "The Pen is called 'the joy of birds,' the Wind 'heaven's tooth,' and the stones of the Ballista the treasure of its womb."[14] If calling a feather "the joy of birds" is to be counted among the most metaphorical moments of the Exeter riddles, it is surprising that Aristotle's statements are so commonly invoked in discussing these Old English texts.

Indeed, it is worth remembering that the statements made by Aristotle and Paris are primarily responses to riddles circulating in oral tradition and

11. Gaston Paris, preface to Rolland, *Devinettes ou énigmes populaires,* viii. The translation here is taken from Georges and Dundes, "Toward a Structural Definition," 111.

12. Williamson, *Old English Riddles,* 26.

13. Paul Sorrell, "Oaks, Ships, Riddles," 107, explains that "the Old English riddle is a metaphorical genre, one thing being described in terms of another. This usually takes the form of a description of an inanimate object in terms appropriate to an animate being (often referred to in general terms such as *wiht* or *deor*)." The discussion of metaphorical Old English riddling provided in Barley, "Structural Aspects," 147–50, also focuses on rather general metaphors, such as "a rake in terms of a rooting animal" or "a riding-well as monster." Wim Tigges, "Signs and Solutions: A Semiotic Approach to the Exeter Book Riddles," in *This Noble Craft: Proceedings of the Tenth Research Symposium of the Dutch and Belgian University Teachers of Old and Middle English and Historical Linguistics,* ed. Erik Kooper, Costerus, n.s., 80 (Amsterdam: Rodopi, 1991), 59–82, discusses "semiotic transformations" such as "a lifeless object described generally in terms of a living being" or an "object or living creature in a social situation." Likewise, Ruth Wehlau, *"The Riddle of Creation": Metaphor Structures in Old English Poetry* (New York: Peter Lang, 1997), 94, 121, is also concerned with general metaphors of animation ("body metaphors") and personification ("Nobles and lords are used as metaphors for mundane objects").

14. Tupper, *Riddles of the Exeter Book,* xiii–xiv.

are not necessarily meant to describe the kind of literary riddles that largely constitute the Exeter collection. It is important to notice the difference between various enigmatic forms, even if medieval compilers of catchall riddle collections seldom make such distinctions. Bearing this in mind, it may nevertheless prove useful to turn now to the work of folklorists on the riddle, since Anglo-Saxonists have offered so few definitions of the Old English genre. Archer Taylor is perhaps the best-known expert on oral traditions of riddling, and he defines "true riddles" (as distinct from numerical conundrums, catechism-style questions, and other interrogative forms) as "descriptions of objects in terms intended to suggest something entirely different."[15] Essentially, then, riddles are to be understood as metaphorical descriptions whose meaning is concealed from an audience—an understanding very near to what we see in Aristotle and Paris. Savely Senderovich, however, points out that Taylor himself found difficulty in aligning his definition with many of the texts found in his monumental, comprehensive anthology of English riddling from oral tradition.[16] This shortcoming seems to call for a more inclusive definition of the traditional riddle, such as the one Georges and Dundes provide: "A riddle is a traditional verbal expression which contains one or more descriptive elements, a pair of which may be in opposition; the referent of the elements is to be guessed."[17]

Georges and Dundes's definition may be inclusive, but it tells us precious little about what makes a riddle a riddle. In fact, Charles T. Scott shows that their definition, structurally speaking, could apply to other genres as well as it does to the riddle.[18] So, in Scott's example, the proverb "money talks" fits Georges and Dundes's definition of a riddle quite well. The only distinction—that "the referent of the elements is to be guessed"—lies in the expected reception of the riddle. In most of these definitions, in fact, the crucial distinction between riddles and other kinds of verbal expression tends to be located in the position of the solver, who is at pains to discover an answer. For Georges and Dundes, the solution is "to be guessed," for Paris the meaning of a metaphor is novel or not evident, while for Taylor what seems to count is that the solver be suspicious of what the text suggests.

A good many other studies, indeed, stress what riddles do to the solver as their defining trait. So, for instance, in another influential definition we are

15. Taylor, *English Riddles from Oral Tradition,* 1.

16. Senderovich, *Riddle of the Riddle,* 55.

17. Georges and Dundes, "Toward a Structural Definition," 113.

18. Scott, "On Defining the Riddle," 129–42. See also Scott, "Study of the Riddle," 120–27.

told that "riddles are questions that are framed with the purpose of confusing or testing the wits of those who do not know the answer."[19] But if we define the riddle in terms of the reader's challenge to solve, we raise all kinds of intractable questions concerning the audience of these texts. While it is true that the rhetoric of riddling often challenges an imagined solver to apply wit and cunning and to unveil an answer, most research (on traditional riddling, at least) concludes that solutions are "to be known" rather than to be guessed or induced by adding up the clues.[20] The fact that the Exeter riddles are found in a manuscript without answers could indicate a greater emphasis on the reader's challenge—or it could indicate that many of its conventional conceits were considered no serious challenge at all. It is hard to say. Perhaps John Frow is close to the truth when he argues that the solution to a riddle "should be both in principle available to the respondent, and in practice not available."[21] On the other hand, it seems possible that readers found pleasure in retrospectively meditating over old solutions or appreciating imaginative variations on old riddling chestnuts. For some Anglo-Saxon readers, then, the solutions could be in principle not available but in practice rather easy to recognize—to turn the tables on Frow's formulation. Others may have needed more help, no doubt. After all, riddling does appear to divide audiences according to those who are in the know and those poor souls who dwell in the dark. Yet Elaine Tuttle Hansen is careful to note that the Exeter riddles "presuppose a *fictional* interaction, a face-to-face situation, which partly determines their meaning in a written form" (emphasis added).[22] Certainly it is worth thinking about how that fiction is inscribed in the rhetoric of the riddles, but in considering the Old English genre we should be wary of taking those fictions too seriously. In practice, both literary and oral riddles offer a range of positions for posers, solvers, and side participants. It is probably better, then, to stress the solver's imagined position less, and put more emphasis on the relationship between a riddle and its solution, for the situation is rather more complex than a simple routine of asking and answering implies.

19. Roger D. Abrahams and Alan Dundes, "Riddles," in *Folklore and Folklife: An Introduction,* ed. Richard M. Dorson (Chicago: University of Chicago Press, 1972), 130.

20. Senderovich, *Riddle of the Riddle,* 19–20, surveys the many studies that support this view.

21. John Frow, *Genre* (New York: Routledge, 2006), 36.

22. Elaine Tuttle Hansen, *The Solomon Complex: Reading Wisdom in Old English Poetry* (Toronto: University of Toronto Press, 1988), 131.

Actually, speaking of riddles in terms of questions and answers may cause some confusion. Riddles seem to be distinct from other kinds of questions in that they set up a relationship of synonymy between the riddle's description and its solution.[23] Other interrogative kinds do not count as riddles, even if the implied poser is thought to occupy a position of authority or superior knowledge. For instance, a text known as *Pharaoh* is found among the disparate materials separating the two major groups of riddles in the Exeter Book:

> "Saga me hwæt þær weorudes   wære ealles
> on Farones fyrde,   þa hy folc godes
> þurh feondscipe   flygan ongunn."
> "Nat ic hit be wihte,   butan ic wene þus,
> þæt þær screoda wære   gescyred rime
> siex hun[........]a   searohæbbendra;
> þæt eal fornam   yþ[...........]
> wraþe wyrde   in woruldrice."
>
> ["Tell me how many troops in Pharaoh's army there were in all, when they in enmity began to pursue God's people." "I do not know anything about it, except that I think there was the number of six hundred armed chariots, which the tumult of the waves swept away; it fiercely destroyed it in the kingdom of the earth."][24]

This kind of dialogue poem is distinct from the riddle in that its question and the answer are not equivalents—a solution does not answer a riddle's query per se. Rather, in a riddle, the solution *names* the description. *Saga hwaet ic hatte,* the Exeter riddles often demand: "Say what I am *called.*"

It is even more important, perhaps, to stress that a riddle is not simply an obscure or unintelligible description. Alice's complaint to the Mad Hatter is paradoxical for this very reason: " 'I think you might do something better with the time,' she said, 'than wasting it in asking riddles that have no answers.' "[25] But riddles without answers are never really riddles. John Frow

23. Frow, *Genre,* 34.

24. Krapp and Dobbie, *Exeter Book,* 223. For a discussion of this text and its genre, see Joseph B. Trahern Jr., "The *Ioca Monachorum* and the Old English *Pharaoh,*" *English Language Notes* 7 (1970): 165–68.

25. Lewis Carroll, *Alice in Wonderland,* ed. Donald J. Gray (New York: W. W. Norton, 1971), 56.

paraphrases Tzvetan Todorov in perceptively defining the riddle as "the unity within a dialogic couplet of a predicate and a subject: a set of properties and the thing they describe."[26] So we might say that riddles join up two texts, one of which is understood to be the compressed equivalent of the other. To be sure, the binary structure of the riddle is one reason why John D. Niles's recent challenge, that we "answer the Exeter riddles in their own tongue," is so important.[27] To offer a solution in modern English is to distort the fundamental relationship between an Old English riddle's subject and predicate (although it is conceivable that a Latin solution might answer a riddle posed in Old English). And so it is also essential to distinguish the *proposition* of a riddle (the description to be posed) from the riddle as a unified whole. A riddle, strictly speaking, comprises two parts and forms a binary structure of one proposition and one solution.[28] The term "proposition" is useful, too, because it allows us to emphasize that one half of the riddle is understood to stand prior to the solution in a fundamental, if fictional, sense (no matter the actual point of view of the solver).

The Exeter riddles are texts that come to us without supplied solutions, so we might say that the riddles, as we find them in the Exeter Book, are not complete riddles but only riddlic propositions. Yet because all generic markers point to their being intended to function as riddles, we are placed in the rather odd position of needing to "finish" these texts before we can interpret how they work, and this is one of the paradoxes that make studying these particular texts a challenge. It also means that our assumptions about the binary structure of riddles will govern much of the way we think about these enigmatic poems. The question is crucial, then, but not at all straightforward, and it is rarely addressed in the countless proposals for solutions offered piecemeal since the time of Tupper. What is the relationship between riddle propositions and their solutions?

This is not an easy question to answer. Nor is the situation likely the same for every riddle in the Exeter Book. In the crowded field of enigmatics,

26. Frow, *Genre,* 34.

27. Niles, *Old English Enigmatic Poems,* 101–48.

28. A single riddle proposition, of course, may be joined with various different solutions, in which case we have more than one riddle. The distinction may seem trivial, but several recent readings of the Exeter riddles posit "double solutions" in a way that is, to my mind, quite inconsistent with any known mode of riddling. Nor is it quite right to speak of double-entendre riddles as having "double solutions," as I discuss further below. Niles reminds us that, whether in unriddling riddles or in interpreting other texts, our readings should be "in harmony with the genre (or nexus of genres) that is at stake" (*Old English Enigmatic Poems,* 30).

there are many different kinds of interrogative riddlic forms—from dialogue questions such as *Pharaoh* to cryptographic puzzles to obscure ekphrastic descriptions. Other forms are often closely associated with riddles in medieval manuscripts, including the proverb, the fable, and dream interpretations.[29] In fact, the dream-riddle connection may be thematized within the Exeter collection itself. Following a solution offered by Stanley Greenfield, Antonina Harbus has shown that Riddle 39's account of dreaming is in line with written authorities on the "true or revelatory dream," and further suggests that the poem draws connections between the visual experience of dreaming and that of solving riddles.[30] Such a connection would be unsurprising, given the close associations of riddling and dreaming in medieval texts.[31] Dreams and riddles are at least once conflated in the Bible,[32] but the *Dream of the*

29. For a discussion of how "riddles and fables had interacted with each other from a very early period," see Jan M. Ziolkowski, *Talking Animals: Medieval Latin Beast Poetry, 750–1150* (Philadelphia: University of Pennsylvania Press, 1993), 41–46. See also Bitterli, *Say What I Am Called,* 68n23.

30. Stanley B. Greenfield, "Old English Riddle 39 Clear and Visible," *Anglia* 98 (1980): 95–100, first made the convincing argument for "dream." The solution is accepted by Hans Pinsker and Waltraud Ziegler, *Die altenglischen Rätsel des Exeterbuchs* (Heidelberg: Carl Winter, 1985), 242–45. Eric Gerald Stanley, "Stanley B. Greenfield's Solution of *Riddle* (ASPR) 39: 'Dream,'" *Notes and Queries* 38 (1991): 148–49, endorses Greenfield's solution and offers a small emendation to clear up the possible difficulty of the creature's stated inability to speak. Antonina Harbus, "*Exeter Book Riddle 39* Reconsidered," *Studia Neophilologica* 70 (1998): 139–48, adds support and refines Greenfield's solution. Niles, *Old English Enigmatic Poems,* 142, accepts the arguments of Greenfield and Harbus and proposes *swefn* 'auspicious dream', corresponding to Latin *somnium,* as an appropriate answer given in the Anglo-Saxon tongue.

31. Artemiodorus, for example, writes that "allegorical dreams are those which disclose their meaning through riddles." *Oneirocritica,* trans. Robert J. White (Park Ridge, N.J.: Noyes Press, 1975), 4.1. Macrobius, the chief medieval authority on dreams, writes, "By an enigmatic dream we mean one that conceals with strange shapes and veils with ambiguity the true meaning of the information being offered, and requires an interpretation for its understanding. We do not explain further the nature of this dream since everyone knows from experience what it is." *Commentary on the Dream of Scipio,* trans. William Harris Stahl (New York: Columbia University Press, 1966), 90. There is some doubt, however, whether Macrobius's *Commentary* was widely known or read in Anglo-Saxon England.

32. For instance, in Numbers 12:6–8 (*Biblia sacra,* 197), God speaks to Aaron and Miriam: "Si quis fuerit inter vos propheta Domini in visione apparebo ei vel per somnium loquar ad illum at non talis servus meus Moses qui in omni domo mea fidelissimus est ore enim ad os loquor ei et palam et non per enigmata et figuras Dominum videt" (If there be among you a prophet of the Lord, I will appear to him in a vision, or I will speak to him in a dream. But it is not so with my servant Moses who is most faithful in all my house. For I speak to him mouth to mouth, and plainly: and not by riddles and figures doth he see the Lord). Here is the highest authority for conflating two types of experience: dreams and visions sent from the divine are equated with *enigmata et figuras* 'riddles and figures'. In the Old English Heptateuch, Pharaoh's dream reads like a riddle in its repetition of the phrase *ic seah.* Joseph too sounds like a riddle solver when he tells Pharaoh, "Þys swefn is anræd" (This dream has a single meaning). S. J.

Rood must be the most famous place in the Old English corpus where the language of riddling overlaps with the language of dreaming.[33] The riddle formula *ic seah* dovetails with the wonders of the dreamer's vision:

> Þuhte me þæt ic gesawe syllicre treow
> on lyft lædan, leohte bewunden,
> bearma beorhtost.
>
> [It seemed to me that I saw a marvelous tree hoisted in the air, wrapped in light, the brightest of trees.][34]

The wonders of dreams, their shifting images and paradoxes, their traditional need for riddle-like interpretation: all of these parallels may have made what Harbus calls "the enigma of the dream" second nature to an Anglo-Saxon reader. On the other hand, the Aesopic fable's binary structure of story and moral creates a kind of equivalency—between a narrative of speaking creatures and a conclusive epimythium—that is also rather reminiscent of riddling. We could go further to say that many fables, like traditional riddles, seem rather disconnected from their assigned morals or "solutions"; such resolutions often fail to satisfy.

That sense of failure, in fact, is an important aspect of the particular dynamic between many riddles' propositions and solutions. In distinguishing riddles from other questions, I have noted that a solution *names* the proposition, but as Andrew Welsh has emphasized, this naming could more properly be called a *mis*naming. As he puts it, the "unknown never completely fits into the known."[35] A riddle couplet inevitably fails—there is usually a kind of friction in the relationship between proposition and solution. Charles T. Scott describes this crucial aspect of traditional riddling in terms of a "partially obscured semantic fit," by which he means that the details of the proposition tend to be unlikely descriptions of the solution. "This unexpected

---

Crawford, ed., *The Old English Version of the Heptateuch, Ælfric's Treatise on the Old and New Testament, and His Preface to Genesis* (London: Oxford University Press, 1922), 41.25.

33. J. A. W. Bennett sees a use of "riddling technique" in the *Dream of the Rood* and compares its opening lines to Riddle 29 in *Poetry of the Passion* (Oxford: Clarendon Press, 1982), 6. A more systematic comparison can be found in Peter Orton, "The Technique of Object-Personification in *The Dream of the Rood* and a Comparison with the Old English *Riddles*," *Leeds Studies in English*, n.s., 11 (1980): 1–15.

34. George Philip Krapp, ed., *The Vercelli Book*, ASPR 2 (New York: Columbia University Press, 1932), 61 (lines 4–6a).

35. Andrew Welsh, *The Roots of Lyric* (Princeton: Princeton University Press, 1977), 32.

relation [between proposition and solution]," Scott writes, "can be attributed to the slim chance that the item specified in the answer will occur in the context provided by the proposition."[36] To clarify what Scott means by a "slim chance," take a look at one of the riddles found in his study:

> A whitewashed tomb,
> In it the soul breathes.

The solution is "egg."[37] Following Scott, we might say that there is only a "slim chance" that an egg can be called a tomb, presumably because there is only a "slim" overlap in the semantic range of tombs and eggs. Both may be recognized as sealed containers, but each has a much more prominent characteristic. Eggs contain new life and serve as food; tombs contain dead bodies and are associated with the supernatural. The status of eggs and tombs as more or less airtight enclosures is a secondary, less "usual" characteristic of each. Likewise, the contents of an egg "breathe" only by a "slim chance" in the semantic range of that verb. In common usage, "to breathe" is more *likely* to mean "to respire" than its extended, metonymic sense of "to live." In Scott's analysis, then, the solution makes contact with the proposition primarily at the backwaters of a given semantic field.

This rather fundamental observation has not always been considered in the practical pursuit of answering the Exeter riddles, though a few solvers have discussed its importance. A. N. Doane, for one, points out that "the trick in solving these riddles is not only to note what is revealed but also to account for the deliberate tendencies of the obfuscation and to discount certain features in just the right amount. Too little discount and we see no other object than the fictional creature that is given; too much and we go for the wrong object altogether."[38] Essentially, then, what Scott calls "partially obscured semantic fit" Doane here calls "obfuscation." Along the same lines, A. J. Wyatt says that the Exeter riddles are "descriptions of an object which are intended to be at once accurate and misleading: the more misleadingly accurate and accurately misleading, the better."[39] What is needed, though, is not an imagined "misled" solver but a clearer picture of how the obfuscated

36. Scott, *Persian and Arabic Riddles,* 72.

37. Ibid., 124.

38. A. N. Doane, "Three Old English Implement Riddles: Reconsiderations of Numbers 4, 49, and 73," *Modern Philology* 84 (1987): 243.

39. Wyatt, *Old English Riddles,* xxviii.

description works. Does it follow any rules or patterns? Another recent solver, Mercedes Salvador Bello, attempts to distinguish between "direct" (or literal) clues and "indirect" clues, those that "must undergo a decoding process." To determine which clues need decoding, Salvador Bello explains, "the solver must use his/her intuition and wit."[40] Similarly, Doane concedes that "the process [of accounting for the obfuscation] is of course very precarious and subjective."[41] Certainly evaluating any of these most difficult Anglo-Saxon poems is a precarious task, particularly because methods of obfuscation are so often evaluated in the context of critics making their best arguments in favor of new solutions. Often in these cases almost anything goes. It would be useful, though, if we could know something about the generic conventions and principles underlying the binary structure of the proposition and solution. I wish to argue, in fact, that the "slim chances" of the Exeter riddles tend to occur according to somewhat regular patterns, although we should not be surprised if the modes of obfuscation vary within the eclectic collection. While each Old English text requires individual study, any reading of an Exeter riddle must provide a coherent answer to this question.

Aside from trusting her own wit, Salvador Bello does offer one identifying mark of obfuscation. This is the presence of explicit paradox, "as it is something that the solver recognizes to be against logic." In other words, if a creature is said to be already born and yet not yet born (to borrow one of Salvador Bello's examples), we must suspect an indirect clue—a metaphor or a slim semantic chance of some kind.[42] More than one miracle of postnatal birth is found in Symphosius's Enigma 14:

> Mira tibi referam nostrae primordia vitae:
> Nondum natus eram, nec eram iam matris in alvo;
> Iam posito partu natum me nemo videbat.

> [I shall tell you the wondrous beginning of my life: Not yet was I born, nor was I still in my mother's womb; though already brought to birth, no one saw me born.][43]

40. Mercedes Salvador Bello, "Direct and Indirect Clues: Exeter Riddle No. 74 Reconsidered," *Neuphilologische Mitteilungen* 99 (1998): 17.

41. Doane, "Three Old English Implement Riddles," 244.

42. Salvador Bello, "Direct and Indirect Clues," 18, 27n24.

43. Ohl, *Enigmas of Symphosius*, 46–47.

One could say, along with Wyatt, that this description is a "misleadingly accurate" description of the oddness (at least from a mammalian perspective) of oviparous reproduction. But we should try not to worry about who is misleading whom. Whether an imagined solver could guess the answer through knowledge of the natural world is not the point. What is important is simply that the semantic slim chances (calling either an egg being laid or a chick being hatched a "birth") are accountable in terms of the genre's built-in love of impossible oppositions. In riddling, as we have seen, the dead carry the living, the daughter bears the mother, the dwelling speaks while the dweller is silent. One way to account for a riddle's obfuscation, then, is simply to show how the semantic slim chances serve a satisfying sense of apparent contradiction.

It is not only the pull of paradox that shapes riddling propositions, however. Outright paradox, in fact, is rather less important than simply the proliferation of neat oppositions and echoes within the description. In other words, many "slim chances" between description and solution arise as a function of the riddle proposition's generic tendency toward formal elegance and, at times, dizzying complexity. Quite a few of Symphosius's *enigmata,* for example, are mostly preoccupied with knotting up intricate, dense descriptions, as here in his riddle on *catena* 'chain':

> Nexa ligor ferro, multos habitura ligatos;
> Vincior ipsa prius, sed vincio vincta vicissim;
> Et solvi multos, nec sum tamen ipsa soluta.
>
> [Fastened with iron am I bound who shall hold many in bonds; first I myself am bound, but when bound I bind in turn; and many I have loosed, nor yet myself am loosed.][44]

Riddling concatenations of this kind are not necessarily "paradoxes" (what is so impossible about a binder being bound?), but the chain of linked variations conveys a pleasing sense of intricacy—one to be unlocked with a single, satisfying click of the answer's key. As Riddle 42, lines 11b–15a, declares,

> Swa ic þæs hordgates
> cægan cræfte þa clamme onleac

44. Ibid., 38–39.

þe þa rædellan wið rynemenn
hygefæste heold, heortan bewrigene
orþoncbendum.

[Thus I have unlocked the chains of the treasure door with the power of the key which held the riddle cunningly against riddle solvers, hidden in its core with clever knots.]

The elaborate craft of the riddle's proposition is inextricably linked to its tolerance for semantic slim chances, and so one way to account for an Old English riddle's obfuscation is simply to demonstrate its place within some kind of formal pattern, whether the detail fits within a chain of oppositions or even simply creates an effect of sound. Riddle 28, lines 4–7b, says that its subject is

corfen, sworfen, cyrred, þyrred,
bunden, wunden, blæced, wæced,
frætwed, geatwed, feorran lædded
to durum dryhta.

[carved, rubbed, turned, dried, bound, wounded, bleached, weakened, adorned, prepared, and brought from afar to the doors of men.]

Do all these descriptors make clear sense in terms of a literal solution? Maybe yes and maybe no, for some of these details may be chosen as much for their rhyme as for their meaning.

Some kind of rhyme or reason, then, should be required whenever solvers of the Exeter riddles appeal to obfuscation in arguing for an answer, for to stress that riddle descriptions are "dark" does not mean that any kind of obscurity makes sense in the context of riddling. For instance, Kevin Kiernan, in the process of solving Riddle 95 as "prostitute," examines the following lines:

Þeah nu ælda bearn,
londbuendra, lastas mine
swiþe secað, ic swaþe hwilum
mine bemiþe monna gehwylcum.

The language of Riddle 95 is in parts very difficult (for further discussion, see chapter 2), but these closing lines are easily translated: "Although now the sons of men, of land dwellers eagerly pursue my tracks, I nevertheless at times conceal my path from each of men." Paired together, the meanings of the nouns *swaþu* 'path, tracks' and *last* 'step, track, trace' in Old English are quite clear. However, Kiernan (relying on a sense of riddling deception) translates them much differently: "Though now the sons of men, of land dwellers, very much seek out my observances [*lāstas*], I will conceal mine with a bandage [*swaþe*]."[45] Kiernan adopts an extremely unlikely meaning for each word in order to support the idea that this section of the riddle refers to the menstrual cycle of prostitutes. I would be surprised if many readers found this interpretation convincing, though the method employed relies on just the sort of semantic "slim chances" we might at first blush expect in riddling. Indeed, many otherwise fine studies of individual Exeter riddles resort on occasion to a similarly arbitrary sense of obscurity—improbable readings offered in the name of riddling's mysteriously unintelligible nature.

Kiernan's reading is also improbable in terms of the conventional range of possible solutions. Solving Riddle 95 as "prostitute" would make it nearly the only riddle in the Exeter collection with a human profession as its solution. An oddball exception to this rule is Riddle 86, a variation on Symphosius's Enigma 94, *Luscus alium vendens* 'one-eyed seller of garlic', which reads:

> Cernere iam fas est quod vix tibi credere fas est:
> Unus inest oculus, capitum sed milia multa.
> Qui quod habet vendit, quod non habet unde parabit?
>
> [Now you may see what you scarcely may believe: one eye within, but many thousand heads. Whence shall he, who sells what he has, procure what he has not?][46]

As Ohl and others have noted, "Were it not for the title, this enigma would probably defy solution!"[47] The same naturally applies to Exeter Riddle 86, and even more so, since all reference to selling is missing in the Old English

45. Kevin Kiernan, "*Cwene:* The Old Profession of Exeter Riddle 95," *Modern Philology* 72 (1975): 387. As Kiernan explains, "The choice of words in most riddles is meant to be deceptive" (385).

46. Ohl, *Enigmas of Symphosius,* 128–29.

47. Ibid., 128.

version. Instead, Riddle 86 emphasizes the status of the text as a "monster" riddle by staging it as a slightly ominous invasion of a space where men are gathered, men who are *mode snottre* 'wise in mind', like the implied solvers of so many formulaic challenges found in the collection:

> Wiht cwom gongan þær weras sæton
> monige on mæðle, mode snottre;
> hæfde an eage ond earan twa,
> ond twegen fet, twelf hund heafda,
> hrycg ond wombe ond honda twa,
> earmas ond eaxle, anne sweoran
> ond sidan twa. Saga hwæt hio hatte.

> [A creature came walking to where men sat, a great many wise ones at assembly. The creature had one eye and two ears and two feet, twelve hundred heads, a back and a belly and two hands, arms and shoulders, one neck and two sides. Say what it is called.]

Riddle 86 amplifies the monstrosity of the creature in question by introducing a series of extra, but ordinary, body parts into the puzzle. In addition to what we learn in Symphosius, we are told that the Exeter garlic vendor has two ears, two feet, a back, a belly, two hands, arms and shoulders, along with a neck and two sides: all normal features for a creature with bilateral symmetry. The text is a nice example of how the riddling imperative for artful elaboration on a theme can lead to a proliferation of perfectly literal clues ("obfuscating" in terms of an imagined solver, but perfectly snug in terms of semantic fit). It is also, as Williamson notes, a "neck riddle" akin to the one Samson posed about the lion swarming with bees.[48] Neck riddles of this kind take their name from their typical role in folktales: a hero saves his neck by posing an elaborate description of a bizarre, singular occurrence—a question that cannot be answered without the solver's "having been there."[49]

48. Williamson, *Old English Riddles,* 377. For more on Samson's riddle, see chapter 4.

49. For more on neck riddles, see F. J. Norton, "The Prisoner Who Saved His Neck with a Riddle," *Folk-lore* 53 (1942): 27–57. Salvador Bello, "Direct and Indirect Clues," 17–18, chooses to illustrate her division between indirect and direct clues with the example of a neck riddle in the Holme collection with the solution of a blind eunuch striking a bat at twilight with a pumice stone while sitting in a mustard tree. Since the neck riddle represents an absurd violation of normal riddling rules, this is perhaps not an ideal example.

In fact, the nasty trick of the neck riddle is that it is, in a sense, no riddle at all. To secure his safety, the fictional riddler violates the basic expectations and generic rules of riddling. This violation, however, is not simply that the solution is impossibly specific, but also that it relies on knowledge about a fluke of happenstance, a chance sighting of something truly strange, such as a partridge sitting on six eggs in the skull of a dead horse.[50] Such trick solutions define how riddling *does not* work, so it is curious when modern solvers treat the Exeter riddles as incidental glimpses into a vanished past, as if the darkness of riddling arises from an "inside story" or a "personal reference" to events witnessed by the riddler.[51] An early example of this kind of reading is found in Stopford A. Brooke's *History of Early English Literature* (1892). Brooke analyzes Riddle 38, one of three riddles in the Exeter Book that reworks a set of riddling motifs borrowed from Latin enigmas on bull-calves.[52] The riddle concludes with a conventional riddling opposition:

> Seo wiht, gif hio gedygeð, duna briceð;
> gif he tobirsteð, bindeð cwice.
>
> [This creature, if it should prosper, will break up the hills. If torn apart, it will bind the living.]

To address this section, Brooke imagines the Exeter poet composing his riddles on a rambling hike through the countryside:

> While he lingered, watching, he saw, perhaps on this very day, a common incident which he made into a riddle. Among the cattle on the pasture, the young bull was tethered. With his close sympathy to animals the poet paints him as rejoicing in his turbulent youth, and fed with the four fountains of his mother. Suddenly he saw the beast dash loose and rush from the pasture into the tilled land. Then he let his imagination loose also, and pictured the bull breaking up the clods of earth left by the plough, as a monster might break up the hills.[53]

50. Norton, "Prisoner Who Saved His Neck," 31.

51. Edward B. Irving Jr., "Heroic Experience in the Old English Riddles," in *Old English Shorter Poems: Basic Readings*, ed. Katherine O'Brien O'Keeffe (New York: Garland, 1994), 206; Shook, "Old English Riddle No. 20: *Heoruswealwe*," in *Franciplegius: Medieval and Linguistic Studies in Honor of Francis Peabody Magoun, Jr.*, ed. Jess B. Bessinger Jr. and Robert P. Creed (New York: New York University Press, 1965), 199.

52. For these analogues in Aldhelm and Eusebius, see Williamson, *Old English Riddles*, 255.

53. Stopford A. Brooke, *The History of Early English Literature* (New York: Macmillan, 1892), 146.

What is particularly odd about this reading is that Brooke shows himself elsewhere to be quite aware of the Latin sources for many Exeter riddles—and yet he persists in interpreting this and the other Old English riddles in terms of chance personal experience, as if imaginative backstories might unlock these texts.

Riddle 38, however, is not an incidental glimpse into Anglo-Saxon England; it is a variation on a set of long-standing riddling conventions. Such conventions are remarkably consistent over time and distinct in their meaning—even when the constituent elements appear very similar. When the dead *binds* the living, there is probably a bull-calf in question. When the dead *carries* the living, it is likely to be an oak ship. When the dead *gives birth* to the living, "the answer is an egg and a chick."[54] On the other hand, as we have seen, when a *daughter* gives birth to her own mother, water is the answer. However, when a *son* is born before his sire, we have smoke and fire.[55] There are exceptions to all of these rules, but such conventions provide a key clue for unriddling many of the Old English enigmas. Note, too, that we can *account* for the semantic slim chances of these traditional riddles in terms of paradoxes and oppositions (living/dead, daughter/mother, son/father), but in many cases only familiarity with the conventions can lead us to the likely answers.[56]

The Exeter riddles are clearly much more than chains of conventional oppositions, however. Let us return, then, to the question of metaphor. Archer Taylor, as we recall, tells us that riddles are "descriptions of objects in terms intended to suggest something entirely different."[57] He also identifies a more particular pattern: "The description in general terms is understood metaphorically; the description in specific terms is understood literally."[58] A simple English "egg" riddle illustrates what Taylor means by this: "A white house full of meat / But no door to go in and eat."[59] The proposition is founded on a core metaphor, in which the house is the "vehicle" and the

54. Taylor, *English Riddles from Oral Tradition,* 306.

55. Ibid., 373.

56. Unfortunately, recognizing the importance of obfuscation in the Exeter riddles does not necessarily provide us with a clear method of inducing their answers, as Salvador Bello, "Direct and Indirect Clues," hopes: "The approach that I propose is as follows: study the direct clues and see what the possible solution is, disregarding the misleading ones for a while; once the direct clues seem to point to a particular solution, we will see if the misleading hints can be decoded in the light of this proposal" (19).

57. Taylor, *English Riddles from Oral Tradition,* 1.

58. Archer Taylor, "The Varieties of Riddles," in Kirby and Woolf, *Philologica,* 3–4.

59. Taylor, *English Riddles from Oral Tradition,* 476.

egg is the hidden "tenor," to use the well-known terms coined by I. A. Richards.[60] But everything else about the proposition is on the mark: eggs are indeed white, full of meat, and without doors. As Salvador Bello would stress, it is important to remember that traditional riddles typically involve a mix of details, some of which are to be taken quite literally, others not.

Taylor's definition, however, tells us that a riddle is not simply a scramble of literal and metaphorical elements: there is a pattern in which "general terms" are metaphorical and "specific terms" are literal. In the egg riddle, then, there is a central metaphor in which the "general" word *house* is substituted for the word *egg,* while the other "specific terms" are literal details that could apply equally to both houses and eggs (except, of course, that most houses are not "full of meat"). In essence, then, a riddle such as this might be thought an extended simile, in which the various likenesses and dissimilarities of eggs and houses are enumerated. Such analysis, as I noted in the Introduction, recalls the medieval grammarian Donatus's definition of the enigma as a text revealing *occultum similitudinem rerum* 'the hidden similarity of things'.[61] Taylor's definition soon breaks down, however, when we examine other egg riddles from his collection. For instance, there is very little that is literal about this egg riddle: "A lady in a boat, with a yellow petticoat."[62] The yolk is literally yellow, yes, but the rest of the proposition is packed with semantic chances of a very slim kind.

They are not arbitrary slim chances, however, and this seems very important to keep in mind. Each detail is explicable in terms of the central metaphor of an egg as a lady: the watertight shell becomes her "boat" and the yolk becomes her "petticoat." In the previous example from Scott's study ("A whitewashed tomb, / In it the soul breathes"), the semantic fit between "egg" and "white" would be snug, but the adjective "whitewashed" is presumably better applied to tombs than to eggs. The metaphor "tomb" exerts a kind of gravitational force on the rest of the proposition, so that the fit between the solution and the proposition is accordingly distorted. In keeping with the tomb's associations of the afterlife, the embryonic life that the egg holds is described as a "soul," which "breathes" primarily in opposition to the tomb's suffocating closeness. In riddles where egg yolks are described as "golden treasure," the eaters of the eggs become "thieves" who "break in and steal the gold," and the eggshell may be a "stronghold" rather than

60. I. A. Richards, *The Philosophy of Rhetoric* (New York: Oxford University Press, 1936).
61. Donatus, *Ars grammatica,* 402 (3.6).
62. Taylor, *English Riddles from Oral Tradition,* 232 (no. 647).

just a house.[63] None of these obfuscations is a random act of obscurity or ambiguity, and there is no need to worry about whether they are "far-fetched." The core metaphor may at times, it is true, seem like a rather arbitrary choice: an egg can be a milestone, a well (with "two kinds of water"), an earthenware jar (full of both honey and butter), a woman cut when her window breaks (bleeding yolk!), a locked chest (full of treasure), a little hill (which cannot be climbed), a "castle on the seaside," or, of course, a person who cannot be healed (Humpty Dumpty).[64]

What is not arbitrary, though, is how the metaphorical core of a riddle organizes the rest of the proposition, in a way reminiscent of Max Black's influential interaction theory of metaphor. Black argues that a metaphor "selects, emphasizes, suppresses, and organizes features of the principal subject by implying statements about it that normally apply to the subsidiary subject." In other words, the metaphor's "focus" (Black's rough equivalent of Richards's "vehicle": the tomb, house, or hill in the examples cited above) evokes a "system of related commonplaces" that reshapes, say, the understanding of an egg.[65] Black here is concerned with the implicit meaning of metaphors, how calling an egg a tomb might create a new sense of embryonic claustrophobia in the mind. In riddles, though, many of these implications (this nexus of associations and commonplaces evoked by the focus) are more or less explicitly represented in the proposition as elements of the description. Bearing this in mind, Black's term is nevertheless a useful one for describing the dark language of metaphorical riddles. A riddle's "focus," as I employ the term in this book, is a core metaphor shaping the proposition's obfuscation. It is a misnaming (whether actually stated or not) that accounts for a larger pattern of semantic "slim chances" in the riddle's description. Or put it this way: the riddle's metaphorical focus is the expected response of an imagined solver who took the riddle much too literally.

In most of the examples cited above, the riddle's focus gives rise to semantic "slim chances" of a kind that probably strike the reader as more or less acceptable extended meanings: living as breathing, eggshell as bone or marble, the yolk as a golden treasure. But in other cases, elements of the proposition may seem utterly inexplicable (such as the notion of the yolk as a

63. Harry Middleton Hyatt, *Folk-lore from Adams County, Illinois* (New York: Memoirs of the Alma Egan Hyatt Foundation, 1935), 660; Taylor, *English Riddles from Oral Tradition,* 476–79.

64. These examples are taken from Taylor, *English Riddles from Oral Tradition;* Hull and Taylor, *Collection of Irish Riddles;* and Basgöz and Tietze, *Bilmece.*

65. Max Black, *Models and Metaphors* (Ithaca: Cornell University Press, 1962), 44–45, 41.

"petticoat"). In fact, we cannot assume that all details of a riddle's proposition must make strict literal sense in relation to a riddle's solution. The riddle's focus may distort the solution's fit with the proposition beyond all recognition—beyond any "reasonable" sense of similarity. Take, for instance, this riddle about a bottle of wine: "As I went over London Bridge / I met old dirty Jay / I cut his throat / and sucked his blood, / and throwed his heart away."[66] How can the bottle be called old dirty Jay's *heart?* Examples like this reveal that, at times, aspects of a riddle proposition may make little literal sense in relation to the solution. Rather, it is more illuminating to stress the way a metaphorical focus *stretches out* those semantic "slim chances" of which Scott speaks. This may account for the obfuscation. Even when the details of a proposition are literally true of the solution, they may not make sense in terms of the answer alone: "My moder have a barrel, haven't got no staves.—Egg."[67] It is accurate to say that eggs have no "staves," but the reference to these missing wooden ribs is explicable only in terms of the metaphorical focus, here stated explicitly (a barrel). Analyzing a riddle of this kind is as much a matter of appreciating its metaphorical obfuscation as of adding up literal clues. It is worth considering, then, whether our typical methods for solving the Exeter riddles would allow for such semantic slim chances as an egg's yolk described as a petticoat, or an empty bottle called a murdered man's heart, or even an embryonic chick seen as "breathing" under its shell. Would such readings stand up to scrutiny? Fat chance.

But perhaps that is the point: the Exeter riddles are *not* simply riddles gathered from oral tradition. Rather, they are carefully crafted literary riddles and, moreover, they show a clear debt to a rich Anglo-Latin tradition of *enigmata.* It may be that the way a proposition is connected to a solution in the Latin literary enigma is more relevant to the study of the Exeter riddles—and indeed that relationship often differs significantly from what we see in oral tradition. The semantic fit of many Latin enigmas, as we have seen, is frequently distorted in relation to symmetrical oppositions and internal contradictions: biters bitten (onions), silent ones who speak when moved (bells), and uncaught quarry carried home (lice!). In quite a few other Latin enigmas, however, there is actually very little semantic distortion, as their "darkness" is mostly a matter of obscure information. Aldhelm, the founding

66. Taylor, *English Riddles from Oral Tradition,* 292 (no. 805k).
67. Ibid., 497 (no. 1171).

father of Anglo-Latin enigmatography, was particularly fond of such "riddling." For instance, he poses this description of the *Pleiades:*

> Nos 'Athlante satas stolidi' dixere priores;
> Nam septena cohors est, sed uix cernitur una.
> Arce poli gradimur nec non sub Tartara terrae;
> Furuis conspicimur tenebris et luce latemus
> Nomina de uerno ducentes tempore prisca.

> [The stupid ancients said that we were the offspring of Atlas. Our company is seven-fold, but one of us is scarcely to be seen. We walk at the summit of the sky and beneath the depths of the earth as well. We are visible in blackest darkness, but are hidden by daylight. We took our former name from that of spring.][68]

As Nicholas Howe has shown, Aldhelm's enigmas are posed with a strong pedagogical purpose, to illustrate the etymology of a word and to impart encyclopedic knowledge.[69] Howe and others have demonstrated that much of Aldhelm's riddling in fact derives from entries in Isidore's encyclopedic *Etymologiae,* and it would not be far off the mark to describe many of Aldhelm's propositions and solutions as akin to the headwords and entries in a reference book. Take, for instance, Aldhelm's enigma on heliotrope:

> Sponte mea nascor fecundo cespite uernans;
> Fulgida de croceo flauescunt culmina flore.
> Occiduo claudor, sic orto sole patesco:
> Vnde prudentes posuerunt nomina Graeci.

> [I am born from the fertile field, flourishing of my own accord; the shining crown grows golden with yellow bloom. With the sun in the west I close up, and open again at sunrise: whence the learned Greeks devised my name.][70]

68. Enigma 8 (Glorie, *Variae collectiones aenigmatum,* 391; translation from Lapidge and Rosier, *Aldhelm: The Poetic Works,* 72).

69. Howe, "Aldhelm's *Enigmata.*"

70. Enigma 51 (Glorie, *Variae collectiones aenigmatum,* 439; translation from Lapidge and Rosier, *Aldhelm: The Poetic Works,* 80).

There is certainly not much paradox here—let alone the extravagant metaphors of traditional riddling. The fit between proposition and solution is complicated only insofar as the description may rely on unusual facts, such as, in this case, Greek etymology. As Howe points out, "If [Aldhelm's] *Enigmata* seem weak or mechanical at times, it is not because they are too learned, but rather because of their assumption that the name and the thing correspond perfectly."[71] The semantic fit is snug—there is no hidden metaphorical focus shaping the proposition.

Of course, this is a tendency in Aldhelm and not an absolute rule. There are certainly moments of metaphor in Latin *enigmata,* if such moments are not usually sustained. I would argue, however, that there is good reason to think that some of the Exeter riddles may be constructed according to a model more akin to traditional metaphorical riddling than Aldhelmian enigmatics. One reason is simply the difficulty we have had accounting for much of what we see in Old English riddling. Two hundred years of scholarly ingenuity—and many an inexplicable detail—demonstrate the limitations of simply adding up the literal clues, though many elegant answers have been accepted. Ironically, too, our very success in establishing some solutions may obscure the extent to which we have not worked out how these texts operate. It is possible to solve a riddle, after all, without fully understanding it, and many of our most confident guesses are based not so much on pure induction as on one or two unambiguous clues—often confirmed through analogues. As far as *solving* goes, this is how it should be: if anything, we need to pay greater attention to what conventional riddling motifs can tell us. But once solved, the Old English riddle is considered solved in a broader sense: the solution provides all the explanation we need. In fact, many of the Exeter riddles that are considered definitively solved feature aspects of the proposition unsatisfied by the literal solution alone. And this is exactly what we would expect if the binary structure of some Exeter riddles resembles that of traditional metaphorical riddles.

And this brings us to one of the most compelling reasons to suspect that the Exeter riddles adopt modes of traditional riddling: the inclusion in the collection of several riddles with patent sexual double meanings. Long perceived as a curiosity in the body of Old English literature, their presence has implications beyond their sexual suggestiveness. In fact, they signal (rather definitively, to my mind) that the Exeter collection has connections to oral

71. Howe, "Aldhelm's *Enigmata,*" 58.

traditional riddling. This notion is vigorously denied by the most recent editor of the riddles, Craig Williamson, who declares that "there is no reason to ascribe the so-called obscene riddles to a folk tradition any more than the 'straight' riddles. The double entendre riddles are carefully crafted; indeed they must be so to carry out the disguise."[72] Williamson is certainly correct to defend the craft of the Old English sex riddles, but their artfulness has nothing to do with their particular mode of riddling, which is found with this intensity in no other Latin literary riddle surviving from Anglo-Saxon England. Andy Orchard's recent efforts to establish that Anglo-Latin enigmas also partake of "levity and occasional crude humour" only serve to support this point. His closest example is a joke from the *Collectanea* of Pseudo-Bede, which he paraphrases: " 'how do you make an ass-hole see?' (answer: add the letter 'o,' to transform *culus* [ass-hole] into *oculus* [eye])."[73] This riddle may be crude, but it is in no way comparable to the kind of sex metaphors we find throughout the Exeter Book. Such metaphors, though, are a hallmark of traditional riddling.

In fact, the sex riddle is the traditional riddle par excellence. It is in no sense a marginal form. Savely Senderovich demonstrates just how pervasive it is in folk riddling (even as represented in mildly bowdlerized anthologies such as Taylor's *English Riddles from Oral Tradition*), while the final two chapters of this book endeavor to show just how firmly rooted in traditional motifs are many of the Old English sex riddles.[74] At present, however, particular motifs are less important to consider than the fundamental mode of riddling for which the sex riddles stand. Take, for example, this riddle from Taylor's collection:

> Long, slim, and slender
> Tickles where it's tender;
> Two heads and nary [a] nose,
> Tickles where the hair grows.[75]

72. Williamson, *Old English Riddles,* 11.

73. Orchard, "Enigma Variations," 287.

74. Senderovich, *Riddle of the Riddle,* esp. 59–115. Taylor, *English Riddles from Oral Tradition,* 687–88, devotes a single page of his exhaustive collection to riddles depicting "erotic scenes." He does not, however, list the indecent propositions but only their "innocent" solutions: "I have deemed it sufficient to cite the answers to these riddles with the references to the places where they have been printed." Readers of the collection, however, may suspect that a few suggestive riddles escaped Taylor's eye.

75. Taylor, *English Riddles from Oral Tradition,* 606 (no. 1465).

If this description of a slender comb appears strange, it is of course because its semantic slim chances are governed by a particular metaphorical focus. Hardened readers of the Exeter riddles will not be fazed by this kind of poem. But rather than assume that the Old English sex riddles are oddball exceptions to the normal rules of riddling in the Exeter Book, I argue that metaphorical modes of riddling are important throughout the collection.

Critics have long noted that some of the Old English sex riddles seem to drift in and out of sexual double entendre, and the metaphorical core of other Exeter riddles may likewise come in and out of focus. Most of the Exeter riddles are much longer than traditional riddles, after all, and it stands to reason that their metaphors may not be consistent or limited to a single focus. As opposed to the clean economy of folk riddles, Taylor characterizes literary riddles as cluttered with clues. I have already quoted this passage in the Introduction: "In order to accumulate details enough to permit the listener to guess the answer, the riddler often sacrifices the unity of his conception. The first assertion and its denial are almost certain to conflict with the next pair. Yet the author goes on and on, while his conception becomes more and more incoherent."[76] By contrast, I would guess that many readers of the Exeter riddles are struck by the internal coherence of their propositions, at least in comparison to the rambling descriptions of many later literary riddles. This observation alone suggests the importance of extended metaphors in Old English riddling. Still, we should not require that a metaphor be sustained throughout the text before we acknowledge its role in the riddle's obfuscation. Nor should we expect the focus to be expressed explicitly. In this shoe riddle from Taylor's collection, for instance, the focus (a dog) is only implied: "All over the hills and back home at night, / Sits under the bed and gapes for bones"[77] (a literal interpretation would be barking up the wrong tree). In many of the Exeter riddles, the focus tends to be similarly implicit, though not always. A notable exception is the explicitly mentioned horses and men of Riddle 22, who seem to represent stars in the sky.[78] But while Riddle 22 is exceptional for its explicit metaphorical focus, its basic mode is nevertheless representative of much riddling in the Exeter Book. As Doane writes, "'Horsemen as stars,' 'stars as horsemen': such poetic equation is at the heart of the Old English riddles."[79] I very much agree.

76. Taylor, *Literary Riddle,* 3.

77. Taylor, *English Riddles from Oral Tradition,* 151 (no. 453b). See also 454–57 (nos. 453a–f).

78. For a discussion of this riddle, see chapter 3.

79. A. N. Doane, "The Other Anglo-Saxons," *Queen's Quarterly* 86 (1979): 309.

All of this suggests that reading the Exeter riddles may demand a more nuanced approach than simply adding up the clues.[80] If many of them are organized not only in relation to a solution but also under the influence of an implicit metaphorical focus, a second look at many "already solved" riddles may reveal evidence of such core metaphors. Another egg riddle, this one in Old English, provides a good first example. Exeter Riddle 13, in fact, has long been considered securely solved as ten chicks hatching from a clutch of eggs. We are able to count our chickens quite confidently, for the proposition opens by announcing:

> Ic seah turf tredan— ten wæron ealra,
> six gebroþor ond hyra sweostor mid—
> hæfdon feorg cwico.

> [I saw walking on the ground ten in all: six brothers and their sisters together. They had living spirits.]

Why six and four? The numbers seem to indicate the number of vowels and consonants in the named solution. I will return to this numbering in due time, but at the moment I am more concerned with how modern solvers have identified these brothers and sisters as chicks. In fact, our assurance of this solution seems to rest primarily on the basis of a single well-worn riddling conceit, expressed in an early section of the proposition:

> Fell hongedon
> sweotol ond gesyne on seles wæge
> anra gehwylces.[81]

> [Skins hung clear and visible on the wall of the hall of each one of them.]

80. One solver of the Exeter riddles who recognized this was Gregory K. Jember, "A Generative Method for the Study of Anglo-Saxon Riddles," *Studies in Medieval Culture* 11 (1977): 33–39. For instance, Jember writes, "The riddles are, after all, more subtly complex than a simple algebraic equation, and solving them involves more than introducing known values into a formula and computing a solution" (33). Jember's own alternative "generative method" for solving the riddles, however, produced such eccentric readings that it is probably safe to say his work has not been very influential.

81. Lines 3b–5a.

The motif of the caul on the wall is a familiar one in Latin *enigmata:* the idea is simply that the inner membrane of the egg (*ægerfelma* in Old English) hangs torn on the shell after the hatchling exits.[82] As a clue, it is unmistakable. For solvers of Riddle 13, then, the writing is on the wall, though the riddle continues for six and a half lines:

Ne wæs hyra ængum þy wyrs,
ne side þy sarre, þeah hy swa sceoldon,
reafe birofene, rodra weardes
meahtum aweahte, muþum slitan
haswe blede. Hrægl bið geniwad
þam þe ær forðcymene frætwe leton
licgan on laste, gewitan lond tredan.

[Nor was it to any of them the worse, nor was his side the more painful, although deprived of their garment and wakened by the might of the guardian of the heavens, they are compelled to tear with their mouths the gray fruit. Clothing will be renewed for those who previous to their coming forth allowed their trappings to lie on the path, to depart and tread the earth.]

As Bitterli and others before him have stressed, elements of this description recall Eusebius's enigma on the chick (*De pullo*):

Cum corio ante meo tectus uestitus et essem,
Tunc nihil ore cibi gustabam, oculisque uidere
Non potui; pascor nunc escis, pelle detectus
Viuo; sed exanimis transiui uiscere matris.

[At first I was clothed and protected in a shell, my mouth then tasted no food, my eyes saw nothing; but now, stripped of my skin, I eat and live, though lifeless I once left my mother's womb.][83]

Eusebius's enigma is essentially a chain of oppositions: once clothed but now stripped, once not tasting food but now eating, once born lifeless but now

82. For analogues, see Erika von Erhardt-Siebold, "Old English Riddle 13," *Modern Language Notes* 65 (1950): 98–99. See also Bitterli, *Say What I Am Called,* 116–18.

83. Enigma 38 (Glorie, *Variae collectiones aenigmatum,* 248; translation by Erhardt-Siebold, in ibid.).

living. A shadow of each of these elements might be detected in Riddle 13's description of stripped creatures who are "wakened" into life by God and compelled in their nakedness to eat gray fruit. Such parallels allow Bitterli to conclude, more or less justifiably, that Riddle 13 "retell[s] a traditional puzzle."[84]

Many aspects of this retelling remain puzzling, however. For instance, most of the oppositions accounting for Eusebius's strategy of obfuscation are absent from Riddle 13. Whereas the feeding of Eusebius's chicken is presented in terms of a linked opposition (it once tasted no food—but now it eats), the chicks of Riddle 13 simply feed because this is the typical behavior "of our various domestic fowls."[85] Is it typical, however, for newborn chicks to eat *haswe blede* 'gray fruit'? Bitterli solves the problem by choosing an unlikely translation ("grey shoots") and explaining that "with their strong bills and claws they eat almost anything they can dig out and pick up, including roots, shoots, seeds, small insects, and cultivated grain and other food they are given by man." The case might be made, but the detail remains a rather arbitrary semantic slim chance. Moreover, we might well wonder why the chicks are being *compelled* to eat this fruit, why the guardian of the heavens is mentioned in this connection, and why the riddle's ending emphasizes both a bitter departure and hope for the future renewal of the creatures' *hrægl* 'clothing'. In fact, Erhardt-Siebold tells us that this second promised clothing "refers, of course, to the growing down."[86] Maybe or maybe not, but accounting for the way the riddle works should involve more than explaining away literal clues.

Some of these clues simply cannot be accounted for, however. Perhaps the oddest detail in Riddle 13 is the assurance we are offered that *ne side þy sarre* 'nor was his side the more painful' on account of the creatures' genesis. The best that Williamson can do with this detail is to analyze it in terms of a riddling incongruity: "The paradox at least is clear: the creature sheds skin, yet feels no pain in the process."[87] That much is indeed clear, but the inconvenient particularity of the creature's "side" makes no good sense. In his translation, Williamson avoids the difficulty: "Though each had been

84. Bitterli, *Say What I Am Called,* 118.

85. Erhardt-Siebold, "Old English Riddle 13," 98. Bitterli elaborates on this point in *Say What I Am Called,* 118–19.

86. Erhardt-Siebold, "Old English Riddle 13," 98.

87. Williamson, *Old English Riddles,* 170.

stripped / Of a gossamer skin, none was nude / Or raw with pain."[88] Other readers have felt compelled to emend the problem away. Most recently, Bitterli follows earlier editors in emending the text to read *ne sið þy sarra* 'nor [their] journey more painful'. This change allows for a more generalized paradox of "skinned" creatures to be "unharmed as they walk from their nest."[89] Much about this riddle, then, must be emended, stretched in translation, or simply ignored to make the standard reading work.

To be clear, I do not doubt that the *solution* here is hatchling chicks (the caul on the wall clinches it); what I doubt is that the standard interpretations of this riddle account for the obfuscation of the poem, which does not seem coherent either as a straightforward description of chicks or as a riddle of paradoxical oppositions. With no other clear way to account for its obfuscation, we might consider metaphor. Bitterli and others have strained to show that Riddle 13 "evokes a vivid picture of a busy hen yard full of scratching and pecking fowl"—a rather hardscrabble scene.[90] In my opinion, though, the text evokes something even less edenic—the loss of Eden itself. To review the basics: in Riddle 13, a group of female and male creatures are stripped naked, forced to depart (*gewitan lond tredan* 'to depart and tread the earth'), and compelled to earn food through their own gritty labors (*sceoldon . . . muþum slitan / haswe blede* 'they are compelled to tear with their mouths the gray fruit').[91] And yet this fate is tempered by a promise of restoration: *hrægl bið geniwad* 'clothing will be renewed'. For any good Anglo-Saxon riddler, the fate of these naked creatures would resonate, recalling a moment told and retold in Old English letters—nowhere more poignantly than in Adam's confession to God in *Genesis A,* lines 865–71:

him þa sylfa oncwæð,
hean hleoðrade hrægles þearfa:
"Ic wreo me her wæda leasne,

88. Williamson, *Feast of Creatures,* 71. A more faithful translation is provided by W. S. Mackie, ed. and trans., *The Exeter Book,* 2 vols. (Oxford: Oxford University Press, 1934), 2:103: "None of them was any the worse, or his side the more painful."

89. Bitterli, *Say What I Am Called,* 115–16.

90. Ibid., 120.

91. Bitterli explains that young chicks, unlike other hatchling birds, feed themselves: "This behaviour is genuinely characteristic of all species of the pheasant family or *Phasianidae,* to which the domestic chicken (*Gallus domesticus*) belongs" (ibid., 118). This is no doubt true, but the *selection* of this detail has as much to do with the riddle's metaphorical focus as with the accuracy of the literal solution.

liffrea min, leafum þecce.
scyldfull mine, sceaðen, is me sare
frecne on ferhðe, ne dear nu forðgan
for ðe andweardne. ic eom eall eall nacod."

[Then he answered him, the miserable one spoke, the one in need of clothes: "My Lord, I hid myself here, lacking garments; I covered up with leaves. A guilty, injured conscience is painfully dangerous to me in spirit, nor do I dare to go forth into your presence. I am utterly, utterly naked."][92]

Adam and Eve have earned a painful exile, but one not without hope, for in the words of Riddle 13, their *hrægl bið geniwad* 'clothing will be renewed'. Indeed, in Genesis 3:21, God outfits the first couple in animal skins as they are expelled from the garden, like the creatures of Riddle 13, *gewitan lond tredan* 'to depart and tread the earth'. Biblical commentators such as Bede saw these garments as significant, "mystically teaching that the elect are to receive in Christ at the end of time the garment of immortality, which they lost in Adam at the beginning of time."[93] The half-line *hrægl bið geniwad,* then, resonates as a dramatic reversal of the elegiac chord struck elsewhere in the Exeter Book, as the famous Wanderer awakens to find that *sorg bið geniwad* 'sorrow is renewed' in his anxious exile: *Cearo bið geniwad.*[94] Surely the half-line in Riddle 13 is charged with more significance than the fluffing of feathers? The forlorn nakedness and promised clothing of the chicks is at the center of the metaphor of this riddle, then, but the focus is also felt throughout the poem in its tone, imagery, and diction. One of the primary meanings of *blēd,* for instance, is "specifically: the forbidden fruit of the Garden of Eden."[95] The fact that the naked chicks are scratching after *haswe blede* 'gray fruit' probably evokes substandard postlapsarian fare, for the word is commonly collocated with cheerier epithets, such as *beorht* 'bright'. In this context, the description of the creatures as "rodra weardes / meahtum aweahte" (wakened by the might of the guardian of the heavens) links the

92. A. N. Doane, ed., *Genesis A: A New Edition* (Madison: University of Wisconsin Press, 1978). In translating 869–870a, I follow Doane's construal of the text, p. 241.

93. Bede, *On Genesis,* trans. Calvin B. Kendall (Liverpool: Liverpool University Press, 2008), 136.

94. *The Wanderer,* lines 50, 55.

95. *Dictionary of Old English,* s.vv. "blēd," "blǣd," 1a.

newborn chicks with the genesis of human life, as we read also in *Genesis A,* lines 169–75:

> ne þuhte þa gerysne rodora wearde
> þæt adam leng ana wære
> neorxnawonges niwre gesceafte
> hyrde and healdend. forþon him heahcyning,
> frea ælmihtig fultum tiode
> wif, aweahte and þa wraðe sealde,
> lifes leohtfruma, leofum rince.

> [To the Guardian of the Heavens (*rodora wearde*) it did not then seem suitable that Adam were long alone the keeper and defender of the new creation of paradise. Therefore the High King, the Lord Almighty, created for him a helper, a woman, the Light-maker of Life animated (*aweahte*) and gave the helper to the dear man.]

Like the hatchlings of Riddle 13, then, Eve is a creature *aweahte* 'wakened/animated' by the *rodora wearde* 'Guardian of the Heavens'. Of course, the Guardian of the Heavens does the same for her mate: "folcmægþa fruman aweahte, æðelinga ord, þa he Adam sceop" ([he] animated/wakened the first of mankind, the original of princes, when he created Adam).[96] The "awakening" of Eve, however, involves a bit of minor surgery, as the poet of *Genesis A* goes on to explain (continuing the passage above, lines 176–180a):

> he þæt andweorc of adames
> lice aleoðode and him listum ateah
> rib of sidan. he wæs reste fæst
> and softe swæf, sar ne wiste,
> earfoða dæl ne þær ænig com
> blod of benne ac him brego engla
> of lice ateah liodende ban,
> wer unwundod.

> [He detached that material from the body of Adam and skillfully drew the rib from his side (*sidan*). He was fast asleep and in a soft slumber,

96. Doane, *Genesis A,* lines 1277–78.

> and did not experience pain (*sar*), a portion of suffering, nor did any blood come from the wound, but the prince of angels drew from his body the living bone, the man unwounded.]

As Doane explains, "It was a commonplace question whether Adam had felt any pain when God extracted the rib."[97] When Riddle 13, therefore, remarks that *ne side þy sarre* 'the side was not the more painful', it is the edenic metaphorical focus that shapes the description in the proposition, not the literal solution. Notice, though, that the detail *is* literally true for the solution: newborn chicks do not feel pain in their sides after exiting their eggshells. And yet referring to an absent pain in the "side" makes no sense if we relate the detail only to the solution, just as saying that an egg has "no wooden ribs" would make no sense outside the metaphor of a barrel in the riddle cited above.

I do not wish to belabor this reading, and I am certainly not arguing here for a "double solution," to avoid a term employed in a few recent studies of the Exeter riddles. The exile of Adam and Eve is not the *solution* to Riddle 13, after all, but rather the metaphorical focus that shapes the proposition, selecting certain aspects of hatchling life (as well as riddling commonplaces, perhaps) for emphasis, distortion, and elaboration. The riddle's focus is one thing, its solution something else altogether, and to speak of "double solutions" (even in the case of riddles involving sexual innuendo) is to confuse the question.[98] A confused solver, however—one who mistook the riddle's

97. Ibid., 236. Doane cites Augustine, *De Genesi ad litteram* 9.15.26. Bede raises the same point; see *On Genesis,* 122. See also John Chrysostom, *Homilies on Genesis,* trans. Robert C. Hill (Washington, D.C.: Catholic University of America Press, 1985), 198, for an extended discussion of how and why Adam "could not feel the loss he was suffering." Adam's *side* 'side' was an object of curiosity, too, in the riddlic dialogue of *Adrian and Ritheus:* "Saga me on hwæðere Adames sidan name ure drihten þæt ribb þe he þæt wif of geworhte.—Ic þe secge, on ðære winstran" (Tell me from which side of Adam did our Lord take the rib from which he made woman.—I tell you, from the left). The text and translation here are taken from Cross and Hill, *Prose Solomon and Saturn,* 35, 128.

98. The phrase "double solution" has been used in several different ways in the study of the Exeter riddles lately. Most commonly, the "double-entendre riddles" are often said to have a "double solution," with the tendency, as Melanie Heyworth, in "Perceptions of Marriage in *Exeter Book Riddles 20 and 61,*" *Studia Neophilologica* 79 (2007), points out, "to devalue the sexual solution of a riddle as incorrect and as in opposition to its non-sexual one" (171). The problem with Heyworth's position, as I argue in chapter 5, is the assumption that the metaphorical focus of a sex riddle actually is a "solution" (which it is not). A related use of the term "double solution" is used by Audrey L. Meaney, "Exeter Book Riddle 57 (55)—a Double Solution?" *Anglo-Saxon England* 25 (1996): 187–200, to describe a riddle without any such innuendo. In "A 'Double Solution' for Exeter Book Riddle 51, 'Pen and Three Fingers,'" *Notes and Queries,*

metaphorical focus for its solution—might guess *Adam ond Eue,* an answer whose letter count gives us six and four siblings to match Riddle 13's opening puzzle.[99] This, however, would be a mistake. In the next chapter I address the complications involved in the precise wording of the solution to Riddle 13, but for the moment I wish to remain focused on patterns of metaphor in the Exeter Book. Are there any patterns?

Actually, upon reflection, newborn chicks in the guise of fledgling humanity is not such an odd pairing. Thus far we have looked at how riddle propositions relate to their solutions. We may wonder, though, if anything coherent can be said about the way a riddle's *focus* tends to relate to its solution. Taylor provides some guidance here, noting that "riddlers do not often compare objects in the same category: a thing is usually compared to a person or an animal and less usually to another thing."[100] A certain degree of semantic friction between focus and solution, then, is common to traditional metaphorical riddling, and at the least is reflected in the familiar pattern in the Exeter Book of inanimate objects taking on a life or a voice of their own. Even when two lifeless objects are compared, though, there tends to be a significant disjunction in terms of scale or abstraction: a pair of trousers may be called "two roads," while a wedding ring might be named "a bottomless tub, full of flesh."[101] Moreover, the metaphorical focus often looms large in the riddle, while the solution tends to be something more simple and domestic. Riddles about riddling often stress this pattern: "When first I appear I seem mysterious, but when I am explained I am nothing serious."[102] For the most part, in riddling, we should be distrustful of outlandish, abstract, or exotic solutions, though there are some likely exceptions

---

n.s., 54 (2007): 16–19, Scott Gwara and Barbara L. Bolt offer a new twist on the idea, apparently arguing that Riddle 51 shifts in the middle of its proposition from describing "Pen and Three Fingers/Scribe (Writing the Gospels)" to a "Priest Performing Mass." Griffith, "Exeter Book Riddle 74," 393, uses the term "double solution" in still another sense, applying it to answers such as "Sun and Moon" and "Soul and Body." These are not "double solutions," though, so much as single solutions phrased as a "doublet," to follow Niles, *Old English Enigmatic Poems,* 108. To my mind, then, this popular phrase is not a useful one in the analysis of the Old English riddles.

99. For reasons that will become clear, it is convenient to continue my reading of Riddle 13 in chapter 2. The phrase *Adam and Eue* makes up half-line 419a of *Genesis B.* Whether or not this "works" as an answer to Riddle 13, however, is beside the point, since it is in fact *not* the solution. For what it is worth, however, the phrase does allow for six vowels and four consonants, if the "u" of *Eue* is classed among the brothers. There does not seem to be any strong reason to suppose that the sisters of Riddle 13 were necessarily vowels or the brothers consonants.

100. Taylor, *English Riddles from Oral Tradition,* 267.

101. Ibid., 464 (no. 1108), 499–500 (nos. 1172a–1173j).

102. Ibid., 40 (no. 100).

in the Exeter Book, especially in texts with clear links to Latin enigmatography. This tendency toward riddlic deflation, though, is not always fully appreciated in the study of the Exeter riddles. If a bird seems devilish, it need not be a demon. If a drifting object presents itself as impressive, it is not necessarily an iceberg. If I catch you in the corner, you may merely be churning a bit of butter.

The friction between focus and solution does not rule out their connection in other ways, however. One pattern that emerges in this study is metonymy. In chapter 2, for instance, I discuss a set of riddles that read various aspects of the written word (whether dark flocks on the page or the flying hand of the scribe) through the lens of avian metaphors. Such riddling can probably be attributed, at least in part, to the material source of the favored medieval writing implement, a feather quill (OE *feþer*). Similarly, chapter 3 examines a celestial enigma (Riddle 22), with a night sky described in terms of a vast sea forded by a constellation of bright riders. The stars in question, I show, are likely to be the very ones famed for guiding literal ships at sea. A second celestial riddle (Riddle 29) begins with the very common association of Christ with the sun and draws out its implications into new territory. In fact, the Exeter riddles often rework commonplace associations in elaborate fashion, as if riddling were a method of discovering the hidden complexity of well-established comparisons. The sex riddles in particular appear to be amplified extensions of some of the oldest jokes in the book. As I argue in later chapters, these artful poems have roots in venerable riddling conceits, whether playing with the associations of root vegetables or with the phallic implications of a warrior's *wæpen*.

The example of *wæpen* 'sword' as a solution raises the possibility of a riddle's proposition and solution being embodied in a single word. In the case of Riddle 20 (discussed in detail in chapter 5), the *wæpen* (sword) in question is read through (and against) the focus of the same word's secondary anatomical meaning (*wæpen* as the male member). A related case may be the vexing Riddle 55, one of five Old English riddles whose solutions are listed by Williamson as "uncertain." The riddle reads:

Ic seah in healle,   þær hæleð druncon,
on flet beran   feower cynna:
wrætlic wudutreow,   ond wunden gold,
sinc searobunden,   ond seolfres dæl,
ond rode tacn   þæs us to roderum up

hlædre rærde, ær he helwara
burg abræce. Ic þæs beames mæg
eaþe for eorlum æþelu secgan:
þær wæs hlin ond acc ond se hearda iw,
ond se fealwa holen— frean sindon ealle
nyt ætgædre; naman habbað anne,
wulfheafedtreo. Þæt oft wæpen abæd
his mondryhtne, maðm in healle,
goldhilted sweord. Nu me þisses gieddes
ondsware ywe se hine on mede
wordum secgan hu se wudu hatte.

[I saw in the hall where men drink four kinds carried onto the floor: a wondrous forest tree, and wound gold, crafted treasure, and a portion of silver, and a sign of the cross of him who raised up for us a ladder to the heavens, before he breached the stronghold of the hell dwellers. I may easily articulate for men the excellences of the tree: there was maple and oak and the hard yew and the yellowish holly; together they were all useful to the lord and had one name, the "wolf's-head tree." It has often received a weapon for his lord, a treasure in the hall, a gold-hilted sword. Let him now reveal the answer of this riddle, he who is so bold to say in words how this wood is called.]

Nearly all recent solvers of Riddle 55 agree that "some sort of sword-rack or -box seems intended, which was perhaps in the shape of a cross and gallows (a *t*-shape)."[103] Krapp and Dobbie explain, "The sword-rack is pictured in the form of a cross (1. 5*a*), and of a gallows (1. 12*a*). There is no inconsistency in this, for to the Anglo-Saxon mind the cross and gallows appear to have been similar in form."[104] Recently, however, Niles has argued that the wooden object in question need not have the "t-shape" of a cross, since the reference to the *rode tacn* 'sign of the cross' in line 5 could refer to the shape of something *on* the structure (such as a sword), rather than the rack itself. Nevertheless, Niles agrees that the "solution can scarcely be anything other than an Old English word that denoted 'a wooden structure used to hang and/or store weapons.'"[105] I agree.

103. Muir, *Exeter Anthology,* 2:662.

104. Krapp and Dobbie, *Exeter Book,* 350.

105. Niles, *Old English Enigmatic Poems,* 75. For a wholly different interpretation of Riddle 55, see Keith P. Taylor, "Mazers, Mead, and the Wolf's-Head Tree: A Reconsideration of Old

There is more to the riddle than its solution, however. There is also its metaphorical focus to consider. Williamson proposes a slightly different solution but also stresses the importance of the underlying metaphor: "My guess is that the creature is an ornamented sword box and that somehow (either by an unknown wordplay or because of some unknown similarity of function or design) the box is being compared to a gallows or rood in the riddle."[106] In fact, this crucial metaphor is so strong in the text that Tupper and others take it for the solution.[107] The sword in lines 12b–14a makes this unlikely, but the wooden structure is clearly read through the lens of the Holy Cross, even if we set aside the overt reference to the *rode tacn* 'the sign of the cross' in line 5a. The *wrætlic wudutreow* 'wondrous forest tree' surely emulates the selfsame *wuldres treow* 'tree of glory' depicted in the *Dream of the Rood,* while its lavish ornamentation evokes the cross as a treasured object of devotion (line 14b). The double focus on its fourfold makeup both in the opening lines and in the middle section seems suggestive of its cruciform nature. And, as many have noted, the list of trees specifically calls to mind a sturdy medieval tradition of listing the four woods from which the holy cross was carpentered.[108] Whether Riddle 55's solution is a scabbard, sword box, or weapon rack, then, surely the metaphorical focus is on the cross.

It may be that this metaphorical focus is enough to explain the puzzling four woods of the middle section, though they appear so enigmatically in error. As Machan and Peterson explain, "the patrological tradition was more than a little eclectic. The four woods [of the cross] could be any of the following seven: cypress, cedar, pine, box, fir, palm, and olive."[109] Many stress this eclectic variability to account for Riddle 55's eccentric list.[110] Still, there is always a good deal of overlap in the other known lists, while not a

---

English *Riddle 55,*" *Journal of English and Germanic Philology* 94 (1995): 497–512. Eric Gerald Stanley, "Heroic Aspects of the Exeter Book Riddles," in *Prosody and Poetics in the Early Middle Ages: Essays in Honour of C. B. Hieatt,* ed. M. J. Toswell (Toronto: University of Toronto Press, 1995), remarks, without further explanation, that "it emerges that this is a poem of the Holy Eucharist" (210). Claire Fanger, "A Suggestion for a Solution to Exeter Book Riddle 55," *Scintilla* 2–3 (1985): 19–28, argues for "reliquary."

106. Williamson, *Old English Riddles,* 303.

107. Tupper, *Riddles of the Exeter Book,* 189–91. See also Hildegard L. C. Tristram, "In Support of Tupper's Solution of the Exeter Book Riddle (Krapp-Dobbie) 55," in *Germanic Dialects: Linguistic and Philological Investigations,* ed. Bela Brogyanyi and Thomas Krömmelbein (Amsterdam: John Benjamins, 1986), 585–98.

108. See Tupper, *Riddles of the Exeter Book,* 190–91.

109. Tim William Machan and Robyn G. Peterson, "The Crux of Riddle 53," *English Language Notes* 24 (1987): 9–10.

110. See also Tupper, *Riddles of the Exeter Book,* 190; Tristram, "In Support of Tupper's Solution," 592–93.

single wood in Riddle 55 is to be found among them. Some solvers account for this riddle of the woods in terms of the actual composition of the wooden object: "An Anglo-Saxon joiner might find this an easy question to answer, but today we can only guess."[111] Others believe that the list simply brings the cross closer to home: "The substitution of woods familiar to the riddler and to his audience would have given the riddle greater immediacy."[112] And yet the section in question seems so very set apart, so oddly precise, and so prominent in the riddle. Aside from the opening general discussion of wood and treasure, the key clue of the stored sword, and the conventional closing challenge, there is really not much else to the riddle. These middle lines, I would argue, seem like the obvious main enigma of the text, its crux:

Ic þæs beames mæg
eaþe for eorlum æþelu secgan:
þær wæs hlin ond acc ond se hearda iw,
ond se fealwa holen— frean sindon ealle
nyt ætgædre; naman habbað anne,
wulfheafedtreo.

[I can easily say for men the excellences of the tree: there was maple and oak and the hard yew and the yellowish holly; together they were all useful to the lord and had one name, the "wolf's-head tree."]

It seems to me that these middle lines may be charged with an implied challenge. They resonate with other such moments in the collection where the solver is expected to decode or unscramble the solution from a set of letters or runes. For instance, the middle section of Riddle 42 reads:

Ic on flette mæg
þurh runstafas rincum secgan
þam þe bec witan bega ætsomne
naman þara wihta. Þær sceal Nyd wesan
twega oþer ond se torhta Æsc,
an an linan, Acas twegen,
Hægelas swa some.

111. Niles, *Old English Enigmatic Poems,* 80.
112. Machan and Peterson, "Crux of Riddle 53," 10.

> [I can on the floor say for men, for those who know about books, through runic letters the names of both those creatures together. There must be a *Nyd* (N), one of two, and the bright *Æsc* (Æ), a single one on the line, two *Acas* (A), and two *Hægelas* (H) as well.]

Unriddle these runes and you get a *hana* 'cock' and a *hæn* 'hen', whose copulating fills out much of the rest of the riddle. Similar scrambles are found in Riddle 24 (where the letters of *higoræ* 'magpie' require rearrangement) and Riddle 23, which opens by giving away the answer: "Agob is min noma eft onhwyrfed" (My name is *agob* turned around backward) (*agob* is *boga* 'bow' spelled in reverse).

Often these word games are not so obvious, however, and the unstated rules can vary from text to text. Riddle 58, for instance, concludes "Þry sind in naman / ryhte runstafas, þara is Rad forma" (There are three right runes in my name, the first of which is *Rad*). The solution seems to be **radrod* 'well sweep' (a medieval apparatus for drawing water), with the trick of the letters being that the r-rune *Rad* stands for both the first word of the compound and the first letter of the second word. In this way the compound can be written with only three runes, "the first of which is *Rad*."[113] Even less guidance is afforded the solver of Riddle 19, whose solution *snac* 'a light, swift ship' is spelled out as an acronym across four common words. The words are spelled backward, so that one takes the "s" from *hors* 'horse', "n" from *mon* 'man', "a" from *wega* 'warrior', and "c" from *haofoc* 'hawk' to find the answer.[114] The path to the solution is not always spelled out, then, but the strange arrangement or wording implies a hidden challenge.

I think this is possibly also the case for the middle section of Riddle 55, and I am not the first to think so. Notice how this sequence of statements

113. Williamson, *Old English Riddles,* 312, first proposed *radrod* as Riddle 58's solution, but Niles, *Old English Enigmatic Poems,* 89–92, was the first to unriddle this elegant trick of the runes.

114. Mark Griffith, "Riddle 19 of the Exeter Book: SNAC, an Old English Acronym," *Notes and Queries,* n.s., 237 (1992): 15–16. The solution is endorsed by Niles, *Old English Enigmatic Poems,* 105; Bitterli, *Say What I Am Called,* 89; and Roberta J. Dewa, "The Runic Riddles of the Exeter Book: Language Games and Anglo-Saxon Scholarship," *Nottingham Medieval Studies* 39 (1995): 32. For further discussion of Riddle 19, see Williamson, *Old English Riddles,* 186–92. See also Jonathan Wilcox, "Mock-Riddles in Old English: Exeter Riddles 86 and 19," *Studies in Philology* 93 (1996), esp. 185–87. Wilcox points out that the unemended text of this third-person riddle concludes with the challenge, "Saga hwæt *ic* hatte." Therefore, Wilcox contends, the proper solution to this "joke riddle" must not be a hidden creature but rather the name of the person posing the riddle!

progresses. First, a challenging list of unusual woods. Second, a statement that these woods (or words?) are all useful for their lord together (*frean sindon ealle / nyt ætgædre*). Finally, the section concludes by declaring that "naman habbað anne, / wulfheafedtreo" (they have a single name, wolf's-head tree).[115] Now, a "wolf's-head tree" is a bit of a riddle in itself, but there is little doubt that this kenning means "a gallows"—a wolf's head referring to the status of an outlaw.[116] From my perspective, then, it seems rather likely that the four named woods encode a single word with the meaning "gallows." A century ago, Felix Liebermann thought the same thing and proposed a way to unriddle the woods: take the first letter of each word (after first removing the "h" from *hlin*), reorder them, and you arrive at *ialh,* a recognizable, if unconventional, way of spelling *gealga* 'gallows'.[117] This reading is often praised for its ingenuity, but most have doubted it as a tortuous and rather unsatisfying way to answer the challenge.[118] And yet some solution meaning "gallows" is clearly indicated by the wolf's-head tree, whatever synonym we choose: whether *gealga, hengen* 'gallows, torture rack', or *rod* 'cross'.[119] The trick, though, would be to find some fairly clean way to make these four woods yield a word with this basic meaning, and for that reason a four-letter word seems most likely.

My own suggestion aims for simplicity: what if we translate these woods into Latin and see if they are "useful together"? Admittedly, it would be easy to pick and choose possibilities until something adds up (as Liebermann found it convenient to lop the "h" off of *hlin*). To be reasonably convincing, then, we ought to select the most obvious Latin equivalents, those words that nearly always gloss the four woods in Anglo-Saxon manuscripts. These are *acer* 'maple' (OE *hlyn*), *quercus* 'oak' (OE *ac*), *taxus* 'yew' (OE *iw*), and *acrifolius* 'holly' (OE *holen*).[120] Are these words useful together? They may be. Let us try lining them up.

115. Notice that it is "they" (the four woods) that have this single name. This tends to undermine the suggestion that "it is also possible that the four woods named in lines 9–10a pertain to the weapons carried on such a structure." Niles, *Old English Enigmatic Poems,* 80.

116. See Tupper, *Riddles of the Exeter Book,* 191; Niles, *Old English Enigmatic Poems,* 65.

117. Felix Liebermann, "Das angelsächsische Rätsel 56: 'Galgen' als Waffenständer," *Archiv für das Studium der neuren Sprachen und Literaturen* 114 (1905): 163–64.

118. See, for instance, Tupper, *Riddles of the Exeter Book,* 189; Williamson, *Old English Riddles,* 301–2; Niles, *Old English Enigmatic Poems,* 68.

119. Niles, *Old English Enigmatic Poems,* 73–77, considers these and other possibilities and settles on **wæpen-hengen* 'weapon-rack'.

120. See Bosworth and Toller, *Anglo-Saxon Dictionary,* s.vv. "ac," "iw," "holen," and "hlyn." The trouble with *hlyn* 'maple', however, is that the word is not known elsewhere in

A	**C**	E	R						
A	C	**R**	I	F	O	L	I	U	S
T	A	X	**U**	S					
Q	U	E	R	**C**	U	S			

This yields OE *cruc* 'cross', an intriguing possibility given the rest of the riddle. Or, by staggering the lineup, we might read the Latin equivalent, *crux,* instead:

	A	**C**	E	R					
A	C	**R**	I	F	O	L	I	U	S
	Q	**U**	E	R	C	U	S		
T	A	**X**	U	S					

By presenting more than one possibility I hope to stress my own uncertainty as to the wordplay involved in Riddle 55. Some other configuration may be called for, Latin may not be the key, and it is also possible that different woods or words altogether are intended, since the exact meanings of the four (and especially the hapax legomenon *hlyn*) are far from clear. Whatever the trick (or even *whether* there is a trick), it seems to me likely that the word in question means *both* "cross" and "weapon rack," in the way that various upright structures (the crosspiece supporting a boiling pot, the frame on a printing press) were later sometimes called a "gallows."[121] Most solutions to date have rested comfortably on this assumption, whether we name the object a *gealga,* a *hengen,* or now a *crux.* Each of these is a good solution, and each might signify for an Anglo-Saxon reader a useful rack, a criminal's gibbet, as well as the Holy Cross itself. And so, leaving aside the uncertainty of codes and acrostics, we are left with the more fundamental question of the riddle's metaphorical focus and its solution. A single word can serve as both—and yet these crucial elements are not the same.

Old English and our translation of its meaning is based on the rare Old Norse word *hlynr* 'maple'. Carole Hough, "Place-Name Evidence for Anglo-Saxon Plant-Names," in *From Earth to Art: The Many Aspects of the Plant-World in Anglo-Saxon England,* ed. C. P. Biggam (Amsterdam: Rodopi, 2003), points out that evidence from place-names indicates that the word *hlin* "was in fairly common use and certainly not restricted to the poetic register" (45). Still, this does not change the fact that, as Niles puts it in *Old English Enigmatic Poems,* our translation of *hlyn* as maple is an "educated guess" (66). If the guess is correct, however, the Latin word for *hlyn* would probably be *acer* (see Bosworth and Toller, s.v. "mapulder").

121. For various extended meanings of "gallows," see the *Oxford English Dictionary,* online ed., s.v. "gallows."

Another possible example of a focus and a solution embodied in a single word occurs in Riddle 5:

> Ic eom anhaga,   iserne wund,
> bille gebennad,   beadoweorca sæd,
> ecgum werig.   Oft ic wig seo,
> frecne feohtan—   frofre ne wene,
> þæt me geoc cyme   guðgewinnes
> ær ic mid ældum   eal forwurðe;
> ac mec hnossiað   homera lafe,
> heardecg heoroscearp   hondweorc smiþa,
> bitað in burgum;   ic a bidan sceal
> laþran gemotes.   Næfre læcecynn
> on folcstede   findan meahte
> þara þe mid wyrtum   wunde gehælde,
> ac me ecga dolg   eacen weorðað
> þurh deaðslege   dagum ond nihtum.

> [I am a solitary one, wounded by iron, gashed by the sword, worn out from martial strife, exhausted by the blade. Often I see war, a terrible battle. I do not expect comfort, that aid in the strife should come, before I should perish among men, but the leavings of hammers strike me, the terribly sharp edges, the handiwork of smiths bite in the dwellings; I must await a nastier meeting. I can never find a physician in the dwelling place, of those who with herbs might heal wounds, but rather the wounds of edges become increased through death blows in the days and in the nights.]

The enduring solution to this riddle is a shield (OE *scild*), which must suffer blows without hope of healing. Williamson puts it well: "Where the shield cannot be easily cured, it cannot also be easily killed. Its strength (wood) is also its weakness. That is the paradox of the riddle."[122] Although this answer is often accepted, a second possibility has attracted support, the idea being that the conventional heroic diction and imagery of the poem conceals

122. Williamson, *Old English Riddles,* 147.

something more prosaic, such as a chopping block.[123] As Anita R. Riedinger has pointed out, certain details may support this alternative solution, such as the "seemingly unnecessary emphasis on 'edges' . . . with never an *ord,* or 'point' in sight," as well as the somewhat odd detail of a physician's inability to cure the creature *mid wyrtum* 'with plants', an instance of herbal healing for which Riedinger can find no parallel in a heroic context such as this.[124] As Wim Tigges explains, these herbs "obtain a humorous ambiguity if they can also refer to the very vegetables that are chopped on the block."[125] It seems, moreover, significant that the creature in question suffers its blows *dagum ond nihtum* 'in the days and in the nights', a fate of continuous cutting seemingly more appropriate to an everyday domestic object than a weapon of war. And since folio 8r of the Exeter Book has been scored as if it was itself used as a cutting board, the solution has a certain built-in appeal.[126]

It would certainly be in keeping with the collection to depict a commonplace chore in heightened heroic language. For instance, a middle section of the fragmentary Riddle 93 appears to describe the process of hollowing out an antler with steel tools in the manufacture of an inkhorn (*blæc-horn*).[127] The passage is sharply reminiscent of Riddle 5:

> Siþþan mec isern innanweardne
> brun bennade; blod ut ne com,
> heolfor of hreþre, þeah mec heard bite
> stiðecg style. No ic þa stunde bemearn,
> ne for wunde weop, ne wrecan meahte
> on wigan feore wonnsceaft mine,
> ac ic aglæca ealle þolige.

123. Moritz Trautmann, "Die Auflösungen der altenglischen Rätsel," *Anglia Beiblatt* 5 (1894): 49, first offered the solution *der Hackeklotz* 'chopping block', and more than one writer on the Exeter riddles has been tempted to agree. See, for instance, Pinsker and Ziegler, *Altenglischen Rätsel,* 155–56; Wim Tigges, "Snakes and Ladders: Ambiguity and Coherence in the Exeter Book Riddles and Maxims," in *Companion to Old English Poetry,* ed. Henk Aertsen and Rolf H. Bremmer Jr. (Amsterdam: VU University Press, 1994), 100–101; Stanley, "Heroic Aspects," 206; and Riedinger, "Formulaic Style," 34. William Sayers, "Exeter Book Riddle No. 5: Whetstone?" *Neuphilologische Mitteilungen* 97 (1996): 387–92, offers a similar argument for a different solution.

124. Riedinger, "Formulaic Style," 34.

125. Tigges, "Snakes and Ladders," 100.

126. Krapp and Dobbie, *Exeter Book,* xiv.

127. To borrow the answer in Old English provided by Niles, *Old English Enigmatic Poems,* 144.

[Then the gleaming iron wounded my insides; blood did not come out, gore from my chest, though the hard, strong-edged steel cut me. Not at all did I then lament, nor weep for the wound, nor could I avenge my misery on the life of the warrior, but I a wretch endured all.]

The next half-line of this section is obscured by damage to the final page of the manuscript, and some of the text is difficult to construe. Two words, though, are clearly legible, *bord biton* 'they bit into the shield', and in context one likely sense seems to be that the cutting tools applied to the inkhorn are being compared to weapons slashing into a shield (*bord*).[128] The word here for shield, *bord,* reappears a few lines later near the end of the extant poem, where apparently a feather pen is lifted out of the inkhorn's "belly" to step across the writing surface: "ofte me of wombe bewaden fereð, / steppeð on stið bord" (often from my belly it goes coated [with ink], steps on the stiff *bord*).[129] The *Dictionary of Old English* defines this instance of *bord* as a table, with a "pun on *bord* 'shield'," wordplay that presumably is detected on account of the earlier appearance of the word in the riddle. Could a similar pun be at play in Riddle 5? OE *bord* could mean "shield," "plank," "board," or "table," with four instances of the last meaning found among the Exeter riddles and maxims.[130] Perhaps a cutting board or table would simply have been called a *bord,* so that the metaphorical focus of the riddle (an embattled *bord*) is summed up in the same word as its solution (a domestic *bord*). Or perhaps the solution is simply *scild* 'shield', as many have thought. Either reading seems plausible.

If, however, the solution is understood to be simply a shield, Riddle 5 is still a metaphorical riddle and in fact displays a particular brand of transfer whereby inanimate objects are animated by the very feelings they typically arouse in those who own or use them in daily life. In this reading of Riddle 5, the riddle's proposition reflects the life of the solution's owner (i.e., the shield bearer), who serves as the riddle's metaphorical focus. Traditional riddles often display this particular kind of relationship between focus and solution. For instance, in Archer Taylor's collection, a walking cane is described

128. See Tupper, *Riddles of the Exeter Book,* 237. For a discussion of the difficulties in construing this passage, see Muir, *Exeter Anthology,* 2:731–32.

129. In my translation of *bewaden* as "coated [with ink]," I follow Williamson, *Old English Riddles,* 396.

130. *Dictionary of Old English,* s.v. "bord."

in terms of its owner: "I have a grandmother who walked all day and when she got home, took up no more space than could be covered by a penny." [131] In another oral riddle, a brandy barrel becomes inebriated: "He travels wrapped in fetters and then comes home drunk, lies down, and vomits what everyone likes."[132] Another riddle describes the sound of a switch as "something going up laughing and coming down crying."[133] It is difficult to separate the whip's complaint from that of its implied victim. In interpreting and solving the Exeter riddles, especially when tools or implements seem to be involved, it may be helpful to keep this pattern in mind.

For instance, this pattern may be relevant to the text immediately preceding Riddle 5 in the Exeter Book. To this day, Riddle 4 continues to bedevil readers, but it is not practical here to address and contest the many other solutions that have been proposed.[134] For the same reason, though, it may serve as a good example of how obfuscation works in Old English riddling. The full riddle reads:

Ic sceal þragbysig þegne minum,
hringan hæfted, hyran georne,
min bed brecan, breahtme cyþan
þæt me halswriþan hlaford sealde.
Oft mec slæpwerigne secg oðþe meowle
gretan eode; ic him gromheortum
winterceald oncweþe. Wearm lim
gebundenne bæg hwilum bersteð,
seþeah bið on þonce þegne minum,
medwisum men, me þæt sylfe,
þær wiht wite ond wordum min
on sped mæge spel gesecgan.

131. Taylor, *English Riddles from Oral Tradition,* 259 (no. 699).

132. Ibid., 247.

133. Ibid., 279 (no. 769a).

134. For a list of solutions proposed for Riddle 4 through 1981, see Donald K. Fry, "Exeter Book Riddle Solutions," *Old English Newsletter* 15, no. 1 (1981): 22. More recent solutions include "dog," by Ray Brown, "The Exeter Book's *Riddle 2:* A Better Solution," *English Language Notes* 29, no. 2 (1991): 1–3; a "devil (distinct from the devil, Satan)" by Melanie Heyworth, "The Devil's in the Detail: A New Solution to Exeter Book Riddle 4," *Neophilologus* 91 (2007): 175–96; and a "plough team" by Shannon Ferri Cochran, "The Plough's the Thing: A New Solution to Old English Riddle 4 of the Exeter Book," *Journal of English and Germanic Philology* 108 (2009): 301–9.

> [Occupied by time, bound as I am with rings, I must eagerly obey my servant and break up my bed, make known noisily that my lord gave me a neck ring. Often a man or a woman has come to encounter me, a sleep-weary one. Cold with winter, I answer those grim-hearted ones. A warm limb at times releases the bound ring, although it is pleasing to my servant, a foolish fellow, and (it would be) to me likewise, if I understood anything and if I were able successfully to tell my tale in words.]

Any analysis of Riddle 4 must begin by noting what Williamson calls its "plenitude of rings": The creature is *hringan hæfted* 'bound with rings', it has been given a *halswriðan* 'neck ring', and its *gebundenne bæg* 'bound ring' is released by a limb of some kind.[135] Some have explained this emphasis on rings in terms of the form or inner workings of various objects, including hand mills, bells, wheeled plows, and buckets. My own reading of these rings is consonant with Williamson's very loose translation of Riddle 4's conclusion: "I sing round / The truth if I may in a ringing riddle."[136] I would suggest that Williamson's translation has it right: Riddle 4 is a bell riddle that produces a chain of ring-related puns, beginning with *hringan* in line 2. The verb *hringan* 'to ring' would serve as a play on *hring* 'ring, circular band' as readily as the "ringing" does in Williamson's translation.[137] There is a very coherent pattern of obfuscated wordplay here: *hring, halswriþa,* and *beag* as "rings" bound up, received, and released. All the "rings" in Riddle 4 chime with the initial pun, and may also recall the basic circular structure of the bell, as for instance we also see stressed in the first line of Symphosius 80: "Aere rigens curvo patulum conponor in orbem" (Rigid with curved bronze I am fashioned in the form of a wide-mouthed circle).[138] Form and function are bound in each *hring*.

135. Williamson, *Old English Riddles,* 141.

136. Williamson, *Feast of Creatures,* 62.

137. Note the compounds *bellhring* 'bell ringing' and *bellhringestre* 'female bell ringer' found in the *Dictionary of Old English*. In relation to a different Exeter riddle, Elisabeth Okasha remarks, "The use of the simplex *hring* to refer to a bell would then embody a neat pun, well suited to a riddle, on *hring,* a circular object, and *hringan,* to ring. An instance of similar deliberate ambiguity occurs in *Beowulf* 1521, where the poet tells us that 'hring-mæl agol' ('the ring-sword rang out')." Okasha does not, however, favor "bell" as the solution of either of the riddles she is studying. "Old English *hring* in Riddles 48 and 59," *Medium Ævum* 62 (1993): 65.

138. Ohl, *Enigmas of Symphosius,* 110–11.

The wordplay of the rings is less interesting, though, than the transfer of the experience and attitudes of the early riser to his rouser, the bell.[139] As Jacques Le Goff puts it, "Medieval time was punctuated by bells."[140] The ringing of the *þragbysig* 'time-occupied' bell marks the daily routine, and often "breaks the bed" of sleepers, who must *georne hyran* 'readily obey'.[141] But a *winterceald* 'sleep-weary slumberer' might find it hard to *hyran* 'obey' the bell's call, as we are warned in one Anglo-Saxon homily: "Deofol us læreð slæpnesse and sent us on slæwðe, þæt we ne magon þone beorhtan beacn þære bellan gehyran" (The devil inculcates drowsiness into us, so that we should not obey the bright sign of the bell).[142] Moreover, the verb *hyran,* here as in Riddle 4, appropriately carries with it the sense of both "to obey" and "to hear." The same double sense seems to be active in many other instances in the Anglo-Saxon corpus where *belle* is the object of the verb *hyran.*[143] But when the bell of Riddle 4 is compelled to obey his *þegn* 'servant', it is to "breahtme cyþan / þæt me halswriþan hlaford sealed" (loudly make known that my lord gave me a neck ring). And so the function of the speaker is restricted to receiving a ring, "making known" the fact of the

139. Although I have arrived at this conclusion independently, I would like to acknowledge that at least two earlier studies suggest a position similar to mine. First, Matthew Marino, "The Literariness of the *Exeter Book* Riddles," *Neuphilologische Mitteilungen* 79 (1978): 264, notes in passing that in Riddle 4 "the *bell* is given human characteristics which are not arbitrarily assigned as part of the deceit but which are transferred from the users of the bell to the bell: *min bed brecan* and *slæp werigne.*" Ann Harleman Stewart, "The Solution to Old English Riddle 4," *Studies in Philology* 78 (1981): 56–57, does not seem aware of Marino when she makes a very similar observation in her own solution of Riddle 4 as "bucket of water." She writes, "the transfer of a state of feeling from a person to an object in the environment is invited here by the use of personification and prosopopoeia." I could not agree more, although I believe that a "bell" solution fits the clues better than "bucket of water," and also sets up a more coherent sense of symmetry between the perceived "sleep-weary" state of the bell and those in bed. Doane, "Three Old English Implement Riddles," 247, also solves Riddle 4 as a "bucket on a chain or rope in a cistern or well."

140. Jacques Le Goff, *Medieval Civilization, 400–1500,* trans. Julia Barrow (Oxford: Basil Blackwell, 1988), 181.

141. Note the compound *bell-tīd* 'a canonical hour (marked by the ringing of a bell)' in the *Dictionary of Old English.*

142. Bruno Assmann, ed., *Angelsächsische Homilien und Heiligenleben* (Kassel: Georg H. Wigand, 1889), 168.

143. For instance, the Old English gloss to Ælfric's colloquy includes the testimony of one sleep-weary young monk: "Hwilon ic gehyre cnyll 7 arise; hwilon lareow min awecþ me stiþlice mid gyrde" (At times I hear/obey the ringing and get up; at times the teacher wakes me harshly with a rod). *Ælfric's Colloquy,* ed. G. N. Garmonsway (Exeter: University of Exeter Press, 1991), 48. For several more instances of *hyran* paired with *belle,* see the *Dictionary of Old English,* s.vv. "belle, bell," "bell-hring," "bell-tācen."

ring, releasing another "bound" ring, and begrudgingly "answering" an action made upon it when it was tired with sleep: "Oft mec slæpwerigne secg oððe meowle, / gretan eode; ic him gromheortum / winterceald oncweþe" (Often a man or a woman has come to encounter me, a sleep-weary one. Cold with winter, I answer those grim-hearted ones). Tatwine's enigma on the bell involves a similar conceit: "I am forced as the 'stricken' widely to release mournful tidings."[144] The tired, cold bell of Riddle 4 answers and obeys by ringing out when struck, just as the tired, cold servant must rise on a dark winter morning at the sound of the bell.

Not everything about the servant is cold, however. In lines 7b–8 we are told that a "wearm lim / gebundenne bæg hwilum bersteð" (warm limb at times releases the bound ring). As it relates to the solution, this may be taken as the arm of the bell ringer as he rings the bell. Or the *wearm lim* may be the clapper of the bell itself, warmed by the pull of a second metaphorical focus. As more than one reader has noted, the phrase *wearm lim* certainly seems suggestive of the OE *sceamlim,* 'shameful limb', or "the private member," to cite Bosworth and Toller's definition. Melanie Heyworth is a bit more blunt when she refers to "a 'hot penis,' so to speak."[145] A moment like this of localized innuendo is quite common in the Exeter collection and may arise partially in response to all the text's rings, a charged image in traditional riddling: "Father's thing stands out, something it cannot do in mother's hole—It is the ring on his finger."[146] Or it may simply be that bell riddles often slip into double entendre, the "penis clapper" being "the essential part of this figure, frequently standing alone or combining with other metaphors."[147] To refer even to the cold metal of the clapper as a *wearm lim* might make sense in terms of the strong pull of the riddle's sexual focus, though of course it rings false in relation to the literal solution.

The challenging language of Riddle 4, then, is accountable in terms of a fairly simple strategy of obfuscation: the symmetrical metaphor of a bell as a creature roused in the same way that a reluctant riser responds to the ringing of a bell. Variations on this pattern reverberate throughout the riddle: the bell, bound with rings, must obey and make known it has been "given a

144. Enigma 7, line 4: "Et cesus cogor late persoluere planctum" (Glorie, *Variae collectiones aenigmatum,* 174; translation adapted from Erhardt-Siebold, in ibid.).

145. Heyworth, "Devil's in the Detail," 188.

146. Peachy, *Clareti Enigmata,* 32 (no. 52). For more on localized innuendo in the riddles, see chapter 5.

147. Gordon Williams, *A Dictionary of Sexual Language and Imagery in Shakespearean and Stuart Literature,* vol. 1 (London: Athlone Press, 1994), s.v. "bell."

ring" (lines 1–4); the man or woman "greets" the silent bell with a blow, and the bell must answer back (lines 5–7a); a "warm limb" releases another bound-up ring, as the riddle drifts into innuendo. This last ring introduces one final variation on the comparison between the bell and the ringer:

> seþeah bið on þonce þegne minum,
> medwisum men, me þæt sylfe,
> þær wiht wite ond wordum min
> on sped mæge spel gesecgan.

> [. . . although it is pleasing to my servant, a foolish fellow, and (it would be) to me likewise, if I understood anything and if I were able successfully to tell my tale in words.]

In other words, even though *both* the ringer and the bell are reluctant to obey the ringing, it is undeniably a bright, pleasing sound. But why is the ringer a "foolish fellow"? He is foolish simply because the *wearm lim* has just evoked a bit of localized innuendo. When Riddle 12 drifts into a similar sexual metaphor, the woman manipulating the creature in question is described as a *dol druncmennen* 'a foolish drunk person'; when the sword of Riddle 20 takes on a local sexual focus, he is described as *wirum dol* 'foolish in filigree'.[148] So the suggestiveness of these images in Riddle 4 is enough to define the ringer's pleasure as "foolish," though this makes no literal sense and requires no elaborate explanation. And why is the bell doubtful of its ability to understand anything or to tell its tale in words? Simply because it is a bell. It is responsive in its ringing, but the speaker cannot really speak. It is a dead ringer.

Such an account might dissatisfy those who would prefer "a doggedly literal reading of the poem, as by far the least forced."[149] Williamson, baffled by Riddle 4, argues that a solution of bell does not "fit, without forcing, all of the descriptive details of the riddle."[150] And yet if the Exeter riddles show any resemblance to traditional riddling, they are quite likely to display "forced" details that do not make literal sense in relation to the solution alone:

148. Riddle 12, line 9a; Riddle 20, line 32a.
149. Brown, "Better Solution," 3.
150. Williamson, *Old English Riddles,* 143.

> beyond the seas there is an oake & in that oake ther is a nest & in that nest there is an egge & in that egge ther is a yolk wch calls together christian folk—the church is taken for the oake the steeple for the nest the bell for the egge and the clapper for the yolk wch calls the people.[151]

As Taylor says of this early modern folk riddle, "the final comparison of the clapper to the yolk cannot be called happy."[152] It is certainly quite as forced as the *wearm lim* of Riddle 4. The key thing in reading the Exeter riddles, though, is that the "forcing" of these clues accounts for the obfuscation in a way consistent with the rich traditions likely available to Old English readers and riddlers. The alternative is to strain in the search for literal accounts of these enigmatic texts. Take, for instance, the most recent reading of Riddle 4, which offers a well-reasoned, attractive account of how a plow team yoked to a wheeled plow "satisfies the criteria for a convincing solution more thoroughly than any of the previous ones that have been proposed."[153] But what are the criteria for a convincing solution? If we are looking for a plausible if improbable hidden scenario to explain away the text, then perhaps we may be convinced. But even if this is how the Exeter riddles work, we must still squint a bit to see the plow. Most notably, we must understand the *wearm lim* in Riddle 4 as "warm mud," which grips and breaks the bound wheel (*bæg*) of a plow. For this to work, an emendation and a "semantic shift in the application" of the noun *bæg* is also needed.[154] *Lim* as "slime" or "mud" in this context seems like a slim chance, too, even were it not for the fact that this warm mud would be mucking up the work of a *wintercealđ* speaker (who is roused in January for winter plowing, as it is explained). Why would the mud be so warm in the winter, though? Conditions might be sloppy in January, but surely the mud would not be *warm*? Another story to heat the mud would be needed, to go along with the following scene imagined in the analysis: "The boy or 'thane' is happy because he can rest while the ploughman (*hlaford*) fixes the plough. The boy is 'foolish' (*medwisum men,* l. 10a) because he cannot make the repairs himself and because he will still have to finish the work, no matter the delay. The ox, too, is happy: *me þæt sylfe* ('and that [circumstance] to me myself,' l. 10b). One can easily imagine its relief when freed from the plough while the wheel is under

151. Tupper, "Holme Riddles," 221 (no. 104).

152. Taylor, *English Riddles from Oral Tradition,* 421.

153. Cochran, "Plough's the Thing," 309.

154. Ibid., 307.

repair."[155] One might just as easily imagine the relief of the bull-calf of Riddle 38, when it dashes loose "in his turbulent youth." The complex motivations and shortcomings of foolish men, boys, and beasts can be shaped into a coherent scenario of plowing accidents, but they lack the riddlic simplicity of a slugabed bell and its unwelcome but pleasing sound. Imaginative inside stories, after all, are not necessarily what are needed to account for the Exeter riddles. What they more likely demand, I would argue, are readings grounded in known modes of riddling obfuscation.

That is not to suggest that there are any easy answers, or that I may not after all be wrong about the plow. Many may likewise doubt the readings I propose here, just as I challenge accepted solutions in the spirit of the game. In many cases, my readings may be in line with the consensus solution, while at the same time offering a revision of the path we take to that answer. A solution, after all, is a common and convenient metaphor in textual analysis in general, which makes it especially important to keep clearly in mind the distinction between a riddle's solution and its interpretation. Interpreting the Exeter riddles involves accounting for their solutions, yes, but it also means attempting to understand their obfuscations in ways consistent with their complex roots in traditional riddling, learned enigmatography, and other varied riddlic forms with currency in Anglo-Saxon England. The influences at play are complex, but the key is to interpret these texts in ways consistent with their likely genre (or nexus of genres).[156] To interpret them instead as literal descriptions or inside stories is to "unriddle" them—to read them as something other than riddles. But it is no paradox to observe that reading these riddles well means to unriddle them in the light of their obfuscations, and I hope that by studying the play of proposition, focus, and solution we may find a new way to track these dark texts.

155. Ibid., 308–9.

156. To borrow the language of Niles, *Old English Enigmatic Poems,* 30.

2

A LITERAL READING OF RIDDLE 57

A folk riddle collected early last century in Adams County, Illinois, challenges the solver:

Riddle me, riddle me, rin-e-go,
My father gave me some seed to sow.
The seed was black, the ground was white,
If you are a good scholar,
You can guess this by tomorrow night.[1]

Good scholars will readily identify this puzzle as an example of a widespread and very old riddlic conceit on writing, whereby the ground is the page and the seed is ink.[2] The answer supplied by the informant, however, makes

1. Hyatt, *Folk-Lore from Adams County,* 666.

2. Taylor, *English Riddles from Oral Tradition,* 435–39, provides a lengthy discussion of this riddle motif. The same metaphor appears in the early ninth-century "Veronese Riddle," a stray text written into a prayer book: "se pareba boves alba pratalia araba & albo versorio tenebra & negro semen seminaba" (he was driving oxen, plowing white meadows and holding a white plow and sowing black seed). The text and translation of this riddle can be found in Giulio Lepschy, "History of the Italian Language," in *Encyclopedia of Italian Literary Studies,* vol. 1, ed. Gaetana Marrone (New York: Routledge, 2007), 967. Aldhelm's Enigma 32 describes a wax writing tablet in very similar terms. For another close medieval analogue, see Frederic Peachy, *Clareti Enigmata,* no. 122. Modern literary riddlers have picked up on such traditional images as well. Kit Wright's contribution to Kevin Crossley-Holland and Lawrence Sail, eds., *The New Exeter Book of Riddles* (London: Enitharmon Press, 1999), no. 99, reads: "I go through the wood in silence / and come out on to the snow / where I leave my prints / though I have no footsteps, / where I speak your heart / though I cannot breathe." The answer is pencil lead.

much more literal sense of the riddle: "The ground was covered with snow and the boy could not plant the seed." This amusing answer is a good example of what we get when we treat metaphorical riddles as straightforward descriptions of fact.[3] The good scholars who puzzle out the Exeter riddles could arrive at similarly literal readings, if they were to mistake a riddle's metaphorical focus for its solution. In this chapter I look at one of the most problematic riddles in the Exeter collection, Riddle 57, a text that has received plenty of attention despite its apparent lack of concrete clues. The poem is short and spare, "a gem of a riddle," as one critic has called it.[4] It describes a flock of emphatically black creatures flying through the air and singing:

> Ðeos lyft byreð   lytle wihte
> ofer beorghleoþa   þa sind blace swiþe,
> swearte, salopade.   Sanges rope
> heapum ferað,   hlude cirmað;
> tredað bearonæssas,   hwilum burgsalo
> niþþa bearna.   Nemnað hy sylfe.

> [The air bears little creatures over the hillsides. Those are very black, dark, swarthy-coated ones. Bountiful of song, they travel in groups, crying loudly. They tread the woody headlands, at times the town houses of the sons of men. They name themselves.]

These creatures have sparked a long and complicated "parliament of fowl solutions" in the critical literature. In accordance with Krapp and Dobbie's judgment that only solutions "which involve birds are at all worthy of consideration," most solvers have focused on the task of pinpointing the exact avian species visualized.[5] Others have thought of insects, though it is difficult

3. I would not assume that Hyatt's informant was necessarily serious. This may be a "joke riddle" variation on the black seed/white field theme, in which the riddler subverts the conventions of the genre by insisting on a ridiculously literal understanding of the puzzle. For other examples of "joke" or "parody" riddles, see Abrahams and Dundes, "Riddles," 139–41. For the possibility of similar types of parody in the Exeter riddles, see Jonathan Wilcox, "Mock-Riddles in Old English: Exeter Riddles 86 and 19," *Studies in Philology* 93 (1996): 180–87.

4. Erika von Erhardt-Siebold, "Old English Riddle No. 57: OE *Cā 'Jackdaw,'" *PMLA* 42 (1947): 1.

5. Krapp and Dobbie, *Exeter Book,* 351. So secure are most solvers in the straightforward bird identity of these creatures that Michael Alexander offers number 57 as an example of those Exeter riddles that are "just poems which need little or no thought to solve." *A History of Old English Literature* (Ontario: Broadview Press, 2002), 100.

to see how consensus on this question could ever be reached. Still, zoological precision has been pursued, and few airborne species have gone unmentioned: swallows, swifts, starlings, house martins, jackdaws, crows, blackbirds, midges, gnats, and bees—each species has its supporter. Among the issues raised in this long debate are whether or not a gnat's vibration could be thought to *cirman* 'cry out, wail', whether jackdaws with fourteen-inch wingspans could be considered *lytle wihte* 'small creatures', the sociability of "gregarious" swallows, and the various color patterns, sizes, and habits of other bees and birds.[6]

Among the recent solvers of Riddle 57 is Audrey L. Meaney, who sets out to demonstrate that, "at least on the literal level, swifts are the only possible answer."[7] Meaney's account of the swift's "appearance, locomotion, habitat and call" is painstakingly precise, but it is worth asking whether this literal approach is what a riddle demands. Traditional riddle propositions, as we saw in chapter 1, do not often relate to their solutions in terms of a smooth semantic fit. Latin enigmas, by contrast, sometimes do provide something like the "precise and accurate (though inevitably incomplete) description" that Meaney would like to extract from Riddle 57, but their propositions still seem quite different. Take Aldhelm's enigma on the midge:

> Corpore sum gracilis, stimulis armatus aceruis;
> Scando cateruatim uolitans super ardua pennis
> Sanguineas sumens praedas mucrone cruento
> Quadrupedi parcens nulli; sed spicula trudo
> Setigeras pecudum stimulans per uulnera pulpas,
> Olim famosus uexans Memphitica rura;
> Nam toros terebrans taurorum sanguine uescor.

> [I am slight in body, (and) armed with sharp stings. I rise in throngs, flying aloft on my wings, taking bloody prey with my gory sword, sparing no four-footed beast; rather, I thrust forth my darts, goading the bristling flesh of flocks with wounds. Once I was notorious for

6. For a discussion of these issues and a list of proposed species, see Williamson, *Old English Riddles,* 307–11. For the solution "blackbird (terdus merula)," see Richard Wells, "The Old English Riddles and Their Ornithological Content," *Lore and Language* 2 (1978): 63. For "swifts," see Meaney, "Exeter Book Riddle 57 (55)," 187–200.

7. Meaney, "Exeter Book Riddle 57 (55)," 187.

> plaguing the Egyptian countryside; and boring through into the muscle, I am nourished with the blood of bulls.][8]

Even if Aldhelm had provided no solution, his precise entomology and biblical allusions point to a very particular creature, and indeed the notes to Lapidge and Rosier's translation reveal that the species in question is "the tiny midge, not the larger gadfly."[9]

How, though, could we ever hope to pin down the creatures of Riddle 57 with similar precision? These creatures seem really unremarkable. They fly, they make noise, they occupy both unsettled and populated areas. They are a study in avian anonymity—quite unlike the quirky birds of Latin *enigmata.* Nor is Riddle 57 very similar to other ornithological Exeter riddles, which tend to emphasize the oddball features of a given species. The barnacle goose speaker of Riddle 10, for instance, assaults the solver with an account of its bizarre ontogeny, while the swan speaker of Riddle 7 describes the unusual qualities of its noisy plumage. The magpie of Riddle 24 demonstrates strange variations in its vocalizations, the coming of age of the cuckoo of Riddle 9 poses paradoxes of kinship, and the songbird of Riddle 8 is notable for its behavior's being compared with that of an *eald æfensceop* 'old evening singer'—a person skilled in human poetic tradition. In each of these first-person bird riddles, the proposition is organized around a special idiosyncrasy of the species in question. In Riddle 57 we simply have dark swarms. As Nigel F. Barley puts it, "the subject is quite firmly assigned to the category *bird,* but no further information to allow narrowing of this category is given until the final sentence."[10]

That final sentence is the somewhat ambiguous half-line *Nemnað hy sylfe.* Early editions of the collection construe this as a plural imperative, an example of the formulaic challenge closing so many of the Exeter riddles: "Name them yourselves."[11] But since other closing riddle formulas of the Exeter Book address a single implied solver, an alternative reading of this half-line has seemed attractive: "They name themselves."[12] Here, then, could be the

8. Enigma 36 (Glorie, *Variae collectiones aenigmatum,* 421; translation from Lapidge and Rosier, *Aldhelm: The Poetic Works,* 77).

9. Lapidge and Rosier, *Aldhelm: The Poetic Works,* 250.

10. Barley, "Structural Aspects," 169.

11. For example, Thorpe, *Codex Exoniensis,* 439, as well as Tupper, *Riddles of the Exeter Book,* 196.

12. This reading has been widely adopted since it was first proposed by Cyril Brett, "Notes on Old and Middle English," *Modern Language Review* 22 (1927): 257–64. For more on the ambiguity of this half-line, see Elena Afros, "Linguistic Ambiguities in Some Exeter Book Riddles," *Notes and Queries,* n.s., 52 (2005): 433–34.

conclusive clue, if onomatopoeia is the name of the game for Riddle 57. But again, a bird of the right size, color, and onomatopoeic name has proved elusive, though a murder of possibilities has been proposed. Some of the best candidates do not have known Anglo-Saxon names, so they must be invented: Erhardt-Siebold's **cā* 'jackdaw' and Meaney's speculations concerning the swift's shrieking "srreee, sreee, sree" fall into this category.[13] Other solvers take a more ingenious route: *fleoge* 'flies' naming themselves by their ability to fly (*fleogan*), or *swealwe* 'swallows' satisfying the clue through their capacity either to swallow food (a rather unremarkable ability!) or to "name a salve" (i.e., an ointment made from the plant swallowwort).[14] Aside from such flights of fancy, there are few good options. But recently John D. Niles has supported the onomatopoeically appropriate solution *crawan,* 'crows', by discounting the importance of absolute size: " 'small' and 'large' are relative terms, and crows are indeed small when compared with many other things."[15] This seems to me a fair argument to make, and the solution *crawan* is in my view the most likely self-naming black bird we are ever likely to snare.

But is the crowing of *crawan* such a distinctive field mark? This apparent key feature of the species comes only in the final half-line, a footnote to the main riddlic description. Nor would such a feature impress a learned birder in the Latin enigma tradition: Eusebius alone attributes self-naming to two different birds, the horned owl (*bubo*) and the stork (*ciconia*), while the cuckoo speaker (*cuculus*) of a pseudo-Symphosian enigma concludes, "Quid tibi vis aliud dicam? me vox mea prodit" (What's the use of saying anything more to you? My voice reveals me).[16] This is not altogether surprising. Birds

13. Erhardt-Siebold, "Old English Riddle No. 57," 1–8; Meaney, "Exeter Book Riddle 57 (55)," 199.

14. For *fleoge* 'flies', see Jonathan Wilcox, " 'Tell me what I am': The Old English Riddles," in *Readings in Medieval Texts: Interpreting Old and Middle English Literature,* ed. David F. Johnson and Elaine Treharne (Oxford: Oxford University Press, 2005), 46–59. Andrew Welsh sees the creatures of Riddle 57 as *swealwe* 'swallows' naming themselves through their capacity to *swelgan* 'swallow': "The swallow 'swallows,' as every living creature does: but it is the only creature that names itself when it does." Welsh, "Swallows Name Themselves: Exeter Book Riddle 55," *ANQ* 3, no. 2 (1990): 91. Mercedes Salvador Bello proposes a pun on the last word of *nemnað hy sylfe* and *sealf* 'salve', thus arriving at an allusion to swallowwort. "*Nemnað hy sylfe:* A Crux in Exeter Riddle 57," *Old English Newsletter* 27, no. 3 (1994): A-21.

15. Niles, *Old English Enigmatic Poems,* 129. The solution "crows" was first proposed by F. Holthausen, "Ein altenglisches Rätsel," *Germanisch-Romanische Monatsschrift* 15 (1927): 453–54. The solution is also accepted in Pinsker and Ziegler, *Altenglischen Rätsel,* 278–80.

16. See Eusebius, Enigma 56, line 1, and Enigma 60, line 5 (Glorie, *Variae collectiones aenigmatum,* 267, 271). For the pseudo-Symphosian cuckoo, see Ohl, *Enigmas of Symphosius,* 134. To

are often named for their calls, just as they often fly through the air or display dark plumage.

Given these doubts, it is worth considering what a less literal solution to Riddle 57 might look like. Aside from a spate of weather-related solutions advanced by Moritz Trautmann near the turn of the twentieth century, metaphorical readings of this riddle have rarely been considered.[17] A notable exception to this is L. K. Shook's answer "musical notes," which Williamson dismisses as "a trifle far-fetched."[18] Shook's defense of his solution, proposed in passing as part of a larger survey of "riddles of the scriptorium," is admittedly rather underdeveloped. Apart from a brief analysis of "þeos lyft," which I discuss below, Shook's entire argument consists of this short explanation: "A glance at any early manuscript containing musical notes is enough to convince one of the aptness of this solution. The scribe's imagination sees his little black notes as singing birds climbing up and down the real or imagined ledges on the page in front of him. They do, of course, name themselves—do, re, mi, etc."[19] Shook's basic idea, that these creatures probably represent written marks of some kind, is attractive. I would, however, revise Shook's solution somewhat. I see the creatures of Riddle 57 as the letters of the alphabet, Latin *litterae* (or *bocstafas* in the Old English tongue), conceptualized according to a tradition of grammatical learning familiar to an Anglo-Saxon literate audience. The dark creatures of Riddle 57, in fact, line up well with accounts of letters found in the works of Priscian, Donatus, Isidore, and other authorities central to the early medieval study of grammar, a subject strongly associated with the enigma in Anglo-Saxon England.[20]

Before turning to a detailed explication of Riddle 57, it is worthwhile to provide a broader context for the particular riddling conceit in question.

---

my knowledge, only one solver of Riddle 57 has noted any of these analogues: Erika von Erhardt-Siebold, "Old English Riddle No. 57," 3. This omission might be explained by the embarrassment they hold for literal readings of Riddle 57. For if the idea of birds "naming themselves" is revealed to be a commonplace convention found in many enigmas (not to mention in numerous Isidorian etymologies for the names of birds and other beasts), it no longer stands out as a distinctive clue for identifying a species. As Erhardt-Siebold herself points out, "Many a bird owes its name to its cry, and a large group of related sound-imitative words in bird nomenclature may be traced throughout numerous groups of languages" (3).

17. Where this possibility has been raised, it is promptly dismissed. Andrew Welsh, for example, simply asserts, "In Riddle 55 [57] there is little metaphorical sense in the description of the 'small creatures.'" "Swallows Name Themselves," 91.

18. Laurence K. Shook, "Riddles Relating to the Anglo-Saxon Scriptorium," in *Essays in Honour of Anton Charles Pegis,* ed. J. Reginald O'Donnell (Toronto: Pontifical Institute of Mediaeval Studies, 1974), 226; Williamson, *Old English Riddles,* 308.

19. Shook, "Anglo-Saxon Scriptorium," 226.

20. As is noted, for example, in Igarashi, "Riddles," 339–40.

The regular appearance of letter enigmas in Anglo-Latin collections makes *bocstafas* a likely solution for an Exeter Book riddle, as does the frequent handling in the Exeter Book collection of other scriptorium-related topics.[21] Yet the riddling strategy of reading written marks through the metaphorical focus of dark birds may indeed seem "a trifle far-fetched," as Williamson noted, and so it is worth providing a bit of context for this argument. I would like to establish both the close associations between these two topics and the specific riddling precedent for my reading. At the same time, there is an opportunity here to comment on a few related Exeter "riddles of the scriptorium."

The connection between birds and writing in the Exeter Book is grounded first in the material link between the *penna* 'feather' of the bird and the *penna* 'quill pen' of the scribe. In Riddle 51, commonly solved as the pen and fingers in the act of writing, this flock of *feþer ond fingras* 'feather and fingers' is figured as aquatic flying creatures,[22] diving in and out of the inkwell and tracing dark tracks across the page:

Ic seah wrætlice   wuhte feower
samed siþian;   swearte wæron lastas,
swaþu swiþe blacu.   Swift wæs on fore
fuglum framra;   fleag on lyfte
deaf under yþe.   Dreag unstille
winnende wiga,   se him wegas tæcneþ
ofer fæted gold   feower eallum.

[I saw four creatures marvelously traveling together. Their paths were dark, their tracks very black. Fast was its movement, bolder than birds; it flew in the air, it dove under the waves. Strove restlessly, did the contending warrior, who pointed to them the way, over the ornamental gold, four of them in all.]

Note the parallels to Riddle 57. The emphatic blackness of the creatures in Riddle 57 is matched by Riddle 51's dark paths, which are "swearte" and

21. Aldhelm (Enigma 30), Tatwine (Enigma 4), Eusebius (Enigma 7), and the Bern collection (Enigma 25) all have riddles with general "letters" for the solution, not to mention enigmas in which an individual letter is described (e.g., Eusebius, nos. 9, 14, 19, 39, and the *Versus de nominibus litterarum*).

22. John D. Niles suggests this neat alliterative doublet, *feþer ond fingras* 'feather [pen] and fingers', for the solution of Riddle 51, in *Old English Enigmatic Poems,* 126.

"swiþe blacu." In each riddle there is a possible punning relationship to *blæc,* the Old English word for ink, and in fact many Anglo-Latin enigmas pun on *atramentum* ("ink").[23] Riddles 51 and 57, of course, also share diction appropriate to their avian personae, such as their flight "on lyfte," as well as an emphasis on the coordinated movements of their flocks: the creatures of Riddle 51 are described as *samed siþian* 'traveling together', while those of Riddle 57 are said to *heapum ferað* 'go along in groups'. These groupings differ in that one refers to the deft collaboration of the scribe's *fingras* with his *feþer,* while the flocks of Riddle 57 are the visible traces of that collaboration on the writing surface. Still, this sense of coordinated dexterity is a theme that might be considered appropriate to both scribal skill and its product.[24]

What we see in Riddle 51 is not unusual, and it is worth looking at a few more related analogues, both from Anglo-Latin riddling and from the Exeter riddles. In the course of providing this context, I would like to kill two birds with one stone (so to speak) by also offering a brief argument concerning the final text in the Exeter Book, Riddle 95:

Ic eom indryhten   ond eorlum cuð,
ond reste oft   ricum ond heanum,
folcum gefræge.   Fereð wide,
ond me fremdes ær   freondum stondeð
hiþendra hyht,   gif ic habban sceal
blæd in burgum   oþþe beorhtne god.
Nu snottre men   swiþast lufiaþ
midwist mine: ic monigum sceal
wisdom cyþan;   no þær word sprecan

23. See, for example, Lorsch Riddle 9, *De penna,* lines 1–2 (Glorie, *Variae collectiones aenigmatum,* 355; my translation): "Candida uirgo suas lacrimas dum seminat atras, / Tetra per albentes linquit uestigia campos" (When the white maiden produces black/inky tears, she leaves behind dark tracks on the white fields), and Eusebius writing on parchment sheets, "Candida sed cum arua lustramur milibus atris" (though white fields, we are illuminated by millions of black/inky figures). Enigma 32, lines 3–4 (Glorie, *Variae collectiones aenigmatum,* 242; translation adapted from Erhardt-Siebold, in ibid.). Cf. Exeter Riddle 93, commonly solved "inkhorn," lines 24b–25a, "Nu ic blace swelge / wuda ond wætre" (Now I swallow the black one/ink, the wood and water). The "wood" here probably refers to the oak galls out of which ink was made.

24. Seth Lerer, "The Riddle and the Book: Exeter Book Riddle 42 in Its Contexts," *Papers on Language and Literature* 25 (1989), writes, "As products of the multiple steps and intricate technologies of inscription and binding, books would have embodied, for a reader of this poetry, an ordering of word and world through human hands" (15).

ænig ofer eorðan. Þeah nu ælda bearn,
londbuendra, lastas mine
swiþe secað, ic swaþe hwilum
mine bemiþe monna gehwylcum.[25]

[I am known to nobles and warriors, and reside often with both the high-born and low, well known to the people. The plunderer's joy travels widely and stands as a friend to me, who was a stranger's before, if I am to have success in the cities or possess the bright Lord. Now wise men feel greatest affection for my company: I must disclose wisdom to many, though I speak no words on this earth. Although the children of men, dwellers on earth, now eagerly seek out my tracks, I at times conceal my path from each of men.]

The rich solving history of Riddle 95 involves a number of elusive and mysterious entities, including the moon, a spirit or soul, "Thought" personified, a "wandering singer," and even (as we saw in chapter 1) a prostitute.[26] In recent years, though, consensus seems to be slowly emerging that Riddle 95 deals in some way with textuality and the technology of writing. In his 1977 edition, Craig Williamson proposed "book," and his basic solution has been endorsed and nuanced by several later authors.[27] There is much to recommend such readings. Notably, the speaker says that while he discloses wisdom to many, he never speaks words. The motif of the written word as a silent speaker is a very well known conceit in Latin *enigmata,* and it is indeed difficult to see how Riddle 95 could refer to something other than writing.[28]

25. The text is Williamson's, but I leave *fremdes* in line 4 and *beorhtne* in line 6 unemended.

26. Fry, "Exeter Book Riddle Solutions," 26.

27. For instance, Helga Göbel solves Riddle 95 as *halig gewrit* 'holy text' in her *Studien zu den altenglischen Schriftwesenrätseln* (Würzburg: Königshausen und Neumann, 1980), 538–606. Pinsker and Ziegler, *Altenglischen Rätsel,* 336–40, propose *Rätselbuch* 'riddle book', a solution that draws on Moritz Trautmann's early solution *Rätsel* 'riddle' ("Cynewulf und die Rätsel," *Anglia Anzieger* 6 [1883]: 158–69). Most recently, Michael Korhammer, "The Last of the Exeter Book Riddles," in *Bookmarks from the Past: Studies in Early English Language and Literature in Honour of Helmut Gneuss,* ed. Lucia Kornexl and Ursula Lenker (Oxford: Peter Lang, 2003), 69–80, specifies Göbel's solution to "the Holy Scriptures."

28. For more on this motif, see Marie Nelson, "The Paradox of Silent Speech in the Exeter Book Riddles," *Neophilologus* 62 (1978): 609–15; Katherine O'Brien O'Keeffe, *Visible Song: Transitional Literacy in Old English Verse* (Cambridge: Cambridge University Press, 1990), 52–54; and Mary Hayes, "The Talking Dead: Resounding Voices in Old English Riddles," *Exemplaria* 20 (2008): 123–42.

I too believe that the basic solution to Riddle 95 is "book," in some sense or other, but I would argue that a related, but neglected, alternative solution helps us understand some of the riddle's more puzzling clues. The solution to which I refer is "quill," proposed more than half a century ago by Erika von Erhardt-Siebold.[29] Its relevance comes into play most notably at the end of the riddle, where the speaker describes wise men attempting to pursue obscure tracks: although they "lastas mine / swiþe secað, ic swaþe hwilum / mine bemiþe monna gehwylcum" (eagerly seek out my tracks, I at times conceal my path from each of men). In passing, it is worth mentioning the possibility that the notion of a text as "tracks" or a "path" may be related to the medieval etymology of *littera* as coming from *legens* 'reading' and *iter* 'path or way'.[30] In fact, inky tracks would be consistent with just about any riddle of the scriptorium, but they are particularly associated in Latin *enigmata* with the path of a bird's quill.

The typical idea seems to be that a bird's feather, once used for flight, continues its journey across the page, and that readers pursue its inky tracks. A brief survey of Latin enigmas dealing with aspects of writing—on topics such as parchment, ink, and wax tablets—reveals that all such metaphors involving the reader's pursuit of textual "tracks" are clustered in riddles solved as quills or *pennae*. For instance, the language of pursuit in Riddle 95 is strongly reminiscent of Eusebius's enigma on the quill:

> Natura simplex stans, non sapio undique quicquam;
> Sed mea nunc sapiens uestigia quisque seqetur.
>
> [Simple by nature, I never acquire any wisdom, but all the wise men follow my traces.][31]

Note that Eusebius's paradox of wisdom here parallels Riddle 95, lines 7–9a: "Nu snottre men swiþast lufiaþ / midwist mine: ic monigum sceal / wisdom cyþan" (Now wise men feel greatest affection for my company: I must disclose wisdom to many). Aldhelm's quill riddle also figures the reader as following the "traces" or "tracks" of the feather pen:

29. Erika Erhardt-Siebold, "Old English Riddle 95," *Modern Language Notes* 62 (1947): 558–59.

30. See Martin Irvine, *The Making of Textual Culture: "Grammatica" and Literary Theory (350–1100)* (Cambridge: Cambridge University Press, 1994), 98–99.

31. Enigma 35, lines 1–2 (Glorie, *Variae collectiones aenigmatum,* 245; translation by Erhardt-Siebold, in ibid.)

Pergo per albentes directo tramite campos
Candentique uiae uestigia caerula linquo,
Lucida nigratis fuscans anfractibus arua.
Nec satis est unum per campos pandere callem,
Semita quin potius milleno tramite tendit,
Quae non errantes ad caeli culmina uexit.

[I move through whitened fields in a straight line and leave dark-coloured traces on the glistening path, darkening the shining fields with my blackened meanderings. It is not sufficient to open up a single pathway through these fields—rather the trail proceeds in a thousand directions and takes those who do not stray from it to the summits of heaven.][32]

A similar set of associations, we have seen, animates the *feðer ond fingras* of Riddle 51, and arguably also informs Riddle 95.

The first half of Riddle 95 is less straightforward than its ending. In particular, lines 3b–6 have presented considerable difficulty for interpretation:

Fereð wide,
ond me fremdes ær freondum stondeð
hiþendra hyht, gif ic habban sceal
blæd in burgum oþþe beorhtne god.

As these lines have been construed in a number of different ways, I will briefly summarize my own understanding of the grammar. I take *hiþendra hyht* 'the joy of the plunderers' to be the subject of both the verbs in the main clause, *fereð* 'travels' and *stondeð* 'stands'. Following Korhammer, I read *me fremdes ær* as "me who was a stranger's before."[33] Following Göbel, I interpret *freondum* as an adverb of manner to be translated 'as a friend'.[34] In the *gif* clause, I leave *beorhtne* unemended, and consequently translate *god* as 'God'.[35] The sense here seems to be that the speaker's success will involve different

32. Enigma 59, lines 3–8 (Glorie, *Variae collectiones aenigmatum,* 455; translation from Lapidge and Rosier, *Aldhelm: The Poetic Works,* 82).

33. Korhammer, "Last of the Exeter Book Riddles," 73.

34. Göbel, *Altenglischen Schriftwesenrätseln,* 561.

35. For a discussion of possible emendations and alternative readings, see Korhammer, "Last of the Exeter Book Riddles," 73–75.

kinds of glory: earthly (*blæd in burgum*) and divine (*beorhtne god*). I therefore translate the lines as "The plunderer's joy travels widely and stands as a friend to me, who was a stranger's before, if I am to have success in the cities or possess the bright Lord."

This rendering remains obscure, and the language is as difficult as anything in the Exeter anthology. The identity of the *hiþendra hyht* 'joy of the plunderers' stands at the center of the problem of interpreting these lines, and those who see a textual metaphor at play here (as I do) have read this as a kenning for either ink, gold leaf, or parchment.[36] I submit, however, that the strong parallels with "quill" *enigmata* we see in the second half of Riddle 95 suggest a fourth possibility: the "joy of plunderers" is simply the quill pen of the scribe. The quill (plundered from its avian owner) travels widely if the book is to be of use to earthly men in their path toward divine wisdom (much as in Aldhelm's metaphor cited above). As we have seen, the fingers and pen of Riddle 51 are said to *samed siþian* 'travel together' (line 2a) and, in an analogue to the folk riddle cited at the opening of this essay, Tatwine's quill of Enigma 6 describes being removed from its journeys through the air and forced to "plow fields" on the earth.[37] The exile of the grounded feather among *bearn londbuendra* 'children of land dwellers' is a common enough theme in quill riddles, as the analogues cited above suggest. That sense of exile may explain the paradox of the "joy of the plunderers" now "standing as a friend" to the speaker, who was previously in the "possession" of a stranger (*fremdes ær*), as all books made of parchment once were. In fact, referring to a feather quill as the "joy of plunderers" neatly parallels another riddle in the Exeter Book that describes the material manufacture of manuscripts, as an animal's skin is prepared and turned into a book. Lines 7b–11a of Riddle 26 read,

. . . ond mec fugles wyn
geondsprengde speddropum, spyrede geneahhe
ofer brunne brerd, beamtelge swealg,
streames dæle, stop eft on mec,
siþade sweartlast.

[. . . and the joy of birds sprinkled drops of success over me, traveled often over the gleaming rim, swallowed tree dye, a portion of liquid, then stepped back onto me, traveled a dark path.]

36. For gold leaf, see Williamson, *Old English Riddles,* 400–401.
37. Enigma 6 (Glorie, *Variae collectiones aenigmatum,* 173).

The kenning for feather as *fugles wyn* 'joy of the bird' may also be paralleled in *The Phoenix,* a poem from the Exeter Book, where in line 155a the word *wyn* may be supplied to complete the sense of a kenning for feather: *fugla wyn* 'the joy of birds'.[38] If my reading is correct, *hyht hiþendra* 'the joy of plunderers' in Riddle 95 is a variation of this kenning that reascribes the traditional "joy" of birds in their plumage to the "plundering" scribes who now take pleasure in their feather pens. If my reading is not accepted, however, the strong riddling associations between birds and writing in Anglo-Saxon England should nevertheless remain obvious.

"Why is a raven like a writing-desk?" the Mad Hatter famously asked Alice. Lewis Carroll left the riddle unanswered, but one of his readers supplied a solution: "Because they both have inky quills."[39] My solution for Riddle 57, however, involves the metaphorical conflation of letters and birds, rather than the substitution of living fowl for feather pens. For a closer analogue to Riddle 57, then, let us return to the chickens of Riddle 13, the opening lines of which I delayed discussing in the previous chapter. It is worth restating the riddle in full:

Ic seah turf tredan— ten wæron ealra,
six gebroþor ond hyra sweostor mid—
hæfdon feorg cwico. Fell hongedon
sweotol ond gesyne on seles wæge
anra gehwylces. Ne wæs hyra ængum þy wyrs,
ne side þy sarre, þeah hy swa sceoldon,
reafe birofene, rodra weardes
meahtum aweahte, muþum slitan
haswe blede. Hrægl bið geniwad
þam þe ær forðcymene frætwe leton
licgan on laste, gewitan lond tredan.

38. Krapp and Dobbie, *Exeter Book,* 275.

39. Lewis Carroll, *The Annotated Alice,* with an introduction and notes by Martin Gardner (New York: Clarkson N. Potter, 1960), 95. Eleanor Cook, *Enigmas and Riddles in Literature* (Cambridge: Cambridge University Press, 2006), 174, explains how Carroll later answered the riddle: "Because it can produce a few notes, tho they are *very* flat; and it is nevar put with the wrong end in front." The word *nevar* is deliberately misspelled so as to read *raven* "with the wrong end in front." A later editor corrected this "error" and the joke was not noted until almost a century later. Meanwhile, many excellent solutions were provided by fans of Carroll, including the one quoted here, as noted in Kamilla Eliot, *Rethinking the Novel/Film Debate* (Cambridge: Cambridge University Press, 2003), 242.

> [I saw walking on the ground ten in all: six brothers and their sisters together. They had living spirits. Skins hung clear and visible on the wall of the hall of each one of them. Nor was it to any of them the worse, nor was his side the more painful, although deprived of their garment and wakened by the might of the guardian of the heavens, they are compelled to tear with their mouths the gray fruit. Clothing will be renewed for those who previous to their coming forth allowed their trappings to lie on the path, to depart and tread the earth.]

We have already discussed the body of this riddle, but what of its beginning? What are these six brothers and four sisters? Once again, Erika von Erhardt-Siebold provides an explanation: "I suggest as the solution to the riddle *Ten Ciccenu* (Ten Chickens). This solution with its ten letters, of which six are consonants (brothers) and four vowels (sisters), would readily explain the number puzzle."[40] Erhardt-Siebold's ingenious answer has been widely accepted, despite its rather odd logic. What is particularly strange about this answer is the way that the number ten refers *both* to the number of *ciccenu* 'chickens' *and* the number of letters spelling—not *ciccenu,* mind you—but *ten ciccenu* 'ten chickens'. It would presumably make greater sense if the number of letters added up to the name of the creatures alone, without forcing the number ten to do awkward double duty. At any rate, it is certainly an offbeat explanation, for which Erhardt-Siebold offers no riddling precedent.

But the basic trick is borne out by a previously unnoticed analogue to Riddle 13 found in the "Cambridge Songs" manuscript (Cambridge, University Library, Gg. 5. 35), an eleventh-century Anglo-Saxon miscellany in which a number of riddle collections are gathered.[41] The final line of the riddle is a bit obscure, but the first two lines can be easily translated:

> Tres proles nantes iuncte genuere sorores:
> Rursus eadem he mature post pepererunt.

40. Erhardt-Siebold, "Old English Riddle 13," 99. It is perhaps worth pointing out that *ten ciccenu* (or *tien cicenu*) could more precisely be translated as "ten chicks" (at least according to the definitions supplied in the *DOE,* s.v. "cicen"). Most follow Erhardt-Siebold in translating her answer into modern English as "ten chickens," but "ten chicks" is actually more appropriate for Riddle 13.

41. For more on this manuscript, see A. G. Rigg and G. R. Wieland, "A Canterbury Classbook of the Mid-Eleventh Century (the 'Cambridge Songs' Manuscript)," *Anglo-Saxon England* 4 (1975): 113–30.

> [Linked sisters gave birth to three swimming offspring: In turn, those mature ones afterward gave birth to the same.][42]

Luckily, this rather obscure bit of riddling has been carefully glossed for the reader (a rare instance of the contemporary explication of a medieval riddle). The lines are explained:

> Ista est constructio—tres iunctae sorores i. tres litterae o. u. a. genuere nantes proles i. tres pullos et iterum maturi pulli genuere easdem scilicet litteras o. u. a. que inucta ova exprimunt.
>
> [That is a construction: three linked sisters—three letters, o, u, a—gave birth to swimming offspring, three chicks, and again mature chickens certainly generated the same: the letters o, u, a, which together articulate "eggs."][43]

The riddling way the letters of *oua* 'eggs' are thought to "give birth" to literal chickens, then, seems to confirm Erhardt-Siebold's inspired hunch for the hatchlings of Riddle 13, though we may remain skeptical of the exact answer she offers.

But how should we answer this puzzle? How can we crack its code? If we took the opening at its literal word, we might simply offer the solution *tien cicenu* 'ten chicks', in the expected West Saxon spelling.[44] To do so, though, would be to ignore the apparent obfuscation of the riddle and presume no conflation of letters and chicks—for this solution gives us five vowels and five consonants. In other words, there would be no riddling reason for the numbers, only an absurdly literal count of ten chickens, six of which happen to be male and four of which happen to be female.[45] Erhardt-Siebold's answer avoids this difficulty by appealing to an unlikely orthography: "*Ten Ciccenu,*" which she claims is evidence for a Northumbrian origin of

42. Tupper, "Riddles of the Bede Tradition," 10; my translation.

43. Ibid.; my translation.

44. As does Niles, *Old English Enigmatic Poems,* 142.

45. Bitterli is tempted by such a reading: "Here, the numbers similarly distinguish male and female birds and perhaps involve a comparable cipher [comparable to Riddle 42, in which runic letters spell the solution *hana ond hæn* 'cock and hen'], but the total of ten also conveys the impression of a lively multitude and may indeed simply refer to one mixed brood of male and female chicks. Should this indeed be the only function of the numbers in this text, then its ten treading siblings have certainly made some modern readers go round and round in circles." *Say What I Am Called,* 120–21.

the Exeter riddles.[46] Now, we might overcome this problem of spelling by appealing to a solution in Latin, which certainly does not seem out of the question. Count the letters in *decem pulli* 'ten chicks', and you find the six and four we are after. As John D. Niles points out, "the possibility should not be ruled out that certain riddles were designed to be answered in Latin even if posed in the vernacular."[47] The possibility seems all the more likely for riddles involving, essentially, a challenge of literacy. But do we really believe that the trick is that ten is *both* the number of chicks and the number of letters in the answer "ten chicks"?

Perhaps more likely is that the numbers refer only to the letters in the plain name of the creatures in question. For instance, Old English *cicen ond æg* 'chick and egg' is a doublet with six consonants and four vowels.[48] In Latin, *oua et pulli* 'eggs and chicks' might also work (depending on how we counted the "u" in *oua*).[49] On the other hand, it is reasonable to guess that the creatures to be named are just the chicks, not their shells. It also seems clear that there is more than one chick involved, if perhaps not exactly ten. In fact, the metaphorical focus of Adam and Eve that I discuss in chapter 1 seems at least to imply a pair of creatures, one male and one female, setting off to tread and populate the earth. Riddle 42 also portrays a couple such creatures, this time engaged in a sex act, and we know the solution to this text because it too is presented in a scramble of letters (more letters and birds!), but one that has been easier to decode.[50] Unscrambled, these letters very clearly yield the solution *hana ond hæn* 'male chicken and female chicken', yet another answer of six and four letters preferable to *ten ciccenu*. There are plenty of good options.

46. Erhardt-Siebold, "Old English Riddle 13," 99.

47. Niles, *Old English Enigmatic Poems,* 103n5.

48. Even when describing multiple creatures, the supplied solutions to medieval riddles are sometimes stated in the singular. See, for instance, Tatwine's Enigma 5 and Eusebius's Enigma 32, both of which parchment riddles are solved in the singular (*De membrano*). Eusebius's enigma, however, has a plural speaker, while Tatwine's is singular (see Glorie, *Variae collectiones aenigmatum,* 172, 242).

49. For this answer to add up, the "u" of *oua* would need to be counted among the vowels, despite its consonantal function here. This would not be surprising. Eusebius has a riddle on the letter "u," Enigma 19: "I am called the fifth cardinal vowel and have a triple function: now I sound as vowel; now as consonant; then, in an intermediate capacity, they say that I am neither" (Glorie, *Variae collectiones aenigmatum,* 229; translation by Erhardt-Siebold, in ibid.). As far as I can make out, there is no reason to assume that the sisters are the vowels and the brothers are the consonants, or vice versa (the analogues cited in Bitterli, *Say What I Am Called,* 114–15, call all the letters sisters, although six—*h, k, q, x, y,* and *z*—are "bastards").

50. For this puzzle, see my discussion of Riddle 55 in chapter 1.

Whatever the wording we prefer, however, the ornithological letters (at once literal birds and "literal" birds in a figurative sense!) of Riddle 13 are seen to *turf tredan* 'tread the ground', much as the dark flocks of Riddle 57 "tredað bearonæssas, hwilum burgsalo / niþþa bearna" (tread the woody headlands, at times the town houses of the sons of men). To account for these strong associations between letters and birds in the Exeter Book, an Anglo-Saxon reader might have looked to the myth of Palamedes, who was thought to have invented certain letters of the Greek alphabet by observing the forms of cranes in flight. Symphosius's Enigma 26, *Grus* 'Crane', alludes to the story: "Littera sum caeli penna perscripta volanti" (A letter of the sky am I, written with flying wing).[51] Widespread evidence from oral tradition offers numerous other birdlike letters. A Russian riddle on writing reads, "The land is nice and white, and the birdies on it are nice and black."[52] A riddle from India translates, "Black crows on a white bank. They are saying '*Caw! Caw!*'"[53] Closer to home, a Welsh riddle asks, "Beth yw ungwys ar gangwys a chan ugain o gwys a chan deryn du o dan bob cwys?" (What is one furrow and a hundred furrows and a hundred score furrows and a hundred blackbirds under each furrow?) Good scholars will see that these creatures are not jackdaws, swifts, or crows. They are "dalennau a llythrennau'r Beibl" (the leaves and letters of the Bible).[54]

Keeping these riddling contexts in mind, let us return to the details of Riddle 57. One point should be made clear from the start. To see how *bocstafas* or *litterae* might solve Riddle 57, we must first understand that the early medieval conception of the *littera* does not line up exactly with the modern notion of the "letter." As Vivien Law points out, the meaning of *littera* familiar to the Anglo-Saxons would include both the written character

51. Ohl, *Enigmas of Symphosius,* 58–59. Andrew Welsh also sees a connection between this enigma and Riddle 57: "At hand was a model for this way of seeing, if the poet needed one, in Symphosius' Riddle 26, which sees in the flight of cranes a letter of the alphabet—Greek Y or Λ, or Latin V—written on the sky with a flying *penna.*" Welsh uses this analogue to argue that Riddle 57 evokes "the airborne image of a vortex or whirlpool," but he does not consider the possibility that the visual comparison of birds specifically to letters is important in both riddles. Welsh, "Swallows Name Themselves," 92–93. In a previous version of this argument, published in *Philological Quarterly* 84 (2005), I note that the myth of Palamedes inventing letters was known to Isidore (*The Etymologies of Isidore of Seville,* trans. Stephen A. Barney et al. [Cambridge: Cambridge University Press, 2006], 40). To clarify, Isidore mentions Palamedes' invention of certain letters, but not the story of the cranes.

52. Sadovnikov, *Riddles of the Russian People,* no. 2146.

53. Cited in Taylor, *English Riddles from Oral Tradition,* 435 (no. 1063).

54. Hull and Taylor, *Collection of Welsh Riddles,* no. 186. See also nos. 184–85.

(the visual mark, what we generally think of as a "letter") and the sound it represents: "it corresponds to both our 'letter' and our 'speech sound,' and upon occasion even to 'phoneme.'"[55] Although *littera* in the sense of written mark was occasionally distinguished from *elementum,* the smallest unit or element of speech sound, the two senses were usually conflated, as Priscian himself acknowledges in making the distinction.[56] In accord with this understanding, the *littera* was commonly defined as having three major "accidents" or properties: *nomen* 'name', *figura* 'shape, written form', and *potestas* 'sound value'.[57] *Littera* thus defined at once as (silent) physical mark and as audible speech sound carries a rich potential for paradox. Indeed, other Latin letter enigmas highlight this threefold characterization. The Bern riddle on letters, for example, groups these three features together in its middle section: "Multimoda nobis facies et nomina multa / Meritumque dispar uox et diversa sonandi" (Multiform is our appearance and our names many, unequal is our value, and our voice diverse of sound).[58] The dark swarms of Riddle 57, I will argue, also reflect an understanding of the letter characterized by these three properties.

55. Vivien Law, *Grammar and Grammarians in the Early Middle Ages* (London: Longman, 1997), 262.

56. "Hoc ergo interest inter elementa et literas, quod elementa proprie dicuntur ipsae pronuntiationes, notae autem earum literae. abusive tamen et elementa pro literis et literae pro elementis vocantur" (There is this difference between elements and letters, therefore, that elements are properly said to be the pronunciations themselves, while the letters are the physical marks of them. However, in casual speech, elements are called letters, and letters, elements). Priscian, *Institutiones grammaticae,* ed. Heinrich Keil, Grammatici Latini, vols. 2–3 (Leipzig: Teubner, 1855), vol. 2, pp. 6–7 (1.2.4–5). That the element/letter distinction did not always hold in the enigma genre is evident from Aldhelm's treatment of the *De elemento* theme (Enigma 30), which, far from excluding the sense of physical mark, focuses on the blackness of the creatures and their paradoxically silent speech. For a classic analysis of how another riddle of the Exeter Book exploits the tension between the written word's material foundations and "the words they symbolize," see Fred C. Robinson, "Artful Ambiguities in the Old English 'Book-Moth' Riddle," in *Anglo-Saxon Poetry: Essays in Appreciation for John C. McGalliard,* ed. Lewis E. Nicholson and Dolores Warwick Frese (Notre Dame: University of Notre Dame Press, 1975), 355–62.

57. For my translations of these terms I follow Law, *Grammar and Grammarians,* 262.

58. Enigma 25, lines 3–4 (Glorie, *Variae collectiones aenigmatum,* 571; my translation). Of the riddles on individual letters of the alphabet found in the medieval collection *Versus de nominibus litterarum,* many are built around these three properties of the letter. One, for example, explicitly mentions "nomen," "figuram," and "potestas" in its discussion of the letter H. See Glorie, *Variae collectiones aenigmatum,* 733. This collection of letter enigmas is found, among other places, in the "Cambridge Songs" manuscript, fols. 381r–382r. Maureen Halsall discusses this collection and related riddles on the letters of the alphabet in *The Old English Rune Poem: A Critical Edition* (Toronto: University of Toronto Press, 1981), 42–45.

It may be helpful here to give a brief overview of my reading of Riddle 57. To begin, the riddle's opening seems to focus on *litterae* as units of sound "carried" in the air: "Ðeos lyft byreð lytle wihte" (the air carries little creatures). Grammarian authorities known to the Anglo-Saxons define letters as the smallest possible units of *vox* 'voice', which in turn is defined as *aer ictus* 'struck air'.[59] Ælfric, following Priscian, puts it this way: "se muð drifð ut ða clypunge, and seo lyft byð geslagen mid þære clypunge and gewyrð to stemne" (the mouth drives out the sound, and the air is struck by it and is transformed into voice).[60] In light of the definition of letters as the smallest indivisible elements of such *vox,* the statement "Ðeos lyft byreð lytle wihte" could apply perfectly well to letters. Eusebius's enigma on speech opens, "Peruolo ualde celer, discurrens per inania missus" (Quick and fierce I fly, once propelled I travel unsupported).[61] The second line of Riddle 57 introduces the property of *figura* 'shape, written form' in its designation of the creatures as *blace swiþe* 'very black'. This is where the riddle, I would argue, begins to exploit the paradox inherent in defining the letter in terms of both its written form and its sound value. The next half-line continues to define the blackness of the small creatures, before the riddle turns to the *potestas* 'sound value' of the individual characters, specifically as they are activated by gathering in *heapum* 'groups', a reference to the many "flocks of letters" (i.e., words) constituting a text. The riddle concludes with the statement that the letters *nemnað hy sylfe* 'name themselves', a detail, as we shall see, that fits quite neatly with medieval discussions of the third and final property of letters, their *nomen* 'name'. Finally, lines 5a–6a are best read in terms of the written word's enigmatic power to carry speech across a literal landscape.

But let us begin with the written form of letters, for if nothing else the creatures of Riddle 57 are inky. Their emphatic, tripled blackness reflects the look of written characters, while invoking the familiar comparison we see so often elsewhere in riddling on books and letters: "What is . . . white as snow, / And yet blacke as any crow?"[62] If inky, though, how exactly can we say that *þeos lyft* 'the air' is supporting them? Shook overcomes this objection by translating these words not as "the air," but as "this thing that

59. See, for example, Donatus, *Ars grammatica,* 367 (1.1.1); Priscian, *Institutiones grammaticae,* vol. 2, p. 5 (1.1.1).

60. Ælfric, *Ælfrics Grammatik und Glossar,* ed. Julius Zupitza (Berlin: Weidmann, 1880), 4.

61. Enigma 22, line 1 (Glorie, *Variae collectiones aenigmatum,* 232; translation by Erhardt-Siebold, in ibid.).

62. This particular bird/writing link is found also in several early modern collections of riddles: *The Booke of Meery Riddles* (London, 1629), no. 52; Tupper, "Holme Riddles," 231; *Ben Johnson's last legacy to the sons of wit, mirth, and jollytry* (London, 1756), 21.

lifts," that is, "the musical scale, the ledges or other devices by means of which a scribe records the rise and fall of musical notes."[63] Williamson rejects this suggestion on the grounds that "*lyft* everywhere else in Old English refers to the actual air or atmosphere in one of its guises."[64] Williamson's objection fails to take into account, however, a notable exception to this rule in *Solomon and Saturn I*. An interesting use of *lyft* occurs near the closing of this poem, at the climax of a battle in which the individual letters of the Pater Noster take on the devil in a kind of typographical brawl.[65] Prior to this passage, the letters of the Pater Noster have been figured as various weapons and implements of torture used against the devil, according to their particular shape:

> Đonne hine on lyfte   lifgetwinnan
> under tungla getrumum   tuigena ordum,
> sweopum seolfrynum,   swiðe weallað,
> oððæt him ban blicað,   bledað ædran;
> gartorn geotað   gifrum deofle.[66]
>
> [Then the twins of life shall torment him mightily in the air under the hosts of the stars with the points of twigs, with silver scourges, until his bones are laid white, the veins bleed; they shall pour the spear wrath on the greedy devil.]

The phrase "twins of life" refers here to the shape of the letter "H," and the visual plain upon which this struggle occurs must be imagined at least partially as the textual space of the written Pater Noster. Here, then, we have a fairly clear instance of *lyft* functioning metaphorically to indicate the spatial position of textual "characters" on the writing surface. That this comparison occurs as a prelude to a riddle contest between Solomon and Saturn makes the passage particularly relevant.

But perhaps more to the point is the observation that the opening lines of Riddle 57 may also be read as referring to the idea of the *littera* as the smallest indivisible unit of speech. As I have stated, *vox* 'voice' is defined as

63. Shook, "Anglo-Saxon Scriptorium," 225.

64. Williamson, *Old English Riddles*, 309.

65. For a discussion of this battle, see Frederick B. Jonassen, "The Pater Noster Letters in the Poetic *Solomon and Saturn*," *Modern Language Review* 83 (1988): 1–9. Jonassen surveys medieval precedent for the personification of letters, including a brief discussion of Riddle 19.

66. Lines 141–45 (Dobbie, *Anglo-Saxon Minor Poems*, 36–37).

aer ictus 'struck air' in the works of the most influential grammarians known to the Anglo-Saxons, while *litterae* are defined as the smallest components of that struck air. Priscian writes, "possumus et sic definire: litera [*sic*] est vox, quae scribi potest individua" (we are able to define it thus: the letter is voice, which can be written as an indivisible particle).[67] The use of the term *elementum* 'atom, particle' as a loose synonym for *littera* in the works of Priscian and other grammarians reflects a perceived similarity between the smallest units of indivisible matter and of voice.[68] In this understanding of the *lytle wihte* 'little creatures', then, we need not worry over the relative sizes of jackdaws and gnats, since the *littera* defined as an *elementum* 'letter, atom' is the smallest of all creatures in an absolute sense. An additional analogue for this type of riddling idea may be found in a literary enigma by Jonathan Swift:

> We are little airy creatures,
> All of diff'rent Voice and Features,
> One of us in Glass is set,
> One of us you'll find in Jet,
> T'other you may see in Tin,
> And the fourth a Box within,
> If the fifth you shou'd pursue,
> It can never fly from you.[69]

The little creatures of Swift's riddle are the vowels, in their double character as both sounds and written marks.

Like Swift's "little airy creatures," the flocks of Riddle 57 have a voice. In lines 3b–4b, the second major property of *litterae* or *bocstafas,* their *potestas* 'force, sound value', is highlighted: "Sanges rope, / heapum ferað, hlude cirmað" (Liberal of song, they travel in groups, they sing loudly). That these characters raise such a ruckus should not come as much of a surprise if we

67. Priscian, *Institutiones grammaticae,* vol. 2, p. 6.

68. According to Martin Irvine, "The term 'element' (*stoicheion, elementum*)—an irreducible part into which all things can be resolved—entered grammatical discourse from physics." *Making of Textual Culture,* 100.

69. Jonathan Swift, *Miscellanies* (London, 1753), 268. This riddle is immediately preceded by another enigma figuring written characters as flying creatures, part of which reads: "Thro' distant Regions I can fly, / Provide me but with Paper Wings, / And fairly shew a Reason, why / There should be Quarrels among Kings." A slightly altered version of Swift's vowel enigma is collected as a riddle from American oral tradition in Karl Knortz, *Streifzüge auf dem Gebiete amerikanischer Volkskunde* (Leipzig: E. Wartigs Verlag E. Hoppe, 1902), 233.

keep in mind the grammatical definition of *littera* as both written mark and speech sound. Eusebius's enigma on the letter "A" begins, "Dux ego linguarum resonans et prima per orbem" (I am the leader of tongues, crying out throughout the world).[70] It is true that many Old English and Anglo-Latin riddles exploit just the opposite conceit, namely, the paradox of writing as "silent speech."[71] This does not preclude the possibility, however, that the loud voices of these characters recall both the understanding of *bocstafas* as elements of voice and, with a touch of irony, the deafening silence of the written word.

This middle section of Riddle 57 is also interesting for the way it associates the ability of the creatures to speak as stemming specifically from their gathering in groups, a detail that past solvers have used to evaluate possible bird species in nature.[72] In riddling, however, it is letters that flock together, as here in this early modern example: "Though a small Troop, we're yet a numerous Throng, The mighty *Persian Host,* not half so strong."[73] The strength of the creatures comes from their thronging, as in another related riddle:

> We are in number not five times five,
> No one of us two handfull long,
> Nor any of us takes care to thrive,
> Yet all together we doe so throng,
> That if a man would list to strive

70. Enigma 9 (Glorie, *Variae collectiones aenigmatum,* 219; translation from Anlezark, "Old English Dialogues," 30).

71. For our purposes, Riddle 48, commonly understood as a chalice bearing an inscription, is the best Old English example here, since it echoes much of Riddle 57's diction: "Ic gefrægn for hæleþum hring gyddian, / torhtne butan tungan, tila þeah he hlude / stefne ne cirmde strongum wordum. / Sinc for secgum swigende cwæð: / 'Gehæle mec, helpend gæsta.' / Ryne ongietan readan goldes / guman, galdorcwide, gleawe beþencan / hyra hælo to Gode, swa se hring gecwæð" (I heard a ring singing for men, bright without a tongue, although strictly speaking it did not utter strong words aloud with a voice. The treasure spoke for men silently: "Heal me, Helper of spirits." Men understood the mysterious saying of the red gold, the incantation, that wise ones should entrust their salvation to God, just as the ring said).

72. For instance, Meaney, "Exeter Book Riddle 57 (55)," 190, writes: "Of these, corvids are black enough, but crows can hardly be described as little, and do not go in flocks unless they are rooks—which do not typically inhabit hills or human dwellings, but trees near arable land." Riedinger, "Formulaic Style," 36, similarly writes, "*Heapum ferað* (4a), eliminates the possibility of the flying creatures being 'eagles,' since they do not fly in flocks or 'bands.' And ravens, their alternative, are not famed for their 'bountiful songs,' nor do they gather near the buildings of the sons of men."

73. *Thesaurus ænigmaticus* (Dublin, 1727), 17.

T'extinguish or to doe us wrong,
Were he the greatest prince alive,
We should be found for him too strong,
And could make him infamous in time to come,
Though most of us beene deafe and dombe.[74]

Note, though, that the creatures of Riddle 57 travel not in a single flock but in plural *heapum* 'groups'. This small detail may be more important than it first appears, referring to the gathering of these creatures into multiple units, that is, the many words making up a text. Moreover, this detail of gathering in groups is nested between the two statements of the creatures' vocality, suggesting a relationship: "Sanges rope, / heapum ferað, hlude cirmað" (liberal of song,[75] they travel in throngs, crying out loudly). This implied link makes good sense, since letters make sound chiefly as they gather together to make words. Latin grammars often devote considerable space to laying out the relationships between letters and how their sounds modulate in combination. Ælfric understood the etymological meaning of "consonants" in this way: "ealle ða oðre stafas syndon gehatene CONSONANTES, þæt is, samod swegende: forðan ðe swegað mid ðam fif clypjendlicum"[76] (all the other letters are called CONSONANTES, that is, making sound together: that is, because they make sound together with the five vowels). Moreover, *potestas* 'force, sound value' was thought to include the ordering and arrangement of letters in groups. According to Priscian, "Potestas autem ipsa pronuntiatio, propter quam et figurae et nomina facta sunt. Quidam addunt etiam ordinem, sed pars est potestatis literarum" (*Potestas,* however, is the pronunciation itself, on account of which both the shapes and names are made. Some add order [as a property] also, but this is part of the *potestas* of the letters).[77] Eusebius too links order with *potestas* in the opening of his enigma on letters:

74. *The Riddles of Heraclitus and Democritus* (London, 1598), no. 20. The solution provided in the back of this riddle book explains, "They are the leters of the alphabet: whereof onely five are vocall, and the rest dumbe."

75. In early editions of the Exeter riddles, the unusual word *rope* was emended to *rowe* 'gentle', or *rofe* 'strong'. Krapp and Dobbie and Williamson retain *rope,* citing glosses that pair *roopnis* or *ropnes* for L. *liberalitas* 'generosity, nobility, liberality' and thus arriving at a meaning of "liberal" or "bountiful" of song. While not pushing this argument too far, I would note that *liberalis* was an adjective frequently associated with *litterae* in the Middle Ages, "liberal letters" being used often as a synonym for "liberal arts." Irvine, *Making of Textual Culture,* 97. For the distinction between "common" and "liberal" letters, see Isidore, *Etymologies,* 40 (1.4.2).

76. Ælfric, *Ælfrics Grammatik und Glossar,* 6.

77. Priscian, *Institutiones grammaticae,* vol. 2, p. 9 (1.2.8).

"Innumerae sumus, et simul omnes queque sonamus, una loqui nequit" (Innumerable we are; we speak in groups, alone we make no sense).[78] Here too, order is considered an integral component of *potestas,* as the description in Riddle 57 artfully suggests.

The third major property of the *littera,* its *nomen* 'name', comes into play in the final half-line of Riddle 57: *Nemnað hy sylfe* 'They name themselves'. Priscian explains the concept of the *nomen* 'name' of the letters quite simply: "Nomen, velut a, b." (The name is, for example, a, b).[79] Thus, in illustrating the names of the *litterae,* Priscian simply gives the letters themselves. Vowels and consonants name themselves in different ways, though. In medieval grammars, the consonant is commonly divided into two types, the "semi-vowel" and the "mute."[80] Both are named "from themselves," since "nichil aliud habet semiuocalis nisi nominis prolationem, que a uocali incipit"[81] (a semi-vowel has nothing else except the pronunciation of its own name, which begins with a vowel), and mutes are letters that "a se incipientes uocali terminantur"[82] (beginning from themselves, are concluded with a vowel). In this way consonants can be said to name themselves, but the case is even more pronounced for vowels. Priscian explains that the names of these come directly from their own pronunciation: "per se prolate nomen suum ostendunt"[83] (through the pronunciation, each one shows its own name). Ælfric renders this idea in language quite similar to that of the final half-line of Riddle 57: "ðas fif stafas æteowiað heora *naman þurh hi sylfe*"[84] (these five letters [the vowels] show their names through themselves). The parallels in diction and meaning are striking. *Bocstafas,* it can scarcely be doubted, name themselves.

Thus a solution of *bocstafas* activates Riddle 57 in many precise and resonant ways, but there is one section of the proposition that may seem difficult to account for. That is the statement that the creatures "tredað bearonæssas, /

78. Enigma 7, lines 1–2 (Glorie, *Variae collectiones aenigmatum,* 217; translation by Erhardt-Siebold, in ibid.).

79. Priscian, *Institutiones grammaticae,* vol. 2, p. 7 (1.2.7).

80. A "mute" is what we today would call a "stopped" or "plosive" consonant. The "semi-vowel" would include consonants we classify today as fricatives, liquids, and nasals.

81. David W. Porter, ed., *Excerptiones de Prisciano: The Source for Ælfric's Latin–Old English Grammar* (Cambridge: D. S. Brewer, 2002), 1.13.

82. Priscian, *Institutiones grammaticae,* vol. 2, p. 8 (1.7.7).

83. Porter, *Excerptiones de Prisciano,* 1.10.

84. Ælfric, *Ælfrics Grammatik und Glossar,* 5 (emphasis added).

hwilum burgsalo / niþþa bearna" (tread the woody headlands, at times the town houses of the sons of men). One might argue that this is merely an extension of the sense of *litterae* as elements of sound, borne aloft on the air. It is more likely, however, that the riddle refers here to the mobility of written *bocstafas*—their ability to carry speech across empty distances to the dwellings of the sons of men, one of the chief wonders of writing technology.[85] The exchange of manuscripts among *burgsalo* 'town houses' is one way such *bocstafas* may travel, as is the sending of written correspondence among centers of power and learning. In fact, it was possible to say that one was sending *bocstafas* or *stafas* 'letters' as an alternative expression for sending an *ærendgewrit* 'letter in the epistolary sense' in the Anglo-Saxon idiom (a use that derives from the Latin meaning of plural *litterae* as "epistle").[86] For example, in the C version of the Anglo-Saxon Chronicle we read, "to þam Lucius Brytene cyng sende bocstafas, bæd þæt he wære cristen gedon" (Lucius, the British king, sent him letters, bade that he should become a Christian).[87]

The idea that *bocstafas* may travel over a literal landscape may seem "far-fetched," but the conceit is well established in riddling traditions. An eighteenth-century riddler finds no problem in emphasizing ink's mobility:

> A greater Trav'ler ne'er was known,
> I visit ev'ry learned Town.[88]

Likewise, the bookish speaker of Exeter Riddle 95 hopes to have *blæd in burgum* 'success in the cities', while a good many oral traditional riddles figure written correspondence as birds flying from dwelling to dwelling. Taylor cites many such riddles: "A little black and white dove flies without wings, talks without a tongue," and "The voice of the raven from the Land of the South can be heard in this land."[89] A Turkish letter riddle reads, "Over very

85. Cassidorus writes of the scribe, "And so, though seated in one spot, with the dissemination of his work he travels through different provinces." *An Introduction to Divine and Human Readings,* trans. and ed. Leslie Webber Jones (New York: Columbia University Press, 1946), 133.

86. *Dictionary of Old English,* s.v. "bōcstæf."

87. Harry August Rositzke, ed., *The C-Text of the Old English Chronicles* (1940; repr., New York: Johnson Reprint Corporation, 1967), 13.

88. *The Merry Fellow: A Collection of the Best Modern Jests, Comic Tales, Poems, Fables, Epigrams, Epitaphs, and Riddles* (London, 1754), 323.

89. Taylor, *English Riddles from Oral Tradition,* 276–78 (no. 760). The latter riddle is solved "telegram" but is clearly related to the scores of letter riddles cited in this section of Taylor's anthology.

long roads a strange bird comes. It talks like cracking almonds. Whatever it says sounds good; it says strange words; tears drop from your eyes."[90] Another riddle from oral tradition reads, "Three hold her while she gives birth, her birds are black, they go all over the world."[91] Athenaeus, writing in the third century, attributes this riddle to Sappho: "There is a feminine being which keeps its babes safe beneath its bosom; they, though voiceless, raise a cry sonorous over the waves of the sea and across all the dry land, reaching what mortals they desire, and they may hear even when they are not there; but their sense of hearing is dull." The solution is explained in this way: "The feminine being, then, is an epistle, the babes within her are the letters it carries round; they, though voiceless, talk to whom they desire when far away; yet if another happen to be standing near when it is read, he will not hear."[92] Literal-minded readers of the Exeter riddles would surely reject the notion that letters "raise a cry sonorous over the waves of the sea," but riddlers know that letters roam.[93]

One further analogue along these lines serves to introduce a feature of Riddle 57 stressed in several recent studies. An Irish riddle collected in Taylor's anthology speaks of "A veinless, bloodless, little, black manikin [coming] across a hill from the East relating his tale."[94] At least to me, the given solution ("letter") is ambiguous. Is the little black manikin a single written character, encountered "from the East" as the reader's eye moves left to right? Or does this strange creature stand in for a full written message, quite literally arriving from the East? The former strikes me as more likely, but at any rate this "veinless, bloodless" creature comes across as a rather sinister character. Several recent studies have detected a similarly dark resonance in the diction of Riddle 57, leading to solutions in which the creatures are identified as either evil spirits (whether damned souls or demons) or various

90. Basgöz and Tietze, *Bilmece,* 436 (no. 438.17).

91. Cited in Taylor, *English Riddles from Oral Tradition,* 435 (no. 1063).

92. Athenaeus, *The Deipnosophists,* trans. Charles Burton Gulick (London: Harvard University Press, 1957), 10.450–51.

93. If the *bearonæssas* 'wooded cliffs' of Riddle 57 seem oddly specific, note that letters in riddles often cross very particular landscapes, as in this example: "I fastened its mouth and nose and had it jump over snowclad mountains" (Basgöz and Tietze, *Bilmece,* 434 [no. 438.9]). It is possible, of course, that the "snowclad mountains" here refer to pages of a book. In the Old English *Solomon and Saturn II* (Anlezark, *Old English Dialogues,* 80–81, line 52), a book riddle begins, "Ac hwæt is se dumba, se ðe on sumre dene resteð?" (But what is the mute thing, which rests in a certain valley?). The valley here is presumably the gutter of the codex in question.

94. Taylor, *English Riddles from Oral Tradition,* 276 (no. 760).

birds with bad reputations (such as the "devilet").[95] While I am somewhat skeptical of the dark implications of Riddle 57's diction, it would not be surprising to find inky creatures sharing in the charged lexicon of devilry.[96]

Take, for instance, a passage from the same section of *Solomon and Saturn I* cited above, in which the devilish enemies of the Pater Noster shift their shapes into a variety of forms (including that of birds). The devil is on the offensive, harassing a warrior as he strives in battle:

> Hwilum he gefeterað fæges mannes,
> handa gehefegað, ðonne he æt hilde sceall
> wið lað werud lifes tiligan;
> awriteð he on his wæpne wællnota heap,
> bealwe bocstafas, bill forscrifeð,
> meces mærðo.[97]

> [At times he fetters and makes heavy the hands of the fated man, when he at battle must contend for his life against a hateful army. He inscribes

95. Gregory K. Jember, "Riddle 57: A New Proposal," *In Geardagum* 2 (1977): 68–71. Jember relies primarily on examples from the prose *Guthlac* and Bede's *Historia* in which *cirman* is used to describe the shrieks of demons. Jember's argument does not acknowledge that the equally frequent association of the word *cirman* in the Old English corpus is with birds, including within the Exeter Book riddle collection itself (number 8, for example, is commonly solved "nightingale"). The later history of the word also suggests its strong association with birds, since "to chirm" is, "in Middle and modern English, chiefly restricted to the melodious chatter of or warbling of birds, or of human beings compared to birds." *Oxford English Dictionary,* s.v. "chirm." In fact, one of Jember's own cited examples from the "beasts of battle" scene in *The Battle of Maldon* (about which he says, "the context is death") seems to have more to do with the *hræfnas* 'ravens' who gather to feed on the coming slaughter than with demons. Still, *cirman*-related words do sometimes carry sinister overtones in the Old English period. The phrase *cirmes dæg* 'day of shrieking, judgment day', for example, testifies to these associations with death and damnation. *Dictionary of Old English,* s.v. "cirm." Phillip Pulsiano and Kirsten Wolf bolster Jember's solution with evidence culled from additional Old English and Old Norse sources: "*Exeter Book* Riddle 57: Those Damned Souls, Again," *Germanic Notes* 22, nos. 1–2 (1991): 2–5. For a list of devilish names for swifts, see Meaney, "Exeter Book Riddle 57 (55)," 199. Riedinger, analyzing such connotations, argues that the "beasts of battle" motif is a disguise for the humbler species of swallow: "The author of *Riddle 57* intends to suggest that the flying creatures in question are birds, but either eagles or ravens, thus misleading and leading simultaneously." "Formulaic Style," 35.

96. In an analysis of Jonathan Swift's literary riddles on topics related to the written word, Luke Powers, "Tests for True Wit: Jonathan Swift's Pen and Ink Riddles," *South Central Review* 7, no. 4 (1990), writes, "While Swift's pen merely abets injustices, ink positively delights in diabolism. Like the papal bulls in *The Tale of a Tub* which 'could outfly any bird,' ink soars more like a demon than the angelic, as yet undefiled, quill (indeed, earlier in the riddle it is described as the 'Son of Pitch and gloomy Night')" (48).

97. Dobbie, *Anglo-Saxon Minor Poems,* lines 158–63.

on his weapon a troop of fatal characters, pernicious letters. He blunts the sword, the glory of the blade.]

Like the creatures of Riddle 57, these *bealwe bocstafas* 'pernicious letters' are described as organized in a *heap* 'flock or troop'. The gathering of evil letters corresponds, in perverse imitation, to the animated letters of the Pater Noster, and the implied comparison, if not equivalence, of the devil's throng (which a few lines earlier is called a *manfulra heap* 'an evil troop') and the written marks (*weallnota heap* 'a troop of fatal letters') makes these characters comparable to the ominous flocks of Riddle 57.

The interpretation I have offered of Riddle 57 illustrates the broader challenge of reading the Exeter riddles. Simply adding up the major field marks of these creatures is hardly sufficient—no matter the nuance of the learned birder—if metaphor is at the heart of the genre. In Riddle 57 we may recognize a riddling mode familiar from oral tradition: a proposition that describes its solution through the metaphorical focus of an ominous flock of birdlike creatures. The Exeter riddles have a tendency to revise such popular themes according to the particular forms of learning available to Anglo-Saxon readers, but the old challenge remains to avoid missing the solution in our preoccupation with the disguise. I would stress, too, that the reverse is also true. It would be quite easy to ignore a riddle's strategy of obfuscation if we believe we already understand its solution. I take up this theme in the next chapter.

For the moment, though, I would like to conclude by commenting on one of the broader paradoxes generated by cloaking written characters in the guise of swarthy fowl. There is, after all, an irony generated in the comparison of the raucous *cirm* 'shrieking' of birds with the *potestas* 'sound value' of the written word. This irony resonates in the grammarian tradition, specifically in distinctions made between articulated and nonarticulated (*articulata/inarticulata*) *vox,* as well as between *vox* that can be rendered in letters and that which cannot be (*litterata/illiterata*). The former distinction involves the ability of the speech to signify: the poetry of the *Aeneid,* for example, gives meaning, while moaning and rattling noises produced by the human voice do not. The latter distinction is a related one. *Vox litterata* is that which is capable of being resolved into letters, while *vox illiterata* is that which is not (for example, hisses or groans). The proper subject of *grammatica,* then, is *vox articulata litterata,* that which can be both written and understood.[98] Priscian

98. For a more complete discussion of these terms, see Irvine, *Making of Textual Culture,* 92–95.

notes, however, a mixed type of *vox* that, while it can be written, cannot be understood: "aliae autem sunt, quae, quamvis scribantur, tamen inarticulatae dicuntur, cum nihil significent, ut 'coax,' 'cra'" (there are other voices which, even though they are written, are nevertheless said to be inarticulated since they do not mean anything, such as "coax" [the voice of a frog] and "cra" [the voice of a crow]).[99] Perhaps, then, in its playful comparison of written characters with dark birds, Riddle 57 does indeed evoke the inarticulate yet "literate" cries of *crawan* 'crows', who stalk the borderlands of human speech and habitation.

99. Priscian, *Institutiones grammaticae,* vol. 2, pp. 5–6 (1.1.2).

3

TRANSFORMATION AND TEXTUAL CULTURE

As I argued in the previous chapter, it would be easy to take a riddle's metaphor for its solution, to mistake a mask for an underlying answer. Much ink, after all, could be spilled in the attempt to sow black seed in the snow, and the dark creatures of the last chapter are surely not alone in their susceptibility to literal-minded readings. On the other hand, however, few of the Exeter riddles offer as few identifying field marks as Riddle 57. Most include a detail, a motif, or a conventional paradox whose relationship with the solution is so strong and so marked by tradition as to erase all doubt. And although we often insist that our solutions must explain "*all* the distinctive features of which account must be taken in any definitive interpretation," most of our confident guesses are grounded not so much in inductive reasoning as in the telltale clarity of a clue or two.[1] When we have a daughter giving birth to her mother, we know we have ice. When we see the dead bearing the living, we know we have a ship. When we have a caul on the wall, we know we have an egg. Once we mark these things, the rest of the riddle can be rescanned. With a little ingenuity (or emendation), Humpty Dumpty can usually be put back together again.

1. Greenfield, "Old English Riddle 39," 96.

Satisfying overt clues is one thing solutions do to propositions, but they also *activate* covert details. Such activation, in fact, is what we often appreciate most in riddles: the "moment" (real or imagined) when a solution remakes the proposition, recontextualizes it, and reveals that the literal words contain more than meets the eye. The solution's function, then, is not simply to satisfy the terms of the proposition, or it would be a bad riddle—no riddle at all, in fact. A solution's more dynamic function is to activate aspects of the proposition that previously appeared incidental or unimportant. I am not so much speaking here of real time, of puzzled solvers suspended in a state of dark mystification, to be followed by the blinding light of the right answer. This could be the case, but it need not be. Rather, the vital observation is that riddle propositions are understood to "come before" solutions in the logic of riddling, and that the answers are understood to overturn prior expectations. This sense of the fundamental structure of riddling would shape the reception and pleasure of these Old English texts whether or not the hearer or reader knows the answer. Michael Riffaterre contrasts the sonnet form with jokes and riddles: "In the joke subgenre there is no way for the reader to get beyond the laugh, once it has been laughed, any more than he can get beyond the solution once he has solved a riddle. Such forms self-destruct immediately after consumption."[2] I am not sure about jokes, but this statement does not seem true of riddling. The Exeter riddles, at least, do not appear to work this way; if anything, they tend to "self-construct" in the presence of the answer.

And yet, if scholarship on the Exeter riddles has been focused primarily on how various solutions might best satisfy the terms of the proposition, it would be easy to miss the focus of the riddle altogether. The danger would be particularly strong in riddles that arrive with telltale conventional clues: if the solution is given away from the get-go, what need to understand how the riddle works? It is already "solved." The assurance of a clear-cut solution can do away with the need to understand its obfuscation. A riddle's solution, however, is not its interpretation. There is potentially more at play, and possibly much more to say about the dynamic between a given riddle's proposition, solution, and metaphorical focus. This chapter, therefore, offers no new solutions for the Exeter riddles, a rather unusual omission in a study on this subject. Instead, I focus on accounting for the metaphorical play in these texts, and how more than one dynamic shapes their propositions.

2. Michael Riffaterre, *Semiotics of Poetry* (Bloomington: Indiana University Press, 1978), 16.

The idea that these poems engage in traditional modes of riddling by no means calls into question their engagement with Anglo-Saxon literary culture, however.[3] In traditional riddling, the metaphorical focus is often on some slice of daily life: a raisin is a wrinkled woman, a nose is a bridge between two lakes, teeth are white horses on a red hill. In the Exeter riddles, however, the "riddle creatures" are just as likely to be informed by the particular forms of learning available to their Anglo-Saxon audience. In unriddling these texts, then, it is necessary to draw on a range of astronomical, exegetical, liturgical, and grammatical works at home in the rich but limited Anglo-Saxon library. Books such as Isidore's *Etymologiae* and Jerome's *Epistulae* would be numbered among the fifty or so books making up the typical monastic library, collections that would probably fit easily within a single *arca* or book chest.[4] In examples already discussed in this study, we have seen riddle propositions shaped by an underlying comparison to the soul and the body, to Adam and Eve in their naked exile, and to the form and function of the Holy Cross. Other related metaphors are considered in this chapter. Just as Aldhelm's riddles are informed by very particular—and from our perspective very unusual—kinds of learning, so too is metaphorical riddling in the Exeter Book indebted to the various forms of specialized knowledge that made up the core curriculum of a tenth-century monastery.

There is perhaps no clearer instance of this than Riddle 22, at once one of the most patently metaphorical riddles in the Exeter Book and one whose interpretation requires the context of a very specific type of astronomical knowledge. This elegant enigma recounts the vision of a grand journey, men and horses crossing a vast sea from shore to shore. Some see a wagon of circling stars in Riddle 22, a solution that accounts well for many of the riddle's darkest clues. I am perhaps putting the cart before the horses, however. The full riddle reads:

> Ætsomne cwom   sixtig monna
> to wægstæþe   wicgum ridan;
> hæfdon endleofan   eoredmæcgas

3. As Orchard points out, "The difference between Anglo-Latin and Old English riddles is often caricatured as that between a handful of churchmen describing largely class-room topics . . . as against the ruder (in every sense) anonymous vernacular compositions, portraying everyday items in unusual ways, and perhaps intended less for the class-room than for the wine-hall." "Enigma Variations," 284.

4. Lapidge, *Anglo-Saxon Library,* 127.

fridhengestas, feower sceamas.
Ne meahton magorincas ofer mere feolan
swa hi fundedon, ac wæs flod to deop,
atol yþa geþræc, ofras hea,
streamas stronge. Ongunnon stigan þa
on wægn weras ond hyra wicg somod
hlodan under hrunge; þa þa hors oðbær
eh ond eorlas, æscum dealle,
ofer wætres byht wægn to lande—
swa hine oxa ne teah, ne esna mægen,
ne fæthengest, ne on flode swom,
ne be grunde wod gestum under,
ne lagu drefde, ne of lyfte fleag,
ne under bæc cyrde; brohte hwæþre
beornas ofer burnan ond hyra bloncan mid
from stæðe heaum þæt hy stopan up
on oþerne ellenrofe
weras of wæge ond hyra wicg gesund.

[Sixty men came riding together on horses to the wave shore; the horsemen had eleven horses (of some kind), four bright steeds. Nor could the warriors make their way over the seas as they aspired, but the waters were too deep, the tumult of waves terrible, the banks steep, the streams strong. The men began then to mount up into a wagon, and they loaded their horses too under the pole. Then the wagon bore the horses, the steeds and the men, resplendent with spears, over the abode of water to the land, so that an ox did not draw it, nor the strength of servants, nor the road horse, nor did it swim on the sea, nor trudge over the ground under its passengers, nor stir up the sea, nor fly from the air, nor reverse its course; nevertheless, it bore the men over the water and their white horses with them from the high shore, so that they mounted back up on the other side, the brave warriors and their horses out of the sea safe and sound.][5]

5. I will have further occasion below to discuss certain features of Riddle 22's diction, but the difficult language of the text makes it necessary to say a few words here about this translation. This riddle contains several hapax legomena, including three words that seem to refer to different types of horses: *fridhengestas* (line 4a), *sceamas* (line 4b), and *fæthengest* (line 14a). The first of these has been variously interpreted as a compound meaning "horses of peace" or "horses of

The solving history of this riddle is fairly thin, and only two proposed solutions deserve serious attention.[6] First, Franz Dietrich solved Riddle 22 as the month of December, with the sixty riders corresponding to half-days and the eleven horses to the seven feast days of that month, plus four Sundays (the four "bright steeds").[7] The far shore, in this reading, would be the new year. The main problem with this interpretation, as Krapp and Dobbie point out, is that if the days of the months are counted according to half-days, it is unclear why the feast days and Sundays are not.[8] Since the strength of the "month" solution presumably lies in its handling of the numbers, this is a real problem. A much more convincing solution was proposed nearly a century later by L. Blakeley, and adopted by Williamson in his edition.[9] Blakeley solves Riddle 22 as "the circling stars," with the point of focus on the *wægn* 'wagon', which corresponds to the constellation known in the Old English vernacular as *carles wæn* or 'Charles's Wain'.[10] This famous asterism is the same as the one known as the Big Dipper in North America today and forms the core of the Ursa Major or Great Bear constellation. In Latin the constellation was also known as Septentriones (the Seven Plow Oxen), a name derived from the number of stars found in the constellation as well as its alternative construal as a plow. It was additionally sometimes referred to as Arcturus, a name more properly applied to a star in the Boötes constellation, which was often associated with Septentriones.[11]

---

war," or as a tautological compound (something like "steed horses"), among other things. My translation retains our uncertainty on this score. See the *Dictionary of Old English,* s.v. "fridhengest." For *sceamas,* see Williamson, *Old English Riddles,* 203–4. I follow Williamson's basic understanding of this word as meaning "bright ones" and translate the phrase "four bright steeds." As for *fæthengest,* the *Dictionary of Old English* seems to omit this word. Bosworth and Toller's *Anglo-Saxon Dictionary* gives "a road horse" and Williamson offers "riding-horse." My translation follows this reading.

6. Alternative proposals include the oddly literal and unconvincing "bridge" as well as the abstracted "rite of passage." See Fry, "Exeter Book Riddle Solutions," 23.

7. Franz Dietrich, "Die Räthsel des Exeterbuchs: Würdigung, Lösung, und Herstellung," *Zeitschrift für Deutsches Alterthum* 11 (1859): 466.

8. Krapp and Dobbie, *Exeter Book,* 333.

9. L. Blakeley, "Riddles 22 and 58 of the Exeter Book," *Review of English Studies,* n.s., 9 (1958): 241–52; Williamson, *Old English Riddles,* 201–4. More recently, Bitterli, *Say What I Am Called,* 59–68, has endorsed this solution.

10. According to the *Oxford English Dictionary,* s.v. "Charles's Wain," "The name appears to arise out of the verbal association of the star-name *Arcturus* with *Arturus* or Arthur, and the legendary association of Arthur and Charlemagne; so that what was originally the wain of Arcturus or Boötes . . . became at length the wain of Carl or Charlemagne. (The guess *churl's* or *carle's wain* has been made in ignorance of the history.)"

11. Constellation names are frequently confused, not least among these associated asterisms: "As the name Arcturus was formerly sometimes applied loosely to the constellation Boötes and

Blakeley's solution makes excellent sense of much of Riddle 22 and remains the consensus reading of the poem.[12] Indeed, I agree with Blakeley's basic picture of Riddle 22 as an enigma of the stars. But there are a few problems with Blakeley's interpretation that need addressing. There is value in attempting to clarify these issues, even if definitive conclusions are difficult to achieve. What is left, one hopes, is a more lucid understanding of an elegant Anglo-Saxon vision of the night sky.

To begin at the beginning, Riddle 22 opens with a group of horsemen riding to a shore:

> Ætsomne cwom sixtig monna
> to wægstæþe wicgum ridan;
> hæfdon endleofan eoredmæcgas
> fridhengestas, feower sceamas.

> [Sixty men came riding together on horses to the wave shore; the horsemen had eleven horses (of some kind), four bright steeds.]

The numbering of these horses is somewhat ambiguous, for it seems that either we might think that the horsemen have eleven horses, four of which are *sceamas* 'bright steeds', or we might interpret the lines as meaning that the horsemen have eleven *fridhengestas* 'horses (of some kind)' as well as four additional *sceamas* 'bright steeds' (for a total of fifteen horses, four of which are particularly bright or prominent). The former reading is the one employed both in Dietrich's and Blakeley's solutions, but, as will become clear, I favor the latter. In any case, Riddle 22 opens with three distinct numbers, sixty, eleven, and four (all of which appear as Roman numerals in the manuscript), and any acceptable solution must take them into account. Before I offer my own explanation, however, a bit more discussion is necessary.

First, what is meant by "sixty" is more open to debate than one might think. In a poem about the celestial wain, of course, these sixty riders most

---

incorrectly to the Great Bear, the name *Carlewayne-sterre* occurs applied to the star Arcturus." Ibid.

12. Blakeley's solution is adopted in Craig Williamson's standard edition of the riddles, for example, and is listed as the correct solution in relevant entries of the *Dictionary of Old English* (s.v. "fridhengest," for example).

probably refer to stars, and this argument relies on that premise.[13] However, *sixtig* may not really mean "sixty" in an Old English riddle. Blakeley takes this number to refer to an indefinite plenitude, translated roughly as "scores." Two main supports bolster this reading: an article on sixty as an indefinite number in Middle English and Alcuin's riddle on a comb, which might make a similar use of that number.[14] Now, in defense of Blakeley's position, we might argue that, as an opening for a celestial riddle, an indefinite reckoning of the stellar multitudes makes sense. The Bern riddle on the stars, for example, opens by stating that "milia conclusae domo sub una sorores" (a thousand sisters are confined inside a single house).[15] Aldhelm's riddle on Arcturus (in the sense of Ursa Major) begins, "Sidereis stipor turmis" (I am crowded by stellar throngs), while many riddles from oral tradition describe the sky as a blanket filled with innumerable coins, buttons, crumbs, or even lice.[16] But the use of *sixtig* as an indefinite number is questionable in Old English. Most of Blakeley's Old English analogues refer to multiples of sixty (as do the Middle English examples cited by Tucker) and may actually refer to precise numbers (the six hundred men in a Roman cohort, by Blakeley's own admission).[17] Blakeley's best shot is a riddle by Alcuin on the topic of a comb whose broad grin bares *dentes lx* 'sixty teeth'. Paul Sorrell, however, has shown recently that this riddle was a piece of occasional verse written in response to Alcuin's receiving an ivory comb from Archbishop Riculf of Mainz. In this context, the count of teeth in Alcuin's comb may reflect an accurate account of a very specific material object and, while Alcuin's own comb is lost, Sorrell is indeed able to instance a comb of ivory found in St. Cuthbert's tomb that has fifty-eight teeth.[18] This is a much more definite reckoning than Blakeley is counting on. Finally, the proverbial uncountability of the stars surely makes sixty a rather low estimate of stellar profusion, given also the frequency of known constellations in Hyginus and Cicero's *Aratea* to number in the upper twenties. If

13. Marijane Osborn, "Old English Ing and His Wain," *Neuphilologische Mitteilungen* 81 (1980): 388–89, accepts Blakeley's larger position on the meaning of Riddle 22's "wain" and proposes that these sixty men are the sixty days after the winter solstice, when Hesiod says that Ursa Major "rises in the evening twilight."

14. Susie I. Tucker, "'Sixty' as an Indefinite Number in Middle English," *Review of English Studies* 25 (1949): 152–53; Blakeley, "Riddles 22 and 58," 244.

15. Enigma 62, line 1 (Glorie, *Variae collectiones aenigmatum,* 609; my translation).

16. Enigma 53, line 1 (ibid., 443; my translation). For a rich collection of folk riddles on celestial topics, see Archer Taylor, "A Riddle for the Sun, Sky, and Stars," *California Folklore Quarterly* 3 (1944): 222–31.

17. Blakeley, "Riddles 22 and 58," 244; Tucker, "'Sixty' as an Indefinite Number."

18. Sorrell, "Alcuin's 'Comb' Riddle," 313.

indefinite throngs of stars are indeed meant by "sixty men," we might view the first line of Riddle 22 as a study in riddlic litotes. Nevertheless, we cannot rule out this reading.

But if Blakeley's account of sixty as scores remains a dark horse in the running, much less likely is his understanding of the eleven *fridhengestas* 'horses (of some kind)' and four *sceamas* 'bright steeds'. Blakeley's reading is as follows:

> The horsemen and horses are the stars near to the Wain, which travel with it. We are told that the eleven horses are loaded under the pole of the Wain. If the horses are stars, this gives perfect sense. . . . Under the pole of the Wain is the constellation now called 'Canes Venatici.' This constellation in fact does consist of eleven stars visible to the naked eye. G. F. Chambers, in his catalogue of the stars visible to the eye, gives a table of the eleven stars, showing that there is one star of the third magnitude, three between magnitudes 4 and 5, and seven between magnitudes 5 and 5.2. This is the only one of the northern constellations which is shown by him to consist of eleven naked-eye stars.[19]

Blakeley goes on to explain that the *sceamas* refer to the four brightest stars since four of the stars in Canes Venatici are slightly larger than the seven smallest ones (how could it be otherwise?). This is a rather dubious argument, since Blakeley's distinction rests on a convenient and arbitrary selection of the top four brightest stars.

The main problem with Blakeley's account, however, is that the constellation Canes Venatici is an early modern invention. According to Morton Wagman, this particular asterism was devised in 1533 by Peter Apian.[20] Blakeley seems aware of this problem when he sidesteps the issue of anachronism with the phrase "the constellation *now called* 'Canes Venatici' " (emphasis added). Constellations such as Canes Venatici are, however, fairly arbitrary collocations of objects in the night sky, not natural groupings.[21] Some groups

19. Blakeley, "Riddles 22 and 58," 243–44.

20. Morton Wagman, *Lost Stars* (Blacksburg, Va.: McDonald and Woodward, 2003), 68. Wagman notes that the astronomer Johannes Hevelius (1611–1687) is commonly and erroneously credited with inventing Canes Venatici.

21. A good illustration of this point is a tenth-century manuscript from China that contains a chart of the stars, with many constellations delineated and labeled. Of the thirty-odd asterisms shown, only one collocation matches up with a Western constellation: the seven stars of Charles's Wain. An image of this chart is found in Ian Ridpath, *Star Tales* (New York: Walker, 1988), 14.

of stars, like those of the Wain, are so prominent as to be recognized across cultures, each of which may see either a bear, a wagon, or a plow in the pattern, but I have not been able to find any evidence to suggest that those eleven stars of Canes Venatici were thought of as a separate and conspicuous unit in Anglo-Saxon England. To claim that the Old English riddler had them in mind and wanted the solver to select their four brighter members as the singled-out *sceamas* 'bright steeds' is not strictly impossible, but it is certainly not very likely without further evidence.[22]

I will offer my own explanation of these numbers presently. First, however, my argument turns on recognizing one additional feature of the night sky in Riddle 22 unmentioned in previous discussions. Lines 8b–10a of Riddle 22 read, "Ongunnon stigan þa / on wægn weras ond hyra wicg somod / hlodan under hrunge" (The men began then to mount up into a wagon, and they loaded their horses too under the *hrunge*). A crucial question here is the meaning of *hrunge,* and once again Riddle 22 does not offer easy answers, as this is the only attested instance of the word in Old English. Bosworth and Toller define *hrung* as "a rung, staff, rod, beam, pole" and give the tentative explanation of its use in Riddle 22 as "the pole that supported the covering?" (of the wagon).[23] Blakeley offers a different explanation: the *hrung* corresponds to the "single pole of the Wain," that is, the three stars that form the "handle" of the Big Dipper, or the "tongue" of the celestial wagon.[24] Blakeley's position is tenable, but there is another likely possibility. This is simply that the *hrung* 'pole' under which the men and horses are loaded into the wain is the celestial pole or axis that lies directly "above" Charles's Wain in the night sky.[25] This is all the more probable since Ursa

22. Bitterli considers whether the numbers could refer to the Wain itself: "The sources agree that Arcturus has seven bright stars, which—according to Isidore—revolve in two groups of three (*tres*) and four (*quattuor*) stars. The latter may account for the 'four white horses' (*IIII sceamas,* 4) in the Old English text, but the remaining numbers simply do not add up." *Say What I Am Called,* 67.

23. Bosworth and Toller, *Anglo-Saxon Dictionary,* s.v. "hrung."

24. Blakeley, "Riddles 22 and 58," 245.

25. In Middle English there is evidence for the use of "rung" to describe both the "shaft of a cart or wagon" and as either the "pin used to hold a wheel on an axle" or "the beam to which the lantern wheel [in a mill] is attached." Hans Kurath and Sherman M. Kuhn, eds., *Middle English Dictionary* (Ann Arbor: University of Michigan Press, 1952), s.v. "rung." With respect to the last of these definitions, it is worth noting that the rotation of the heavens is compared to a wheel driven by a watermill in Aldhelm's Enigma 48. The celestial pole or axis was not necessarily always identified with the star today known as Polaris: "During the Anglo-Saxon period the Pole did not correspond with any star but was the geometrical point at the centre of stars revolving in circles around it." Wesley M. Stevens, "Astronomy," in *The Blackwell*

Major's proximity to the heavenly pole is considered one of its essential features in many works known to the Anglo-Saxons. For example, the speaker of Aldhelm's riddle on the subject of Ursa Major says,

> In giro uoluens iugiter non uergo deorsum
> Cetera ceu properant caelorum lumina ponto.
> Hac gaza ditor, quoniam sum proximus axi [. . .]
>
> [Revolving continually in a circle I never incline downward, as do the other stars of the heavens (which) hasten to the sea. I am enriched by this endowment, since I am nearest to the pole . . .][26]

Isidore says of Ursa Major that "in coeli axe constitutus semper uersatur, et numquam mergitur" (it turns forever positioned on the axis of the sky, and is never submerged below the horizon).[27] Including the celestial pole in a riddle of the Wain would be a likely choice for an Anglo-Saxon riddler.

In fact, this makes better sense of the relevant lines quoted above: "Ongunnon stigan þa / on wægn weras ond hyra wicg samod / hlodan under hrunge" (The men began then to mount up into a wagon, and they loaded their horses too under the pole). Blakeley's reading implies that the horses are "hitched under" the shaft of the wagon, but this conflicts with the overarching fiction of Riddle 22 that the horses and men ride *inside* the protective enclosure of the wain from one shore to another, unaided by oxen or horses. Rather, the lines indicate that the men are beginning to *stigan* 'mount up' and then to *hlodan under hrunge* 'load under the pole' their horses together with them in the wagon.[28] This is pivotal because it marks out a space in the

---

Encyclopaedia of Anglo-Saxon England, ed. Michael Lapidge et al. (Oxford: Blackwell, 2001), 51. Nevertheless, some authorities known to the Anglo-Saxons did seem to identify the pole with a particular star. Martianus Capella, for instance, puts these words into the mouth of a personified Astronomy: "At the very pole of the universe I have set a brilliant star." See *Martianus Capella and the Seven Liberal Arts,* vol. 2, *The Marriage of Philology and Mercury,* trans. William Harris Stahl and Richard Johnson, with E. L. Burge (New York: Columbia University Press, 1977), 322.

26. Enigma 53, lines 3–5 (Glorie, *Variae collectiones aenigmatum,* translation from Lapidge and Rosier, *Aldhelm: The Poetic Works,* 81).

27. Isidore, *De natura rerum,* ed. G. Becker (Berlin: C. Schutzii, 1857; repr., Amsterdam: A. M. Hakkert, 1967), 26.3.4–5.

28. The sense of *hladan* in Old English is "to heap, pile up, build, place, lade, load, freight." This does not bear out Blakeley's picture of the horses "hitched under" the wain. Bosworth and Toller, *Anglo-Saxon Dictionary,* s.v. "hladan."

night sky above the celestial Wain and *under hrunge* 'below the pole' as the area where these riders join up with Ursa Major.

This orientation, in turn, will now allow us to move back retrogressively through the numbers problem as outlined above. There is only one feature of the night sky that lies "above" the Wain and "under" the celestial pole. This is the tail end of the constellation Draco, which, in Cicero's *Aratea* (8.16), is described as flowing like a river *has inter* 'between these' (i.e., between the greater and lesser Wains: exactly the spot in the night sky suggested by Riddle 22). Martianus Capella tells us that Draco "winds about and glides between" them.[29] Quite conveniently for the argument I am making here, this constellation consists of fifteen stars, according to Hyginus.[30] Moreover, four of these fifteen make up the "head" portion of the dragon, a distinctive group that also contains the brightest stars of the constellation.[31] These, arguably, are the four *sceamas* 'bright steeds' of Riddle 22, while the remaining stars of Draco (strung out in a line that runs into the space between the Wain and the pole) make up the other eleven horses mentioned.[32] A constellation known to medieval readers to have fifteen stars, of which four were marked off as especially prominent, is thus found exactly where the riddle tells us it will be: coming up under the pole (*under hrunge*) and "up into" the Wain: "ongunnon stigan þa / on wægn."

29. Martianus Capella, *Seven Liberal Arts,* 326.

30. "Hic habet in utroque tempore stellas singulas, in oculis singulas, in mento unam et toto corpore reliquo passim dispositas decem; ita omnino est stellarum XV" (This [constellation] has single stars on each temple, single stars in its eyes, one on its chin, and ten are dispersed along the rest of the whole body. Therefore in all there are fifteen stars). Hyginus, *De astronomia,* ed. Ghislaine Viré (Leipzig: Teubner, 1992), 3.2.25–27.

31. In most descriptions of Draco, medieval and modern, the head forms the most prominent feature of the constellation, including its brightest and most readily recognizable stars. As the passage above indicates, Hyginus identifies two stars on the "temples" of the dragon's head, two for its eyes, and one on its chin. The *Aratea* highlights the head stars of Draco as the most prominent and bright: "Huic non una modo caput ornans stella relucet, uerum tempora sunt duplici fulgore notata, e trucibusque oculis duo feruida lumina flagrant atque uno mentum radianti sidere lucet" (The head does not give light only through a single adorning star, but the temples are marked by a double clarity, and from his menacing eyes two glowing lights blaze forth and the chin is lit with one shining star). Cicero, *Les aratea,* ed. Victor Buescu (Hildesheim: Georg Olms, 1966), 8.19–22. Arguably, this passage stresses the blazing "double clarity" of Draco's temples and eyes, somewhat less his "chin." It may be that Riddle 22 also has these four in mind as the "bright steeds," marked by their twinned arrangement and perceived brilliance. Modern depictions of Draco's head tend to view it as a strained square of four stars. See, for example, Julius D. W. Staal, *Patterns in the Sky* (London: Hodder and Stoughton, 1961), 174.

32. Aside from its star count and position in the sky, Draco is a likely candidate here on account of the traditional order of constellations listed in astronomical works: in both the *Aratea* and Hyginus, Draco is the first constellation mentioned after an opening discussion of Ursa Major and Ursa Minor.

But what about the sixty men who are said to be riding these horses? These could quite possibly be indefinite throngs. There is another possibility, however. Positioned immediately "on the back" of Draco are four constellations known to the Anglo-Saxons through authorities such as Hyginus and Cicero's *Aratea.* The number of stars in these constellations as given in Hyginus's *Poetic Astronomy* (Ursa Minor with seven, Cepheus with nineteen, Cassiopeia with fourteen, and Andromeda with twenty) add up to exactly sixty.[33] Thus this portion of the night sky, as an Anglo-Saxon might tally it up, balances nicely an equation with the opening lines of Riddle 22: sixty stars "riding" a constellation of fifteen (with four marked as distinct) snaking its way into the gap between the pole and the Wain.

With this picture clarified, it is now possible to comment more confidently on the riddling language of this poem. One of the beauties of Blakeley's solution is its restoration of the manuscript reading *ne of lyfte fleag* 'nor did it fly from the air', which has often been emended to read *ne on lyfte fleag* 'nor did it fly in the air'.[34] The artful variation on the expected phrase *on lyfte* 'on the air' is a nice example of the riddler manipulating the reader's expectations.[35] Moreover, while none of the fixed stars fly out of the air, the statement is particularly true of the Wain, which is famed for never "plunging" below the horizon. For example, Ælfric, following Isidore, writes in his *De temporibus anni,*

> Arcton hatte an tungel on norðdæle se hæfð seofon steorran ond is forði oðrum naman gehatan Septemtrio þone hatað læwede men

33. Hyginus, *De astronomia,* 3.1.14; 3.8.105; 3.9.118–19; 3.10.20. Of course, any such count involves a certain degree of selectivity. But these constellations and star counts were known to the Anglo-Saxons and do arguably constitute the cluster of asterisms that is most immediately "riding on the back" of Draco. Moreover, the close association of the Wains and Draco in early medieval astronomical treatises, as well as the fact that Cepheus, Andromeda, and Cassiopeia are named after members of the same mythological family, makes this arrangement not altogether random.

34. Blakeley, "Riddles 22 and 58," 245–46. Ironically, Williamson, who followed Blakeley in restoring the manuscript reading *of lyfte,* was later criticized for supposedly rendering *on lyfte* as "down from the air" in order unfairly to support the celestial solution to Riddle 22. See Carol L. Edwards, Review of *A Feast of Creatures: Anglo-Saxon Riddle-Songs,* trans. Craig Williamson, *Western Folklore* 43, no. 2 (1984): 146.

35. A simple search of the online *Dictionary of Old English* produces twenty-six matches for the phrase *on lyfte* and only four for *of lyfte.* Of the latter, two refer to light or objects becoming visible "from the air," and one occurs in a homiletic context discussing the four elements out of which the body is made ("of eorþan, ond of fyre, ond of wætere, ond of lyfte" [from earth, and from fire, and from water, and from air]). This leaves only a single instance in *Guthlac A* that parallels the meaning of *of lyfte* found in Riddle 22: something traveling down "out of" the air. http://ets.umdl.umich.edu/o/oec/ (accessed January 2006).

> Carles wæn se ne gæð næfre adune under ðissere eorðan swa swa oðre tunglan doð. Ac he went abutan hwilon up hwilon adune ofer dæg ond ofer niht.
>
> [A constellation in the northern part of the sky is called Arcturus, which has seven stars and is therefore also called Septemtrio, which unlearned men call Charles's Wain and which never goes down under the earth as other constellations do. Rather, at times it goes up and at times down, by day and by night.][36]

This of course is very similar to Aldhelm's words on the Wain, which I have already had occasion to cite: "Revolving continually in a circle I never incline downward, as do the other stars of the heavens (which) hasten to the sea."[37]

It is perhaps this unsinkable aspect of Ursa Major that helps inspire the broad conceit of the night sky as vast sea. Charles's Wain, as the one constellation never to be submerged in the oceanic horizon, becomes the means of crossing the open waters of the sky. The seafaring metaphorical focus of the poem is an artful heels-over-head inversion of the solution—for the stars in question are the very ones used for guiding ships through the sea. In fact, the celestial pole was identified in at least one Old English text as the *scip-steorra* 'ship-star', the navigator's key point of reference in the night sky. Given Riddle 22's emphasis on guiding the passengers safely from shore to shore, it is also intriguing to note the punning potential of the words *steora* 'one who steers or directs the course of a ship' and *steorra* 'star'. The path of the seafarers is reflected in their celestial guide. Also influenced by the metaphorical focus is the description of the stars as *æscum dealle* 'resplendent with spears', a description that I read as evoking the clusters of points forming a star-shaped asterisk. Isidore understood that the * symbol was called an asterisk because of the Greek word for star, and representations of the night sky in early medieval manuscripts often represent the stars of constellations with similar marks.[38] The pull of the metaphorical focus is enough to transform these points of light into warriors "resplendent with spears."

36. Ælfric, *De temporibus anni,* ed. Heinrich Henel (Oxford: Oxford University Press, 1942), 9.6.

37. Enigma 53, lines 3–4 (trans. Lapidge and Rosier, *Aldhelm: The Poetic Works,* 81).

38. Isidore, *Etymologies,* 50 (1.21.2). For early medieval manuscript representations of constellations, see Stephen C. McCluskey, *Astronomies and Cultures in Early Medieval Europe* (Cambridge: Cambridge University Press, 1998), 107, 136.

The basic inversion of sea and sky opens up further riddling play. The depths of the sky become the profundity of the sea: Ursa Major's position near the pole makes it the asterism capable of crossing the waters *to deop* 'too deep' for the others. The horizons that Ursa Major may graze but never sink under become inverted *ofras hea* 'high shores' onto which the Wain's passengers *stopan up* 'stepped up' as they dip out of sight. Surely the unchanging rotation of the heavens is referenced in the statement *ne under bæc cyrde* 'nor did [the Wain] turn back', but this may also wink at the Wain's apparent "backward" movement through the sky, for the wagon's "tongue" trails behind in the counterclockwise motion of the stars. Truly, the riddling strategy of inversion is at full tilt in Riddle 22.

To close my discussion of Riddle 22, I would like to come full circle and touch again on Dietrich's reading of the poem as a puzzle of the calendar, its feast days, and other features. Blakeley framed his own solution as a rejection of this reading, as well as of the comparative methods that led Tupper and others to assume that Riddle 22 is, "of course, a variant of the Year problem."[39] For a number of reasons, I accept Blakeley's basic solution as the best. And yet acceptance of this answer need not mean ignoring the relevance of the evidence linking Riddle 22 to the extremely widespread pattern of time riddling cited by Dietrich, Tupper, and others. As Taylor documents, such time riddles are amazingly diverse and widespread, but as a group they share a marked resemblance to Riddle 22 in their multiple numbers and in their sense of a cyclical journey. The numbered creatures are sometimes the spokes of a wheel, animals ("there are three hundred and sixty-six oxen and twelve yokes, all tied to one pole"),[40] riders on horseback, or even passengers in a wagon.[41] These voyagers often embody days, nights, weeks, and months, or other less abstract signs of the passing of time, such as lunar months or the paths of the sun and moon. The movements of the celestial Wain would be another such sign of cyclical time for Anglo-Saxon stargazers, its circling positions in the dark sky marking out both the hours of the night and the passing of the year. The nightly rotation of the stars provided a key guide

39. Frederick Tupper Jr., "Originals and Analogues of the *Exeter Book Riddles*," *Modern Language Notes* 18, no. 4 (1903): 102. See also Tupper, *Riddles of the Exeter Book*, 117–19. Blakeley declares, "It is a mistake to rely too much on the finding of analogues to give a solution." "Riddles 22 and 58," 242.

40. Taylor, *English Riddles from Oral Tradition*, 412–21 (nos. 1037–38).

41. See Tupper, "Originals and Analogues," 102.

for regulating schedules of monastic sleep and prayer, and the shifting positions of the stars with the seasons were central to agricultural timing.[42] While embracing Blakeley's solution, then, it seems to me quite consistent also to accept Tupper's basic view of Riddle 22 as indeed a "time riddle"—as, in a very strong sense, a "variant of the Year problem." To do so emphasizes the haunting sense of symmetry conveyed in the Wain's enigmatic annual voyage from shore to shore, for surely in Riddle 22 the eternal motion of the stars and the swift course of the year are tightly yoked together.

Riddle 22 shares its celestial theme with another elegant poem found nearby in the Exeter Book, Riddle 29. Few would quibble with J. A. W. Bennett's judgment that this text is one of the "finest, and most teasing" of the collection, and yet despite its popularity in anthologies, Riddle 29 remains a text little studied, as if its secrets are self-evident.[43] The full riddle reads:

> Ic wiht geseah   wundorlice
> hornum bitweonum   huþe lædan,
> lyftfæt leohtlic   listum gegierwed,
> huþe to þam ham   of þam heresiþe.
> Walde hyre on þære byrig   bur atimbran,
> searwum asettan,   gif hit swa meahte.
> Ða cwom wundorlicu wiht   ofer wealles hrof
> seo is eallum cuð   eorðbuendum;
> ahredde þa þa huþe,   ond to ham bedraf
> wreccan ofer willan—   gewat hyre west þonan
> fæhþum feran,   forð onette.
> Dust stonc to heofonum;   deaw feol on eorþan;
> niht forð gewat.   Nænig siþþan
> wera gewiste   þære wihte sið.

[I saw a creature strangely bearing booty between its horns, an air vessel brightly decked out with cunning, carrying plunder home from its war journey. It wished to build for it a chamber in that fortress, craftily to set it up, if it was so able. Then came over the roof of the wall a marvelous creature well known to all earth dwellers; it rescued

42. See McCluskey, *Astronomies and Cultures,* 97–113.

43. Bennett, *Poetry of the Passion,* 6.

> then that booty and drove it (the first creature) into its home, the exile against its will—one who departed from there to the west, bearing enmity, and it made haste. Dust rose to the heavens, dew fell on the earth; night departed. No one then knew the journey of that creature.]

The solving history of this riddle essentially begins and ends with Dietrich's answer, "sun and moon," a solution so satisfying that certain puzzling aspects of the poem have gone largely undiscussed.[44] The moon is depicted as an ambitious warrior, whose plunder of borrowed light is intercepted by another creature (the sun), who drives it off as night departs. This much is clear, though aspects of the poem remain dark. Among other things, the meaning of the poem's ending, with its rising dust and falling dew, seems far from self-evident. Dew of course comes with dawn, but why the rising dust? Riddle 29 may be an instance in which the obvious solution of a riddle discourages inquiry into other aspects of its interpretation. As I have argued, however, solutions do not solve everything when it comes to these texts. As with other riddles of the Exeter Book, the proposition of Riddle 29 may be illuminated as much by considering its metaphorical focus as by guessing its undisputed answer.

To address this question, I propose to revive and revise F. H. Whitman's argument for a Christian reading of the poem, which seems to me quite persuasive.[45] Whitman's interpretation has been largely ignored and is dismissed in Williamson's influential edition of the Exeter riddles. Yet Whitman's basic claim is convincing in its simplicity. He argues that the strife depicted in Riddle 29—between a horned, plundering Moon and an illustrious Sun that rescues the plunder and drives the usurper into exile in the west—would be read by an Anglo-Saxon audience as symbolic of Christ's victory over Satan. Williamson rejects this argument simply by asserting that "the treatment in the riddle seems more heroic than Christian. The moon is a plundering warrior and not a Satanic prince."[46] In fact, there should be no difficulty about detecting in the poem a blend of heroic and Christian elements, the mixing of which is, after all, a hallmark of Old English poetry.

44. Dietrich, "Räthsel des Exeterbuchs: Würdigung," 468–69. For a very few (rather unconvincing) alternatives to the solution of "sun and moon," see Fry, "Exeter Book Riddle Solutions," 23. Also see Pinsker and Ziegler, *Altenglischen Rätsel,* 215–19, for Riddle 29 interpreted as "a star-riddle—'Venus carried off.'"

45. F. H. Whitman, "The Christian Background to Two Riddle Motifs," *Studia Neophilologica* 41 (1969): 93–98.

46. Williamson, *Old English Riddles,* 228.

Presumably, the real trouble is that Whitman's thesis does not square with the expectations many modern readers have about the riddling genre or, more specifically, about the Exeter collection.

One of these expectations is that the Exeter riddles, if they are good riddles, should reflect an image of nature with almost scientific precision. For instance, Stopford A. Brooke, one of the earliest commentators on Riddle 29, wonders at its "vivid natural description" and declares, "That there should be so much deliberate nature-poetry, written for the sake of nature alone, and with an evident and observing love, is most remarkable in vernacular poetry of the eighth century, and very difficult to account for."[47] Daniel G. Calder cites this very discussion of Riddle 29 to illustrate how Brooke "endows Old English literature with Romantic effulgence," and yet Brooke's reading of the poem is not far off what we find in Williamson's edition, where we read, "The notion of 'earthlight' does not enter into medieval discussions of the moon, but the Old English riddler in true scientific fashion told what he saw."[48] In raising the question of "earthlight," Williamson is endorsing a solution to a perceived problem in the poem, a reading that Brooke himself first suggested. The issue is that the moon's "plunder," which Tupper and others naturally assume to be its borrowed light, is carried *hornum bitweonum* 'between the horns', rather than *on* the horns. Therefore, the booty cannot be light but must rather be "the earthlit dark portion of the moon cradled by the crescent light."[49] Williamson credits A. J. Wyatt for this bit of ingenuity, but Wyatt seems to have actually borrowed it uncredited from Brooke's analysis of the riddler's "observing love."[50] It is curious to observe, in fact, that the most authoritative discussion of a famous Old English poem can be traced back to Brooke's idiosyncratic vision of the riddler's "personal love of nature."[51] Regardless of its origin, however, the suggestion of "earthlight" clearly runs counter to the larger narrative of a sunlike creature rescuing its plundered light. Moreover, if there

47. Stopford A. Brooke, *English Literature: From the Beginning to the Norman Conquest* (New York: Macmillan, 1898), 95–96.

48. Daniel G. Calder, "Histories and Surveys of Old English Literature: A Chronological Review," *Anglo-Saxon England* 10 (1982): 221; Williamson, *Old English Riddles*, 228.

49. Williamson, *Old English Riddles*, 227.

50. Ibid.; Wyatt, *Old English Riddles*, 88; Brooke, *English Literature*, 95.

51. Brooke, *English Literature*, 97. As Michael Lapidge stresses, it is important to avoid reading the Exeter riddles as if they were "the lyric outpouring of an illiterate poet warbling native woodnotes wild." Lapidge, "Stoic Cosmology and the Source of the First Old English Riddle," *Anglia* 112 (1994): 25.

really is a difficulty to be overcome here, it might simply be that the plundering creature is a full moon, whose imagined lunar "horns" are thus packed with plundered light, much as Chaucer once described the full moon as "schynynge with hir fulle hornes."[52]

It is this insistence on viewing Riddle 29 as pure "nature poetry" that blinds us to its central metaphorical focus: Christ's Harrowing of Hell.[53] In a moment, I will provide a close examination of how this works in the text. First, though, it is hardly news to note that the medieval association of Christ with the sun is ubiquitous. Examples are not difficult to produce, and probably the most relevant are found in the Exeter Book itself. Take, for instance, Riddle 6:

> Mec gesette soð   sigora waldend,
> Crist to compe.   Oft ic cwice bærne
> unrimu cyn   eorþan getenge,
> næte mid niþe,   swa ic him no hrine,
> þonne mec min frea   feohtan hateþ.
> Hwilum ic monigra   mod arete;
> hwilum ic frefre   þa ic ær winne on
> feorran swiþe—   hi þæs felað þeah
> swylce þæs oþres,   þonne ic eft hyra
> ofer deop gedreag   drohtað bete.

> [The true lord of victories, Christ, set me up for battle. Often I burn the living, innumerable peoples near to the earth, oppress them with enmity, just as I do not touch them, when my lord commands me to fight. At times I gladden the minds of many; at times I comfort those I previously contended against from afar—they will feel that, though, and the other as well, when I again improve their condition over the deep expanse.]

The solution here is clearly the sun, which Christ establishes to "do battle." This riddle not only links the sun with Christ; it crosses their identities, as

52. Chaucer, *Boece,* 1.m.5–6, in *The Riverside Chaucer,* ed. Larry D. Benson (Boston: Houghton Mifflin, 1987), 404. Kurath and Kuhn, *Middle English Dictionary,* s.v. "horn," 6b, confirms that Chaucer means by this the full moon.

53. In "Exeter Latin Riddle 90: A Liturgical Vision," *Viator* 23 (1992), James E. Anderson notes that "the harrowing of hell appears often enough in Exeter Book poetry to be considered perhaps a central theme of the codex" (78).

Williamson himself argues in his edition.[54] Most notably, the description of the sun is shaped by a metaphorical focus of the Son in his twin aspects as scourge of the sinful and comfort to the faithful. Williamson rightly connects this riddle to another passage in the Exeter Book, lines 905–9 of the poem *Christ III,* where Christ is compared to the sun:

Cymeð wundorlic Cristes onsyn,
æþelcyninges wlite, eastan fram roderum,
on sefan swete sinum folce,
biter bealofullum, gebleod wundrum,
eadgum ond earmum ungelice.[55]

[Comes the amazing presence of Christ, the beauty of the noble king, in the east from the heavens, sweet in the heart to his people, bitter to the evil ones, varied in his wonders, to the blessed and to the wretched quite unlike.]

The warmth of the sunlike Christ is pleasant for the blessed and painful for the sinful, just as the sun speaker of Riddle 6 at times comforts and at times scorches dwellers on earth. This Christian paradox is the clear metaphorical focus of Riddle 6—a poem, by the way, also featuring a war-minded creature. The Christian and heroic elements, of course, are not in conflict.

Christ as the sun invites any number of potential comparisons, then, but one very basic pattern is that Christ is envisioned as the sun that set on Good Friday but rose to conquer darkness and death on Easter Sunday. This much is not surprising at all.[56] In the context of Riddle 29, in which the moon is the sun's foe, the moon would betoken Satan, and in fact Whitman is able to cite a few Christian writings in which the moon is identified with the devil.[57] The search for such sources is the focus of Whitman's article. Patristic

54. Williamson, *Old English Riddles,* 149.

55. Krapp and Dobbie, *Exeter Book,* 28. The coming of the Son in this passage also echoes the advent of the second creature in Riddle 29: "Þa cwom wundorlicu wiht ofer wealles hrof / seo is eallum cuþ eorþbuendum" (Then came the amazing creature over the roof of the wall, who is well known to all earth dwellers).

56. For a full account of such associations, see Hugo Rahner, *Greek Myths and Christian Mystery* (London: Burns and Oates, 1963), 89–128.

57. Whitman, "Christian Background," 97–98. The more obvious heavenly body associated with Satan is of course the morning star (the planet Venus, also known as Lucifer), another "light-bearing" creature, as we read in Vercelli Homily 19: "Lucifer [. . .] þæt ys on ure geþeode 'leohtberend' gereht" (Lucifer, that is to say in our language "light-bearer"). See Don-

precedent is not necessary, however, to see a pattern emerging in Riddle 29, for the poem clearly presents the moon's journey in terms consonant with the arc of Satan's overweening career. To make a few initial observations: the horned plunderer, like Satan, attempts to make off with spoils not his own.[58] Also like Satan, the creature wishes to establish a chamber for his stolen booty in his citadel: "Walde hyre on þære byrig bur atimbran, / searwum asettan, gif hit swa meahte" (It wished to build for it a chamber in that fortress, craftily to set it up, if it was so able).[59] Appropriate too is the moon's carrying out of this endeavor by means of *searwum* 'contrivances', a word that often connotes craftiness, sinister cunning, and devilish treachery.[60] But the moon's ambitions are soon interrupted by the coming of the sun, who

ald Scragg, ed., *The Vercelli Homilies and Related Texts* (Oxford: Oxford University Press, 1992), 316. Lucifer the morning star is the subject of Aldhelm's Enigma 81, whose clues point to both the celestial object and the devil: "How happy I once was when God's law was being obeyed! Alas, I subsequently fell, proud in my impudent arrogance" (Lapidge and Rosier, *Aldhelm: The Poetic Works,* 88). Pinsker and Ziegler, *Altenglischen Rätsel,* 215–19, in fact argue that "Venus carried off" is literally a third celestial creature in Riddle 29 (and its solution), but their reading is not very compelling. It seems clear that there are only two creatures in this question, though the figural description of the horned moon as a proud Luciferian "light-bearer" (cf. line 3: "lyftfæt leohtlic listum gegierwed") does seem appropriate.

58. The detail of the creature's horns appears a giveaway of its devilish identity, but this connection may not have been as obvious to an Anglo-Saxon riddler. Depicting the devil as a creature with horns does not appear to have been common until around the eleventh century. See Jeffrey Burton Russell, *Lucifer: The Devil in the Middle Ages* (Ithaca: Cornell University Press, 1984), 131. But the devil with horns was not unknown in Anglo-Saxon iconography. Perhaps most interesting for this discussion is an image of "Satan-Mors" found in the Leofric Missal (Oxford, Bodleian Library, MS. Bodley 579), a manuscript believed to be referenced in Leofric's list of donations in the Exeter Book (Förster, "Donations of Leofric to Exeter," 17). The image depicts "Satan-Mors" with "a beastly face with long pointed ears, horns, and massive wings." See Louis Jordan, "Demonic Elements in Anglo-Saxon Iconography," in *Sources of Anglo-Saxon Culture,* ed. Paul E. Szarmach, with Virginia Darrow Oggins (Kalamazoo: Medieval Institute Publications, 1986), 290–93. Peter Dendle, *Satan Unbound: The Devil in Old English Narrative Literature* (Toronto: University of Toronto Press, 2001), writes that "the portrayals of the devil in Anglo-Saxon literature, as opposed to the visual arts, know little of the dramatic flourishes that would characterize the later devil of medieval drama and Renaissance witch trials—the horns and spines, multiple faces, bestial proportions and features, etc. Anglo-Saxon authors devote little attention to his physical description" (11).

59. I have been unable to find many instances of an analogously ambitious moon in English riddling traditions, with the following exception: "I am ambitious to obtain / A certain Pitch of Glory; I fail so soon's my End I gain, / And yet I am not sorry." Alexander Nicol, *Nature without art: Or, Nature's progress in poetry. Being a collection of miscellaney poems* (Edinburgh, 1739), 111. Compare, however, the first creature of Riddle 29 to the desire of Lucifer in Vercelli Homily 19: "him þrymsetle on norðdæle heofona rices getimbrian wolde" (he wished to build for himself a stronghold in the northern region of the kingdom of the heavens). See Scragg, *Vercelli Homilies,* 316.

60. See Bosworth and Toller, *Anglo-Saxon Dictionary,* s.v. "searu."

drives him westward, into the region traditionally associated with hell.[61] The tidal pull of the metaphorical focus is felt throughout the surface of the poem.

It is also present in less conspicuous aspects. For instance, as the plunderer is driven into the west, we are presented with a subtle but telling paradox. This comes as we are told that the sun "to ham bedraf / wreccan ofer willan" (drove it [the first creature] into its home, the exile against its will). At first glance, this might seem straightforward enough, and in fact the verb *bedrifan* has as one of its primary meanings "to drive (the wicked) into hell."[62] But still these lines should give us pause. As Marckwardt and Rosier point out, this second use of *ham* 'home' in Riddle 29 is "apparently in some contrastive sense to" *þam ham* 'that home' to which the moon leads the plunder back in line 4.[63] The confusion of these "homes" could be ironic in light of the devil's loss of a heavenly home and his new (less homey) residence. Satan's proper sphere, his home, is defined in contrast to the true home of heaven. More intriguing, however, is the paradox of driving an exile (*wreccan*) *into* (rather than *away from*) his "home." The devil is in this detail, for that is precisely who is paradoxically most "at home" in exile. This paradox is exploited elsewhere in Anglo-Saxon riddling. Eusebius's enigma on the topic of a fallen angel begins: "Incola sum patriae, cum sim miserabilis exul" (I am an inhabitant of my native land, while at the same time I am a wretched exile).[64]

These details are suggestive, but it is important to understand that Riddle 29's handling of its theme goes well beyond a vague sense of the moon as satanic. Specifically, the metaphorical focus of the Harrowing of Hell seems primarily to inform the main conflict of the poem. As noted above, Christ's identification with the sun is bound up with the idea that his death was a type of sunset that preceded his rising on Easter Sunday. Holy Saturday, then, represents a time of darkness, the "nocturnal" moment during which Christ visits the underworld and plunders hell. It makes perfect sense, then, for a riddle of the sun and moon to reenact these events in terms of night yielding to day.[65]

61. Whitman, "Christian Background," 94–95.

62. *Dictionary of Old English*, s.v. "bedrifan."

63. Albert H. Marckwardt and James L. Rosier, *Old English Language and Literature* (New York: W. W. Norton, 1972), 199.

64. Enigma 3, line 1 (Glorie, *Variae collectiones aenigmatum*, 213; my translation).

65. It is also worth noting that images of the sun and moon were common features of early medieval crucifixion iconography. Such images seem to have held a different significance from

To confirm this reading of Riddle 29, detailed attention must be paid to the poem's diction. Let us begin with the *huþ* 'booty' that the plundering moon has captured in the opening lines. On the celestial level, this "plunder" is best understood as the light the moon borrows from the sun. The word *huþ,* however, also resonates in Old English poetry as a vivid term for the souls who were rescued at the Harrowing. In the Exeter Book poem *The Creed,* it is said that Christ "of helle huðe gefette, / of þam suslhofe, sawla manega, / het ða uplicne eþel secan" (brought plunder back from hell, fetched from that place of torment many souls and commanded them to seek out the celestial homeland). Also in the Exeter Book is a moment in *Christ II* where a troop of angels describe how Christ, at the Harrowing,

> of hæfte ahlod   huþa mæste
> of feonda byrig,   folces unrim,
> þisne ilcan þreat   þe ge her on stariað.

> [led forth from captivity nearly all of the spoils from the stronghold of the fiends, innumerable people, this same troop which you look upon now.][66]

In his discussion of a related compound in a homiletic text, Donald Scragg recognizes the "traditional nature" of *huþ* used in this way and writes, "The word *herehuðe,* normally translated 'booty' or 'plunder,' has the sense of 'booty recovered' for the elect which Christ leads triumphantly from hell."[67] Clearly, *huþ* resonates with a Christian heroic sense.[68]

Let us move on to the liberation of that *huþ.* The coming of the sun in line 7 is marked by language that recalls the formulaic openings of individual riddles: *Đa cwom wundorlicu wiht* 'Then came a wondrous creature'. The rhetoric here is thus appropriate to the sun's/Christ's power of renewal, as well as

---

what we find in Riddle 29, however, tending to represent Christ's divinity and power over the natural world, among other things. See Barbara C. Raw, *Anglo-Saxon Crucifixion Iconography* (Cambridge: Cambridge University Press, 1990), 129–36.

66. Krapp and Dobbie, *Exeter Book,* 568–70.

67. Donald Scragg, "A Late Old English Harrowing of Hell Homily from Worcester and Blickling Homily VII," in O'Brien O'Keeffe and Orchard, *Latin Learning and English Lore,* 2:206.

68. See Williamson, *Old English Riddles,* 228 (cited above). More recently, Daniel Donoghue also considers *huþe* a key word in establishing the heroic tone of the poem, conjuring "the kinds of treasure that legendary Germanic warriors would bring back from a successful battle." Donoghue, *Old English Literature: A Short Introduction* (Oxford: Blackwell, 2004), 121.

the dramatic reversal of the moon's fortunes and the astonishment of the satanic host at the Harrowing. The brightness of Christ's penetrating light on that occasion was notable, as the fiends confess in *Christ and Satan:* "Him beforan fereð fægere leoht / þonne we æfre ær eagum gesawon" (He [Christ] bears before him a more splendid light than we have ever yet seen with our eyes).[69] Next, the sun comes *ofer wealles hrof* 'over the roof of the wall' and *ahredde þa þa huþe* 'recaptured/rescued then that plunder'. The celestial meaning of the *wealles hrof* 'roof of the wall' is not entirely transparent, some seeing this as the sun's rising above the horizon and others suggesting that "within the (figurative) terms of the poem the roof's wall refers back to the *byrig* in line 5."[70] These readings are not mutually exclusive, but the important thing to notice is the sun's act of breaching the usurper's stronghold. The famous rupture of hell at the Harrowing is noted in Exeter Riddle 55, where Christ's death on the cross is said to have occurred "ær he helwara / burg abræce" (before he breached the city of the hell dwellers).[71] *The Descent into Hell,* a poem positioned between the first and second sections of riddles in the Exeter Book, describes the Harrowing in similar language: "wolde heofona helm helle weallas / forbrecan ond forbygan, þære burge þrym / onginnan reafian, reþust ealra cyninga" (the lord of the heavens, the most fierce of all kings, wished utterly to break and lay low the walls of hell, to begin to plunder the multitude from that city). With so many such parallels in the Exeter Book alone, could an Old English solver fail to see the connection?

There is no shortage of evidence. *Ahreddan,* the verb used in Riddle 29 to describe the rescue of the plunder, also turns out to have strong associations with Christ's power to redeem. Williamson's glossary obscures this somewhat, as he provides only the meaning "recapture."[72] In conjunction with *huþe* this may be considered an accurate rendering, but the far more common sense of the word is "to save, rescue, or set free."[73] Moreover, the

69. *Christ and Satan,* lines 387–88. George Philip Krapp, *The Junius Manuscript,* ASPR 1 (New York: Columbia University Press, 1931), 148.

70. Marckwardt and Rosier, *Old English Language and Literature,* 198. See also Earl R. Anderson, "The Uncarpentered World of Old English Poetry," *Anglo-Saxon England* 20 (1991): 71.

71. Riddle 55, lines 6a–7a. Constance B. Hieatt considers the breaching of the *weallas* of Mermedonia in *Andreas* evidence of a typological connection between that episode and the Harrowing. Hieatt, "The Harrowing of Mermedonia: Typological Patterns in the Old English 'Andreas,'" *Neuphilologische Mitteilungen* 77 (1976): 51.

72. Williamson, *Old English Riddles,* 409.

73. *Dictionary of Old English,* s.v. "ahreddan."

examples cited in the *Dictionary of Old English* strongly suggest that this sense of *ahreddan* is found most commonly in the context of the divine redemption of mankind. A few examples will suffice. Note, for instance, *Christ I,* lines 16–18: "nu sceal liffrea / þone wergan heap wraþum ahreddan, / earme from egsan, swa he oft dyde" (now the Lord of life shall rescue the accursed people from their enemies, the wretched from fear, just as he many times has done).[74] Wulfstan says that Christ "ahredde us þurh his deað of ecan deaðe" (rescued us from eternal death through his death).[75] In Middle English, *ahreddan* seems to lose altogether the secondary sense of "recapture" and retain its sense of spiritual deliverance: "To save (souls, mankind); deliver (sb., as from hell or eternal death)."[76]

The metaphorical focus of Riddle 29 appears to shape the poem's language and imagery nearly as much as its solution (which, not to be misunderstood, is clearly "sun and moon"). And this leads us back to the question of Riddle 29's brief but haunting coda: "Dust stonc to heofonum, deaw feol on eorþan; / niht forð gewat. Nænig siþþan / wera gewiste þære wihte sið" (Dust rose to the heavens, dew fell on the earth; night departed. No one then knew the journey of that creature). The elegance of the lines, with their balanced phrasing, motion (rising/falling), and elements (earth/water), tempts us to gloss them over without paying much heed to what they actually mean.[77] Dew "falls" in the morning, but, again, why the rising dust?

74. Lines 16–18. Krapp and Dobbie, *Exeter Book,* 3.

75. Wulfstan, *De fide catholica,* 73, in *The Homilies of Wulfstan,* ed. Dorothy Bethurum (Oxford: Clarendon Press, 1957), 160. See also Ælfric: "Þæt egypta land hæfde getacnunge þyssere worulde and pharao getacnode þone ðwyran deofol þe symle godes gecorenum ehtnysse on besett on andwerdum life; Swa swa se ælmihtiga god ða his folc ahredde wið þone cyning pharao and hi lædde to ðam earde þe he abrahame and his ofspringe behet" (That land of Egypt signified this world and Pharaoh signified the evil devil who has always attacked God's chosen ones in this present life; in the same way, Almighty God rescued his people from the king Pharaoh and led them to the land which he promised to Abraham and his offspring). *Ælfric's Catholic Homilies: The Second Series,* ed. Malcolm Godden (London: Oxford University Press, 1979), 12.178–82.

76. Kurath and Kuhn, *Middle English Dictionary,* s.v. "aredden."

77. John J. Joyce, "Natural Process in *Exeter Book* Riddle #29: 'Sun and Moon,'" *Annuale Mediaevale* 14 (1974): 5–8, for example, finds the equilibrium achieved by these "opposing elements" to form a fitting conclusion to the ordered "natural process" depicted in the poem. Kevin Crossley-Holland, trans., *Storm* (New York: Farrar, Straus and Giroux, 1970), 69, explains: "In the last three lines the poet creates a sense of mystery without, in the end, being too mysterious. Or is he?" Andrew Welsh, "Riddle," 828, would agree: "There the riddle could end. But the poet added three final lines of quiet mystery."

The issue has hardly been "clouded . . . by the dust of the quarrying researchers."[78] Williamson does not address this question in his notes, and very few others have made an attempt to explain this rather odd ending. Stopford A. Brooke, however, can be counted on for an explanation in terms of nature poetry: "Then the sun also would hasten westwards, and the night would come again with mist like dust and falling dew."[79] In other words, the dust is also dew? This seems like a slim chance.[80] Frank Walter's account also raises more questions than it answers, although he and Brooke deserve credit for addressing the problem:

> Dust rose to heaven, but when? Dew fell on earth—last night? Clearly, dew-laden earth would give no dust. . . . *Deaw feol on eorthan:* the insemination of nature, life giving water for things that grow; at various times in his life the speaker has witnessed this half of the process. *Dust stonc to heofonum:* the death of nature, the remains of things dead; he has seen all this, too. Now they are all thrown together in a frenzied effort by the speaker to get to the heart of earthly experience.

Walter finally concludes this analysis by attributing the lines to "the persona's irrational state."[81] Walter is understandably confused. As he points out, dust would not puff up from a "dew-laden earth" any more than we might expect warm mud in the winter. The discrepancy, though, does not bother Tupper, who explains that the dust is "probably raised by the cool wind that, in early Germanic poetry, blows at the rush of day."[82]

78. J. R. R. Tolkien, "Beowulf: The Monsters and the Critics," in *Interpretations of Beowulf: A Critical Anthology,* ed. R. D. Fulk (Bloomington: Indiana University Press, 1991), 15.

79. Brooke, *History of Early English Literature,* 154.

80. Similarly, Pinsker and Ziegler, *Altenglischen Rätsel,* 219, read the dust as "night fog": "Es handelt sich wahrscheinlich um den Nachtenebel, der sich vor Tagesanbruch als Tau auf der Erde niederschlägt." To make the case, they consult the *Oxford Dictionary of English Etymology* to detect an original sense of *dust* as "vapour." The numerous citations in the *Dictionary of Old English,* s.v. "dūst," however, include nothing along those lines but rather reveal that *dust* invariably elsewhere meant something quite like modern "dust": particles of earth or ashes or powder made from crushed dried leaves or other dry, decaying matter.

81. Frank Walter, "Language Structure and the Meanings of the *Exeter Book* Riddles," *Ball State University Forum* 19 (1978): 52–53.

82. Tupper, *Riddles of the Exeter Book,* 139. Burton Raffel implies a similar idea in "Six Anglo-Saxon Riddles," *Antioch Review* 20, no. 1 (1960): 53, in his loose translation of the line to read, "The morning / Dust scattered away."

Although I have been able to track down no other instances of such dust storms at dawn, Tupper's suggestion seems more plausible given Isidore's etymology: "Dust (*pulvis*) is so named because it is driven (*pellere*) by the force (*vis*) of the wind, for it is carried on the breath of the wind, neither resisting nor able to stay put, as the Prophet says (Psalm 1:4): 'Like the dust, which the wind driveth from the face of the earth.'"[83] There is also an intriguing parallel in a later alliterative poem. In the second fitt of the fourteenth-century *Sir Gawain and the Green Knight,* the passing of the seasons is described with "the imagery of summer-winter contention."[84] One passage is particularly relevant to our discussion:

After þe sesoun of somer wyth þe soft wyndez
Quen Zeferus syflez hymself on sedez and erbez,
Wela wynne is þe wort þat waxes þeroute,
When þe donkande dewe dropez of þe leuez,
To bide a blysful blusch of þe bryȝt sunne.
Bot þen hyȝes heruest, and hardenes hym sone,
Warnez hym for þe wynter to wax ful rype;
He dryues wyth droȝt þe dust for to ryse,
Fro þe face of þe folde to flyȝe ful hyȝe;
Wroþe wynde of þe welkyn wrastelez with þe sunne,
þe leuez lancen fro þe lynde and lyȝten on þe grounde,
And al grayes þe gres þat grene watz ere. [85]

[After the season of summer with the soft winds, when Zephyrus blows himself gently on seeds and herbs, very pleasing is the plant that grows out of them, when the moistening dew drops from the leaves, to await the happy glance of the bright sun. But then autumn hurries on and hardens them at once, warns them because of the winter to grow full ripe; it drives with drought the dust to rise, from the face of the earth to fly very high; the angry wind from the sky wrestles with

83. Isidore, *Etymologies,* 317 (xiv.i.1).

84. Derek A. Pearsall, "Rhetorical 'Descriptio' in 'Sir Gawain and the Green Knight,'" *Modern Language Review* 50 (1955): 131.

85. J. R. R. Tolkien and E. V. Gordon, eds., *Sir Gawain and the Green Knight,* 2d ed. (Oxford: Oxford University Press, 1967), 15 (Fitt 2, lines 516–27). I would like to thank Britton Harwood for bringing this analogue to my attention. Elizabeth Brewer, *Sir Gawain and the Green Knight: Sources and Analogues* (Cambridge: D. S. Brewer, 1992), 61–77, offers no parallels to the imagery of the rising dust in her chapter on this passage of the passing year.

> the sun, the leaves fly from the trees and fall to the ground, and all gray is the grass that previously was green.]

Here we have a loose conjunction of dropping dew and dust raised high by the wind, although the context in this poem is the passing of the seasons (a fertile summer followed by an arid autumn) rather than the coming of dawn. Intriguing, too, is the sun's prominent role in the passage, both to shine on the dew and to "wrestle" with the winds that kick up the dust. In fact, the sun played an important role in raising winds in several texts known to medieval readers. Pliny, for instance, explains that some winds "may be caused by the driving force of the sun," while in Seneca's *Quaestiones naturales,* we read, "When the sun rarefies at his rising the thick dank morning air, then a breeze springs up."[86]

If wind from the sun *might* raise dust, the moon could easily drop dew. Dew is condensed water vapor, but it was formerly thought to fall imperceptibly from the heavens, hence the old compound "dewfall."[87] Dew fell, moreover, from the moon according to many authorities known to early medieval readers.[88] For instance, Macrobius explains:

> Aer ipse proprietatem lunaris umoris et patitur et prodit. Nam cum luna plena est vel cum nascitur—et tunc enim a parte qua sursum suspicit plena est—aer aut in pluviam solvitur, aut si sudus sit, multum de se roris emittit, unde et Alcman lyricus dixit rorem aeris et lunae filium.[89]

> [The very air not only feels but also shows the effect of the moon's quality of moistness; for when the moon is full, or when it is waxing—

86. Pliny, *Natural History,* trans. H. Rackham (Cambridge: Harvard University Press, 1979), 255 (2.114); Seneca, *Physical Science in the Time of Nero: Being a Translation of the Quaestiones naturales of Seneca,* trans. John Clarke (London: Macmillan, 1910), 195–96 (book 5.3). Lapidge, "Stoic Cosmology," argues that the *Quaestiones naturales* is the source for Exeter Riddles 1–3, though in *Anglo-Saxon Library* Lapidge also notes that "no Anglo-Saxon manuscript [of this text] survives" (68). Barbara Obrist, "Wind Diagrams and Medieval Cosmology," *Speculum* 72 (1997), explains that, "following the Aristotelian view, winds were defined as dry, earthly exhalations. As to what caused the movement of air (and of exhalations), a multitude of theories was put forth, with the sun as the overall efficient cause but with the planets playing a role as well" (36).

87. *Oxford English Dictionary,* s.vv. "dew," "dewfall."

88. Charles D. Wright, "The Persecuted Church and the *Mysterium Lunae,*" in O'Brien O'Keeffe and Orchard, *Latin Learning and English Lore,* 2:296–97, first noted in passing the connection of Riddle 29 to the tradition of the dew-producing moon.

89. Jacob Willis, ed., *Saturnalia* (Leipzig: Teubner, 1994), 7.16.31.

> since then its upper part is full—the air either dissolves in rain or, if the weather be fine, gives out an abundance of dew, a circumstance which led the lyric poet Alcman to speak of dew as the son of the air and the moon.][90]

The notion of the *rorifera luna* 'dew-bearing moon' or *roscida luna* 'moon full of dew' was common enough to show up in the questions of the *Disputatio Pippini,* riddlic queries that Martha Bayless describes as "embryonic riddles" and Paul Sorrell as "riddles-in-reverse."[91] The exchange of number 51 reads: "Quid est luna? Oculis noctis, roris larga, praesaga tempestatum"[92] (What is the moon? The eye of night, the one bountiful of dew, the foreboding of storms). Thus, the dew, if not *quite* as much the dust, makes perfect sense at the end of a riddle on the sun and the moon. The point of the ending, though, may not be so much to imagine a literal dawn of dewfalls and dusty winds as simply to suggest a loose association of these elements with the riddle creatures in question.

And yet this description of rising dust and falling dew is much too strong an image to imply only a vague sense of the weather. Something else about the riddle influences the *selection* of these images for one of the most resonant endings in the Exeter collection. That "something else," you may have guessed, is the metaphorical focus. In the context of Riddle 29's focus on the Harrowing of Hell, it is worth remembering that rising dust in an Old English poem most immediately recalls the eventual resurrection of redeemed humanity.[93] Any Anglo-Saxon riddler would know that "Þu eart dust & ðu awentst to duste" (you are dust and you will revert to dust). The theme was taken up in riddlic fashion in the various versions of the Middle English poem *Erthe upon Erthe,* where "earth" (man) inhabits the earth, covets earthly things, and, being mortal, reverts to earth:

90. The translation is that of Percival Vaughan Davies, in *Macrobius: The Saturnalia* (New York: Columbia University Press, 1969), 517.

91. Bayless, "Alcuin's *Disputatio Pippini,*" 160; Sorrell, "Oaks, Ships, Riddles," 112. For epithets of the dewy moon, see *Oxford Latin Dictionary,* s.vv. "rorifer," "roscidus," esp. 2b. For an account of the transition from the medieval notion of a "dewfall" to a modern understanding of dew, see W. E. Knowles Middleton, *A History of the Theories of Rain and Other Forms of Precipitation* (New York: Franklin Watts, 1965), chapter 9, "Theories of Dew and Hoar Frost," 177–93.

92. Lloyd William Daly and Walther Suchier, eds., *Altercatio Hadriani Augusti et Epicteti philosophi* (Urbana: University of Illinois Press, 1939), 139. Wright, "Persecuted Church," 308n21, cites this and other analogues to Riddle 29.

93. See *Dictionary of Old English,* s.v. "dūst," 5b; s.v. "dūstscēawung": "observation or contemplation of dust (referring to a visit to a grave)."

And God ros ought of the est this erth for to spede,
And went into hell as was gret nede,
And toke erth from sorowe þus erth for to spede,
The ryght wey to heuen blys Iesus Cryst vs lede![94]

Other versions of the widespread poem conclude with a prayer:

But that erthe in this erthe
Be doynge euer thi wille,
So that erthe for the erthe
Stye vp to thi holy hille.[95]

The *Dictionary of Old English* devotes a full section to dust in the sense of "the material out of which the human body is made, to which it returns, and from which it will arise again."[96] For most of humanity, the rising of the corporeal dust is slated for the Second Coming, but in the case of the patriarchs, their bodies along with their souls are rescued and delivered into heaven at the Harrowing.[97] The rest must bide their time, as we are assured in *Christ and Satan,* lines 603–5: "Þonne of þisse moldan men onwecnað; / deade of duste arisað þurh drihtnes miht" (Then out of this dust men shall awake; the dead will arise from the dust through the strength of the Lord). Such statements recall the prophecy of Isaiah 26:19:

vivent mortui tui interfecti mei resurgent
expergiscimini et laudate qui habitatis in pulvere,
quia ros lucis ros tuus

[Your dead will live, my slain will rise back up. Arise from sleep and give praise, you who dwell in the dust, for your dew is a dew of the light.][98]

94. Hilda M. R. Murray, ed., *The Middle English Poem, Erthe upon Erthe* (London: Oxford University Press, 1911), 34 (lines 79–82).

95. Ibid., 23 (lines 129–32).

96. *Dictionary of Old English,* s.v. "dūst," 5b.

97. Judith N. Garde explains that patristic writings influential to the Anglo-Saxons frequently stress that the Harrowing involved not only the freeing of souls but also the resurrection of the physical bodies of the captive patriarchs. Garde, *Old English Poetry in Medieval Christian Perspective: A Doctrinal Approach* (Cambridge: D. S. Brewer, 1991), 117–24.

98. *Biblia sacra,* 1121. For the book of Isaiah's probable influence on Riddle 90 (the single instance of a Latin riddle in the Exeter collection), see Stanley, "Heroic Aspects," 198–99.

Here, then, we have the rising dust in conjunction with the morning dew, an image quite in keeping with Riddle 29's ending. But what has this to do with the Harrowing of Hell? For an Anglo-Saxon riddler, the answer might well be "everything," for this passage from a Christian perspective clearly forecasts Christ's coming to rescue the patriarchs from hell. In the Gospel of Nicodemus, the hell-shackled Isaiah himself makes this clear as Christ arrives to liberate the hell dwellers. His satisfaction is evident as he declares his prophecy fulfilled:

> Nonne ego cum essem in terris uiuus predixi uobis: "Exsurgent mortui et resurgent qui in monumentis sunt et exultabunt qui in terris sunt, quoniam ros qui est a domino sanitas est illis?"
>
> [While I was alive on earth did I not foretell to you: "Let the dead arise and let those in the tombs arise and let those on earth rejoice, since the dew which is salvation from the Lord is in them?"][99]

Clement of Alexandria, too, links the dew of salvation to the Easter sun:

> To us, who were buried in darkness and shut in by shadows of death, there shone a light from heaven, purer than the sun and sweeter than this earthly life; for the light that shone on us is life eternal and whatsoever has a part in it is alive. But night draws back from this light, it hides itself in fear and makes way for the day of the Lord. All creation has become a light that will never be extinguished and sunset has become the rising of the sun. This is what is meant by "the new creation." As the Father makes the sun shine upon all men, and causes the dew-drops of truth to fall upon them all, so the Sun of Righteousness upon his journey passes over all mankind.[100]

It is this context that allows us to understand how the metaphorical focus selects the dust and dew as a fitting conclusion to Riddle 29. The dust of mortality rises as the dew of salvation falls. Night departs. No one on earth knows the path of either being. With these final lines of Riddle 29, the

99. J. E. Cross, ed., *Two Old English Apocrypha and Their Manuscript Source: The Gospel of Nichodemus and the Avenging of the Saviour* (Cambridge: Cambridge University Press, 1996), 216. The translation is that of Cross's edition.

100. Quoted in Rahner, *Greek Myths and Christian Mystery,* 119.

standard riddling challenge to solve merges with a grander Christian mystery. None of this changes Riddle 29's *solution,* of course, but it does illuminate its rather dark ending, as well as account for the elegant obfuscation of a brilliant poem.

The first two readings of this chapter rise to the challenge of celestial riddles, but the final section involves a more down-to-earth example. Riddle 83 reads:

> Frod wæs min fromcynn [..................]
> biden in burgum, siþþan bæles weard
> [...........] wera lige bewunden,
> fyre gefælsad. Nu me fah warað
> eorþan broþor, se me ærest wearð
> gumena to gyrne. Ic ful gearwe gemon
> hwa min fromcynn fruman agette
> eall of earde; ic him yfle ne mot,
> ac ic hæftnyd hwilum arære
> wide geond wongas. Hæbbe ic wunda fela,
> middangeardes mægen unlytel,
> ac ic miþan sceal monna gehwylcum
> deogolfulne dom dyran cræftes,
> siðfæt minne. Saga hwæt ic hatte.

> [Ancient was my ancestry . . . awaited in the strongholds, when the guardian of fire . . . a man . . . wound about with flame, purified by fire. Now the cursed brother of the earth guards me, he who first among men became an affliction for me. Very readily do I remember who in the beginning brought ruin on my race, (extracted us) all out of the earth; yet I must do him no evil, though I at times raise up thralldom, widely through the plains. I have many wounds and no small power in this middle earth, yet I must conceal from each of men the mysterious power of my precious strength, my journey. Say what I am called.][101]

Despite the manuscript burn holes riddling Riddle 83's fiery opening, its basic sense seems straightforward. The poem tells of a substance ripped from

101. One aspect of this translation is under probation. I translate *warað* (4b) as "guards," following the editions of both Tupper and Williamson. In the course of my argument, however, I will have occasion to question this translation.

the ground, purified by fire, and crafted into items possessing special power. The solution must be metal of some kind, manufactured from ore into objects. The innate power of wealth or weapons might suggest gold or iron as the most likely veins of thought, but I believe that Frederick Tupper was correct in his assessment when, in his 1910 edition, he wrote: "Ore, of whatever metal, fulfills all conditions."[102] Accordingly, I favor John D. Niles's answer *ora* 'ore, metal'—although my reading resists the pun he sees as central to his solution.[103]

In depicting the origins of ore, Riddle 83 shows an affinity with several other riddles of the Exeter Book that focus on the transformation of raw materials into wrought objects. Of these, the most well known is Riddle 26, which describes the painful particulars of a sheep's passage from beast to parchment page.[104] Other examples in this group include Riddles 12 (an ox becomes leather), 28 (grain becomes alcohol), 60 (a reed becomes a pen), and 88 and 93 (antlers become inkhorns). By lending a single voice to a material across its multiple stages of manufacture, such riddles draw attention to the underlying origins of fabricated things. The pattern is a familiar one in oral tradition, where a "series of tortures" describe the preparation of an object.[105] In the Exeter riddles, parallels are also sometimes drawn between the creature's past and present. In Riddle 88, for instance, the *wonn ond wonderlic* 'dark and marvelous' contents of the inkhorn recall its previous wanderings *wonnum nihtum* 'in the dark nights' as the antler of a stag.[106] The inkhorn's companion, the pen of Riddle 60, also remembers its roots as a reed:

> Ic wæs be sonde   sæwealle neah
> æt merefaroþe;   minum gewunade
> frumstaþole fæst.

102. Tupper, *Riddles of the Exeter Book,* 221.

103. Niles, *Old English Enigmatic Poems,* 133–35. Niles argues that the creature of Riddle 83 is unified by the potential meanings of *ora,* including both "ore" and "a small silver coin." While not an outright rejection of this view, the reading I offer below interprets Riddle 83 as functioning according to a somewhat different strategy of riddling.

104. For more on Riddle 26, see Richard Marsden, "'Ask What I Am Called': The Anglo-Saxons and Their Bibles," in *The Bible as Book: The Manuscript Tradition,* ed. John L. Sharpe III and Kimberly van Kampen (London: British Library, 1998), 145–46; Shook, "Anglo-Saxon Scriptorium," 219–20; G. A. Lester, "*Sindrum Begrunden* in Exeter Book Riddle No. 26," *Notes and Queries,* n.s. 38 (1991): 13–15.

105. Taylor, *English Riddles from Oral Tradition,* provides an extensive discussion of this pattern in a section entitled "A Series of Tortures or Punishments Describing a Manufactured Object," 247–49.

106. See lines 19a and 13b, respectively.

> [I was by the shore, near the seawall at the edge of the deep; in my original state, I was in a fixed position.]

But the ore of Riddle 83 traces its *fromcynn* 'lineage' even further back than the *frumstaþol* 'original state' of Riddle 60's reed. In fact, the remarkable thing about Riddle 83 is the way it extends the basic form of the transformation riddle beyond its common borders—and in fact all the way back to the beginning.

To make this case, we need to focus on the middle section of the riddle and a series of statements that have sometimes been downplayed or glossed over in the critical literature on Riddle 83. The first of these comes after the riddle's opening description of fiery purification:

> Nu me fah warað
> eorþan broþor, se me ærest wearð
> gumena to gyrne.

> [Now the cursed brother of the earth *guards* me, who first among men became an affliction for me.]

There is much that is enigmatic about this statement. Who is this *eorþan broþor* 'brother of the earth'? Why is he *fah* 'cursed'? I will return to these questions, but first I would like to focus on the second clause. Who was it who first became an affliction for the speaker? For Williamson and others, this is a reference to humanity at large, who is "brother" to the earth in a variety of senses.[107] Williamson identifies this person as "man in all his guises—miner, smelter, forger, and artisan."[108] But this is not very satisfying. The riddle seems clearly to be pinpointing a particular man—*ærest . . . gumena* 'the first of men'—who harms the speaker, rather than humanity in general. In his translation, Williamson avoids this problem by loosely rendering the lines as "Now a fierce earth-brother stands guard / The first to shape my sorrow." Marie Nelson, more conscientiously, produces the following tangled translation: "Now the brother of the earth / who was first as a sorrow of men to me / guards me."[109] Whatever this may mean, the much

107. Williamson, *Old English Riddles,* 367. Marie Nelson, "The Rhetoric of the Exeter Book Riddles," *Speculum* 49 (1974): 427, identifies the "earth's brother" as "either a human being or a dragon guarding treasure."

108. Williamson, *Old English Riddles,* 367.

109. Williamson, *Feast of Creatures,* 141; Nelson, "Rhetoric of the Riddles," 427.

more straightforward conclusion is that we have here a reference to the first human being who became an "enemy" to the speaker.

Franz Dietrich long ago pointed out who that enemy in Riddle 83 must be: Tubalcain, the grandson of Cain in the Bible.[110] Tubalcain is the traditional founder of the foundry and metalworking. His reputation as the first smith originates in a brief remark in Genesis: "Sella quoque genuit Thubalcain qui fuit malleator et faber in cuncta opera aeris et ferri" (Zillah gave birth to Tubalcain who was a hammerer and metalsmith in all kinds of works in brass and iron).[111] Tubalcain's reputation spread, in part, through collections of dialogue questions that circulated alongside riddles throughout the medieval period.[112] Moreover, as Tupper points out, there exist medieval illustrations of Tubalcain at work on his anvil, including one in the Anglo-Saxon manuscript Cotton Claudius B. iv, which includes the inscription: "Tubalcain se wæs ægþer ge goldsmið ge irensmið" (Tubalcain, who was both a goldsmith and an ironsmith).[113] Regardless of which kind of metal Riddle 83 describes, Tubalcain was simply known to be the first to plunder the earth for ore. Also in support of Dietrich's reading, Tupper quotes lines 1082–89 of *Genesis A*. Note their similarity to Riddle 83:

> Swylce on ðære mægðe   maga was haten
> on þa ilcan tid   tubalcain.
> se þurh snytro sped   smiðcræftega wæs
> and þurh modes gemynd   monna ærest,
> sunu lamehes,   sulhgeweorces
> fruma wæs ofer foldan   siððan folca bearn
> æres cuðo   and isernes,
> burhsittende,   brucan wide.

> [Likewise, in that same time, there was born from that woman a kinsman called Tubalcain. Through his wise ability and through the intelligence of his mind, he was the first of men skilled in the craft of metalsmithing, the son of Lamech, and he was the originator of plow

110. Dietrich, "Räthsel des Exeterbuchs: Würdigung," 484.

111. Genesis 4:22 (*Biblia sacra,* 9).

112. Archer Taylor, "Biblical Conundrums in the *Golden Era,*" *California Folklore Quarterly* 5 (1946), writes, "Such questions as 'Who slew the fourth part of the world?—Cain' and 'Who was the first smith?—Tubal Cain' fixed the facts of Biblical history in the hearer's mind" (273).

113. Quoted in Tupper, *Riddles of the Exeter Book,* 221.

> making in the world. Thereafter, it was widely known to the sons of men, to city dwellers, how to use brass and iron.][114]

Just as in *Genesis A* Tubalcain was the *ærost monna* 'first of men' and the *fruma* 'originator' of metalsmithing, so too does the ore speaker of Riddle 83 describe the *ærest . . . gumena* 'first of men' who *fruman* 'in the beginning' plundered his race from the earth. It seems to me that Dietrich, the first great solver of the Exeter riddles, was on the right track from the beginning.

There is certainly precedent for the events of Genesis to be recast as riddles in the Exeter collection. My reading of the chicks of Riddle 13 is one example.[115] Another is Riddle 46, which enumerates the incestuous paradoxes bred when Lot procreated with his daughters:

> Wær sæt æt wine   mid his wifum twam
> ond his twegen suno   ond his twa dohtor,
> swase gesweostor   ond hyra suno twegen,
> freolico frumbearn.   Fæder wæs þær inne
> þara æþelinga   æghwæðres mid,
> eam ond nefa.   Ealra wæron fife
> eorla ond idesa   insittendra.

> [A man sat at wine with his two wives and his two sons and his two daughters, dear sisters and their two sons, good-looking firstborn children. The father was in there with each of those princes, uncle and nephew. All in all there were five men and women sitting inside.]

The main pleasure of this text is unraveling the kinship knots, and these are particularly complex in comparison to the many analogous riddles on Lot and his family found in later tradition. For instance, the early modern Holme Riddle 10 reads:

> 2 sisters standing on a tombe thus bewaled the dead ther in alas here lys our mothers husbant our husband our childrens father & our father how can this bee[116]

114. Doane, *Genesis A,* 131. Tupper quotes the same passage in *Riddles of the Exeter Book,* 221–22.

115. See chapter 1.

116. Tupper, "Holme Riddles," 221.

Do we simply have here a roomy tomb to hold several corpses? No, the answer is of course the same as that of Riddle 46. The Old English version, however, goes beyond the standard set of paradoxes generated by the daughters' relationship with their father. One of the more notable tangles is the designation of the princes as *eam ond nefa* 'uncle and nephew', a phrase that neatly encapsulates the strange relationship established between the inbred cousins, Moab and Ben-ammi (each child is both uncle and nephew to the other). But the solution to Riddle 46 not only untangles the explicit paradoxes; it also activates details from the text that seem unimportant or trifling. The poem's opening is a good example: "Wær sæt æt wine mid his wifum twam" (A man sat at wine with his two wives). The setting of the riddle might seem conventional and irrelevant. If anything, it suggests a vaguely heroic situation of drinking in the hall, as we saw in Riddle 55's opening: "Ic seah in healle, þær hæleð druncon" (I saw [something] in the hall where men were drinking). In Riddle 46, however, the opening is sharply ironic in relation to its source: Genesis 19 tells us how Lot is tricked into committing incest by his daughters, who first ply him with wine. This seduction, too, takes place in a cave in which the threesome take refuge after the destruction of Sodom and Gomorrah, making the epithet *insittende* 'sitting within' particularly appropriate for this close-knit family. In other words, Riddle 46 expects a reader who knows these stories inside and out as bedrock texts of Anglo-Saxon Christian culture. Such a reader would readily know which man was the first to extract ore from the earth.

Williamson, however, raises a serious objection to identifying this man in Riddle 83 as Tubalcain, suggesting that the adverb *nu* 'presently' directs us away from a figure of the past.[117] Williamson has a point, but for the sake of argument let us try for the moment to dig our way out of this difficulty with an alternative translation. Perhaps the solution is simply to take *warian* in its sense of "to occupy" rather than "to guard." Compare this passage from *Beowulf,* in which the dwelling-places of Grendel's Cain-cursed kin are described: "Hie dygel lond / warigeað wulfhleoþu, windige næssas, / frecne fengelad" (They occupy secret lands, the retreat of wolves, gusting headlands, the dangerous fen-tract). If we take *warian* in the sense of "to occupy," we could activate a neat, balanced paradox of just deserts: "Nu me fah warað / eorþan broþor, se me ærest wearð / gumena to gyrne" (Now the

117. Williamson, *Old English Riddles,* 367. Williamson's rejection of this reading is stated less directly than suggested here, but this seems to be the upshot of his objection. I discuss his note on this section further below.

cursed brother of the earth occupies me, he who first among men became an affliction for me). The irony would be closely comparable to what we find in the riddling Middle English poems of *Erthe upon Erthe,* which I have already cited in my discussion of Riddle 29 above. Elsewhere in these poems, various former rulers of the earth are said to now occupy it: "now, as erth within erth, þei lye pale & wan."[118] Variations on this theme form a favorite riddling conceit in these poems: "Vnder erthe for lust of erthe / Thou schalt haue sorow and woo," we are warned, in a lesson that would surely apply to Tubalcain: "Erth gose on erth glytteryng in golde, / ȝet shale erth to þe erth, raþer þen he wolde."[119] The first miner's present dwelling in the earth would involve the same neat symmetry often favored in riddling. Furthermore, the lines immediately following are also clarified: "Ic ful gearwe gemon / hwa min fromcynn fruman agette / eall of earde" (Very readily do I remember who in the beginning brought ruin on my race, [ripped us] all out of the earth). Here the speaker seems focused on the original miner of ore as someone remembered from the past, not as a present guardian.

That leads us to consider the "cursed brother of the earth." Naturally, Tubalcain's profession is closely associated with the earth, not only because of his occupation as a miner but also because of his reputation for inventing the plowshare (as evident in the quotation from *Genesis A* above). It is also worth bearing in mind that Tubalcain's great-grandfather, Adam, was quite literally the *offspring* of the earth. Indeed, Adam, who was *of eorðan geworht* 'created from the earth', owes his very name etymologically to the Hebrew word for "earth" (*'adamah*), a circumstance that the poet of *Genesis B* knows and emphasizes, according to Roberta Frank.[120] The close familial ties of Adam and his family to the earth were often brought up in dialogue questions, such as the following example from *Adrian and Ritheus:*

> Saga me hwilc man wære dead and nære acenned and æfter þam deaðe wære eft bebyried in his moder innoðe.
>
> Ic þe secge, þæt wæs Adam se æresta man, for þam eorðe wæs his moder and he wæs bibiriged eft in þære eorðan.
>
> [Tell me which man was dead and yet was never born and after his death he was buried in the bowels of his mother. I tell you, that was

118. Murray, *Erthe upon Erthe,* 28 (line 32).

119. Ibid., 22 (lines 83–84) and 24 (lines 21–22).

120. Roberta Frank, "Some Uses of Paronomasia in Old English Scriptural Verse," *Speculum* 47 (1972): 217.

> Adam who was the first man, because the earth was his mother and he was buried again in the earth.][121]

Tubalcain, then, as a not-so-distant descendant of Adam, is at the very least a "great-grandson" of the earth, and of course everyone is of the earth from a Christian perspective. But why would Tubalcain specifically be the earth's "brother" and why *fah* 'cursed'? The best solution to this problem, I think, is that Riddle 83 is simply connecting two closely associated figures from Genesis: Tubalcain and his grandfather, Cain himself. Isidore notes the relationship, referring to "Tubal, who was of the stock of Cain before the flood."[122] But aside from lineage, we might note several other reasons to connect these figures, beginning with the similarity of their names. In the *Ioca monachorum,* an early medieval collection of riddling wisdom questions, we find the following: "Quis primus fauer [faber] fuit? Tobal et Cain, fratres Iobas" (Who was the first metalsmith? Tubal and Cain, brothers of Jobas).[123] Tubalcain and Cain were also tied together by a linked tragedy: in the popular apocryphal story, Tubalcain mistakes Cain for a beast and advises his blind father Lamech to shoot him with an arrow. When Lamech realizes his mistake, he claps his hands together in fury and kills Tubalcain.[124] Finally, and most significantly, the two figures are linked in their signature innovations: Cain invents murder, and Tubalcain invents weapons for more efficient murder.[125] As David

121. Cross and Hill, *Prose Solomon and Saturn,* 38.

122. Isidore, *Etymologies,* 95 (3.15.1).

123. Max Förster, "Das älteste mittellateinische Gesprächbüchlein," *Romanische Forschungen* 27 (1910): 346. My translation of *faber* as "metalsmith" is supported by Isidore's designation of "blacksmith" as the word's primary meaning, as noted by James Bradley, "St. Joseph's Trade and Old English *smiþ,*" *Leeds Studies in English* 22 (1991): 25. "Jobas" I take here to be Jubal, the half-brother of Tubalcain and the first player of musical instruments (for this reason the two were sometimes paired in illustrations). There was often difficulty in keeping Cain's kin straight. In two Anglo-Saxon manuscripts (*Junius 11* and *Cotton Claudius* B. iv), illustrations of Jubal are mislabeled "Jabal." Jabal was Tubalcain's *other* half-brother. See Thomas H. Ohlgren, "Five New Drawings in the *MS Junius 11:* Their Iconography and Thematic Significance," *Speculum* 47 (1972): 230. Note also the long tradition of confusing Cain with Ham; see John Block Friedman, *The Monstrous Races in Medieval Art and Thought* (Cambridge: Harvard University Press, 1981), 100–107.

124. For the death of Cain and Tubalcain, see Friedman, *Monstrous Races,* 97–98.

125. Cross and Hill, *Prose Solomon and Saturn,* discuss medieval guesses for Cain's murder weapon: "other weapons were chosen, such as stone, sword, axe or hoe, cane or rod, club, ploughshare, but those who chose iron weapons had forgotten their scripture as the dialogue-question (I:ii) implies: 'How did he cut his head off?' 'With his teeth because he did not have "ferrum" (sword or iron).' It was Cain's descendant Tubalcain who was presumably the first 'malleator et faber in cuncta opera aeris et ferri'" (102–3).

Williams writes, "The activity of the first smith is especially significant when related, as it always was, to Cain."[126]

If Tubalcain is associated with Cain in Riddle 83, the meaning of the "cursed brother of the earth" is greatly clarified. Unsurprisingly, Cain is more than once referred to as *fah* 'cursed' elsewhere in Old English poetry. In lines 1037–39 of *Genesis A,* for instance, God assures Cain, "ne þearft ðu þe ondrædan deaðes brogan, / feorhcwealm nu giet, þeah þu from scyle / freomagum feor fah gewitan" (you need not dread the fear of death, nor yet the end of life, although you must go far away, cursed [*fah*], on account of the crime against your kinsman).[127] In *Beowulf,* lines 1262b–1265a, we read:

Cain wearð
to ecgbanan angan breþer,
fæderenmæge; he þa fag gewat,
morþre gemearcod mandream fleon,
westen warode.

[Cain became the killer of his own brother, his own paternal kinsman; he then departed, cursed (*fag*), marked with murder, to flee human joys. He dwelled in the wilderness.]

As the passage in *Beowulf* stresses, the cursed Cain is the most famous fratricide in scripture, and his malediction is closely associated with his act of concealing Abel in the earth:

dixitque ad eum quid fecisti
vox sanguinis fratris tui clamat ad me de terra

126. David Williams, *Cain and Beowulf: A Study in Secular Allegory* (Toronto: University of Toronto Press, 1982), 29. Williams continues, "Cain had been the first murderer, first to shed human blood, and according to tradition he thus originated not only homicide but war, as well, and all forms of blood-lust. Just as his ancestor had taken the first step in the post-lapsus degeneration of the race, so Tubal-Cain continues the process in inventing the weapons by which Cain's particular evil could be effected. Tubal-Cain also prefigures the giants of Genesis 6 in his physical strength and prowess." Andy Orchard, *Pride and Prodigies: Studies in the Monsters of the Beowulf-Manuscript* (Cambridge: D. S. Brewer, 1995), similarly writes: "One is reminded that in the Book of Enoch it is the fallen Angels of Genesis VI who are specifically credited with teaching metalwork and weapon-smithying to men, just as Genesis IV.22 describes how one of Cain's descendants, Tubal-cain, was a master at the working of brass and iron. It was presumably some such tissue of connections between the art of the weapon-smith and the giants of the Flood that led the *Beowulf*-poet to describe the sword with which Beowulf kills Grendel's mother and decapitates Grendel as a work of just such giants" (66).

127. Doane, *Genesis A,* 129.

nunc igitur maledictus eris super terram
quae aperuit os suum et suscepit sanguinem fratris tui de manu tua

> [And (the Lord) said to him, "What have you done?" The voice of your brother's blood calls to me from the earth. Now, therefore, you will be cursed from the earth, which opened its mouth and received the blood of your brother from your hand.][128]

If anyone is a "cursed brother of the earth," it is Cain and his kin. These traditions of Cain and Tubalcain, then, are the likely materials from which Riddle 83 is forged.

And yet it remains difficult to make this all add up literally. Let us take another look at the middle section of Riddle 83:

Nu me fah warað
eorþan broþor, se me ærest wearð
gumena to gyrne. Ic ful gearwe gemon
hwa min fromcynn fruman agette
eall of earde; ic him yfle ne mot,
ac ic hæftnyd hwilum arære
wide geond wongas.

> [Now the cursed brother of the earth guards (occupies?) me, he who first among men became an affliction for me. Very readily do I remember who in the beginning brought ruin on my race, (extracted us) all out of the earth; yet I must do him no evil, though I at times raise up thralldom, widely through the plains.]

This description of the speaker's enemy is curious, because it at once seems to suggest a persecutor from the distant past—the "first among men" who "in the beginning" caused the speaker's affliction—and, at the same time, a present enemy who "now" guards the speaker. And even if we attempt to avoid this confusion, as I have done above, by translating *warað* as "occupies," we still cannot avoid the prohibition against the speaker's seeking revenge: "Yet I must do him no evil." As Williamson would surely point

128. Genesis 4:10–11 (*Biblia sacra,* 8).

out, such a statement implies that the enemy is still around, not dead and occupying the earth. How can these contradictions be resolved?

Williamson grapples with these complications in a single note, and he begins by debunking the link to Genesis: "Dietrich . . . and Tupper take the *eorþan broþor* at 5*a* to be Tubal-Cain, the legendary first smith . . . but it does not seem likely that the smith who presently (*Nu me . . . warað*) guards and heats (lines 1–4*a*) the creature is the same man of the past—presumably a miner and not a smith—who stole the creature from its home in the ground." In other words, Williamson argues that we need to distinguish these various, particular enemies: a miner from the past as distinct from a smith in the present (*nu*). After further discussion of the associations of humanity and the earth, however, Williamson concludes, "Essentially I agree with Trautmann that the enemy here is man in all his guises—miner, smelter, forger, and artisan."[129]

The inconsistency of Williamson's reading arises because no literal explanation of Riddle 83 really makes sense—whether we appeal to a generalized "man in all his guises" or attempt to pinpoint the identities of the various enemies as particular craftsmen or as particular figures from the Bible. Once again, it is often not useful to read riddles as if they were literal descriptions of consistent, coherent events. The entwined biblical narratives of murder and metalsmithing are not the *solution* of Riddle 83—nor are they literally "present" in the text—but they clearly influence the riddle's proposition, from the characterization of the metalsmith as a "cursed brother of the earth" to the emphasis on origins: what the "first of men" did "in the beginning." In other words, the enemy of the speaker is indeed "man in all his guises," but the slim chances of the proposition can only be accounted for in terms of an unspoken metaphor.

Riddle 83 remains a transformation riddle about the manufacture of metal objects, then, but it is also a text inflected through a sense of history that traces the origin of ore back to its biblical roots. The events of Genesis are a favorite theme both in the Exeter riddles and in riddling more generally, suggesting a thematic link between "riddle creatures" and the larger sense of creation they embody. In the case of Riddle 83, though, a rich set of mysteries animates the speaker's story: the secrecy of Abel's murder, the hidden power of metal as weapons or cash, the concealed solution to the riddle itself. These correspondences lend a new complexity to the transformation

129. Williamson, *Old English Riddles,* 367.

riddle subgenre, as the murder of Abel bleeds into the violence done to the earth in extracting its ore. Like many a manufactured object in riddling, the speaker is unable to exact revenge on its persecutor (*ic him yfle ne mot* 'I may do him no evil'), but here the ore's helplessness sounds more like obedience to a law, a proscription akin to the Lord's protection of Cain: "omnis qui occiderit Cain septuplum punietur" (anyone who kills Cain will receive sevenfold punishment).[130] The earth of Riddle 83 cries out through the riddling trope of prosopopoeia, yet it is forbidden to do (Tubal)Cain harm.

Nevertheless, the speaker of Riddle 83 does continue to exert power in the world: "hæftnyd hwilum arære / wide geond wongas" (I at times raise up thralldom, widely through the plains). Whether through the subtle strength of gold or the brutal force of iron, Tubalcain's legacy travels widely through the world.[131] In one final comment on Riddle 83, I would like to relate this spread of thralldrom to a passage in *Maxims I,* another poem of the Exeter Book:

> Wearð fæhþo fyra cynne, siþþan furþum swealg
> eorðe Abeles blode. Næs þæt andæge nið,
> of þam wrohtdropan wide gesprungon,
> micel mon ældum, monegum þeodum
> bealoblonden niþ. Slog his broðor swæsne
> Cain, þone cwealm serede; cuþ wæs wide siþþan,
> þæt ece nið ældum scod, swa aþolwarum.
> Drugon wæpna gewin wide geond eorþan,
> ahogodan ond ahyrdon heoro sliþendne.

> [Strife has existed among the race of men, ever since the earth swallowed Abel's blood. Nor was that enmity limited to a single day, but rather from it widely sprang crime drops, much evil for men, enmity mixed with violence for many people. Cain killed his own dear brother, contrived that death. Thereafter it was widely known that unending violence did harm to men, as to dwellers in a pestilence. They suffered the strife of weapons widely throughout the earth, devised and tempered the cruel blade.][132]

130. Genesis 4:24.

131. Bloodlust and desire for gold are hardly separable, as Boniface's enigma on avarice (*De cupiditate*) stresses. Glorie, *Variae collectiones aenigmatum,* 317.

132. Lines 192–200. Krapp and Dobbie, *Exeter Book*, 163. I follow John C. Pope, "A Supposed Crux: Old English *apolwarum* in Maximus I," *Modern Philology* 93 (1995), 205–6, in emending "nerede" in line 197 to "serede."

Writing on this passage, John C. Pope says of the poet, "He is content to have looked into the past, uncovered the source of the trouble, traced its ever-widening spread, and compared it to an equally widespread, uncontrolled, and presumably uncontrollable affliction. The invention of weapons seems destined to make matters worse: Men have learned how to harden the *heoro sliþendne* 'the destroying sword'."[133] Riddle 83 too connects the innovations of Cain and his kin with the spread of evil in the world. In transforming the transformation riddle, Riddle 83 extends the conventional form while unearthing many wounds of human craft and history.

133. Pope, "A Supposed Crux," 211. Of the same passage, Charles D. Wright writes, "the general sense is that violence began to spread after the earth received the blood of Abel." Wright, "The Blood of Abel and the Branches of Sin: *Genesis A, Maxims I,* and Aldhelm's *Carmen de uirginitate,*" *Anglo-Saxon England* 25 (1996): 13–14.

4

RIDDLE 17 AS SAMSON'S LION

In the previous chapter I offered no new solutions for the Exeter riddles but focused instead on how their propositions are shaped under the influence of complex metaphors. Such revision of metaphorical riddling in the light of new learning makes a lot of sense for a genre so characterized by variation within established traditions. Topics and motifs in the Exeter collection often overlap, while basic conceits are riddled and re-riddled. Some of the Exeter riddles appear almost redundant, paired in the anthology with closely related companion texts: we find two on keys, two on onions, two on ice, two on swords, several horns (two for holding ink), a pair of bellows, and a couple cups. Although the solutions are questionable, three separate texts develop the venerable riddling image of a hawk-holding rider and the puzzle of his body parts. Three others offer novel versions of a single bull-calf riddle, each iteration quite distinct from the last. That such is the case is not surprising, perhaps, given the curious conservatism of riddling when it comes to traditional motifs and the range of likely solutions.[1]

By contrast, what is not limited in the Exeter anthology is the variety of enigmatic kinds gathered together. The closing section of the manuscript is

1. On the limited range of traditional riddling themes, see Taylor, *English Riddles from Oral Tradition,* 4–5.

a repository for riddlic forms of every stripe. Close translations of Aldhelm stand side by side (or even overlap) with "sex riddles"—texts with deep roots in popular riddling.[2] Even beyond that clear divide, though, the Exeter compilation seems to reflect a notably inclusive definition of what counts as a riddle, a situation that both enriches the collection and raises questions about its boundaries, the divisions to be drawn between the Exeter riddles and other "enigmatic poems" such as *Wulf and Eadwacer* or *The Husband's Message.*[3] Even within the Exeter riddles "proper," we suspect that some texts are little more than runic puzzlers, while others resist our impulse to assign them a solution. For instance, it seems less important to name Riddle 47's obvious answer (this is the famous "Book-Moth" riddle) than to appreciate its playful sense of wonder at the marvelous qualities of the written word. In much the same way, the expected closing challenges of some Exeter riddles seem to merge with more subtle mysteries, whether the nature of dreams (in Riddle 39), the riddle of textual interpretation (in Riddle 95), or even a sense of religious awe, as in Riddle 29: "Nænig siþþan / wera gewiste þære wihte sið" (No one then knew the journey of that creature). Such are enigmas beyond common riddling.

The eclecticism of the collection might lead us to expect the influence of genres outside the ambit of traditional riddling. A small detail in Riddle 40 is an interesting example. This text is a fairly close translation of the last enigma in Aldhelm's collection, *De creatura* 'On creation', a sprawling, sweeping description of the created world. In accordance with its grand theme, *De creatura* is by far the longest enigma of Aldhelm's collection. Riddle 40, too, is the longest riddle in the Exeter miscellany. It is therefore not practical to cite fully either Aldhelm or Riddle 40, but only a small selection. Aldhelm's text describes the world in terms that emphasize its paradoxical totality:

> Dulcior in palato quam lenti nectaris haustus
> Dirior et rursus quam glauca absinthia campi.
>
> [I am sweeter on the palate than a taste of smooth nectar; yet again, I am more bitter than the grey wormwood in the field.][4]

2. For discussion of which, see chapters 5 and 6.
3. See Niles, *Old English Enigmatic Poems,* 46–48.
4. Enigma 100, lines 31–32 (Glorie, *Variae collectiones aenigmatum,* 533; translation from Lapidge and Rosier, *Aldhelm: The Poetic Works,* 93).

Exeter Riddle 40, lines 58–61, translates Aldhelm thus:

> Ic eom on goman gena swetra
> þonne þu beobread blende mid hunige;
> swylce ic eom wraþre þonne wermod sy
> þe her on hyrstum heasewe stondeþ.

> [I am sweeter still on the palate than when you blend honeycomb with honey; likewise I am more bitter than is the gray wormwood which stands here in the woods.]

There is a slight but interesting difference in Riddle 40's translation that I would like to highlight: the change from *nectaris haustus* 'a taste of nectar' to *beobread* 'honeycomb', which is blended *mid hunige* 'with honey'. Admittedly, this alteration is pretty inconsequential in the grand scheme of Riddle 40's creation. What is worth noting, though, is that the shift probably reflects deep familiarity with the language of the Psalms, a central text for Anglo-Saxon readers. In fact, the psalm in question, number 18, is a hymn of praise for God's order that in many ways echoes these riddles of creation. And it is intriguing that Psalm 18 has been interpreted elsewhere as a kind of riddle, with some of its stylistic features recalling the language of riddling.[5] The echo in Riddle 40 comes from the second half of the psalm, where God's ordinances are said to be "desiderabilia super aurum et lapidem pretiosum multum et dulciora super mel et favum" (more to be desired than gold and many precious stones and sweeter than honey and honeycomb).[6] King Alfred's translation of these lines echoes Riddle 40's statement that creation is "swetra / þonne þu beobread / blende mid hunige" (sweeter than when you blend honeycomb with honey):

> Hy synt ma to lufianne þonne gold oððe deorwurðe gimmas, and hi synt swetran ðonne hunig oððe beebread

> [They are more to be desired than gold or precious gems, and they are sweeter than honey or honeycomb][7]

5. D. G. Blauner, "The Early Literary Riddle," *Folklore* 78 (1967): 51.

6. Psalm 18:11 (*Biblia sacra,* 790).

7. Patrick P. O'Neill, *King Alfred's Old English Prose Translation of the First Fifty Psalms* (Cambridge, Mass.: Medieval Academy of America, 2001), 120.

The Vespasian Psalter similarly glosses the psalm: "swoetran ofer hunig ond biobread" (sweeter than honey and honeycomb), and in fact nearly all Old English glossed Psalters use the same words to translate these lines.[8] The psalms were one of the best-known texts in Anglo-Saxon monasteries, and they were studied, glossed, and memorized by novices as a first step toward literacy.[9] As Pierre Riché puts it, "to know how to read was to know one's Psalter."[10] With this in mind, one can easily see how this language works its way into the Exeter riddles.

But if the riddle of a psalm finds a place in the collection, it is curious to note that the most famous biblical riddle, that of Samson's lion, is missing from the Exeter Book. Samson's riddle, in fact, is to be found translated or reworded in several medieval and early modern riddle anthologies, and is especially common in those collections that seem most varied in their assortment.[11] Given the penchant of the Exeter riddles to revise venerable riddling themes, we might expect to find an Old English reimagining of this most famous riddle creature. And our expectations may very well hold true, for in this chapter I again offer no original solutions but rather advance an old answer as applied to a new proposition. Riddle 17 reads:

Ic eom mundbora   minre heorde,
eodorwirum fæst,   innan gefylled
dryhtgestreona.   Dægtidum oft
spæte sperebrogan;   sped biþ þy mare
fylle minre.   Freo þæt bihealdeð,
hu me of hrife fleogað   hyldepilas.
Hwilum ic sweartum   swelgan onginne
brunum beadowæpnum,   bitrum ordum,
eglum attorsperum.   Is min innað til,

8. Sherman M. Kuhn, *The Vespasian Psalter* (Ann Arbor: University of Michigan Press, 1965), 18.10. For variations, see Phillip Pulsiano, *Old English Glossed Psalters: Psalms 1–50* (Toronto: University of Toronto Press, 2001), 228.

9. George H. Brown, "The Psalms as the Foundation of Anglo-Saxon Learning," in *The Place of the Psalms in the Intellectual Culture of the Middle Ages,* ed. Nancy van Deusen (Albany: State University of New York Press, 1999), 1–24.

10. Pierre Riché, *Education and Culture in the Barbarian West,* trans. John J. Contreni (Columbia: University of South Carolina Press, 1976), 463.

11. The early modern Holme Riddles collection, for instance, poses Samson's riddle as a follow-up to two sexually suggestive riddles. Tupper, "Holme Riddles," 229. See also the medieval Latin riddles of Claret (Peachy, *Clareti Enigmata,* 50), and William Bagwell, *Sphynx Thebanus, with his Oedipus: or, Ingenious Riddles, with their Observations, Explications and Morals* (London, 1664), 3.

wombhord wlitig, wloncum deore;
men gemunan þæt me þurh muþ fareð.

[I am the protector of my flock, firmly attached to lordly wires, filled on the inside with noble treasures. During daylight hours I often spit out spear terrors; when I have filled my belly, prosperity is the greater. A lord beholds how from my belly battle spears fly. At times, I begin to swallow black ones, dark battle weapons, bitter points, fearsome poison spears. My guts are good, a beautiful belly hoard, precious to the high born; people remember what goes through my mouth.]

The text of this riddle is supplemented by a pair of runes, *lagu* (L) and *beorc* (B), which are found between Riddle 16 and Riddle 17 on folio 105r of the Exeter Book.[12] As is the case with other such marginal runes that occur among the Exeter Book riddles, they are usually taken to indicate the solution of a nearby riddle.[13] Since the only other candidate, Riddle 16, is almost certainly best solved as *ancor* 'anchor' (a variation on a Symphosian theme that would not suit the runes in either Latin or Old English), the "B" and "L" runes most probably refer to the answer of Riddle 17.

Consequently, the runic marks have shaped both the interpretation of Riddle 17 and the wording of proposed solutions. The most popular of these has been Latin *ballista* 'siege engine', an answer first suggested in 1859 by Franz Dietrich.[14] Though finding favor in some later editions, the solution is considered unlikely today. Problems include its inability to account adequately for the "noble treasures" in the speaker's belly, the fact that such siege engines did not eject arrows or darts, and the doubtful use of such engines of war in Anglo-Saxon England.[15] Other proposals included in Donald K. Fry's 1981 survey of solutions are not much more convincing.[16] They

12. For a facsimile reproduction of these runes, see Williamson, *Old English Riddles,* 55.

13. For example, the rune *sigel* ("S") is found before and after Riddle 6, which is best solved as OE *sigel* 'sun' or L. *sol* 'sun'. See Williamson, *Old English Riddles,* 151. The use of first letters to indicate the solutions of Latin enigmas in several known manuscripts of the Anglo-Saxon period makes it difficult to doubt the intended function of these marginal runes (although they may, of course, indicate the guesses of later readers). See Orchard, "Enigma Variations," 284–304.

14. Dietrich, "Räthsel des Exeterbuchs: Würdigung," 465.

15. Williamson, *Old English Riddles,* 180. Tupper argues most extensively for the solution of *ballista* in his edition, *Riddles of the Exeter Book,* 105–7. Wilcox also objects that "such a war-machine does not adequately account for the disjunction between the visible expulsion and the separate (nightly) filling described in the riddle." The "nightly" filling referred to here is based on reading *sweartum* (line 7a) as "by night." Jonathan Wilcox, "New Solutions to Old English Riddles: Riddles 17 and 53," *Philological Quarterly* 69 (1990): 395.

16. Fry, "Exeter Book Riddle Solutions," 23.

include "fortress," "forge," "oven," and "inkwell" (*blæchorn*).[17] Finally, two additional solutions for Riddle 17 have been proposed since the appearance of Fry's list. Peter Bierbaumer and Elke Wannagat offered the solution "beehive," a reading that has been taken up and expanded in a swarm of subsequent articles.[18] Also recently, Jonathan Wilcox has proposed *cocer* 'quiver'.[19] Since Wilcox's argument is perhaps the most persuasive alternative to "beehive," it is necessary here to give his solution some attention before we proceed.

The strongest evidence in support of Wilcox's reading is the resemblance of Riddle 17 to Riddle 23, which is best solved as *boga* 'bow'. The solution of Riddle 23 is fairly certain, since it is provided in the riddle's first word, spelled backward.[20] Wilcox efficiently sums up the relevant parallels:

> The paradoxes central to the "bow" riddle are analogous with those of Riddle 17. An object is described in terms of an animate creature with body parts—a bosom or stomach ("bosme," 3b, "hrife," 12b) and, in this case, a limb ("liþ," 7b). The creature spits ("ic spæte" 8b) and takes into its bosom ("me on bosme fareð" 3b). The thing ingested and expelled is again poisonous ("ættran onga" 4a, "ealfelo attor" 9a) and, indeed, can lead to the death of any man whom it touches.[21]

The first of these perceived similarities rests on the unfounded if understandable assumption that the speaker of Riddle 17 is an inanimate object, but the

17. For "fortress" (*Burg*), see Franz Dietrich, "Die Räthsel des Exeterbuchs: Verfasser, weitere Lösungen," *Zeitschrift für Deutsches Alterthum* 12 (1865): 237. For "forge" (*Schmelzofen*), see Hans Pinsker, "Neue Deutungen für zwei altenglische Rätsel (Krapp-Dobbie 17 und 30)," *Anglia* 91 (1973): 11–17. For "oven," see Trautmann, "Die Auflösungen der altenglischen Rätsel." For "inkwell" (*blæchorn*), see Shook, "Anglo-Saxon Scriptorium," 222–24. For "phallus," see Gregory K. Jember, "An Interpretive Translation of the Exeter Riddles" (PhD diss., University of Denver, 1975), 94.

18. Peter Bierbaumer and Elke Wannagat, "Ein neuer Lösungsvorschlag für ein altenglisches Rätsel (Krapp-Dobbie 17)," *Anglia* 99 (1981): 379–82; Tigges, "Signs and Solutions," 70–76; Paul Sorrell, "A Bee in My Bonnet: Solving Riddle 17 of the Exeter Book," in *New Windows on a Woman's World: Essays for Jocelyn Harris,* ed. Colin Gibson and Lisa Marr (Dunedin, New Zealand: University of Otago Press, 2005), 544–53; Marijane Osborn, "'Skep' (*Beinenkorb, *beoleap*) as a Culture-Specific Solution to *Exeter Book* Riddle 17," *ANQ* 18, no. 1 (2005): 7–18. See also Osborn's follow-up article, "Anglo-Saxon Tame Bees: Some Evidence for Bee-Keeping from Riddles and Charms," *Neuphilologische Mitteilungen* 107 (2006): 271–83. Niles, *Old English Enigmatic Poems,* 145, advocates "either 'quiver' or, even better, 'skep.'" Bitterli, *Say What I Am Called,* 165–66, accepts "beehive" as the likely answer.

19. Wilcox, "New Solutions," 393–408.

20. The manuscript reading, in fact, is *agof.* For an explanation of this spelling, see Williamson, *Old English Riddles,* 204–5.

21. Wilcox, "New Solutions," 394.

other points seem valid. These resemblances, though, do not on their own justify the solution *cocer* 'quiver'. Indeed, this solution was raised and immediately dismissed long ago by Dietrich on solid grounds: "Bei dem wesen das mit kampfzeug gefüllt ist, nr 18, liefse sich an den köcher (ags. *cocere*) denken, wenn es nicht hiesse 'ich speie den schrecken der speere, kampfpfeile fliegen aus meinem innern'" (By the way the creature of number 18 [K-D 17] is filled with war gear, one might think of a quiver '*cocere*', if it did not claim that "I spit the terrors of spears, and war darts fly from my innards").[22] Wilcox asserts, however, "Despite Dietrich's objection . . . spitting from a mouth is as appropriate for a quiver as it is for the bow of Riddle 23."[23] This does not seem to me altogether convincing; a bow violently ejects projectiles, while a quiver passively awaits their extraction. Moreover, the solution *cocer* does not satisfy the contrasting contents of the speaker's stomach. Spearlike objects enter and exit the speaker, but a good, memorable *wombhord wlitig* 'beautiful belly hoard' is also found within. Wilcox explains that the belly hoard, too, refers to the arrows, but he is unable to provide any instances of arrows described as treasure.[24]

A solution that better accounts for these major aspects of the riddle is the "beehive" proposed by Bierbaumer and Wannagat. The bees and the honey account for the contrastive contents of the speaker's belly, while the creature's spitting of copious poisonous projectiles fits well the swarming issue of a hive. In fact, this solution lines up so well with the basic terms of the riddle proposition that it has swiftly gained favor in several recent articles. Wim Tigges explicates many of the clues in the riddle, including the imagery of war and the material makeup of the traditional hive. Marijane Osborn and Paul Sorrell also add valuable background to these readings (both giving rich accounts of the traditional straw-woven hive, the so-called skep, discussed below), and Osborn proposes the unattested Old English word **beoleap* 'bee basket' as a solution to fit the marginal runes.[25]

Despite these useful studies, however, many of Riddle 17's mysteries remain unresolved. My purpose here is not to overthrow the growing consensus on this text but to rethink and revise it in several respects. In doing so, I draw on the valuable work of previous solvers, but I also hope to add much

22. Dietrich, "Räthsel des Exeterbuchs: Würdigung," 465.

23. Wilcox, "New Solutions," 406.

24. Wilcox mentions other weaponry found in the dragon's hoard of *Beowulf* but admits, "such treasure hoards rarely explicitly include bows and arrows" (ibid., 406).

25. See note 18 above.

that has remained hidden in the diction and imagery of the poem.[26] This will involve examining a group of related metaphors concerning bees, honey, and beehives, a set of associations well known to the Anglo-Saxons. Such materials, I believe, are essential for establishing the conceptual environment of this riddle. First and foremost, though, my task here is to offer a new solution to Riddle 17 that accounts both for the terms of the riddle proper and the marginal runes. As I will show, the trick is to see the speaker of Riddle 17 as the most famous of riddle creatures known to the Anglo-Saxons, Samson's lion.

To begin, it may be helpful to recall the biblical account of Samson's encounter with the lion. On the road to visit his betrothed, Samson is attacked by a lion, which he succeeds in tearing to tatters through God's gift of strength. He leaves the body to rot but later revisits the place and finds a swarm of bees occupying the lion's carcass, which is now filled with their honey. Taking some honey and eating it, he goes on his way but does not tell anyone of the strange spectacle. When his in-laws, following custom, assign him thirty companions for the wedding feast, he poses them a riddle, which they must answer in seven days or pay Samson a certain amount of textile goods. The riddle reads: "De comedente exivit cibus et de forte est egressa dulcedo" (Out of the eater came forth food and, from the strong one, sweetness). Under threat, Samson's bride pesters him into telling her the secret, which she then reveals to the thirty companions. When time is up, the thirty ask Samson, "What is sweeter than honey? And what is stronger than a lion?" Enraged, Samson replies, "If you had not plowed with my heifer, you would not have guessed my riddle."[27] The marriage arrangement sours and the match falls apart.

Samson's riddle is the most obvious example of the riddle genre in the Bible, and it stands out as the enigma par excellence of the Christian tradition. It is cited in the definition of enigma found in the Christianized *Ars maior* of Donatus, as well as in Isidore's discussion of the difference between enigma and allegory.[28] The riddle has been sometimes been mentioned in

26. In the recent spate of articles on Riddle 17, there is considerable overlap in the conclusions and the evidence brought to bear on this text. An earlier version of this chapter, for example, appeared in *English Studies* before I was aware of Sorrell's work, which touches on points raised also by Osborn and Tigges. At the moment, Riddle 17 seems to be the focus of much critical buzz.

27. Judges 14:14, 18 (*Biblia sacra,* 345): "et illi dixerunt ei die septimo ante solis occubitum quid dulcius melle et quid leone fortius qui ait ad eos si non arassetis in vitula mea non invenissetis propositionem meam."

28. Irvine, *Making of Textual Culture,* 230–31.

introductions to modern editions of the Exeter Book riddles as part of the general context of medieval riddling, and yet no reference to the bee-infested lion has been found in the collection.[29] This is a surprising fact, given the fame of that enigma and the tendency of the Exeter Book riddler(s) to rework and revise popular themes. But while the solutions are stable, delight is taken in giving a well-worn answer a new twist in the telling, and it would be in keeping with the collection to see Riddle 17 offering a fresh variation on the venerable matter of Samson's riddle: a lion serving as a "skep."

My reading begins simply with the observation that the victim of Samson's strength squares well with the basic description of Riddle 17's creature. The speaker's main claim is that he is the lord of a herd, which presumably consists of the spearlike and poisonous objects flying in and out of his body. Such a picture strongly resembles the spectacle of Samson's lion. In addition, the speaker is said to have a "belly hoard" of something good and memorable, a "lordly treasure." This could easily refer to honey. Finally, the creature is said to be observed by a "lord," who might be identified as the most famous of riddlers, Samson himself. Now, I must admit here that there is one potential sticking point in my solution. This is a detail found in half-line 2a: the speaker says that he is *eodorwirum fæst,* that is, in the translation I favor, "attached to lordly wires." But setting aside this detail—momentarily—it is easy to see that Riddle 17 describes with uncanny precision the lion that Samson tears apart and later revisits to find swarming with bees and dripping with honey.

In a closer analysis of these similarities, the first thing we notice is that the creature in question is distinguished by a regal, lordly persona. This is somewhat unusual, for in the Exeter Book collection, inanimate objects more commonly speak from a position of servitude or victimhood. Riddle 17's speaker is attached to *eodorwirum* 'lordly wires' and is also a *mundbora* 'lord, protector' of his herd. Both terms of lordship, *eodor* 'lord, one who enfolds or surrounds' and *mundbora* 'lord, one who offers a protective hand', connote a sense of protective enclosure. Needless to say, Samson's lion as speaker makes good sense of these connotations, since that creature literally embosoms his herd and hoard. Moreover, as "king of the beasts," a lion subject fits well such a regal persona, for indeed the association between kingship and lions is no modern innovation. In early medieval bestiaries, the lion

29. See, for example, Paull F. Baum, trans., *Anglo-Saxon Riddles of the Exeter Book* (Durham: Duke University Press, 1963), ix; Kevin Crossley-Holland, trans., *The Exeter Book Riddles* (New York: Penguin Books, 1993), x.

often comes first and is described as a king.[30] Isidore explains that "the Greek word *leo* is translated as 'king' in Latin, because he is the ruler of all the beasts,"[31] while the speaker of Aldhelm's enigma on the lion declares, "haud uereor regali culmine fretus" (I am not fearful, reliant as I am on my royal stature).[32] Arguably, the noun *mundbora* befits a lion more than most other creatures or objects.

In keeping with the fate of Samson's lion, Riddle 17 offers a riddlic dissection of the speaker's anatomy. In particular, the belly of the beast is emphasized. The spearlike creatures fly *of hrife* 'from the stomach', the *innað* 'guts' of the beast are said to be good, and its *wombhord* 'belly hoard', beautiful. Wilcox proposes that this imagery may suggest a sense of impregnation: "*Fyllo,* 'filling, fullness' (line 5), is the word used for the impregnation of the copulating hen in Riddle 42, which suggests a reason why prosperity will be the greater on account of that filling: a 'wombhord wlitig' will be engendered inside the 'innað.'"[33] This would suit Samson's lion, for bees, as a learned Anglo-Saxon solver might well know, are born from the bodies of dead animals. Isidore, for example, reports: "Many people know from experience that bees are born from the carcasses of oxen, for the flesh of slaughtered calves is beaten to create these bees, so that worms are created [from] the putrid gore, and the worms then become bees."[34] This notion is widely reported in a variety of classical and medieval sources and was taken seriously as late as 1842.[35] Moreover, at least one medieval source explicitly understands the wonder of Samson's lion as an example of such spontaneous generation: Enigma 126 of the Benedictine monk Claretus (fl. 1355–65) reads, "De comedente cibus, de forti dulce fit intus. Agmen apum natus leo fert saevus generatus" (From the devourer comes forth food, and sweetness from inside the strong.—A lion, fierce in his birth, gives birth to a swarm of bees).[36]

This background allows us to reconsider how a medieval audience might understand the subject of Samson's riddle. A modern reader probably assumes that Samson's lion is colonized by a chance migrating swarm. Thus

30. Margaret Haist, "The Lion, Bloodline, and Kingship," in *The Mark of the Beast: The Medieval Bestiary in Art, Life, and Literature,* ed. Debra Hassig (New York: Garland, 1999), 3–5.

31. Isidore, *Etymologies,* 251 (12.2.3).

32. Enigma 39 (Glorie, *Variae collectiones aenigmatum,* 423; my translation).

33. Wilcox, "New Solutions," 396.

34. Isidore, *Etymologies,* 269 (12.8.2).

35. For a discussion of the "ox-born" theory of bee generation, see H. Malcolm Fraser, *Beekeeping in Antiquity* (London: University of London Press, 1931), 8–12.

36. Peachy, *Clareti Enigmata,* no. 126. The translation is Peachy's.

the lion-hive appears a fluke of happenstance, a random slice of Samson's private experience and so a rather unfair subject of a riddle: something akin to the ring in Bilbo's pocket.[37] Craig Williamson, for one, compares Samson's riddle with the notorious "one-eyed seller of garlic" topic of Riddle 86: both riddles are "grotesque" for the freakish particularity of their solutions.[38] On the other hand, if bees were commonly thought to spring from the corpses of animals, then Samson's lion is not so much a special case along the lines of Riddle 86 as it is a description of a commonplace creature (the bee) with a notable—even marvelous—mode of regeneration. It might in this way seem analogous to Riddle 10, which describes the peculiar beginnings of a barnacle goose. But in fact Samson's riddle is probably best understood as a cross between these types, since, although the idea of bees inhabiting an animal corpse might seem more plausible to a medieval audience than it does to us, a dead lion in place of a bull-calf corpse might also seem a rather novel variation on a notable aspect of natural history. The main point, though, is that an Anglo-Saxon reader would probably assume that the bees in the corpse of Samson's lion did not settle in their new home by chance but arose there in a process of spontaneous generation. This background is therefore helpful in explaining why Riddle 17 figures the host lion as pregnant with its spiky guests.

Turning now to what issues from the *wombhord* 'belly hoard', we see that it is easy to read these pointed flying objects as the bees residing in Samson's lion. The creatures or objects exiting and entering the innards of the speaker are described variously as *sperebrogan* 'spear terrors', *hyldepilas* 'battle spikes', *sweartum* 'dark ones', *brunum beadowæpnum* 'brown or burnished battle weapons', *bitrum ordum* 'bitter points', and *eglum attorsperum* 'fearful poison spears'. This imagery is in keeping with Latin enigmas on the subject of bees and other stinging insects, which tend to elaborate on their martial prickliness and poisonous venom. The bee speaker of Aldhelm's Enigma 20, for example, declares, "Semper acuta gero crudelis spicula belli" (I always brandish the sharpened arrow-points of fierce warfare).[39] Aldhelm's Enigma 75, *De*

37. Such riddles, as in the case of Tolkien's Bilbo, often fall into the category of "neck riddles," which in folktales are posed by a prisoner to save his or her neck. When the captors cannot name the impossibly idiosyncratic answer, the captive gains freedom. See Dorothy Noyes, "Riddle," in *Encyclopedia of Folklore and Literature,* ed. Mary Ellen Brown and Bruce A. Rosenberg (Santa Barbara: ABC-CLIO, 1998), 551.

38. Williamson, *Old English Riddles,* 377.

39. Enigma 20, line 4 (Glorie, *Variae collectiones aenigmatum,* 403; translation from Lapidge and Rosier, *Aldhelm: The Poetic Works,* 74). Osborn, " 'Skep,' " 12, notes the similarities between Aldhem's enigma on the bee and Riddle 17, and she proposes that the *spicula belli* 'arrows of war' of the former may have inspired the *hyldepilas* 'battle points' of the latter.

crabrone 'On the hornet', also uses similar language to describe swarms of hornets defending their nest:

> Dumque cateruatim stridunt et spicula trudunt,
> Agmina defugiunt iaculis exterrita diris:
> Insontes hosti sic torquent tela nocenti
> Plurima, quae constant tetris infecta uenenis.
>
> [And when, together, they buzz in rage and thrust out spears, the invaders flee, terrified by their sharp stings; guiltless they thrust into the harmful enemy many spears, which are dipped in black poisons.][40]

The bellicose bees of Latin enigmas are clearly quite comparable to the pointy, poisonous, and dark ejecta of Riddle 17. The coloration of these spearlike creatures, though, has been used to argue against their possible apiarian interpretation, but it is in fact a strong point in favor of that reading. The creatures are described as *sweartum* 'black ones' as well as *brunum beadoweapnum* 'dark (or perhaps burnished) battle weapons'. Although these epithets seem appropriate enough, Jonathan Wilcox (citing N. F. Barley's article "Old English Colour Classification") argues that the spearlike creatures' *brun* coloration is not suitable for bees: "He [Barley] shows that the word is used of glossy things such as helmets, swords, waves, and feathers; hence it is more appropriate to an arrow than a bee."[41] I find this conclusion puzzling. What could be more "glossy" than the chitinous exoskeletons of insects? To quote one modern observer, Edwin Way Teale describes a similar species, the cicada-killer wasp, in this way: "They emerge into the sunshine, their black and yellow bodies gleaming as though they had been glazed in a pottery furnace."[42] Moreover, if *brun* is a word best used to describe glossy objects such as feathers, we need only look to Riddle 27 of the Exeter Book (commonly solved as "mead") for bees described as *feþre on lifte* 'feathers in the air'.[43] Far from a problem, a dark sheen on these potential bees seems a point in their favor.

40. Enigma 75, lines 9–12 (Glorie, *Variae collectiones aenigmatum,* 487; translation from Stork, *Through a Gloss Darkly,* 196).

41. Wilcox, "New Solutions," 21.

42. Edwin Way Teale, *The Strange Lives of Familiar Insects* (New York: Dodd, Mead, 1964), 170.

43. For more on this riddle, see Williamson, *Old English Riddles,* 217–18.

Teale's emphasis on the wasps' emergence into the sunshine introduces an additional detail worth noting about the pointy ones of Riddle 17: they are said to leave the speaker's belly *dægtidum* 'by day'. The bee solution activates this small detail. The diurnal habits of bees are a commonly stressed feature in medieval sources, as here in Aldhelm's *Prosa de virginitate:* "roscido facessante crepusculo et exorto limpidissimi solis iubare densos extemplo tripudiantium turmarum exercitus per patentes campos gregatim diffundunt" (at the coming of dewy dawn, when the first light of the very clear sun has risen, they [the bees] quickly spread out dense armies of reveling troops, travelling in flocks through the open fields).[44] On the other hand, Pliny stresses the bees' disinclination to fly at night in this charming moment: "noctu deprehensae in expeditione excubant supinae, ut alas a rore protegant" (if on an expedition they [the bees] are caught out at night, they will camp out lying on their backs, so as to protect their wings from the dew).[45] The bees of Riddle 27, mentioned above, also take to flight in the daylight hours: "Dæges mec wægun / feþre on lifte, feredon mid liste / under hrofes hleo" (By day, feathers carry me [honey from which mead is made] in the air, transport me with skill under the shelter of a roof).[46] Reading the ejecta of Riddle 17 as bees thus makes sound sense of the fact that these pointy ones are emitted only in the daylight hours.

One further objection to reading these ejecta as bees should be mentioned. Wilcox asserts that all bee riddles must "exploit the paradox of the potentially poisonous bees producing sweet honey, yet there is no reference to sweetness of any form in [Riddle 17]."[47] Yet it does seem that Riddle 17 makes use of this paradox. To be sure, the basic set of oppositions in the poem are between sharp, poisonous objects flying in and out of the speaker's belly, which is nevertheless full of *dryhtgestreona* 'lordly treasure', a filling that is *til* 'good' as well as memorable and makes the speaker more prosperous with its increase. What could be more appropriate to these details than the honey flow of a stinging swarm? This pattern comes close to the poison-honey paradox Wilcox expects, and also echoes more or less distantly the second element of Samson's riddle: "Out of the eater came forth food and,

44. Aldhelm, *Prosa de virginitate,* ed. Scott Gwara (Turnhout: Brepols, 2001), 4.4–6.

45. Pliny, *Natural History,* 11.8.21–22.

46. For more on this riddle, see Williamson, *Old English Riddles,* 217–18.

47. Wilcox, "New Solutions," 396. An exception that disproves this rule is Bern Riddle 21, *de ape* 'about the bee', which fails to exploit this contrast and does not in fact even mention the poison or stings of the bees. See Glorie, *Variae collectiones aenigmatum,* 567.

from the strong one, sweetness." The dilution or "blurring" of well-worn enigmatic conceits is a strategy of obfuscation the Exeter Book riddler employs at times, and seems to be what we have here in Riddle 17. An analogous situation might be cited in Riddle 25, an onion riddle discussed in depth in chapter 6. The speaker of that riddle declares, "Nængum sceþþe / burgsittendra nymþe bonan anum" (I harm no citizens save my slayer alone). The statement is best explained as a vague and perhaps deliberately obscured restatement of a motif elaborated extensively in Symphosius 44 (*cepa* 'onion'): *Mordeo mordentes* 'I bite the ones who bite'.[48] If we posit a similar transformation at play in Riddle 17, we can perceive both elements of Samson's riddle given a distant echo, for the first element too, "Out of the eater came forth food," may be seen reflected in the poem's focus on ejecta both ingested and actively issuing forth from the mouth of the consumer.

Let us now turn to what is perhaps the most puzzling aspect of Riddle 17, the statement that the speaker is *eodor wirum fæst.* First, it is necessary to think about what *fæst* means in this context. Its semantic range includes "secure" or "bound" and is often found in phrases translated as "secure with fetters" or "secure with cords." For this reason, most translate it here as meaning that the speaker is "bound (with wires)." The entries for *fæst* in the *Dictionary of Old English,* however, include the meanings "firmly attached / held fast (to or by something); that cannot easily escape or be extricated; with *be / on* or the dative."[49] This is the meaning I favor for Riddle 17, so that in my translation the lord is "firmly attached to lordly wires." This interpretation is in keeping with my larger understanding of the mysterious wires, which turns on a pair of additional cruces in this half-line. First, are we to take *eodor* in the sense of "lord" or of "enclosure"?[50] I prefer the former, since this meaning links to the speaker's role as *mundbora* 'lord', but the latter sense also reinforces the speaker's role as a lord who protects and guards his *wombhord* 'belly hoard'. Second, we have to decide whether one is intended to read *eodor wirum* as two words or as a compound. If two words, the half-line translates, "a lord (or enclosure) secure with (or attached to) wires." If a compound, it might mean either "secure with protective wires" or "attached to lordly wires." Williamson finds the half-line's construal as a

48. Ohl, *Enigmas of Symphosius,* 176 (my translation). The relationship between these riddles is discussed in Orchard, "Enigma Variations," 295–97.

49. *Dictionary of Old English,* s.v. "fæst," 2a.

50. Williamson, *Old English Riddles,* 182–83. The *Dictionary of Old English* favors the latter, with a possible pun on the former: s.v. "eodor," 1.

compound more satisfying on metrical grounds, and I tend to favor this reading also, partly because the sense "firmly attached to lordly wires" allows for a nice riddling parallel with the apposite phrase, "innan gefylled dryhtgestreona" (filled on the inside with lordly treasures).

This parallelism is important to my solution because it helps explain a potential sticking point in my interpretation: why and how Samson's lion is attached to or secured with wires. A conventional beehive might be described as *wirum fæst* on account of the look of the traditional hive used in England at least from the times of Roman occupation to the present day. Such "skeps" are typically fashioned by weaving hay into a cone-shaped basket, which is then plastered with mud. Such an object would seemingly fit the description in Riddle 17 well, at least in terms of its visual texture, and Marijane Osborn has provided a full and detailed argument in favor of this reading.[51]

There is reason to remain skeptical about this, however. While Osborn's reading stresses the modern sense of "wires" as extending to almost any material of fibrous or stringy texture, the Old English word *wir* meant metal, specifically precious metal, and especially *gold.* Its semantic range includes "ornaments" or "gold trappings," as the entry in Bosworth and Toller indicates.[52] Elsewhere in the Exeter Book riddles, *wir* denotes the metal ornaments either of lavish books or of swords.[53] In *Beowulf* the word describes the various golden treasures of the dragon's hoard, which "wæs innan full / wrætta ond wira. Weard unhiore, / gearo guðfreca goldmaðmas heold / eald under eorðan" (was full on the inside of artful treasures and ornaments. The monstrous guardian, the old vigilant warrior, kept watch over his golden treasures below the earth).[54] In this light, the riddlic meaning of *wir* is likely to lie in its sense of delicate, golden, metallic brightness, rather than in a comparison to the bulky coils of a mud-covered skep.

A better reading of Riddle 17's opening lines, then, emphasizes the parallels set up between *eodorwir* 'lordly wires or ornaments' and *dryhtgestreona*

51. Osborn, "'Skep,'" esp. 8–11. Tigges, "Signs and Solutions," 75, first suggested this reading, though he did not provide the name "skep" or go into much detail.

52. "*Wire, metal thread:* often used apparently in ornamental work, so, *an ornament made of wire.*" Bosworth and Toller, *Anglo-Saxon Dictionary,* s.v. "wīr."

53. An exception to this statement in Riddle 40 compares the splendor of God's creation with the ornamentation of a master metalworker: "Ic eom fægerre frætwum goldes, / þeah hit mon awerge wirum utan" (I am fairer than trappings of gold, though one should cover it with wires on the outside). Williamson, *Old English Riddles,* 92 (lines 46–47).

54. Lines 2412–15.

'lordly treasures'. The speaker is *fæst* 'attached to' lordly trappings and *innan gefylled* 'filled inside' with lordly treasures. I suggest that these treasures and trappings both refer to the bright, clinging, and precious contents that make up the speaker's *wlitig wombhord* 'beautiful belly hoard': that is, the golden honey in the lion's belly. Honey, unsurprisingly, is often figured as a golden treasure in Anglo-Latin *enigmata*. Aldhelm's bee boasts, "Arte mea crocea flauescunt fercula regum" (Through my art, the dishes of kings are made golden).[55] And the speaker, honey, concludes his sweet discourse in a riddle of the Bern collection thus: "Milia me quaerunt, ales sed inuenit una / Aureamque mihi domum depingit ab ore" (Thousands search for me, but only a single winged creature finds me. And he paints my golden house from out of his mouth).[56]

As these quotations suggest, the bee is often figured as a master artificer in *enigmata* known to the Anglo-Saxons, and his special art is crafting honey. Archer Taylor points out that this idea is also found in both riddles and proverbs from oral tradition, citing one of the latter: "The little smith of Nottingham, who doeth the work no man can."[57] One of the Holme riddles calls the bee "a Bird of great renown, usefull in citty & town, none work like unto him can doe," while a riddle in Wynkyn de Worde's *Demandes Joyous* says of the bee: "he dothe that no man can."[58] Moreover, the special craft of the bee is often figured as a kind of metalwork, an idea that is in keeping with his product, the golden honey. And so the bee becomes a smith of honey, as in the following early modern example: "I have a smith without a hand, / he workes the worke that no man can. / He serves our God, and doth man ease / without any fire in his furnace."[59] We find the same idea of honey-making as metallurgy at the conclusion of Aldhelm's bee enigma: "Atque carens manibus fabrorum uinco metalla" (And, lacking hands, I surpass the metalwork of smiths).[60]

This emphasis on the special, delicate craftsmanship of the bee helps to explain the riddler's characterization of honey as *eodorwir* 'lordly wires/ornaments'. First, of course, this is a matter of obfuscation: figuring honey

55. Enigma 20, line 3 (Glorie, *Variae collectiones aenigmatum,* 403; my translation).

56. Enigma 20, lines 5–6 (ibid., 566; my translation).

57. Taylor, *English Riddles from Oral Tradition,* 512.

58. Tupper, "Holme Riddles," no. 140; Wynkyn de Worde, *Demandes Joyous* (London, 1511), no. 40.

59. *Booke of Merrie Riddles* (London, 1631), no. 64.

60. Enigma 20, line 5 (Glorie, *Variae collectiones aenigmatum,* 403; translation adapted from Rosier and Lapidge, *Aldhelm: The Poetic Works,* 74).

as gold is in keeping with venerable riddling metaphors. But presenting honey as *eodorwir* also draws out its famous ductility. Common experience reveals that honey's viscosity produces delicate golden threads. Such flow is highlighted in the Bern riddle on honey: "Lucida de domo lapsus diffundor ubique" (Fallen from my bright house, I am poured everywhere).[61] Thin strands of dripping honey might easily evoke golden wires. A closer analogue is found in Pliny's *Naturalis historia,* where the author explains the particular qualities of honey produced from thyme pollen: "thymosum non coit et tactu praetenuia fila remittit, quod primum bonitatis argumentum est" (the thyme variety does not congeal, and when touched emits very delicate threads, which is the most important proof of its goodness).[62] Arguably, some such *fila* 'threads' of honey are the lordly wires that cling to Samson's lion in Riddle 17.

It seems likely as well that the conclusion of Riddle 17 refers to honey: "men gemunan þæt me þurh muþ fareð" (people remember what goes through my mouth). Although it is not explicitly stated in Judges that Samson drew the honey from the lion's mouth in particular (presumably one might find several points of exit from its torn body), commentators frequently made the reasonable assumption that he did so. For example, the Christianized *Ars maior* explains Samson's riddle as "significans ex ore leonis favum extractum" (signifying that honeycomb was extracted from the mouth of the lion).[63] Prudentius sees the honey as more actively issuing from the lion's mouth, explaining: "Invictum virtute comæ leo frangere Samson aggreditur; necat ille feram: sed ab ore leonis mella fluunt" (A lion undertakes to tear apart Samson, who is invincible thanks to his hair; he therefore kills that beast, but honey flows out of the mouth of the lion).[64]

Moreover, the reading I propose brings into sharper focus the concluding statement that people *remember* what comes from the creature's mouth. Indeed, this detail has posed no problem for Riddle 17's many solvers, for what variously emerges from siege engines, quivers, and phalluses might all be considered "memorable" in one way or another. The line has therefore been an invitation for free speculation: Marijane Osborn, for one, proposes that this line might refer to a "fierce honey of rhetoric," that is, "loving and no

61. Enigma 20, line 1 (Glorie, *Variae collectiones aenigmatum,* 566; my translation).

62. Pliny, *Natural History,* 10.15.39.

63. Quoted in Irvine, *Making of Textual Culture,* 230–31.

64. Prudentius, *Dittochæum,* ed. Jacques-Paul Migne, Patrologi;ae Cursus Completus: Series Latina 40 (Petit-Montrouge [Paris]: J.-P. Migne, 1847), 98.

doubt sometimes scolding advice."[65] The solution of Samson's lion, however, activates a much more well attested set of associations. Namely, people remember this extraction because bees, honey, and hives figure prominently in a set of common medieval metaphors for the faculty of memory.[66] These metaphors are ubiquitous throughout the medieval period, but I will confine myself to a few suggestive examples.

Commenting on the prophet's obedient consumption of a book (which in his stomach becomes sweet like honey) in Ezekiel 3:1–3, Jerome writes: "Principia lectionis, et simplicis histori;ae, esus voluminis est. Quando vero assidua meditatione in memori;ae thesauro librum Domini condiderimus, impletur spiritualiter venter noster, et saturantur viscera" (The foundation of reading, and of basic history, is the consumption of books. When we truly hoard the book of the lord in the treasury of our memory for constant meditation, our belly will be spiritually swollen and our guts full).[67] Jerome then connects this exegesis of Ezekiel with the riddle of Samson's lion as well as with a line from Proverbs advising one to "look to the bee." Maximus of Turin uses a similar set of metaphors in explaining why a community of priests are comparable to a swarm of bees: "Bene dixi examine sacerdotum, quia sicut apis de diuinarum scripturarum flosculis suauia mella conficiunt, et quidquid ad medicinam pertinet animarum oris sui arte conponunt" (I spoke well when I said "a swarm of priests," for just like bees they confect sweet honey from the flowers of divine scripture, and they hoard through the craft of their mouths whatever is of concern to the healing of souls).[68] Many other examples of this might be cited, but the important thing to note is that the bee's process of storing and transforming its harvest into concentrated honey is a widespread medieval metaphor for the mind's ability to retain, organize (in the "cells" of memory), and refine the material it gathers from "the flowers of divine scripture."

Isidore also draws on related metaphors in his commentary on Samson's lion in his *Mysticorum expositiones sacramentorum,* a text Michael F. Krouse describes as "a sort of *summa* of all the allegorical interpretation developed

65. Osborn, "'Skep,'" 11, 16.

66. In a thorough study of these metaphors, Mary Carruthers, *The Book of Memory: A Study of Memory in Medieval Culture* (Cambridge: Cambridge University Press, 1990), writes, "one should be very alert in medieval discussions of honey-bees, for a trained memory may well lurk within the meadows and flowers, chambers, treasure-hoards, and enclosures of the hives/books" (38).

67. Jerome, *Commentary on Ezechiel,* in *Opera omnia,* ed. Jacques-Paul Migne, Patrologi;ae Cursus Completus: Series Latina 25 (Petit-Montrouge [Paris]: J.-P. Migne, 1845), 35–36.

68. Maximus of Turin, *Maximi episcopi Taurinensis sermones,* ed. Almut Mutzenbecher (Turnhout: Brepols, 1962), 515A.

during the first seven centuries of Christianity."[69] Isidore writes that Samson's lion signifies those converted kings "qui adversus Christum ante fremuerunt, nunc iam , perempta feritate, dulcedini evangelicae praedicandae etiam munimenta praebent" (who growled against Christ in the past, but now, their wildness having been slain, they supply protection for the sweetness of the preaching of the Gospel).[70] Here we have Samson's lion figured as a guardian of the Gospel's sweetness, a picture that lines up quite closely with the regal *mundbora* 'protector' of Riddle 17, who keeps watch over his memorable *wombhord* 'belly hoard'.

Apart from the lion speaker and his herd and hoard, Riddle 17 also includes an observer who beholds that unusual sight. Naturally, in the reading I have proposed, the lord who "þæt bihealdeð, / hu me of hrife fleogað hyldepilas" (beholds how from my belly battle spears fly) can be identified as the person who had unique visual access to that spectacle, Samson himself. If this is correct, he would not be the only biblical figure to appear in the collection. The *wær* 'man' who sits at wine with his unusual family in Riddle 46 is universally accepted as Lot, and his "suno twegen, / freolico frumbearn" can be identified as Moab and Ben-ammi, the offspring of his incest. Also, John D. Niles has suggested that the book consumed by the bookworm of Riddle 47 is most probably a Psalter (OE *sealm-bōc*), and thus that the man mentioned in the phrase *wera gied sumes* 'the song of a certain man' is probably King David, the traditional author of the Psalms.[71] Other biblical figures make an appearance in the Exeter riddles, including Tubalcain, as I argued in chapter 3. It is certainly in keeping with the conventions of the Exeter Book riddles that Samson, the famed riddler of the Bible, should make a brief cameo as the *freo* 'lord' in line 5.

Identifying this lord as Samson also explains his strange passivity in relation to the creatures' activities. If the correct solution were a bake oven or a weapon of some kind, we might well expect the *freo* to be actively engaged with the creature in its work. Of course, there are manmade objects described in the collection as operating autonomously: the rake of Riddle 34, for example, does its rooting around on its own. But where human beings

69. Michael F. Krouse, *Milton's Samson and the Christian Tradition* (Princeton: Princeton University Press, 1949), 42.

70. Isidore, *Opera omnia,* ed. Faustino Arevalo, Patrologi;ae Cursus Completus: Series Latina 83 (Paris: J.-P. Migne, 1850), 390.

71. Niles, *Old English Enigmatic Poems,* 119–22.

are included in the picture, they tend to be dynamically involved in the activity. This is true in such cases as the Old English plow riddle (number 21), where back-breaking human assistance is required to till the earth, or the bawdy churn riddle (number 54), where a young man's strength peters out before that of his dash.[72] The integral—and often antagonistic—relation between master and implement seems indeed to be a major theme in the Old English riddles, so why does the *freo* of Riddle 17 merely behold the creature? Judges 14:12 provides us with an answer. Samson's detour is described in the Vulgate in this way: "declinavit ut videret cadaver leonis et ecce examen apium in ore leonis erat favus mellis" (he made a digression in order to see the body of the lion and, behold, a swarm of bees was in the mouth of the lion and combs of honey). It is this wonder to behold, of course, that Samson turns into his famous riddle, and I wish to stress here that the emphasis Judges 14 places on Samson's lion as a visual spectacle matches well the language of Riddle 17: "Freo þæt bihealdeð, / hu me of hrife fleogað hyldepilas" (A lord beholds how from my belly battle spears fly). It is easy to see the gaze of Samson and that of this *freo* 'lord' as one and the same.[73] Moreover, this interpretation of the unnamed observer may also help to account for an additional oddity of Riddle 17, the unique spelling of *frea* 'lord' as *freo,* which Williamson explains as "probably archaic."[74] Some editors, among them Tupper and Krapp and Dobbie, emend this unusual spelling away, but it may serve as a subtle and playful clue in reaching the riddle's solution: the *freo* 'lord' beholds the *leo* 'lion' and *beon* 'bees'.

This brings us finally to the wording of Riddle 17's solution, for which I propose the Old English phrase *leo ond beo* 'lion and bee'. This doublet is

72. Also, Riddle 23, which is commonly solved as *boga* 'bow' and which is, as I have discussed, often cited as an analogue to Riddle 17, includes the figure of a *waldend* 'master', whose actions cause the arrows to fly.

73. Arguably, in Riddle 17 the stress on Samson as the one who *sees* the creature squares with both the narrative crux of the biblical story (centered around a riddle based on something Samson alone has seen) and a dominant convention in the Exeter Book riddles—that is, figuring the riddler as an authoritative eyewitness to wonders with the formula "Ic seah wundorlicu with" (I saw a wondrous creature). Elaine Tuttle Hansen, *Solomon Complex,* views such "ic seah" riddles as symptomatic of "the riddler's exclusive powers of seeing" (135). Samson's case, then, would be the paradigm for such powers.

74. Williamson, *Old English Riddles,* 183. The *Dictionary of Old English* gives a definition of *frēo* as "woman," citing a single instance in *Genesis B.* This might seem to indicate that the assumed lord in Riddle 17 could actually be a woman. However, Alfred Bammesberger, "*Freo* 'Woman' in *Genesis,* Line 457a," *Notes and Queries,* n.s., 52 (2005): 282–84, has argued cogently that this instance of *freo* is a "transposition of the Old Saxon genitive plural *frio*" found in *Genesis B*'s source material, and is not a part of the "genuine lexicon of Old English." In this light, it remains our best bet to take *freo* in Riddle 17 as a curious spelling of *frea* 'lord'.

attractive for a number of reasons. It has, for example, the advantages of being a simple, balanced, and rhyming Old English phrase. Although in most cases solutions proposed for the Exeter Book riddles have been stated as single items, several favored solutions come in the form of alliterative doublets, such as *hana ond hæn* 'cock and hen' (Riddle 42) and *feðer ond fingras* 'pen and fingers' (Riddle 51).[75] A rhyming doublet such as *leo ond beo* would not be out of place among such solutions. Indeed, it may be that some of the absent answers of the Exeter riddles rival the propositions themselves in their fondness for wordplay and artful economy. Moreover, the solution *leo ond beo* makes the best sense yet proposed for the marginal runes L (*lagu*) and B (*beorc*) that have so long baffled solvers. To date, explanations for these runes have either been incomplete, involved unattested words, relied on bilingual or otherwise clunky explanations, or failed to make good sense of the riddle proper.[76] Yet where consensus has been reached on how runes work in the Exeter Book riddles, favored solutions are often more elegantly contrived than what has so far been proposed for Riddle 17.[77] In this light, the rhyming doublet *leo ond beo* seems a nice fit for both runes and riddle.[78]

75. For *hana ond hæn,* see Williamson, *Old English Riddles,* 276. For *feðer ond fingras,* see Niles, *Old English Enigmatic Poems,* 126, who develops the idea of the potential importance of "doublet" solutions in the Exeter riddles. Here also Niles argues for the solution *hund ond hind* 'hound and hind' for Riddle 75/76, which he arrived at independently of Dewa, "Runic Riddles," 26–36, who reached the same conclusion.

76. Incomplete explanations include Tigges's *beohyf* 'beehive', which does not address the *lagu* rune, while unattested words include Tigges's **beohyf* 'beehive' and Osborn's **beoleap* 'bee basket'. Tupper's double solution, Latin *ballista* 'siege engine' and OE *(stæf)-liðere* 'an engine for casting stones, a kind of sling', is bilingual and very awkward, while Dietrich's *ballista* 'siege engine' and Shook's *blæchorn* 'inkhorn' both involve a rather arbitrary reversal of the order of the runes as found in the manuscript. Moreover, as Williamson, *Old English Riddles,* 181, has pointed out, Shook's solution fits the runes better than it does the actual terms of the riddle proposition. Finally, Wilcox, "New Solutions," 395, avoids the question of the runes altogether by discounting their relevance.

77. For example, the solution that Griffith, "Riddle 19 of the Exeter Book," provides for nearby Riddle 19—*snac* 'swift-sailing vessel'—explains several difficulties of the text in a neat Old English acronym: the reverse order of the runes in that riddle, the odd redundancy of runic words meaning "man," as well as the conventional imagery found in the poem. This is the sort of pat and satisfying solution we have come to expect from riddles of the Exeter Book. Niles's discussion of a probable solution to Riddle 58 (*rad-rod* 'riding well') further supports this notion. *Old English Enigmatic Poems,* 89–92.

78. My choice of singular *beo* 'bee' instead of plural *beon* 'bees' may seem inaccurate; there is not a single bee in the lion's belly but many bees. Still, I preserve the felicity of the rhyming doublet *leo ond beo,* noting that in the Latin tradition of *enigmata,* supplied solutions often fly in the face of grammatical number. The speaker of Aldhelm's Enigma 20, *de apibus* 'about bees', for example, is a single insect.

5

INNUENDO AND ORAL TRADITION

If you had not ploughed with my heifer," Samson tells the Philistines, "you had not found out my riddle." A response like this is its own riddle, of a kind that English readers would no doubt recognize in this taunting of a cuckold: "your Horns are a growing, your Bed is a going, your Heifer's a Plowing."[1] Something similar is perhaps behind the imagery of Exeter Riddle 21, where the speaker (presumably a plow) explains how,

> hlaford min
> woh færeð, weard æt steorte,
> wrigaþ on wonge, wegeð mec ond þyð,
> saweþ on swæð min.

> [my lord goes bent over, a guardian at the tail, shoves forward on the surface, shakes and presses me, scatters seed in my path.]

The suggestiveness of these images is clear enough, even if plowing were not such a rich field for double entendre. In his 1842 edition of the Exeter

1. Williams, *Dictionary of Sexual Language,* s.v. "plough."

Book, for instance, Benjamin Thorpe too seems to have had second guesses about this plowing creature with an *orþoncpil* 'curious stick' that *hangað under* 'hangs under'.[2] Perhaps this is, ironically, the very reason he offers an answer for Riddle 21—in the single instance of riddle solving in his edition. In a note, he assures the reader of Riddle 21's proper meaning: "By this, no doubt, a plough is intended."[3] No doubt Thorpe is on to something here, but students of these Old English poems may also wonder if one of the earliest solutions to an Exeter Book riddle was actually motivated by a desire to suppress the text's suggestiveness.

In a genre so rich with metaphor, innuendo is always on the verge of budding up, if it is not always in full bloom. And yet Old English specialists share a certain understanding. It is clear which of the Exeter riddles betray an erotic edge—consensus on this question rises up on its own, as phallic onions, swelling dough, and dangling keys are easy to grasp and do not require further explanation. All that is needed is a knowing wink, and we have been winking for a while. Thorpe declined to make "an effort at translation" for a small selection of the Exeter riddles, prudently preserving their salty wit for those who could read them in their original tongue. Thorpe's dirty half-dozen include Riddles 25 (commonly solved as an onion), 37 (commonly solved as a pair of bellows), 42 (commonly solved as a cock and a hen), 44 (commonly solved as a key), 45 (commonly solved as rising dough), and 54 (commonly solved as a butter churn). Nowadays we would probably add the plow, as well as Riddles 12 (commonly solved as leather), 61 (commonly solved as some kind of garment, possibly a shirt or helmet), and 62 (commonly solved as a poker for the fire or a woodworker's boring tool). Quite possibly, these last three suggest acts and images (of female sexuality, for instance) that Thorpe would not have wished to acknowledge even through omission. There are others, too, that occasionally raise eyebrows.

For the most part, though, the innuendo is hard to hide. While a few of the riddles mention sexual intercourse (*hæmedlac*) explicitly, most of those mentioned above employ a clearly charged set of words—a very recognizable lexicon of dirty riddling. Conspicuous members of this set include the related *nathwæt* 'I-know-not-what' and *nathwær* 'I-know-not-where', terms that pack the force of an ironic leer.[4] Verbs and adjectives describing male

2. Riddle 21, lines 11–12.

3. Thorpe, *Codex Exoniensis,* 527.

4. A discussion of these words is found in Matti Rissanen, "*Nathwæt* in the *Exeter Book Riddles,*" *American Notes and Queries* 24, nos. 7–8 (1986): 116–20.

tumescence are also common (*stican* 'to stick, penetrate', *stondan* 'to stand', *weaxan* 'to grow', *stiþ* 'stiff'), as is a focus on the phallus's firm foundations (the creature of Riddle 44 "has a good foundation," and the *staþol* 'foundation, trunk' of the speaker in Riddle 25 is *steapheah* 'lofty'). The man's role in sexual intercourse is often described in terms of service or use (the onion is *neahbuendum nyt* 'useful to the neighbors' and the churning man "wæs þragum nyt / tillic esne" [was useful at times, a good servant]). And while sexual penetration is suggested in many riddles, equal emphasis is laid on manual stimulation. Often it is a *modwlonc meowle* 'haughty maiden' who *gripeð* 'grasps' the male member in an act described in terms of inflated pride or "haughtiness." Compound adjectives with the element *wlanc* 'proud' are also particularly common, as are epithets and implications of foolishness: the woman of Riddle 12 is a *dol druncmennen* 'foolish drunk woman' with a *hygegalan hond* 'foolish hand', while the sexually aggressive lady of Riddle 25 suffers an oniony and apparently satisfying comeuppance at riddle's end. To be sure, the grip of a proud woman is explosively suggestive in these riddles, even when the creature in question remains cloaked in mystery. A case in point is the amorphous innuendo of Riddle 45:

> Ic on wincle gefrægn   weaxan nathwæt,
> þindan ond þunian,   þecene hebban.
> On þæt banlease   bryd grapode,
> hygewlonc hondum;   hrægle þeahte
> þrindende þing   þeodnes dohtor.

> [I heard about a certain-such-thing growing in the corner, swelling and standing out, hoisting up its covering. A cocksure young bride got a grip on that boneless thing with her hands; the daughter of a great man wrapped that rising thing in a garment.]

The object to be guessed (dough, according to most modern solvers) is given scant description, even less than with this early modern riddle on dough:

> Back bent Smock rent
> Slippery it was, And in it went.[5]

5. *Delights for young Men and Maids,* no. 11. The solution provided at the bottom of the page is "Neading Dough."

For the Old English riddle, a formless sense of swelling is sufficiently suggestive—along with the idea that something is in need of concealment, and the riddle emphasizes this last point with not one but two coverings—a redundancy with a difference, if the *hrægl* 'clothing' of the daughter is to be read with a double meaning similar to the woman's offered garment in Riddle 61:

> Oft me fæste bileac freolicu meowle,
> ides on earce, hwilum up ateah
> folmum sinum ond frean sealde,
> holdum þeodne, swa hio haten wæs.
> Siðþan me on hreþre heafod sticade,
> nioþan upweardne on nearo fegde.
> Gif þæs ondfengan ellen dohte,
> mec frætwedne fyllan sceolde
> ruwes nathwæt. Ræd hwæt ic mæne.

> [Often a comely lady kept me close under wraps, held me in a coffer. But at other times she brought me forth in her hands and presented me to her lord, her devoted master, just as she was told. Then he pushed his head into my bosom, jammed upward from below smack dab into a tight spot. If the strength of the receiver held out, he had to fill fancy me up fully, a some-such-thing with hair. Riddle out my meaning.]

Riddle 61 resembles in several respects a riddle found in the early modern rhetorical primer *The Arte of English Poesie,* in which George Puttenham poses a riddle on the subject of a "furd gloove" that "may be drawen to a reprobate sence": "My mother had an old woman in her nurserie, who in the winter nights would put us forth many prety ridles, whereof this is one: *I Have a thing and rough it is / And in the midst a hole Iwis: / There came a yong man with his ginne, / And he put it a handfull in.*"[6] The opening of this riddle

6. George Puttenham, *The Arte of English Poesie* (1589), ed. Gladys Doidge Willcock and Alice Walker (Cambridge: Cambridge University Press, 1936), 188. The line "There came a young man with his ginne" seems to mean that a young man approaches "with cunning or craft," but it could also be taken to mean that the youth approaches with a tool that has been fashioned with particular art or ingenuity. In the latter case especially, the idea reminds us of Riddle 44's description of a key/penis as *wrætlic* 'cunningly adorned or fashioned'. The word "prety," used here to describe the riddle, has the sense of "ingenious" or "artful," as it does in the title of the early modern collection *Prettie Riddles*. See the *Oxford English Dictionary,* s.vv. "gin," "pretty."

could fairly translate Riddle 61, line 9a, *ruwes nathwæt* 'some-such-thing with hair', while the general riddling strategies and conceits involved are very close to the Old English text. Puttenham presents this riddle as circulating in oral tradition, and this is corroborated by the existence of a similar riddle apparently once to be found in the now fragmentary *Book of a Hundred Riddles*. The solution to this lost riddle is found on a single page surviving from the book, a sheet left over from the answer key: "A furred gloue. But this ryddyl must be put by a woman or it is not proper."[7] In this case, in fact, we may be able to guess something of an improper riddle by noting its proper solution.

We might also guess that these riddles represent variations on a traditional bawdy conceit with considerable durability in oral tradition. In fact, the patterns of riddling we see in these suggestive Exeter riddles are remarkably consistent with innumerable later riddles collected from oral tradition. And the similarities are not limited to general words and images but extend also to the very particular metaphors employed. Riddle 44 is another good example:

> Wrætlic hongað bi weres þeo
> frean under sceate: foran is þyrel.
> Bið stiþ ond heard; stede hafað godne.
> Þonne se esne his agen hrægl
> ofer cneo hefeð, wile þæt cuþe hol
> mid his hangellan heafde gretan
> þæt he efenlang ær oft gefylde.

> [A remarkable thing hangs along a man's thigh, under that lord's garment: it has a hole in the front. It is stiff and tough, and it has a firm foundation. When that man hikes up over his knee his own garment, he desires to encounter that well-known hole with the head of his dangler—a hole which it, equally long, often filled up before.]

Analogues for this basic comparison abound, but a few examples will suffice. The relating of keys dangling on a belt to the position of the penis is a standard joke, as in this riddle from oral tradition: "Hips says I, / Hangs by

7. *Book of a Hundred Riddles* (London: W. Rastell, [1530?]).

my side; / One went in, / Two hung by" (answer: keys).[8] The phallic object's *efenlang* length (line 7a) is also a favored subject of traditional riddling: "What I speak of seeks to keep the master's measure in the mistress's hole.— The mistress's ring is a perfect fit on the master's finger."[9] Certainly the keyhole as well as the key could be suggestive, as in this riddle (solved "door peg"):

> Uncle and Aunt went to bed;
> Uncle left a thing undone;
> Uncle clumb over Aunt
> And put it in the hole.[10]

Further examples of this would be easy to produce, and such close similarities suggest that a comparative study of the conventions and motifs of oral riddling may potentially provide an essential context for understanding this aspect of the Exeter collection.

Surprisingly, however, comparative work of this kind has not yet been carried out, perhaps partly because the needed approach falls awkwardly between the two most influential editions of the Exeter riddles. Although Frederick Tupper's edition of 1910 is the strongest statement we have in favor of the comparative study of Old English riddles and oral tradition, questions of decorum would have prevented Tupper from dealing in a substantial way with what he dismisses as the "smut and horse-laughter" of the erotically charged subgenre.[11] On the other hand, later students of the Exeter riddles find themselves under fewer constraints of propriety, but by the time of Williamson's 1977 edition, Tupper's comparative method seems to have fallen from favor. Or at least Williamson's position is clear: "As I have indicated elsewhere in the notes and commentary to several riddles, the relevance of late medieval, renaissance, or early modern English folklore to Old English riddles (which are, incidentally, literary creations) is doubtful at

8. Hyatt, *Folk-lore from Adams County,* 663.

9. Peachy, *Clareti Enigmata,* 28. Williamson, *Old English Riddles,* offers an alternative translation, in which the hole is "often filled (when he was) just as long as before" (281). Edward L. Risden, "Script-Based Semantic Theory of Humor and the Old English Riddles," *Publications of the Medieval Association of the Midwest* 8 (2001), suggests "a pun on *æfenlang;* that is, the familiar hole which the lord has often filled for a whole evening long, a kind of locker-room style performance joke" (65).

10. L. W. Chappell, "Riddle Me, Riddle Me, Riddle Me Ree," in *Folk-Say: A Regional Miscellany,* ed. B. A. Botkin (Norman: University of Oklahoma Press, 1930), no. 34.

11. Tupper, *Riddles of the Exeter Book,* xxv.

best." At worst, comparative study could be perceived as a pointless scavenger hunt, and Williamson sees "no reason to ascribe the so-called obscene riddles to a folk tradition any more than the 'straight' riddles. The double entendre riddles are carefully crafted; indeed they must be so to carry out the disguise."[12] Such statements may have done much to discourage research into the traditional roots of the genre.

It seems needless to point out, however, that the crafted quality of the Exeter riddles has very little to do with their possible relationship to oral traditional riddling motifs, conventions, and forms. What is needed is a critical stance between the reticence of Tupper and the skepticism of Williamson. For if we suspect that some of the Exeter riddles may show the influence of oral tradition, it is well worth taking a look at existing analogues to see if our modern wits line up with traditional modes of riddling. The durability of riddle forms in oral transmission has often been noted, and the monumental collecting efforts of such scholars as Archer Taylor provide us with a great wealth of materials for comparison and analysis (the riddle has been a particularly well studied form in the field of folklore). At the same time, other medieval and early modern riddle books both in print and in manuscript may also prove invaluable. But the worth of such materials to the study of the Exeter riddles can only be determined by examining the evidence. And what the evidence reveals, I would argue, is indeed a set of carefully crafted "sex riddles" that show strong familiarity with traditional riddling motifs. Any modern solver is at a disadvantage reading such riddles, even if the upshot of these enigmas seems obvious. In fact, many of these riddles rely on an allusive relationship to well-worn riddling conceits, some of which are quite elusive to a modern sense of wit. Far from simple jokes, these poems are best read as literate, layered reworkings of conventional materials—a unique response to a shared currency of common innuendo. To grasp these riddles, then, we must look for their roots.

Before we begin uprooting these riddles, however, there is the practical matter of deciding what to call them. Often these texts are described as "dirty" or "obscene," but one wonders whether there would be anything truly obscene about these texts from an Anglo-Saxon perspective. In fact, Mercedes Salvador Bello has recently made the case for reading the key riddle (number 44) and its surrounding texts allegorically, "as a section focused on the body, ultimately warning a potential audience against the dangers of relying on the carnal/literal dimension of the texts and, by extension,

12. Williamson, *Old English Riddles*, 24, 11.

of life."[13] Whether or not Salvador Bello's argument is accepted, her reading highlights the crucial question of perspective in these texts. Arguably, the riddles in question do tend to portray sex as absurd, undignified acts carried out by persons who are slaves to their own passions. Salvador Bello points out that in the manuscript several of the sexually charged riddles are clustered together around Riddle 43, a text that has been invariably solved as "the soul and the body." Lines 4–11 of Riddle 43 declare the proper relationship of the soul and the body in a statement that is relevant to our interpretation of the sex riddle subgenre:

> Gif him arlice
> esne þenað se þe agan sceal
> on þam siðfate, hy gesunde æt ham
> findað witode him wiste ond blisse;
> cnosles unrim care, gif se esne
> his hlaforde hyreð yfle,
> frean on fore, ne wile forht wesan
> broþor oþrum.

> [If the servant honorably serves the one who must control him on the journey, they will be safe and sound, and find at home their appointed sustenance and joy. But they will find a countless progeny of sorrow if the servant poorly obeys his lord, his master on the journey, if the one brother is unwilling to fear the other.][14]

As Salvador Bello contends, this perspective on the body's properly servile role is key to understanding those Exeter riddles dealing in implied sexual acts. For in fact the main thrust of these riddles is often to depict sexual activity in terms of the body's brash revolt, as a master paradoxically and problematically serving a servant.[15] Such a view of sex would hardly be considered "obscene" from the perspective of a Christian Anglo-Saxon

13. Mercedes Salvador Bello, "The Key to the Body: Unlocking Riddles 42–46," in *Naked Before God: Uncovering the Body in Anglo-Saxon England,* ed. Benjamin C. Withers and Jonathan Wilcox (Morgantown: West Virginia University Press, 2003), 96.

14. In my translation of line 8, I follow Williamson, *Old English Riddles,* 280.

15. Jonathan Wilcox stresses this pattern in his paper "Masters and Slaves: Servants of Desire in the Old English Riddles," presented at the Thirty-fifth International Congress on Medieval Studies, Kalamazoo, Michigan, May 2000. The text is currently available online at http://www-2.kenyon.edu/AngloSaxonRiddles/Wilcox.htm (accessed April 15, 2010).

audience. To argue that these texts grow out of oral traditional riddling motifs, then, is not to deny the fresh role they may assume in the literary riddling of the Exeter Book. In fact, the stress the Exeter sex riddles place on servant-master paradoxes is one thing that distinguishes them notably from so many analogous folk riddles. Perhaps, then, these texts may be interpreted to some extant as old jokes serving a new master, though even the most conscientious readers might derive mixed messages, as well as somewhat problematic pleasures, from such playfully suggestive texts.

And yet the problem of naming the subgenre remains. More neutrally, some identify these riddles as those that have "double solutions." The metaphorical focus of a riddle, however, is not the same thing as its solution. It may be more accurate to speak of a double meaning or a "double entendre" in these texts but, as I argue in this book, many other Exeter riddles display "double meanings" with no hint of sex. On the other hand, to refer to these texts as "erotic riddles" or even "sexual riddles" may imply unwarranted and limiting assumptions about these riddles' actual or intended reception, as much as if we were to label them simply "obscene" or (alternatively) "moralizing." Perhaps the best solution is simply to call these texts "sex riddles," much in the same way some have studied Old English "ship riddles" or "riddles of the scriptorium" as sets of related texts.

To fuss over nomenclature may seem unnecessary, but the labels we give these riddles often shape their reception. For instance, speaking of "double solutions" can mistakenly suggest that the implied sexual acts in these texts *can* be "solved" with explicit names. Nailing down erotic imagery was never an issue for commentators on the collection as late as Williamson, who for obvious reasons of decorum might simply appeal to the "shared mutual understanding of the hidden meaning."[16] However, more recent studies have often been bolder in naming the "real" meanings of these riddles, and this seems to me a mistake for reasons that have nothing to do with modern propriety. We might say, in fact, that the exact sexual acts and organs described in these texts are, by their very nature, unresolvable. Savely Senderovich makes this important point about traditional riddling: "While the explicit target [of a riddle] is identified by a verbal, pronounceable answer, the implicit target remains under the veil of taboo not simply because its naming is proscribed, but because there is no name for this strange image.

16. Williamson, *Old English Riddles,* 299.

And it is not a withheld answer but a matter of intuitive, eidetic knowledge."[17] That is not to deny the phallic upshot of keys and onions or the vaginal implications of the sheaths of swords, but at the same time we should certainly not assume that the sex riddles always describe coherent sexual events. No single backstory necessarily accounts for these beasts with two backs.

In fact, even in the most self-evident sex riddles, the images are not easily resolvable. The upshot of Riddle 54, for instance, seems fairly obvious. Here is the text as found in Williamson's edition, although I will have reason to question one of its words in the discussion below.

> Hyse cwom gangan   þær he hie wisse
> stondan in wincle;   stop feorran to
> hror hægstealdmon,   hof his agen
> hrægl hondum up,   hrand under gyrdels
> hyre stondendre   stiþes nathwæt,
> worhte his willan: wagedan buta.
> Þegn onnette;   wæs þragum nyt
> tillic esne;   teorode hwæþre
> æt stunda gehwam   strong ær þonne hio,
> werig þæs weorces.   Hyre weaxan ongon
> under gyrdelse   þæt oft gode men
> ferðþum freogað   ond mid feo bicgað.

> [A young man came walking along to where he knew it stood in the corner; the sturdy young bachelor stepped up from afar, lifted up his own clothing with his hands, thrust something stiff under the belt of it (her) standing there. He worked his will and they both jerked around. The handyman was in haste: at times useful, a good servant. However he, though strong, petered out at times before it did, weary as he was of the work. Below the belt, something then began to grow in it which good people love in their hearts and buy with money.]

For a long time now, we have enjoyed a satisfying solution for this text. Trautmann's "churn" (*cyrn*) is accepted by all later editions, and has never

17. Senderovich, *Riddle of the Riddle*, 85.

been seriously challenged.[18] Numerous analogues from oral tradition confirm the likelihood of this reading, including this Irish riddle (solved "churn dash," the paddle-shaped implement used in churning): "Put it in dry, bring it out wet. / Move your fundament and keep it busy."[19] With this folk riddle, we might feel free to speak of "double entendre" without hedging: images of penetration and butter churning are nicely balanced. Other analogues also display a sexual focus but are more difficult to resolve: "Big at the bottom and little at the top; / Right in the middle it goes flippity-flop."[20] And a Turkish churning riddle reads, "A rock below, a rock above. Its end is moist. It goes in and out between your mother's legs."[21] The two "rocks" here raise an eyebrow, although they are oddly positioned. As with so many traditional sex riddles, the image is suggestive but difficult to anatomize.

And yet many readers of Riddle 54 have found little difficulty in resolving its "anatomical solution": a young man (*hyse*) approaches a lady in a corner, where they enjoy sex in a fully upright position. We might note, too, that the woman outperforms the man, who *teorode* 'petered out' before she does, in a possible punning deflation of the man's *teors* 'penis'. Something then begins to *weaxan* 'grow' under the woman's belt: in the words of Williamson, this product is the "*butere,* the child of the churn." For Williamson, in fact, all of this is self-evident to the sophisticated reader: "In most of the double entendre riddles the anatomical solution is more covert; the game seems to be a shared mutual understanding of the hidden meaning. Here the love play seems center stage, and one might speculate that the original game consisted of inducing the riddle-solver to guess the 'wrong solution,' that is the anatomical one, in order to offer him the 'plain' solution and proof of his salacious imagination."[22] Recently, Melanie Heyworth has cited this passage in challenging Williamson's fanciful vision of a naïve solver, arguing that "it is impossible to distinguish which solution, the sexual or the non-sexual, is 'right' (innocent) or 'wrong' (harmful), or even whether *either* of

18. James E. Anderson, Review of *Die altenglischen Rätsel des Exeterbuchs,* ed. and trans. Hans Pinsker and Waltraud Ziegler, *Speculum* 63, no. 4 (1988): 981, offers in passing "cow milking" as an alternative solution for Riddle 54. Anderson has not to my knowledge yet explained the details of his reading.

19. Hull and Taylor, *Collection of Irish Riddles,* no. 405.

20. Arthur Palmer Hudson, "Some Folk Riddles from the South," *South Atlantic Quarterly* 42 (1943): 86. A close analogue of this riddle can be found in Elsie Clews Parsons, *Folk-lore of the Sea Islands, South Carolina* (Chicago: Afro-Am Press, 1969), 157.

21. Basgöz and Tietze, *Bilmece,* 210 (no. 164.27).

22. Williamson, *Old English Riddles,* 301, 299.

them is 'wrong' or 'harmful' in terms of Anglo-Saxon ways of thinking."[23] Now, Heyworth is right to be wary of quick assumptions about Anglo-Saxon attitudes toward the "anatomical" implications of the riddle. But if we follow what we find in folk riddling, it is fairly clear that the sexual meaning is not the solution to be guessed but is rather the unspoken disguise (by definition it is indeed "wrong" in that sense). This is not a matter of moralizing so much as a matter of recognizing the conventions of the genre. In fact, I would argue that there is no clear-cut "sexual solution" to the sex riddles, even in such an apparently obvious text as Riddle 54.

At any rate, it is worth measuring textual foundations against received opinion, if only because translating Riddle 54 inevitably obscures real ambiguities in the language of the text. The first point I would like to make concerns the way translators have handled feminine pronouns in the poem. The first line of Riddle 54 reads: "Hyse cwom gangan þær he hie wisse / stondan in wincle." In all the translations I have been able to consult, the pronoun *hie* is rendered "she," though as Paull Baum and others have noted, the apparent solution *cyrn* is a feminine noun and so might be the antecedent of the pronoun. As Baum explains, "This makes for an awkward handling of the pronouns: 'she' is too obvious; 'it' too misleading."[24] But it is not simply the gender of *cyrn* that makes the pronoun difficult to translate. It is also the generic conventions of the Old English third-person riddle, in which the unknown answer is nearly always described as a *wiht* 'creature', a feminine noun. For this reason, the creatures in question in Old English riddles (when they are not speaking for themselves) are often described with feminine pronouns. Even the *wiht . . . wæpnedcynnes* 'creature of the kind that has a penis' of Riddle 38 (the bull-calf riddle mentioned in chapter 1) is described with a feminine pronoun:[25]

> "Seo wiht, gif hio gedygeð, duna briceð;
> gif he tobirsteð, bindeð cwice"
>
> [The creature, if *she* prospers, will break up the hills; if *he* is rent apart, he will bind the living.]

In this stock livestock paradox, the bull-calf is described both as a he and as a she, a contradiction that demonstrates just how strong a pull grammatical

23. Heyworth, "Perceptions of Marriage," 172.
24. Baum, *Anglo-Saxon Riddles,* 58.
25. See Niles, *Old English Enigmatic Poems,* 137n87.

gender has in such riddles. The underlying, implied question is always *saga hwæt hio hatte* 'say what *she* (the creature) is called'.

And so the pronouns in Riddle 54 are more ambiguous than one might at first assume. In the context of a riddle, their feminine gender would, at least initially, simply signal a *wiht* to be guessed, and not necessarily the presence of a literal woman. Moreover, in those other sex riddles in which women appear, the woman is always described in more detail than a pronoun, be she a *ceorles dohtor* 'man's daughter' or a *freolicu meowle* 'noble woman'.[26] It is therefore best to translate the feminine pronouns of Riddle 54 as "it" even if, as Baum says, this is an imperfect choice. In fact, it may be impossible to translate Riddle 54 without unjustifiably resolving its ambiguities—and perhaps that is the point. But let us move on to the main action of this encounter, the moment in Riddle 54 where contact is first made between the dashing young man and the object of his attentions. Here is the text as found in Williamson:

> stop feorran to
> hror hægstealdmon, hof his agen
> hrægl hondum up, hrand under gyrdels
> hyre stondendre, stiþes nathwæt,
> worhte his willan: wagedan buta.

> [The sturdy young bachelor stepped up from afar, lifted up his own clothing with his hands, thrust something stiff under the belt of it (her) standing there. He worked his will: they jerked around together.]

I have reason to call into question other aspects of this text and translation, but first I simply wish to highlight one unambiguous fact about the text: it is the young man who *hof his agen hrægl* 'lifted up his own clothing'. There is no mention of any woman's *hrægl* (or the *hrægl* of any creature), although it is possible to take *hyre stondendre* as possessive, modifying *under gyrdels,* translating "under the belt of her who is standing [there]." Nevertheless, translators of Riddle 54 often choose to attribute loosely the *hrægl* to the woman. Baum, for example, renders the passage:

> Forth he strode,
> a vigorous young man, lifted up her own

26. Riddle 25, line 6b; Riddle 61, line 1b.

dress with his hands, thrust under her girdle
something stiff as she stood there;
worked his will.[27]

As we can see, Baum (willfully?) reworks the riddle's clear statement that the young man *hof his agen hrægl* 'lifted up his own clothing'. Crossley-Holland, too, attributes the dress to the woman:

this strapping youth
had come some way—with his own hands
he whipped up her dress, and under her girdle
(as she stood there) thrust something stiff,
worked his will.[28]

Here the text is rearranged so that *his agen* refers to the man's hands, a reading in active revolt from the manuscript. Williamson alone faithfully attributes the garment to the young man, but his translation involves changes of its own:

He stepped up,
Eager and agile, lifted his tunic
with hard hands, thrust through her girdle
Something stiff, worked on the standing
One his will.[29]

Admittedly, Williamson's aim in *The Feast of Creatures* is not literal translation, so his loose rendering here can be defended. As he puts it, "a translator must attempt to reproduce not only primary meanings, but also ambiguities, textures, and tones."[30] But the effect of Williamson's rearrangement is to resolve an ambiguity, not to reproduce it. He struggles to rearrange the text (reversing the order of *hyre stondendre* and *stiþes nathwæt*) to suit his understanding of a sexual act "slightly surreal in its ravishing treatment of the passive woman in the corner."[31] If Williamson sees Riddle 54 as intended to

27. Baum, *Anglo-Saxon Riddles,* 58.
28. Crossley-Holland, *Exeter Book Riddles,* 58.
29. Williamson, *Feast of Creatures,* 114.
30. Ibid., 50.
31. Ibid., 196.

fool a naïve solver, translators and commentators are eager to show that they know exactly what is going on. For instance, John Miles Foley asserts that the *hyse* 'young man' is the "plunge-stick" personified (but fails to explain how a churn dash might lift up his clothing with his *hondum* 'hands'). He also explains that the personified churn dash "enters the woman," a detail I do not find mentioned anywhere in the riddle.[32] Perhaps it is not so easy to put this riddle to bed.

As Thomas D. Hill has emphasized in regard to the bawdy kneading of Riddle 45, we cannot afford to lose track of the fact that our understanding of the Exeter riddles is in many cases heavily reliant on conjecture and emendation.[33] Riddle 54 is no exception, and Williamson's edited text involves three distinct alterations of what we find in the manuscript. One of these is particularly critical to construing the meaning of Riddle 54, for it comes at the moment of contact between the young man and the object of his affections, the same lines translated in the examples above. As the meaning of these lines is precisely what needs to be determined, this time I leave the text unemended and the translation inconclusive:

stop feorran to
hror hægstealdmon, hof his agen
hrægl hondum up, *rand* under gyrdels
hyre stondendre, stiþes nathwæt.

[The sturdy young bachelor stepped up from afar, lifted up his own clothing with his hands, (did something to) it (her?) standing (there) under the belt, a stiff one of some kind.]

The crux here is the meaning of *rand,* a word that does not mean anything (as a verb) in Old English, nor does it fit the alliterative needs of the poem. The obvious solution has seemed to emend *rand* to *hrand,* the third singular preterite form of *hrindan,* a verb that is further interpreted to mean "to thrust." The lines then may be translated, "He thrust something stiff under the girdle of her standing there." This small emendation greatly shapes our

32. John Miles Foley, "Riddles 53, 54, and 55: An Archetypal Symphony in Three Movements," *Studies in Medieval Culture* 10 (1977): 28.

33. Thomas D. Hill, "The Old English Dough Riddle and the Power of Women's Magic: The Traditional Context of Exeter Book Riddle 45," in *Via Crucis: Essays on Early Medieval Studies and Ideas in Memory of J. E. Cross,* ed. Thomas N. Hall (Morgantown: West Virginia University Press, 2002), 50–60.

interpretation of the lines and all that follows in the riddle, yet it is not beyond all questioning. First, we should bear in mind that this instance of the verb *hrindan* would be our *only* example of this word in the extant Old English corpus: our emendation is based entirely on the Old Norse verb *hrinda*. Moreover, we may also doubt the meaning commonly assigned to *hrand*—"he thrust"—for Old Norse *hrinda* means "to push, kick, throw" with a dative object.[34] Thus, in order to resolve this key moment in the poem we must first invent an Old English word and then make up its meaning.

That does not rule out this reading of a difficult text, but other possibilities are perhaps worth considering. I would suggest that one attractive alternative emendation would be to change *rand* to *hran* 'he touched'. This involves a minimal change to the text as we have it, and has the advantage of being a common Old English verb (*hrinan*) often employed elsewhere in the Exeter riddles collection and the corpus at large. If we were to accept this emendation, the lines would then read:

stop feorran to
hror hægstealdmon, hof his agen
hrægl hondum up, hran under gyrdels
hyre stondendre.

[The sturdy young bachelor stepped up from afar, lifted up his own clothing with his hands, and under the belt touched it standing there.][35]

In this reading, the joke would be that the young man finds an erect object standing up under his own clothing, which he touches and begins, in the next lines, to caress vigorously.

To support this reading, let us return to the beginning of Riddle 54. The opening is crucial because it introduces the main participants in this suggestive encounter: "Hyse cwom gangan, þær he hie wisse / stondan in wincle" (A young man came walking along to where he knew it stood in the corner).[36] Of course, the "it" here could be a "she." But it does seem worth

34. Richard Cleasby and Gudbrand Vigfusson, eds., *An Icelandic-English Dictionary,* 2d ed., s.v. "hrinda."

35. In this reading, *hyre stondendre* 'her standing [there]' is taken to be the dative object of *hran*.

36. I follow most editions (including those of Tupper, Williamson, Pinsker-Ziegler, and most recently Muir) in emending MS *Inwinc sele* to *in wincle* 'in the corner'.

asking what we more commonly do find standing "in the corner" in sex riddles. Most relevant to this question is the opening line of Riddle 45, which includes the only other extant instance of the word *wincle* 'corner' in the Old English corpus (with the exception of place-names): "Ic on wincle gefrægn weaxan nathwæt, þindan ond þunian, þecene hebban" (I heard about something growing in the corner, swelling and sticking up, raising up its covering). Presumably, the dough is "in the corner" simply to rise in a draft-free nook. If we dared to resolve the "double meaning" of this poem, the image would be plain: the penis grows "in the corner," that is, between the legs or in the man's crotch. Reading this meaning back into Riddle 54, the humor involved in the opening of the churn riddle would be evident, too: the young man *wisse* 'knew' the location of the thing that stands in the corner as well as he knows the back of his own hand.

It is also worth noting that the object in the corner of Riddle 45's dough joke is said to be sticking or standing up, a detail we also find in the crucial passage from Riddle 54 discussed above. Now, the particular verb *stondan* is used at least once elsewhere in the Exeter riddles to suggest male erection: the onion riddle's phallic speaker says *stonde ic on bedde* 'I stand up in the bed', a phrase I also discuss in my analysis of Riddle 25 (in chapter 6). More generally, describing the "standing" posture of a penis is par for the course in the English tradition of sex riddling. The standing posture in some early modern riddles is enough to suggest the penis: "Though he want legs, yet he can stand, With the least touch of your soft hand." Another reads, "There came in a Lad from I cannot tell whence, with I cannot tell what in his hand; it was a live thing that had little sence, but yet it could lustily stand."[37] Indeed, in English traditions recorded after the Anglo-Saxon period, the "word's proneness to innuendo was clearly hair-triggered."[38] Moreover, "standing" and "stiff" were closely associated epithets for the erect penis. See, for example, this early modern riddle of a distaff: "Stiff standing, ruff hanging / Betwixt a Maids Legs in a froosty Morning."[39] The close ties between these words in the later history of English innuendo supplies a firm foundation for reading *stiþes nathwæt* 'something stiff' as one and the same as *hyre stondendre* 'the one standing there'. Yet in the case of Riddle 54,

37. Quoted in Williams, *Dictionary of Sexual Language,* s.vv. "stand" and "thing," respectively.

38. Ibid., s.v. "stand."

39. *Delights for young Men and Maids,* no. 71.

the creature standing in the corner has never been associated with the stiff, unknown thing nearby.

Let us turn to the churner. Regardless of how we emend and translate *rand,* the epithets attributed to the man working the implement seem to stress both his youth and his inexperience. He is a *hyse* 'young man', a word that seems to connote late childhood and immaturity. The word glosses Latin *puer* 'boy' and is found in such contexts as a scene in the *Battle of Maldon* where Byrhtnoth is accompanied by a raw young soldier in the hour of his death: "Him be healfe stod hyse únweaxen, / cniht on gecampe" (By his side stood a young man not fully grown, / a boy in the battle).[40] The young man of Riddle 54 is further described as a *hror hægstealdmon* 'a stout bachelor'. The precise meaning of *hægstealdmon* is difficult to determine precisely but seems to indicate a young man in an unmarried state. The word may further suggest a lack of sexual experience: note the related words *hægstealdhad* 'virginity' and *hægstealdnis* 'virginity'. In Riddle 20 (discussed further below), the sword speaker relates his lord's prohibition on sex to this particular state:

Ic wiþ bryde ne mot
hæmed habban, ac me þæs hyhtplegan
geno wyrneð se mec geara on
bende legde; forþon ic brucan sceal
on hagostealde hæleþa gestreona.

[I am not allowed to have sexual intercourse with a bride, but he who once laid bonds on me denies me that joyous romp; therefore I must (instead) enjoy the treasures of warriors in celibacy.]

As the action of Riddle 54 gets under way, the youth's ridiculous position is emphasized. The stiff thing "worhte his willan: wagedan buta" (worked its will: they both shook together). Of this line Williamson writes, "The dichotomy between active and passive, male and female, man and churn, disappears in a moment of lyric frenzy—'*Both* swayed and shook.'"[41] Indeed, these categories do collapse in the coordinated event, but if an onanistic act is suggested here the joke may have more to do with the implied potential independence of the man's own implement (as in so many other

40. Donald Scragg, ed., *The Battle of Maldon: AD 991* (Oxford: Basil Blackwell, 1991), lines 152–53.

41. Williamson, *Feast of Creatures,* 196.

sex riddles). In the next lines, indeed, the young man continues to serve as a solitary agent of the action: He *onnette* 'hurried' and "wæs þragum nyt / tillic esne" (was at times of use, a worthwhile servant). Such "useful" self-service is, of course, ironic in terms of church strictures against sexuality not purely directed at reproduction, as well as in terms of the servile attention he may be paying to his own member: is this a case of the tail wagging the dog?

What tickles commentators on Riddle 54 the most, however, is that the young man "teorode hwæþre / æt stunda gehwam strong ær þonne hio, / werig þæs weorces" (at times became tired before it (she?) did, weary of the work, although he was strong). Of this, Wilcox says, "The churn as insatiable lover reverses a world of male dominance: the young man is a servant to the woman because her desire lasts longer than his and so his actions are ultimately for her pleasure."[42] Nina Rulon-Miller agrees: "*Riddle 54* (Churn) resonates with the fear of an insatiable woman."[43] But could it instead be a small joke about the young man's failing arm strength compared to his desire for manual stimulation, a predicament that squares well with the chore of churning?[44] In either case, the joke is directed at a youth whose strength cannot keep up with his passions.

A butter metaphor finishes off Riddle 54:

Hyre weaxan ongon
under gyrdelse þæt oft gode men
ferðþum freogað ond mid feo bicgað.

[Below the belt, something then began to grow in it (her?) which good people love in their hearts and buy with money.]

These lines have been consistently interpreted as referring to two incongruous products of the double-entendre action: butter and child. Williamson writes that "the lady's power is in the making: she bears the butter," while Tanke locates Riddle 54 within a "circuit of production and procreation"

42. Wilcox, "Masters and Slaves."

43. Nina Rulon-Miller, "Sexual Humor and Fettered Desire in Exeter Book Riddle 12," in *Humour in Anglo-Saxon Literature,* ed. Jonathan Wilcox (Cambridge: D. S. Brewer, 2000), 111.

44. Wyatt notes the "tiring and tedious work" of churning as a major point in its favor as a solution to Riddle 54. Wyatt, *Old English Riddles,* 106.

largely in response to these lines.[45] Still, this "double entendre" strains not a little, relating the thickening and separation of oily globules in a churn to the telltale signs of a woman great with child.

These days, every fresh reader of the Old English sex riddles grows bolder and more explicit in spelling out their dirty secrets, and I do not wish to be distasteful. Still, there is much to suggest that what the riddler might have in mind is not babies but *semen*. For obvious reasons, this comparison is much more precise than one involving pregnancy, and it is in keeping with other Exeter riddles that end with such an allusion (compare my discussion below of Riddle 25's conclusion, *Wæt bið þæt eage* 'That eye will be wet'). Moreover, the butter/semen comparison is quite widespread in English bawdy traditions, and as Wyatt observes, "to the argument drawn from tradition great weight must be assigned."[46] Indeed, the "greasy innuendo" of Riddle 54 is confirmed by copious early modern references to, for example, the "Butter of Joy" (with which a cheating wife is "anointed") and descriptions of intercourse as a woman "makinge butter with her tayle."[47] The colorful epithet "buttered bun" was used to describe a woman who had recently had sex, while milk and cream were also common metaphors, not for babies but for semen. An early modern joke-riddle reads, "Why is an old man's wife like a hot bun?—Because she wants to be well butter'd." It makes perfect sense, too, for the semen to *hyre weaxan* 'rise up/grow within it', as we see in this common modern "submarine" riddle: "What is long, smooth, and filled with se(a)men?" Note too that the conclusion of Riddle 54 makes no indication of time having passed since the vivid encounter in the corner: the product of this action seems as immediate as the forced tears of Riddle 25's ending.

Having flirted with this "onanistic" reading of Riddle 54, I will now turn tail and admit that the standard reading is at least as compelling as my vision of solitary sex. For one thing, there is plenty of support in later recorded bawdy play for "corner" as a secluded place for sexual activity. In the late

45. Williamson, *Feast of Creatures,* 196; John W. Tanke, "*Wonfeax wale:* Ideology and Figuration in the Sexual Riddles of the Exeter Book," in *Class and Gender in Early English Literature: Intersections,* ed. Britton J. Harwood and Gillian R. Overing (Bloomington: Indiana University Press, 1994), 37.

46. Wyatt, *Old English Riddles,* 106.

47. The former is found in "The Cimmerian Matron," in Charles C. Mish, ed., *Restoration Prose Fiction: 1666–1700* (Lincoln: University of Nebraska Press, 1970), 155. The latter comes in "The Fourth Mountebank's Songe" of the *Gesta Grayorum,* ed. Desmond Bland (Liverpool: Liverpool University Press, 1968), 335.

medieval morality play *Mankind,* for example, Mischeff (Mischief) boasts, "The chenys I brast asundyr, and killyde the jailere, / Yea, ande his fayer wiff halsyde [embraced] in a cornere."[48] Early modern examples of such furtive nooks abound, with many an amorous young man wishing to "haue his wench in a corner."[49] Furthermore, even if we accept "semen" over "pregnancy" as the implication of Riddle 54's conclusion, this of course in no way rules out conventional coitus. At the same time, we might still argue for a "pregnant" conclusion to Riddle 54, noting that the idea of a masculine churn dash and feminine churn vat giving birth to a butter baby is not unattested in riddling traditions. This German churning riddle, for instance, might be cited: "Eine hohle Mutter, ein dürrer Vater, ein fettes Kind" (A hollow mother, a skinny father, a fat child).[50] Perhaps the ending of Riddle 54 reflects a similar idea.

The point, though, is that even in this most "overt" of the Old English sex riddles, the "sexual solution" is not resolvable. Our naïveté or squeamishness is not to blame—nothing is to blame for our inability to "solve" this riddle with anatomical precision. In fact, the point may well be that the sex images involved are not to be solved, because the nature of such a metaphorical focus is fundamentally different from a solution. The "double meaning" of such a poem may speak most loudly by staying silent. In fact, the idea that we should in theory be able to pinpoint the sex act or organ in question has sometimes left us puzzled by texts that stubbornly resist this expectation. Riddle 12 is an interesting case in point:

> Fotum ic fere, foldan slite,
> grene wongas, þenden ic gæst bere.
> Gif me feorh losað, fæste binde
> swearte Wealas, hwilum sellan men.
> Hwilum ic deorum drincum selle
> beorne of bosme; hwilum mec bryd triedeð
> felawlonc fotum; hwilum feorran broht
> wonfeax wale wegeð ond þyð,
> dol druncmennen deorcum nihtum,

48. David Bevington, ed., *Medieval Drama* (Boston: Houghton Mifflin, 1975), 927.

49. Williams, *Dictionary of Sexual Language,* s.v. "corner."

50. Richard Wossidlo, *Mecklenburgische Volksüberlieferungen* (Wismar: Hinstorff'sche Hofbuchhandlung Verlagsconto, 1897), 71 (no. 138c). My translation. The given answer is *Butterfass* 'butter churn'.

wæteð in wætre, wyrmeð hwilum
fægre to fyre; me on fæðme sticaþ
hygegalan hond, hwyrfeð geneahhe,
swifeð me geond sweartne. Saga hwæt ic hatte
þe ic lifgende lond reafige
ond æfter deaþe dryhtum þeowige.[51]

[While carrying a spirit, I go on foot and slit the earth, the green fields. Should I lose my life, I securely bind dark slaves, and sometimes better men. At times I dispense drinks to bold men from my bosom; at times a bride treads on me with her proud feet; at times a dark-haired slave woman brought from afar, a foolish drunken woman, who moves and presses me in the dark nights, wets me in water, turns me at times, beautiful before the fire; she thrusts into my center a wanton hand, turns me about a good deal, sweeps me through a dark thing. Say what I am called, I who living ravage the land and after death serve lords.]

A few pages back, in my discussion of Riddle 38, we saw a variation of the opening and closing paradoxes of Riddle 12, which recall a stock motif familiar from Latin *enigmata:* Living, the creature breaks up the soil, while dead he binds men (as strips of leather). One other Exeter riddle (Riddle 72) develops this idea, which is also found in Aldhelm and Eusebius, and so the solution of "bull-calf" (in its transformation from living beast to useful products) seems settled. But what has unsettled some readers of Riddle 12 is the patent innuendo of the middle lines, in which the creature apparently describes its unwilling participation in a sex act with a dark-haired (*wonfeax*) drunken slave woman in front of a fire. Nothing like this is found in the other Exeter bull-calf riddles, nor do the Latin texts imply any such innuendo. Analogues from oral tradition, however, suggest that a heated hearth alone could raise the temperature in riddling: "I saw a little thing sitting by the fire: / Red lips, black beard. / Cuss the thing, how I was skeered.—An old-fashioned copper teakettle sitting by the fire."[52] Or consider this early modern riddle:

A Maid in neat Attire, was occupy'd by the fire:
She took a thing and put it too,

51. In line 8 of Williamson's text, I leave *wale* uncapitalized.
52. Taylor, *English Riddles from Oral Tradition,* 199 (no. 548).

It was so limber it would not do;
She try'd again, it did not miss,
Ah, quoth she, I'm glad of this.[53]

In both this kettle riddle and Riddle 12, the most obvious interpretation of the unspoken metaphorical focus is that a woman's vagina is compared to the creature in question. In fact, similar comparisons to leather are well attested in later texts. The term "leather stretcher" was popular early modern slang for a penis, and in Sir David Lindsay's sixteenth-century play *Ane Satyre of the Thrie Estaitis,* a tailor's wife complains of her husband, "it is half ane yeir almaist / Sen ever that loun laborde my ledder."[54] The joke probably reflects the tailor's profession involving literal leatherwork, and a similarly riddlic context is established in an American folktale collected in the twentieth century. A "smart-aleck" tells the local tanner, "I got a piece of skin at home, that ain't no bigger than your hand. I've been a-working on it for twenty years, and it still ain't what you could call leather." The smart-aleck's intention is to embarrass, but the tanner is equal to the innuendo and responds, "You fetch that skin down here . . . and leave it all night. I'll tan it, easy enough. And I won't charge you a cent."[55]

Of course, the tanner's reply may not strike one as particularly funny, and several recent commentators on Riddle 12 have also found much to say about the rather unsettling ways in which this Old English enigma binds together images of sexuality, violence, gender, and race.[56] Much of this work has been quite illuminating. But in parsing the slave woman's wanton acts, readers have also found themselves puzzled by the literal sex acts implied. In particular, it has been difficult to visualize several of the woman's most suggestive acts. At half-lines 11b–12a, the speaker complains that "me on fæðme sticaþ / hygegalan hond" (she sticks into my bosom a wanton hand). The implication of this seems confirmed by Riddle 61's apparent description of

53. *Delights for young Men and Maids,* no. 9.

54. Greg Walker, ed., *Medieval Drama: An Anthology* (Oxford: Blackwell, 2000), 568.

55. Vance Randolph, *Pissing in the Snow and Other Ozark Folktales* (Urbana: University of Illinois Press, 1976), 17–18.

56. See Tanke, "*Wonfeax wale*"; Rulon-Miller, "Sexual Humor," 99–126; Sarah L. Higley, "The Wanton Hand: Reading and Reaching into Grammars and Bodies in Old English Riddle 12," in Withers and Wilcox, *Naked Before God,* 29–59; Peter Robson, "'Feorran Broht': Exeter Book Riddle 12 and the Commodification of the Exotic," in *Authority and Subjugation in Writing of Medieval Wales,* ed. Ruth Kennedy and Simon Meecham-Jones (New York: Palgrave Macmillan, 2008), 71–84.

intercourse: "me on hreþre heafod sticade" (he stuck his head into my bosom). Surely, then, the innuendo of Riddle 12 implies a vagina penetrated by a "wanton hand." The next half-lines, 12b–13a, however, seem to contradict this image: "swifeð me geond sweartne" (she sweeps me through a dark thing). This now sounds as if the speaker is a penis, "swept through" the vagina. Here is a confusing switch, to say the least, and one that has seemed to require various special explanations. I would contend, though, that resolving the images of sex in these poems is not necessary and in fact runs counter to the way the sex riddles operate.

The perceived need to anatomize such dark acts is implicit in the way the sex riddles have often been analyzed as a group. It is no accident that the most popular, most commonly anthologized Old English sex riddles (the key riddle, for example, or the onion riddle) also conform to a highly symmetrical model of "double entendre," in which a perfectly balanced "doubleness" is seemingly achieved. A classic formulation of this structure is provided by the folklorists Roger D. Abrahams and Alan Dundes, who define it in this way: "details are provided that lead to an ability to discern a referent, and thus call for an answer, but the answer is wrong. This answer is often an embarrassing, obscene reference."[57] Drawing on this definition, Ann Harleman Stewart admires the artful construction of double entendre in the Exeter riddles: "This requires a great deal of skill—the more so, the longer the riddle, since the composer will be forced into more detail—and is a balancing act so preoccupying in itself that, as we might expect, comparatively little attention can be given to mystifying the reader."[58] For texts such as Riddle 12, however, the expected "balancing act" seems to collapse at the edges of the poem, where we strain to posit a double meaning for the stock motifs of the dead binding the living.

Nevertheless, an artful balancing act is what we are conditioned to look for in these poems, and this may be one reason why Riddle 12's innuendo was so long ignored.[59] It simply did not fit the expected mold of balanced duplicity. The pole must never tip too far in one direction (toward the solution) or the other (toward the metaphorical focus)—or else the "double entendre" is invalidated. Take, for instance, Riddle 52, a text tilted in its own, slightly asymmetrical way:

57. Abrahams and Dundes, "Riddles," 131.

58. Ann Harleman Stewart, "Double Entendre in the Old English Riddles," *Lore and Language* 3 (1983): 40.

59. As late as 1977, Craig Williamson felt that Riddle 12 was "not usually classified as 'obscene.'" *Old English Riddles,* 167.

Ic seah ræpingas   in ræced fergan
under hrof sales   hearde twegen
þa wæron genumne   nearwum bendum,
gefeterade   fæste togædre.
Þara oþrum wæs   an getenge
wonfah wale,   seo weold hyra
bega siþe   bendum fæstra.[60]

[I saw servants carried into the hall, under the roof of the hall, two hard ones which were held by tight bonds, bound tightly together. Near to one of them was a dark servant, who controlled both of them on their journey fixed in their bonds.]

Readers have solved this riddle as some type of flail or threshing tool, or perhaps as two buckets suspended on a pole. Which is the answer? It is hard to say. There is very little to get a grip on—only two hard objects bound together to a dark slave, who controls their movements. It is not surprising that only two tentative solutions have been offered with so few available clues. What is surprising, however, is that this riddle has never been grouped together with the other sex riddles, for in traditional riddling, the configuration here is unmistakable. I have already mentioned one analogue, solved as "key": "Hips says I, / Hangs by my side; / One went in, / Two hung by." The pattern of two objects plus one other pops up again and again, and the implication is quite clear: "What is two things flapping and one going in and out?" (a hog with his ears flapping and his nose going in and out).[61] The pattern holds whether for keys, hogs, needles (and thread), barrels, or boots.[62] It is the oldest joke in the book, and yet Riddle 52 remains unsullied by any such implication by those who have commented on it.

60. In line 6 of Williamson's text, I leave *wale* uncapitalized.

61. Taylor, *English Riddles from Oral Tradition,* 354 (no. 960).

62. See, for instance, this boot riddle: "Got two ears. Hoist up yer foot, sho' it in, go flippity flop. What's dat?—boot." Or this needle riddle: "With one I penetrate, and two hang down behind." Taylor, *English Riddles from Oral Tradition,* 576 (no. 1417). The basic pattern is so recognizable that Chris Tully, trans., *Old English Poems and Riddles* (Manchester, UK: Carcanet Press, 2008), 29, seems to see it even in the list of body parts of Riddle 86 (of notorious one-eyed-seller-of-garlic fame, discussed in chapter 1). He translates the third line: "He had only one eye, but ears. . . . Yes, two." In his notes, Tully supplies the answer: "a one-eyed onion [*sic*] seller (though there are other probable, but much less decent answers" (92). For the record, I do not see much of a sexual focus in Riddle 86, though perhaps a slight suggestiveness is always present in riddles that catalogue body parts.

I suspect the reason why is that the basic configuration of one plus two is slightly askew in Riddle 52. As has been noted in the debate over the solution, the *wonfah wale* 'dark slave' is said in particular to be near to only *one* of the two other objects, and this would seem to rule out "double entendre" on the basis of strict anatomical correctness. For if the Old English sex riddles are posed according to a model of perfectly balanced doubleness, the metaphorical focus of this poem fails to perform. And yet anatomical coherence is not what traditional riddles of this kind lead us to expect. For instance, it is difficult for me (unless I must again play the role of naïve solver) to explain all the sex imagery of this twelfth-century Latin riddle: "My riddle consists of living baths, their entrances covered with hair: one washes within, two strike without.—The tongue inside the mouth, and the eyes in their two recesses."[63] Once again, the simple addition of one plus two is easy enough to grasp, but these multiple living baths (the same as the bathers and strikers?) strike me as more difficult to define. And yet if we suppose that the sex riddles simply function like other traditional riddles, with the slim chances of a riddle's proposition governed by a shaping metaphorical focus, it is easy to see how Riddle 52 works (even if the solution remains dark). In fact, it is fair to say that the sex riddles work much like any of the other metaphorical riddles in the Exeter Book. They do not have coherent, painstakingly balanced "double solutions," but they do have a coherent strategy of obfuscation.

The *wonfah wale* 'dark-colored slave woman' of Riddle 52 leads us back to the *wonfeax wale* 'dark-haired slave woman' of Riddle 12. This *wonfeax wale* plays the title role in a recent article by John W. Tanke, who argues that "social order is perverted when the *wonfeax wale* assumes the power to satisfy her own desire, and reaffirmed through the repudiation of her pleasure."[64] But Tanke's discussion of the *wonfeax wale*'s gender, sexuality, "status as a servant," and ethnicity is complicated, though certainly not invalidated, by Riddle 12's relationship to Riddle 52, a text that Tanke mentions twice but never discusses. A crucial point here is the *wonfah wale*'s position in Riddle 52, where we may see both a slave woman at work and the dark skin of a male member. The darkness of the *wonfah wale,* then, may have as much to do with the pull of the sexual metaphorical focus as the imagined ethnicity or race of the servant in question. Likewise, the description of the *wonfeax*

63. Peachy, *Clareti Enigmata,* 27 (no. xxxvii).

64. Tanke, "*Wonfeax wale,*" 38.

wale 'dark-haired slave' of Riddle 12 may reflect something more private than the hair on the woman's head. In the frenzy of fireside activity in Riddle 12, as we have seen, it is quite impossible to clarify the dark images of sex organs and sexual activity, to the point where we may easily mistake a body part for its owner. And as Riddle 43 (the "soul and body" riddle cited above) makes clear, the Anglo-Saxon owner of a body part at least *ought* to be its master. If, as Tanke observes, the *wonfeax wale* of Riddle 12 "serves herself," so do many other rebellious members of the Old English sex riddle corpus.

Both the *wonfeax wale* and the *wonfah wale,* then, must be read primarily in the context of the Old English sex riddles' overwhelming concern with masters and servants. The dashing young man of Riddle 54 (discussed below) "wæs þragum nyt / tillic esne" (was at times useful, a good servant), the suggestive onion of Riddle 25 (discussed in the following chapter) is *neah-buendum nyt* 'useful to the neighbors', while the obedient wife of Riddle 61 does *swa hio haten wæs* 'just as she was commanded'. The relationship of service is often flipped in paradoxical fashion, as when the bell speaker of Riddle 4 (discussed below and in chapter 1) declares, "Ic sceal þragbysig þegne minum, / hringan hæfted, hyran ġeorne" (Preoccupied with time and bound with rings, I must readily obey my servant). Similarly, the *frea* 'lord' of the key riddle (number 44) becomes an *esne* 'servant' at the very moment he first hikes up his *hrægl.* In the case of Riddle 21's plowman, Jonathan Wilcox has noted that there is "something faintly unseemly about the guard-ian being at the tail" in lines 3–4: "hlaford min / woh færeð, weard æt steorte" (my lord goes along bent over, a guardian at the tail).[65] A similarly unseemly position is assumed by the servant who must follow the phallic bellows of both Riddle 37 and Riddle 87, as if forced to serve a body part with a mind of its own. In nearly all such texts, then, sex is associated with service or use, and quite often the servant seems to be serving the commands of his own body.

The effect of many such riddles, in fact, is to detach the sex organ from its owner. Prosopopoeia, common in both traditional riddles and Anglo-Latin *enigmata,* contributes to this sense of separation. A suffering onion or speaking shirt is a lively creature with a will of its own, often (as with the plow) somewhat stubbornly dedicated to pursuing its own path. The sex riddles in particular seem focused on men struggling with rebellious tools.

65. Wilcox, "Masters and Slaves."

Riddle 62, usually solved as a poker for the fire or a woodworker's boring tool, is another prime example:

> Ic eom heard ond scearp, hingonges strong,
> forðsiþes from, frean unforcuð;
> wade under wambe ond me weg sylfa
> ryhtne geryme. Rinc bið on ofeste
> se mec on þyð æftanweardne,
> hæleð mid hrægle: hwilum ut tyhð
> of hole hatne, hwilum eft fareð
> on nearo nathwær; nydeþ swiþe
> suþerne secg. Saga hwæt ic hatte.[66]

> [I am hard and sharp, strong in my going, bold in my enterprise, in no way despised by a lord; I make headway under the belly and prise my own way open, dead ahead, direct. A man is in high gear who presses me from behind, a fellow with a garment: at times he draws out of the hot hole, at times he goes back into a tight spot, somewhere, and a southern man earnestly urges on. Say my name.]

This piece is another dark moment of riddling where it grows difficult to separate the bold enterprise of the implement from the man in motion who "presses . . . from behind."

Worker and implement come together and come apart, nowhere more intriguingly than in the riddle's hot and heavy conclusion:

> hwilum ut tyhð
> of hole hatne, hwilum eft fareð
> on nearo nathwær; nydeþ swiþe
> suþerne secg.

> [At times he draws out of the hot hole, at times he goes back into a tight spot, somewhere, and a southern man earnestly urges on.]

The subject of the *hwilum* clauses appears clearly to be the *rinc* 'man' mentioned above, a figure distinct from the speaker. Yet notice that it is the man

66. In line 7b, I have restored MS *fareð* to Williamson's text.

who *eft fareð* 'travels back' into the narrow spot. Williamson and others emend *fareð,* since it "makes little sense" for the man himself to be traveling into the hole. But of course it makes perfect sense if Riddle 62 is switching freely between the implied penis as a distinct (and humorously autonomous) implement and the implied penis as an integral part of the man (with which he may "travel" into tight spots). This leads us to the man who is "southern," an epithet some have thought puzzling. Tupper sees it in terms of race and class: "As an actor in one of the obscene riddles, 'the southern man' is obviously in the same class as 'the dark-haired Welsh,' the churls and esnes, often people of un-English origin, who figure in these folk-products."[67] Williamson is noncommittal but suggests that *suþerne* may be "meant to indicate somewhat obliquely the direction of the thrust."[68] Certainly we would expect something along these lines in a sex riddle, but the simplest explanation may be to identify the *suþerne secg* as an accusative object of the action: "He [the man] earnestly urges on his southern fellow [by which is understood the penis]."

If this "southern fellow" joins the ranks of the *wonfah wale* and *wonfeax wale* as figures who are at least partly to be understood, darkly, as stand-ins for sexual parts, there is plenty of precedent for this strategy in traditional riddling. For instance, an early modern penis riddle is worth noting here:

> *Collosus* like, between two Rocks,
> I have seen him stand and shake his locks.[69]

This colossal fellow, with his impressive locks of hair, may remind us of the dark-colored servant of Riddle 52 who stands yoked to "two hard things," or of the of dark-haired slave woman of Riddle 12. In the following chapter I argue for yet another member of this class, the oniony *wif wundenlocc* 'woman with braided hair' of Riddle 25, another text firmly rooted in traditional riddling motifs.

For the moment, though, it is important to remember that the identities of these dark-haired women and southern men are not finally resolvable in the sex riddles, for the same reason that other images in these texts are not

67. Tupper, *Riddles of the Exeter Book,* 203.

68. Williamson, *Old English Riddles,* 323.

69. From "A Present to a Lady" (essentially a riddle to be solved "penis"; the text early on assures the reader, "Name I will not, nor define it, / Sure I am you may devine it"), in *The Second part of Merry drollery* (London, 1661), 55–57.

easily named. In fact, the unwarranted expectation of "double solutions" has probably contributed to our ignoring clear instances of localized innuendo in the riddles. As in any Exeter riddle, the metaphorical focus of the sexually charged subgenre need not be active throughout the text. And, in fact, many of the riddles drift in and out of such focus. The opening and ending of Riddle 12 is a good example, as is the plow riddle. Another notable instance is Riddle 4, discussed in chapter 1, where I support Dietrich's bell solution. Double entendre, conceived as a sustained balancing of one sexual and one nonsexual meaning, is not credible in this riddle's proposition, and yet certain moments in the text seem shaped by an implicit metaphorical focus. For example, the verb *gretan* 'approach, draw near' has an established euphemistic meaning of "to engage (someone) in sexual intercourse" and serves to introduce an encounter in which the speaker's *wearm lim* 'warm member' is mentioned.[70] The image here chimes with the Old English compound *scamlim* 'shame limb, penis' and with the phrase *wæpnedlic lim* 'male member', while the bell clapper has a similar ring in a later medieval English lyric, in which a clerk named Jack takes the speaker to bed: "wan iak had don, þo he rong the belle; / al nyȝt þer he made me to dwelle."[71]

Moments such as these suggest that the sex riddles are not easily separable from other texts in the Exeter collection. A given riddle proposition may drift in and out of "double entendre" as easily as it might assume any other metaphorical focus. The sex riddles, then, are not a marginal form but rather can be considered representative of a kind of obfuscation found throughout the collection. They are in many senses at the center of the collection. In fact, a pair of sex riddles take pride of place in the second major riddling sequence in the Exeter Book: Riddle 61 (the suggestive shirt riddle discussed above) and Riddle 62 (the hot poker riddle featuring the "southern man"). The next text, Riddle 63, is also quite suggestive, though less obvious in its innuendo than some. Its ending has been largely destroyed by a burn hole

70. For the sexual connotations of *gretan,* see Roberta Frank, "Sex in the *Dictionary of Old English,*" in Amodio and O'Brien O'Keeffe, *Unlocking the Wordhord,* 306.

71. For the terms *scamlim* and *wæpenlic lim,* see Frank, "Sex in the *Dictionary,*" 303, 311. For *gretan,* see also Riddle 44 (regularly solved as "key" described in terms of a penis): "wile þæt cuþe hol / mid his hangellan heafde gretan" (he wished to encounter that familiar hole with his well-hung head). The use of *lim* to describe "one of the sexual parts of man or woman" is attested in Middle English from the twelfth to fifteenth centuries, as well as in the early modern period. *Dictionary of Middle English,* s.v. "lim"; *Oxford English Dictionary,* s.v. "limb." For the Middle English lyric "A Midsummer Day's Dance," see Rossell Hope Robbins, ed., *Secular Lyrics of the Fourteenth and Fifteenth Centuries* (Oxford: Clarendon Press, 1952), 23.

in this portion of the manuscript (damage possibly caused by a hot poker left resting on the book!), but the beginning of the riddle reads:

> Oft ic secgan seledreame sceal
> fægre onþeon þonne ic eom forð boren,
> glæd mid golde, þær guman drincað.
> Hwilum mec on cofan cysseð muþe
> tillic esne þær wit tu beoþ,
> fæðme on folm[.....]grum þyð,
> wyrceð his willa[.......][72]
>
> [Often I must serve men well in their hall joy, when I am brought forth, bright with gold, to where men drink. At times a useful servant kisses me on the mouth in my chamber where we two are. In the embrace of his hands, he presses (me) with his (fingers); he works his will.]

This text has rarely been categorized among the "obscene riddles," but the focus of the second half of the surviving text is clear enough if we compare the images to other sex riddles in the collection. Once again we find here confusion as to who is serving whom, with the speaker habitually compelled to serve men but also itself attended at times by a *tillic esne* 'useful servant'. In fact, the innuendo seems sparked by that servant's kissing of the cup in lines 4–5, an image paralleled in Aldelm's Enigma 80, which also displays some limited localized innuendo.[73] After kissing the speaker, the servant *þyð* 'presses' him with his fingers in an act that repeats what we see elsewhere in the sex riddle subgenre: the foolish handler of Riddle 12 *wegeð ond þyð* 'moves and presses' the leathern creature in question, while the plowing speaker of Riddle 21 complains that the plowman *wegeð mec ond þyð* 'moves and presses me'. As with so many Old English sex riddles, manual manipulation is stressed, as the servant *wyrceð his willian* 'exercises his desire', a euphemism for sexual activity paralleled in Riddle 54 (discussed above) where a

72. Fragments of Riddle 63 indicate that it continues on for several more lines.

73. The middle section of Aldhelm's riddle on a "glass goblet" reads, "To be sure, many people wish to grasp my neck with their right hands and to seize my delightfully smooth body with their fingers. But I change their minds as I give kisses to their lips, applying these sweet kisses to their tightly-pressed mouths." The translation here is that of Lapidge and Rosier, *Aldhelm: The Poetic Works,* 87. Readers as early as Dietrich have noted these parallels, for a discussion of which, see Williamson, *Old English Riddles,* 323–24. Notable too are the differences, such as Riddle 63's stress on servants and masters.

young man *worhte his willan* 'exercised his desire' with a cornered creature. The underlying focus of this riddle is plain, and yet the creature's golden sheen has seemed to rule out "double entendre" in the sense of a sustained balancing act.

If the cup is half-empty of innuendo in Riddle 63, the suggestiveness of Riddle 20 is apparently confined to its concluding section, the last lines of which have also been lost (in this case from a missing leaf and not a hot poker):

Ic eom wunderlicu wiht,   on gewin sceapen,
frean minum leof,   fægre gegyrwed.
Byrne is min bleofag;   swylce beorht seomað
wir ymb þone wælgim   þe me waldend geaf,
se me widgalum   wisað hwilum
sylfum to sace.   Þonne ic sinc wege
þurh hlutterne dæg,   hondweorc smiþa,
gold ofer geardas.   Oft ic gæstberend
cwelle compwæpnum.   Cyning mec gyrweð
since ond seolfre   ond mec on sele weorþað,
ne wyrneð wordlofes,   wisan mæneð
mine for mengo   þær hy meodu drincað,
healdeð mec on heaþore,   hwilum læteð eft
radwerigne   on gerum sceacan,
orlegfromne.   Oft ic oþrum scod
frecne æt his freonde.   Fah eom ic wide,
wæpnum awyrged.   Ic me wenan ne þearf
þæt me bearn wræce   on bonan feore,
gif me gromra hwylc   guþe genægeð;
ne weorþeð sio mægburg   gemicledu
eaforan minum   þe ic æfter woc,
nymþe ic hlafordleas   hweorfan mote
from þam healdende   þe me hringas geaf.
Me bið forð witod,   gif ic frean hyre,
guþe fremme,   swa ic gien dyde
minum þeodne on þonc,   þæt ic þolian sceal
bearngestreona.   Ic wiþ bryde ne mot
hæmed habban,   ac me þæs hyhtplegan
geno wyrneð   se mec geara on

bende legde; forþon ic brucan sceal
on hagostealde hæleþa gestreona.
Oft ic wirum dol wife abelge,
wonie hyre willan; heo me wom spreceð,
floceð hyre folmum, firenaþ mec wordum,
ungod gæleð. Ic ne gyme þæs,
compes * * *

[I am a marvelous creature, shaped in battle, beloved to my lord, decorated beautifully. My mail coat is many-colored; likewise, bright wire rests around the slaughter gem that my lord gave me, he who at times guides me to battle in my wandering. Then I carry treasure through the bright day, the handiwork of smiths, gold over the plains. Often I kill soul bearers with war weapons. A king decks me out with treasure and silver and honors me in the hall; nor does he refuse a word of praise, but rather talks up my nature in front of the men where they drink mead. He holds me in confinement, yet at times allows me in my stir-crazy state to go again to battle. Often I fiercely harmed another by means of his ally. I am widely hated, accursed among weapons. There is no need for me to expect that a child will avenge me on my killer, if a fierce one assails me in battle. Nor will my kind from which I was born be increased by my offspring, unless I, lordless, should turn from that guardian who gave me rings. It is decreed for me, if I obey my lord and do battle, just as I still willingly did for my lord, that I must do without offspring. I am not permitted to have sexual intercourse, but he who previously placed bonds on me denies me that joyful play. Therefore, I must instead, in celibacy, take my pleasure in the treasures of men. Often I, foolish in my filigree, enrage a woman, diminish her desire. She speaks me ill, claps her hands together, reviles me with words, shouts curses. I do not care for *that* battle.]

Riddle 20 is probably a sword riddle, though it takes a sharp, unexpected turn toward its ending. In fact, some have felt that the riddle cannot be solved with a single solution. Paull F. Baum, for instance, asserts that "the piece is thus one half a transparent riddle and then a kind of heroic lay in the best tradition."[74] John Tanke argues that the riddle "is constructed in two

74. Baum, *Anglo-Saxon Riddles,* 42.

parts, each of which supports one solution and disallows the other. The unifying principle . . . lies on the subjective level: first as a sword and then as a phallus, the speaker represents himself throughout the poem as a bachelor-warrior."[75] Similarly, Edward B. Irving finds the "macho" speaker's voice so central to the riddle that "one good solution might be simply 'Testosterone.'"[76] There is no cause to wag a finger at Irving's facetious "solution," but I would continue to insist that it is best not to conflate a riddle's solution with its metaphorical focus. When Donald Kay proposes to solve Riddle 20 as "phallus," for instance, he is doing just that.[77] Like most, then, I accept Franz Dietrich's "sword" as answer enough for the full riddle. Those who cannot swallow the sword solution, however, have considered an alternative answer: "hawk." Possibly the most unusual approach to Riddle 20 was proposed by L. K. Shook, who attempted to unite both of these solutions through a rare kenning for the hawk, *heoruswealwe* 'sword swallow'. Through this compound, Shook was able to satisfy those clues that seemed in keeping with swords, as well as those clues that struck him as hawkish.[78]

But if Shook's solution has failed to catch on, his approach may have something to tell us about the way this riddle works. Shook's notion that a compound word may serve to solve a riddle, where its concrete referent in reality fails, anticipates John D. Niles's recent call for us to think of the Exeter riddles' solutions as words and not things. And in fact both Niles and Tanke independently offer the solution *wæpen,* a word that can mean both sword and penis in the Anglo-Saxon tongue.[79] This is certainly an apt solution, and one that I accept as the best proposed so far, but it seems to me

75. John W. Tanke, "The Bachelor-Warrior of Exeter Book Riddle 20," *Philological Quarterly* 79 (2000): 409.

76. Irving, "Heroic Experience," 206.

77. To make his case, Kay posits a number of unlikely readings (including *wælgim* 'slaughter gem' as a "death-orgasm archetype"). Donald Kay, "Riddle 20: A Revaluation," *Tennessee Studies in Literature* 13 (1968): 137.

78. Moritz Trautmann's alternative solution, "hawk," primarily aimed to address clues near the conclusion of the riddle (where a tercel's enforced chastity might be considered appropriate). L. K. Shook, in "*Heoruswealwe,*" attempted to revise Trautmann's solution by way of the hawk kenning *heoruswealwe* 'sword swallow', which allows for a double solution bound together by the elements of the compound: a description of a sword turns into a description of a hawk, and so the only way to answer the riddle is with this unique kenning. Williamson, *Old English Riddles,* 193, concludes that, as a hapax legomenon, *heoruswealwe* is an unlikely solution. Bitterli, *Say What I Am Called,* 19, 128–29, tentatively accepts "a falcon or a hawk" but does not provide a full reading of the riddle.

79. The importance of the two meanings of OE *wæpen* for Riddle 20 is first mentioned by Ruth Wehlau, *"Riddle of Creation,"* 112–13, who seems to credit Williamson with the idea. Williamson, however, never mentions the Old English word *wæpen* in his commentary, though

that past discussions of Riddle 20 have not recognized the way its local innuendo develops within the riddle's proposition. This sword riddle, in fact, has something in common with Riddle 63 (the cup riddle discussed above), where the metaphorical focus seems occasioned initially by the conceit of "kissing" the cup. Like Riddle 63, the innuendo of Riddle 20 can be thought of as proceeding coherently from a "straight" motif of the earlier section.

I contend that the innuendo of Riddle 20 tumbles out of a string of related paradoxes, beginning near the middle of the poem, and that these need some explication if we are to understand the poem's suggestive conclusion. Since these paradoxes are best read as a coherent sequence, each linked to the next, it is best to parse them in order. As I am mainly concerned with Riddle 20's handling of a localized metaphorical focus and how it develops, I will pass over the first half of the poem, noting only that the speaker describes himself in a heroic context, centered around service and the creature's reciprocal relationship with a generous lord. Like the *bord* of Riddle 5, which suffers endless blows with no hope of healing (see chapter 1), Riddle 20's speech grows paradoxical when incongruities arise in the comparison of a warrior to his gear. Here, however, the sword compares poorly with the warrior's ideal: "Oft ic oþrum scod / frecne æt his freonde. Fah eom ic wide, / wæpnum awyrged" (Often I fiercely harmed another by means of his ally. I am widely hated, accursed among weapons). The sword's indiscriminate potential for slaughter is considered paradox sufficient to form the core of some Latin sword enigmas, and there is little reason to doubt that this is the main import of these lines. For example, the opening paradox of Eusebius 36 (*De gladio* 'about the sword') reads:

> Sanguinis humani reus et ferus en ero uindex:
> Corpora nunc defendere nunc cruciare uicissim
> Curo;
>
> [Guilty of bloodshed, I will also be the fierce avenger: it is my business at times to defend bodies, at others to do them great injury][80]

he does provide an excellent analysis of the "two weapons in the last part of the poem" (194). Tanke, "Bachelor-Warrior," 413, independently notes the potential significance of OE *wæpen* in Riddle 20, as does Niles, *Old English Enigmatic Poems,* 137–39, who argues that the solution *wæpen,* with a pun on its two meanings as a sword and as phallus, provides a satisfying solution for Riddle 20.

80. Enigma 36, lines 1–3 (Glorie, *Variae collectiones aenigmatum,* 246; my translation).

In the heroic context, the sword's difficulty in making distinctions between enemies and allies is easily linked to the issue of revenge, which is brought up in the next few lines:

Ic me wenan ne þearf
þæt me bearn wræce on bonan feore,
gif me gromra hwylc guþe genægeð

[There is no need for me to expect that a child will avenge me on my killer, if a fierce one assails me in battle]

Such a paradox simply turns, once again, on the differences between a warrior and his sword, and it is best read as a rather straightforward bit of oppositional riddling (a warrior who can never be avenged, like the cut *bord* that can never be healed). The issue of offspring, however, introduces a further paradox, one that is often misread, in my opinion:

ne weorþeð sio mægburg gemicledu
eaforan minum þe ic æfter woc,
nymþe ic hlafordleas hweorfan mote
from þam healdende þe me hringas geaf.

[Nor will my kind from which I was born be increased by my offspring, unless I, lordless, should turn from that guardian who gave me rings.]

The next few lines reiterate this paradox, explaining that the speaker may not have children *gif ic frean hyre* 'if I obey my lord'. In the hawk reading, this and subsequent clues supposedly refer to the oddly literal "enforced celibacy" of a captive bird, but if the speaker is understood as a sword, the riddling implication is fairly clear: a sword can fail its lord either by refusing to bite, or by breaking into pieces.[81] Such pieces could be reforged into new

81. As is famously the case in Beowulf's battle with Grendel's mother: "seo ecg geswac / ðeodne æt þearfe" (the sword failed the lord in his time of need). Frederick Klaeber, ed., *Beowulf and the Fight at Finnsburg,* 3d ed. (Lexington, Mass.: D. C. Heath, 1950), lines 1524–25.

weapons.[82] Therefore the sword sires offspring only in death, as a bull-calf binds the living only in death: such paradoxes are a firmly attested aspect of Old English riddling and the genre at large. In my opinion, the reading is much more convincing than has generally been acknowledged.[83]

This strategy of paradoxical procreation, a typical riddling motif, provides a turn in the riddle, shifting focus from the difference between swords and warriors to the connections to be drawn between a *wæpen* 'sword' and a *wæpen* 'penis'. Such associations, of course, go well beyond the level of wordplay, and are well known in traditional sex riddling, as in the Holme riddle describing a maid with a thing "aboue my knee, long it is & deep it is, & in the midst a hole there is: for came a yong man & put in a thing two handfulls long." The solution is "a maid that hath a sheath, & a yong man put a knife into it."[84] That an Old English riddle develops a similar metaphor is not surprising. What is interesting to note, however, is how the introduction of explicit sexuality in Riddle 20 develops in a coherent progression out of the conceit of reforging as reproduction. Having riddled on its procreative limitations, the speaker turns to the pleasures he must therefore forgo:

Ic wiþ bryde ne mot
hæmed habban, ac me þæs hyhtplegan
geno wyrneð se mec geara on
bende legde;

82. Williamson adopts this reading from H. R. Ellis Davidson, *The Sword in Anglo-Saxon England* (Oxford: Clarendon Press, 1962), 153–54. Of course, since the speaker seems to be referring to the *mægburg* 'kin or kind' *from which* it sprang, we may not even need to introduce the notion of reforging to explain the paradox. The unmaking of the weapon gives birth to its raw material origins, in much the same way that ice gives birth to its mother, water, through the process of melting (as in Riddle 33). Still, in my opinion, the idea of reforging is probably at play here.

83. Attempts to undermine this reading include Tanke, "Bachelor-Warrior," who writes, "The problem here is that if a sword can beget 'children,' it can also hope—*unlike* the subject of Riddle 20—that a son might avenge its death" (412). This argument, it seems to me, misunderstands the way riddling language works: the logical implications of one paradox need not be squared with other aspects of the proposition. As Jember, "Generative Method," rightly remarks, "Separate clues . . . might not make sense cumulatively" (33). The sword, as a weapon and not a warrior, will never have its "death" avenged by a son. Also, the sword, as an inanimate object, only has offspring when it is unmade, "failing" its lord. The two riddling statements stand on their own or, better yet, create a sense of paradox in their clashing. Taylor, *Literary Riddle Before 1600,* explains that in riddling, "The first assertion and its denial are almost certain to conflict with the next pair" (3). What Tanke interprets as a problem is exactly what we should expect in a riddle.

84. The solution to this riddle is found in Tupper, "Holme Riddles," 236 (no. 130), where the indecent proposition has been tastefully omitted. The proposition, but not the full solution, can be found in Williams, *Dictionary of Sexual Language,* s.v. "knack."

> [I am not permitted to have sexual intercourse, but he who previously placed bonds on me still denies me that joyful play][85]

It is worth emphasizing that there is no "double solution" here. What is stated is quite literally true of the solution: an iron *wæpen* is forbidden sexual intercourse. But still the *selection* of this detail is not governed simply by its relationship to a solution. It arises from an underlying metaphorical focus, which might select differences as well as similarities for emphasis (just as we saw in chapter 1 that an egg has "no staves" on account of its comparison with a barrel).

The focus continues to be felt in the following lines, where the speaker concludes, "forþon ic brucan sceal / on hagostealde hæleþa gestreona" (Therefore, I must instead, in celibacy, take my pleasure in the treasures of men). The verb *brucan* 'to use, to enjoy', can also mean "to have sexual relations with,"[86] but again this is a statement of contrast, not "double entendre": the speaker *cannot* enjoy sexual intercourse; *therefore* he must take pleasure instead in the less carnal treasures of a sword's lavish trappings. Coupled with the references to celibacy (*hagosteald*), this assertion can be read as a "straight" clue but one that nevertheless plays on the kinds of pleasures a flesh-and-blood *wæpen* might enjoy.

Riddle 20's strange conclusion is therefore not explicable in terms of "two solutions," a situation that may have led to some critical confusion. In lines 32–33b a woman is abruptly introduced, who reacts with anger and aggression toward the speaker: "Oft ic wirum dol wife abelge, wonie hyre willan" (Often I, foolish in my filigree, enrage a woman, diminish her desire). The root sense of the verb *abelgan* is "to swell" or "to cause to swell," and its meaning here connotes a puffed-up sense of rage or anger.[87] The woman's displeasure, then, swells up in a way reminiscent of imagery we often encounter in the Old English sex riddles, with their emphasis on distended body parts. The creature's self-description as being "foolish in my filigree," also deserves a bit of discussion, if only for its peculiarity. The sword's decorative *wir* 'gold trappings, filigree' are mentioned early on in

85. For a much different interpretation of these lines, see Tanke, "Bachelor-Warrior," 414–17.

86. *Dictionary of Old English,* s.v. "brūcan," 2a.i. A particularly relevant example here is the first half of Antiochius's self-referential incest riddle in the Old English *Apollonius of Tyre:* "Scylde Ic þolige, moddrenum flæsce Ic bruce" (I suffer guilt, I enjoy the flesh of the mother). In Elaine Treharne, *Old and Middle English: An Anthology* (Oxford: Blackwell, 2000), 236.

87. *Dictionary of Old English,* s.v. "ābelgan."

the riddle, but here they are paired with the epithet *dol* 'foolish', which we might assume to be some kind of inexplicable criticism of the weapon's adornments. On the other hand, *dol* is a word used to describe the wanton leather worker of Riddle 12, and in this context, framed by an explicit discussion of *hæmed* 'sexual intercourse', it is no stretch to see the meaning of *dol* 'foolish' as connoting sexual folly.[88] And yet it is hard to force a "double meaning" on the golden *wir* of the creature in question—in fact, there does not even seem to be a *literal* explanation for this odd phrase.

Indeed, the strangeness of the phrase *wirum dol* is instructive in that it demonstrates the advantage of analyzing the sex riddles in terms of a shaping metaphorical focus. The pull of the localized focus influences the proposition, producing a semantic "slim chance": the idiosyncratic characterization of the creature as "foolish in my filigree" (might we even say, "filthy in my filigree"?). As this section closes, too, the focus continues to be felt—but with a twist. So, for instance, the speaker says of the angry woman, *wonie hyre willan* 'I diminish her desire'. The phrase reverses the expected, charged formula *worhte his willan* 'he exercised his desire', which shows up in two other Exeter sex riddles.[89] The verbs *wyrcan* 'to work, perform, produce' and *wanian* 'to diminish, decline, decay' are near opposites, and so the sword's poor reception from the enraged woman is defined in contrast to her potential erotic satisfaction from a phallus. One disturbing but clear implication of this manipulation of convention, it should be noted, is the suggested comparison of sexual penetration with the violence of a sword. Thankfully, though, this brutal brand of sex riddling does not emphasize similarities so much as it highlights differences through an inverted sexual idiom. The remaining description of the woman's rage may be read as continuing this riddling strategy. The woman "me wom spreceð, / floceð hyre folmum, firenaþ mec wordum, / ungod gæleð" (speaks me ill, claps her hands together, reviles me with words, shouts curses). Our understanding of the verb *flōcan* depends on its being glossed once elsewhere with *complodere* 'to strike or clap (the hands) together (as a sign of various emotions)'.[90] What particular emotions in Riddle 20 are being expressed? Critics have offered several guesses, but however we interpret the literal gesture, emphasis on a woman's hands are a staple of Old English sex riddling. It is hard to discount an allusion here to the *hygegalan hond* 'wanton hand' so common in these texts

88. See also my discussion of Riddle 4 in chapter 1.

89. Riddle 54 (churn), line 6a; Riddle 63 (cup), line 7a.

90. *Dictionary of Old English,* s.v. "flōcan"; *Oxford Latin Dictionary,* s.v. "complodere."

and not always known for its gentle touch.[91] There is no "double solution" to this sword riddle, then, but an underlying focus most certainly shapes this section.

But, again, *why* is the woman is so upset? Advocates of a hawk solution have imagined intriguing backstories to explain her wrath. Shook claims that "there seems to be a personal reference: some friend of the king, possibly the poet himself, perhaps even several of the king's friends, have been injured by this particular *wiht* which seems to be no respecter of persons."[92] Edward B. Irving agrees that "it seems very much an inside story."[93] Among advocates of the sword solution, too, there are many who invent motivations for the woman with no basis in the text. More than one critic imagines her as a "scold, who insults, chides, and speaks evil to the celibate sword for his avoidance of women," while the sword is imagined as something of a lout, "shrugging off her usual complaints."[94] Another sees her as "resentful at her husband's lack of attention."[95] Raising the stakes, another argues that "the woman at the end of Riddle 20 is accusing the speaker of a sexual crime."[96] Citing many of these examples, Melanie Heyworth worries that "none of these interpretations is particularly complimentary to the distressed wife, nor are they supported by the text itself." Heyworth, however, offers her own backstory: "A more satisfactory reading is that the sword is self-condemnatory because he has diminished the wife's joy—her marriage—presumably by killing her husband."[97] Heyworth's guess is as satisfactory as any tale we might imagine, but the darkness of riddling is not best explained by storytelling of this kind. The rage of the woman in Riddle 20 could be explained by any number of unfortunate incidents: swords can slaughter enemies and friends, husbands and wives, children as well as kings. Perhaps the sword has slaughtered the hawk? The riddling point, however, is simply that one kind of *wæpen* causes pleasure, another causes pain. One can be conventionally desired, the other painfully reviled. Whatever its imagined literal cause, the displeasure the woman takes in the solution (a sword) is described in terms that echo the pleasures of the riddle's phallic focus.

91. For a discussion of the emphasis on hands in the obscene riddles, see Glenn Davis, "The Exeter Book Riddles and the Place of Sexual Idiom in Old English Literature," in *Medieval Obscenities,* ed. Nicola McDonald (York: York Medieval Press, 2006), 39–54.

92. Shook, "*Heoruswealwe,*" 199.

93. Irving, "Heroic Experience," 206.

94. Rulon-Miller, "Sexual Humor," 109; Tigges, "Snakes and Ladders," 102.

95. Crossley-Holland, *Exeter Book Riddles,* 93.

96. Tanke, "Bachelor-Warrior," 419.

97. Heyworth, "Perceptions of Marriage," 176.

I have argued that in Riddle 20 a localized sexual focus develops from a motif of reproduction (a sword "siring" its reforged offspring) that would not necessarily be suggestive, in itself, of sex. Scores of such "riddles of reproduction" might be cited from popular tradition, whether a tree mothering her leaves (which die of old age while she lives on) or a bread shovel begetting "smooth children." It would be a stretch to call such texts sex riddles: the emphasis is clearly on generation and not fornication. And yet this is how some Exeter riddles choose to treat these stock riddling motifs: as foreplay to a decidedly more graphic form of charged riddling. In fact, the Old English sex riddles are notable not only for the way they artfully extend sexually charged images from oral tradition but also for the way they adapt less suggestive materials to their purpose. Riddle 37 is another example of this, and one that again demonstrates the importance of unriddling these texts in relation to riddling traditions and not simply in accordance with modern wit. The full riddle reads:

> Ic þa wihte geseah— womb wæs on hindan
> þriþum aþrunten. Þegn folgade,
> mægenrofa man, ond micel hæfde gefered
> þær þæt hit felde fleah þurh his eage.
> Ne swylteð he symle þonne syllan sceal
> innað þam oþrum, ac him eft cymeð
> bot in bosme; blæd biþ aræred.
> He sunu wyrceð; bið him sylfa fæder.

> [I saw that creature—its belly was in behind—greatly swollen. A servant followed, a very strong fellow, and he had quite an experience when that which filled it flew through its eye. Nor does he ever die when he has to empty his filling for the other, but a restoration comes back into his bosom; glory (or breath) is raised up. It makes a son; it is its own father.]

The preferred solution for Riddle 37 has been "bellows" ever since it was first proposed by Dietrich.[98] Recently, John D. Niles has advocated answering Riddle 37 in Old English as *blæst-belg* 'windbag or bellows', but we might also consider *blæd-belg* 'windbag or bellows' for the satisfaction of

98. "Der *schmiedebalg*." Dietrich, "Räthsel des Exeterbuchs: Verfasser," 238.

bringing out a pun in line 7b: *blæd biþ aræred* 'glory (or wind) is raised up'.[99] The general focus here on wind (*blæd*) rather than fire (*blæst*) makes this especially attractive. Of course, *blæst-belg* is a much better attested word than *blædbelg,* as is, more simply, *belg* 'bellows'.[100] All of these Old English words tend to bring to the fore a connection between the swollen *womb* 'belly' of this creature and Old English *belgan* 'to swell', as well as the Latin *uter* or *uterus* 'belly, womb, bellows'.[101] In any case, a bellows solution is all the more likely since the middle portion of the poem matches up very closely with a bellows enigma of Symphosius, as Dietrich notes. Symphosius's Enigma 73 reads:

> Non ego continuo morior, dum spiritus exit;
> Nam redit adsidue, quamvis et saepe recedit:
> Et mihi nunc magna est animae, nuc nulla facultas.
>
> [I do not straightaway die while breath departs; for repeatedly it returns, though often too departs again: and now my store of vital breath is great, now none.][102]

In addition, no discussion of Riddle 37 may proceed without reference to the very similar Riddle 87 (confidently solved "bellows" as well, largely owing to its parallels with Riddle 37):

> Ic seah wundorlice wiht;   wombe hæfde micle,
> þryþum geþrungne.   Þegn folgade,
> mægenstrong ond mundrof;   micel me þuhte
> godlic gumrinc;   grap on sona,
> heofones toþe   * * *
> bleowe on eage;   hio borcade,
> wancode willum.   Hio wolde seþeah
> niol [...............]

99. Niles, *Old English Enigmatic Poems,* 112. See also David Hill, "Anglo-Saxon Mechanics: 1. blæstbel(i)g—The Bellows," *Medieval Life* 13 (2000): 9–13.

100. *Dictionary of Old English,* s.vv. "blǣdbelg," "blǣstbelg," "belg, bylg."

101. As well as the later development of *belg* 'pouch, sack, bellows' down to our modern "belly." We seem to be dealing with a rather overdetermined set of images.

102. Ohl, *Enigmas of Symphosius,* 104–5.

[I saw an amazing creature; it had a mighty belly, greatly swollen. A servant followed, a powerful one with strong hands; he seemed to me a fine stout man. Straightaway he gripped it, . . . with the tooth of heaven . . . it would blow in its eye; it yelped, shook willingly. It nevertheless wished underneath . . .]

Riddle 87 is fragmentary, and the problematical verbs *borcade* (or *boncade*?) and *wancade* make its ending particularly mystifying.[103] It goes without saying, though, that its opening is clearly related to Riddle 37, though positing one as the source of the other would be dangerous. Riddle 87 tends to be thought of as the "straight" bellows riddle, but it is probably better to say that its innuendo is more localized than that of Riddle 37.[104] At any rate, the *heofones toþe* 'tooth of heaven' introduced in the second half of Riddle 87 seems empty of innuendo. Apparently, this is a kenning for wind, as Tupper explains with reference to other instances of the "biting wind" mentioned in Latin analogues.[105] To be sure, it would be difficult to attribute an erotic sense to this half-line, and in the next line the verb *bleowe* 'it would blow' encourages the reader to keep an eye on the literal wind alone. By contrast, Riddle 37 keeps the eye's ejaculate suggestively ambiguous: "þær þæt hit felde fleah þurh his eage" (when that which filled it flew through its eye). Somewhat unexpectedly, Riddle 37 develops this suggestiveness through the conversion of a motif clearly indebted to Symphosius, as mentioned above:

Ne swylteð he symle   þonne syllan sceal
innað þam oþrum,   ac him eft cymeð
bot in bosme;   blæd biþ aræred.

[Nor does he ever die when he must release his filling into the other, but a restoration comes back into his bosom; glory (or breath) is raised up.]

Within this erotic context, the Symphosian paradox of reinspiration is converted to an endless cycle of sexual appetite and release. Desire never

103. For more on these verbs, see Williamson, *Old English Riddles,* 379–80; Tupper, *Riddles of the Exeter Book,* 227; *Dictionary of Old English,* s.v. "*boncian, *borcian."

104. Williamson refers to it as "a plain *bellows* riddle" in comparison to "its bawdier cousin." *Feast of Creatures,* 214.

105. Tupper, *Riddles of the Exeter Book,* 227.

dies and, once again, a man is subservient to his own tool. It is notable that those Exeter riddles that depict awkward, undignified manual labor—be it churning butter, plowing fields, or pumping bellows—are often the same texts that betray a sexual edge. It is very neat, the way this works. The convention of Old English riddling is to animate inanimate objects of all kinds—to imagine the stoic endurance of a shield or the graceful flight of a feather pen—but in sex riddles this translates into a sense of anatomical autonomy as the implied sex organ works its own will. Body parts take on a will all their own. Herein lies much of the humor of these texts, and the best reason why they should probably not be labeled "obscene." These riddles deflate the puffed-up *blæd* ('glory' or 'wind') of sexual pride and emphasize the ridiculous, awkward, and even slavish position of men and women who serve their own implements. At the same time, it goes without saying, the sex riddles might also arouse other feelings. Charged texts of this kind might easily inspire a contradictory and complex response.

They also can have complex roots. The Old English enigmas often astonish in the way they fuse and rework their materials, so we should not be surprised if the solving of these poems trips up the wit of modern solvers. The last line of Riddle 37 is a case in point: "He sunu wyrceð; bið him sylfa fæder" (It makes a son; it is its own father). This clipped, capping paradox comes without much context, but Williamson unriddles it by extending the implications of the rest of the riddle: "The bellows creates wind; wind in turn 'recreates' (sustains, lends substance to) the bellows."[106] The advantage of this interpretation is that it flows out of the previous lines involving the Symphosian conceit of the "reinspiration" of the bellows (though not without straining). David Hill has a different take, however: "The last line alludes to the creation of new tools in the forge and to the fact that the bellows themselves have been made by use of tools forged by the smith with the aid of bellows."[107] Hill's solution seems just as plausible as Williamson's, and indeed recalls the sword siring of Riddle 20. So how should we choose between them?

In fact, the much more likely reading is that the final line refers not to wind or tools but to the most immediate offspring of a bellows: fire and smoke. I offer this not as an intuitive guess but as a conclusion grounded in riddling precedent. Indeed, there exists a rather strong and long-standing

106. Williamson, *Old English Riddles,* 254. Williamson's guess has often been adopted by later critics. See, for instance, Wehlau, *"Riddle of Creation,"* 116.

107. Hill, "Anglo-Saxon Mechanics," 9–10.

strand of riddling wherein smoke is said to sire fire (in the sense of coming beforehand in the act of kindling), and fire to sire smoke (in the obvious causal sense). What is more, the smoke-and-fire paradox is consistently gendered male, just as the very similar riddle on ice and water (discussed in the Introduction) quite regularly refers to a mother and daughter.[108] For instance, a medieval riddle reads: "The son is caught above the house in which the father is born—Smoke leaps upward before a good fire burns."[109] Taylor lists many variations of this pattern in a range of European languages.[110] The pattern, indeed, was known to an Anglo-Saxon audience also through Symphosius's smoke (*fumus*) enigma: "Et qui me genuit sine me non nascitur ipse" (and he who gave me birth without me is not born himself).[111] The capping paradox of Riddle 37, then, conforms nicely to riddling conventions in the gender of the smoke and fire, the wording of the paradox, and the larger context of the poem.

Needless to say, the siring of fire need be no more sexualized than the birth of water from ice or any other riddling trope where generation is equated with procreation. It is a striking choice, then, to fuse this traditional conceit of paradoxical offspring to the charged images of Riddle 37's swollen innuendo. And this deft recontextualization of the fire-and-smoke riddle is certainly not unique within the Exeter collection. As we have seen, Riddle 54 may be up to something quite similar, while other, rather innocent Latin motifs of binding bull-calves are transformed in the context of Riddle 12's dark imagery. On the other hand, innuendo in the Exeter riddles is often momentary and localized, as a suggestive image drifts into focus. The taboo image appears to be always, potentially, just on the tip of the riddler's tongue: a constant concern, even where no "double solution" could possibly be defended. In that sense, the sex riddles are really no different from many other riddles of the Exeter Book, for they display a dynamic of proposition, solution, and metaphorical focus that represents something much more than an offbeat corner of Old English poetry. No, these curious texts stand at the center of the Exeter collection.

108. Taylor remarks that "the references to father and son usually concern fire and smoke, and those to mother and daughter usually concern ice and water." *English Riddles from Oral Tradition,* 373.

109. Peachy, *Clareti Enigmata,* no. 110.

110. Taylor, *English Riddles from Oral Tradition,* 373–75.

111. Ohl, *Enigmas of Symphosius,* 40–41 (no. 7).

6

THE ROOTS OF RIDDLE 25

We have grown used to reading the sex riddles both as a special case in Old English studies and as an oddball exception to the enigmatic poems of the Exeter Book. But part of my argument throughout this study has been that this suggestive subgenre offers, on the contrary, a central clue to the way so many of the other Exeter riddles work: not as bland challenges of inductive reasoning but rather as artful variations on a traditional riddling structure of proposition, solution, and metaphorical focus. All of the Exeter riddles, of course, are not best read in this way, but it may be surprising to find that "double meanings" inform so many texts that show no sign of sex. In this final chapter, though, I hope to propose one last eye-opener with respect to the Exeter sex riddles. It may be that those Old English riddles that seem best suited to a standard, straightforward model of "double meaning and coarse suggestion" have in fact some of the most complex roots in the collection.[1] Readings in the previous chapter confirm this claim, but Riddle 25 is perhaps one of the most interesting cases:

> Ic eom wunderlicu wiht,   wifum on hyhte,
> neahbuendum nyt.   Nængum sceþþe

1. Tupper, *Riddles of the Exeter Book,* xxv.

burgsittendra nymþe bonan anum.
Staþol min is steapheah; stonde ic on bedde,
neoþan ruh nathwær. Neþeð hwilum
ful cyrtenu ceorles dohtor,
modwlonc meowle, þæt heo on mec gripeð,
ræseð mec on reodne, reafað min heafod,
fegeð mec on fæsten. Feleð sona
mines gemotes se þe mec nearwað,
wif wundenlocc— wæt bið þæt eage.[2]

[I am a marvelous creature, a joy to the ladies, a handy thing for neighbors. I harm no citizens save my slayer alone. My trunk is lofty; I stand up in bed. Down below there's hair—I can't say where. Once in a while, some man's very toothsome daughter, a haughty maid, plucks up her courage and takes me in her hand. She pounces on poor reddish me, seizes my head, and tucks me into a tight spot. Lickety-split, she'll feel the full force of my contact, the one who confines me, a woman with braided hair. That eye will be wet.]

This poem is no poser: it smells of onions, whether we give an answer of *cipe* or *ynneleac* (two words for onion in the Anglo-Saxon tongue). And no doubt "the obscene implication is obvious," as Tupper would say.[3] But although it is in some respects an obvious text, Riddle 25 is nevertheless well loved and often anthologized, a model example, for many critics, of the "balancing act" we expect from the sex riddles. John W. Tanke is not alone in viewing Riddle 25 as a "classic double-entendre riddle" in which every detail "points simultaneously to two possible solutions—onion and penis."[4] Such balanced duplicity, moreover, suggests a neat division between a knowing riddler and an unknowing solver—some poor dupe dwelling in the dark. As Stewart explains, "The riddler carefully feeds his listener details that clearly point to a sexual referent. At the same time, with the same details, he is describing some harmless non-sexual referent which, much to the decipherer's embarrassment, turns out to be the 'real' solution."[5]

2. The text here is from Williamson's edition, with the exception that I retain the MS reading *se þe* rather than the emendation *seo þe*. I discuss this decision below.

3. Tupper, *Riddles of the Exeter Book,* 126.

4. Tanke, "*Wonfeax wale,*" 31.

5. Stewart, "Double Entendre," 39.

It is certainly harmless to imagine such a naïve solver—the text itself invites the knowing reader to at once dream up and scoff at a straw man along these lines. I would argue, however, that a more useful solver to imagine for Riddle 25 is one much more sophisticated and aware of riddling traditions. It is true that this text is remarkably coherent both as a description of onion plucking and penis fondling, but to think in terms of a "balancing act" may be to miss the remarkably aggregate quality of this text. Far from a simple joke, in fact, Riddle 25 is a highly allusive poem that seems to place trust in the reader's sage knowledge of riddling conventions and conceits—both literary and from oral tradition.

It would certainly take a sharp eye to pick out the allusion in lines 2b–3 to a paradox plucked from a Latin riddle by Symphosius: "Nængum sceþþe / burgsittendra nymþe bonan anum" (I harm no citizens save my slayer alone). As many have noted, this line really only makes sense in reference to Symphosius's Enigma 44 (solved *cepa* 'onion'):

> Mordeo mordentes, ultro non mordeo quemquam;
> Sed sunt mordentem multi mordere parati.
> Nemo timet morsum, dentes quia non habet ullos.

> [I bite the biters, of my own accord I bite no one; but many are ready to bite me even though I bite. No one fears my bite, for teeth it has none.][6]

The motif of the "bitten biter" is generalized in Riddle 25, but the underlying idea of the onion's mordant revenge is recognizable, all the more so because another Exeter Book text, Riddle 65, also draws on the Symphosian conceit:

> Cwico wæs ic—ne cwæð ic wiht; cwele ic efne seþeah.
> Ær ic wæs—eft ic cwom; æghwa mec reafað,
> hafað mec on headre, on min heafod scireþ,
> biteð mec on bær lic, briceð mine wisan.
> Monnan ic ne bite nympþe he me bite:
> sindan þara monige þe mec bitað.

6. Ohl, *Enigmas of Symphosius,* 76–77.

[I was alive—I said nothing; even so, I die. I was before—I came back again; everyone plunders me, holds me in confinement, cuts into my head, bites me on my bare body, breaks my stalk. I do not bite anyone unless he bites me: many there are who bite me.]

Both Riddle 65 and Riddle 25 probably derive directly or indirectly from Symphosius, though the chain of influence is murky. Both texts also elaborate on the basic Symphosian conceit of a bitten biter by enumerating a series of additional tortures. The onion of Riddle 25 complains that a woman *reafað min heafod* 'plunders my head', while everyone *reafað* 'plunders' the speaker of Riddle 65 and *scireþ* 'cuts' its head. Each speaker suffers confinement. And in both texts these tortures are enumerated in a distinct section: a rapid-fire listing off of sufferings strongly reminiscent of patterns we see elsewhere in oral traditional riddles, especially those that Archer Taylor classifies under the heading "a series of tortures."[7] This pattern is not prominent in Anglo-Latin enigmatography, but it shows up again and again in the Exeter Book, where innumerable suffering riddle creatures endure the process of manufacture from raw material to useful product. Examples abound, none more famous than Riddle 25's manuscript neighbor, Riddle 26—the painful story of a calf skinned, stretched, and scraped into vellum. The two Old English onion riddles, then, can be read as related adaptations of a Symphosian theme to a new context: the traditional riddle of torture.

However, as Andy Orchard writes, Riddle 25 is plainly distinct from Riddle 65 in that it "appears to have developed considerably the onion's complaints of its treatment, all the while giving its moaning a sexual spin."[8] But Riddle 25 is not *only* a sexualized and fleshed-out version of Riddle 65. Rather, Riddle 25 uses the "bitten biter" as a shaping conceit for a fully articulated narrative of sexual tit for tat, as the plucky and toothsome daughter seems to suffer a fitting comeuppance at riddle's end. Moreover, and most significantly, Riddle 25 does not simply offer the knowing solver a series of double meanings to decipher. Instead, this onion riddle is layered with allusions to a common currency of traditional innuendo that the knowing solver is probably meant to recognize. The reference to a bitten biter is only darkly evident in Riddle 25, but the poem seems to anticipate an audience that might well discern its upshot. As I hope to show in the following discussion, this buried Latin motif is joined by many other secrets.

7. Taylor, *English Riddles from Oral Tradition,* 240–53 (nos. 674–80).

8. Orchard, "Enigma Variations," 296.

But let us return to the riddle itself. Following its generalized Symphosian opening, the middle section of Riddle 25 introduces a more particular conflict between the speaker and an aggressive woman:

> Staþol min is steapheah; stonde ic on bedde
> neoþan ruh nathwær. Neþeð hwilum
> ful cyrtenu ceorles dohtor,
> modwlonc meowle, þæt heo on mec gripeð,
> ræseð mec on reodne, reafað min heafod,
> fegeð mec on fæsten.
>
> [My trunk is lofty; I stand up in bed. Down below there's hair—I can't say where. Once in a while, some man's very pretty daughter, a haughty maid, plucks up her courage and takes me in her hand. She pounces on poor reddish me, seizes my head, and tucks me into a tight spot.]

The language of this section is clearly charged. Notice, for instance, the prominent pun in line 4b on *bedd* in its various senses of "garden plot" and "a place or piece of furniture on which sexual activity takes place." Such a pun would be as active in Old English as it is in modern English translations.[9] And the word is indeed a loaded one, forming the base of euphemisms such as *gebeddscipe* '(carnal) intercourse' and *beddgemana* '(carnal) intercourse'.[10] The creature's *heafod* 'head' continues the wordplay. In the case of the onion and other plants with a bulbous root, the "head" usually designates the buried globular root rather than the leafy stalk above.[11] This could be the sense in Riddle 25, for it is the buried bulb of the onion plant that would be harvested. In Old English, the top of a *heafdehtes porres* 'a head-having leek' is mentioned in a remedy for bellyache, while the term *leaces heafod* 'head of a plant' glosses the Latin word *cartilago* 'the tough, fleshy substance of a

9. See *Dictionary of Old English,* s.v. "bedd," 2.

10. See Julie Coleman, "Sexual Euphemism in Old English," *Neuphilologische Mitteilungen* 93 (1992): 93, 96.

11. See the Welsh-Gypsy riddle, for example: "Q. What grows head down and feet up? *A.* An onion." Robert Petsch, "Fifty Welsh-Gypsy Folk-Riddles," *Journal of the Gypsy Lore Society,* n.s., 5 (1911–12), no. 20. Chaucer's Reeve says of lecherous old men, "For in oure wyl ther stiketh evere a nayl, / To have an hoor heed and a grene tayl, / As hath a leek; for thogh oure myght be goon, / Oure wyl desireth folie evere in oon." *Reeve's Prologue,* 3877–80.

plant'.[12] Heads also pop up in many a sex riddle, including Exeter Riddle 61, in which the speaker tells how a lord "me on hreþre heafod sticade" (stuck his head into my breast). Indeed, the words employed in Riddle 25 are frequently hair-triggered for innuendo. The suggestive onion "stands up" in bed, and is hairy below *nathwær* 'I know not where'—a compound common to the sex riddles and reminiscent of the comic uncertainty of Alisoun's *berd* in the *Miller's Tale*. Much of the humor in Riddle 25 comes from a phallic speaker who portrays himself as a passive victim of an eager woman, one who *ræseð mec on reodne* 'attacks me who am red', a rather tortuous expression that blurs the causal relationship between the creature's blushing redness and the woman's aggressive fondling.

Often in the reading of such Anglo-Saxon sex riddles, a mischievous riddler is imagined as "juggling two different referents, sustaining a description," but such incidents in Riddle 25 are best conceived of not so much in terms of an inventive juggling act but rather as an artful joining of traditional elements.[13] In fact, this middle layer of Riddle 25 may be read as a discrete riddle embedded in the text. There is a long record of later analogues for this section, dating back at least to the eclectic riddle books of the early modern period. These riddles parallel the middle section of Riddle 25 with remarkable precision. The 1629 *Booke of Meery Riddles,* for instance, includes a riddle solved "eglantine berry": "What is that that is rough within & red without, and bristled like a bares snout: there is never a Lady in this land, but will be content to take it in her hand."[14] Here we have the woman's desire to grasp the object in her hand, as well as the redness and roughness found in Riddle 25. This strawberry riddle from an eighteenth-century collection also bears a close resemblance:

> Pleasant growing in a Bed,
> With complection white and Red:
> The fairest Lady in the Land
> Desires to have it in her hand.[15]

12. Oswald Cockayne, ed., *Leechdoms, Wortcunning, and Starcraft of Early England,* 3 vols. (London, 1864–66), 2:230; Bosworth and Toller, *Anglo-Saxon Dictionary,* s.v. "leac."

13. Stewart, "Double Entendre," 40.

14. *Booke of Meery Riddles,* no. 6.

15. *Delights for young Men and Maids,* no. 7. Another early modern riddle book, the *New Booke of Merry Riddles,* includes a strawberry riddle identical to this, aside from the final line, which reads "Desires to have'um at Command." Yet another strawberry riddle, this collected from oral tradition, reads: "First white, then red, / There isn't a lady in the land, / Who

In this example we find a pun on *bed* similar to Riddle 25's *bedd,* as well as the creature's redness and the lady's desire to hold it in her hand. These are close analogues, and there are others. Examples collected in the twentieth century from oral tradition include this carrot riddle:

> Stiff standing on the bed,
> First it's white, an' then it's red.
> There's not a lady in the land,
> That would not take it in her hand.[16]

Here we have something remarkable, I think. The opening line of this riddle is virtually identical in diction and conceit to Riddle 25's line 4b, *stonde ic on bedde* 'I stand up in bed'. It appears, too, in a context that parallels the riddling situation of Riddle 25 with uncanny precision: a woman grasping a reddish, phallic vegetable that stands in the bed. This pattern seems to be one of the oldest jokes in the book and is found in many other related oral riddles. Another carrot riddle reads: "What lies in bed, and stands in bed, / First white and then red, / The thicker it gets the old woman likes it better?"[17] An even more explicit version reads:

> Stiff standing in the bed,
> Sometimes white and sometimes red;
> Every lady in the land,
> Takes it in her hand,
> And puts it in the hole before.

The answer provided ("radish") includes this explanation: "The 'hole before' is the mouth."[18] A very similar radish riddle is found among the mid-seventeenth-century Holme Riddles: "in a bed . . . stife stand: first white then red & the fairest La[dy] in this land will take it in her lilly whit hand

wouldn't take it in her hand." Hyatt, *Folk-lore from Adams County,* 668. In an offhand footnote, Barley remarks, "I have recently come across a modern parallel to this sort of riddle in the form: 'What's long and thin / And covered in skin / Red in parts / Shoved in tarts? / Answer: "Rhubarb.'" "Structural Aspects," 161. Barley offers no source for this analogue.

16. Elsie Clews Parsons, *Folk-lore of the Antilles, French and English* (New York: American Folk-lore Society, 1943), 446.

17. S. Rosamond Praeger, "Rimes and Riddles from County Down," *Béaloideas: The Journal of the Folklore of Ireland Society* 8 (1938): 171.

18. Hyatt, *Folk-lore from Adams County,* 665.

and put it in the hole before."[19] The apparent comparison of the woman's mouth to her vagina is yet another link to Riddle 25, and among these carrots, radishes, and berries, there are also onions. For instance, a Jamaican onion riddle goes, "Green as grass, not grass; stiff standing in the bed; and the best young lady is not afraid of handling it."[20] The young lady's fearless handling of the onion lines up with the boldness of the woman in Riddle 25 who *neþeð* 'dares to' grasp the creature. Another riddle, this one in Welsh on the subject of a leek, also emphasizes a lady's desire for thick produce:

> Mewn gwely 'rwyf yn cysgu,
> Fy mlaen sydd wedi ei gladdu;
> A pha frasaf byddaf fi,
> Gore i gyd i wraig y ty.
>
> [In a bed I sleep, / My end has been buried; / The fatter I am, / The better for the housewife.][21]

As these examples illustrate, emphasis in such riddles often falls on the desire the woman feels to hold the produce in her hand. This squares well with Riddle 25, and several other Exeter sex riddles involve similar vignettes of women grasping dough or leather with a *hygegalan hond* 'wanton hand'.[22] It is notable, however, that of these only Riddle 25 refers explicitly to the creature as *wifum on hyhte* 'a joy to women' or some rough equivalent. This is particularly interesting because, in sex riddles in the English tradition, explicit statements of a woman's desire for an eroticized object seem to occur almost exclusively in riddles about vegetables or fruits.[23] While (as we have seen) examples are readily available of phallic churn dashes, keys, ink pens,

19. This similar strawberry riddle is also found in the Holme collection: "first white then red; the fairest lady in the land, may be seen to take it in her hand, & put it in her hole before." These are among the riddles "dismissed in disgrace" from Frederick Tupper Jr.'s edition of the Holme collection, "Holme Riddles," 216. I am therefore able to quote them only from their appearance in Williams, *Dictionary of Sexual Language,* s.vv. "berry" and "radish."

20. Martha Warren Beckwith, *Jamaica Anansi Stories* (New York: American Folk-Lore Society, 1924), 202 (no. 173). Beckwith notes in her introduction that riddles from this collection seem to owe a strong debt to "old English folk riddling" in both traditional formulas and motifs (xii).

21. Hull and Taylor, *Collection of Welsh Riddles,* no. 117.

22. Riddle 12, line 12.

23. The one exception I am able to cite comes as the opening line to a rather polished early modern riddle about a rolling pin: "What's that in which good Houswifes take delight." *Ben Johnson's last legacy,* 20.

horsewhips, wagon poles, and even pigs' snouts (the list goes on), I am hard pressed to find any of these referring directly to the woman's *desire for* the phallic object. All that do so inevitably seem to deal with vegetables or fruits, and these tend to be remarkably similar to Riddle 25. What this suggests is that a seemingly throwaway epithet such as *wifum on hyhte* may be much more resonant than we suppose. Rather than a mere vague, salacious bit of suggestiveness, such a detail may bring to mind a very specific riddling idea associated with the perceived erotic potential of a common domestic task.

These analogues suggest that the middle section of Riddle 25 is working with a set of closely associated riddling conceits that may have been well known in Anglo-Saxon oral tradition. While there is no way to prove this idea, it seems to be the simplest explanation for the available evidence. In his edition, Tupper cites another analogue to Riddle 25, a long onion riddle appearing in the *Royal Riddle-Book,* a collection published in 1820:

> In the bed it stands, in the bed it lies,
> Its lofty neb looks to the skies:
> The bigger it is the good wife loves t'better,
> She pluckt it and suckt it, till her eyes did water.
> She took it into her hand, and said it was good.
> Put it in her belly and stirred up her blood.[24]

Tupper says of this analogue that it "reads like a literal translation of the Anglo-Saxon."[25] It is reasonable to guess that this example from the *Royal Riddle-Book* is essentially an orally derived riddle put together from materials culled from the same enduring tradition that informed Riddle 25 nearly a thousand years earlier. The evidence in this case argues strongly against Williamson's position that later analogues have nothing useful to say about Old English riddling. At the very least, awareness of these roots complicates the vision of a duped solver and the text's obvious duplicity. And in fact I am inclined to think that a knowing solver might pick out these layers of allusion, while also relishing the tidy way in which the composite text hangs together.

Another visible layer might be the dry wit of the riddle's conclusion: *wæt bið þæt eage* 'that eye will be wet', a salty, deadpan deictic, and one that points

24. The riddle is also included in Mark Bryant's anthology, *Riddles: Ancient and Modern* (New York: Peter Bedrick Books, 1984), no. 604.

25. Tupper, *Riddles of the Exeter Book,* 123.

in many directions at once. In the context of the riddle's narrative, the eye in question may be one moistened by tears of regret or repentance from the plucky young lady. Or it may be "that eye" that is irritated by onion fumes. Or it may be the lady's "nether eye," her vagina. We might even consider it the "eye" of the penis, as some have seen it.[26] Traditional sex riddles, however, tend to look at wet eyes in a particular way. For instance, Taylor records one suggestive eye riddle as asking, "Hairy on top, an' hairy below, with a round thing in the middle. What is that?"[27] Another describes "A little, long thing, with hair all around it, / Sorta red on the inside, an' water comes outa it."[28] These motifs are old and persistent over time.[29] Other examples mention a "slit in the middle," and, despite my skepticism about giving a name to what sex riddles suggest, in most cases the eye is a vagina. Here, then, is perhaps another embedded riddle to be peeled back from Riddle 25—one more allusive layer for a riddler to relish. As an early modern riddle asks, what is "the eye that weeps most when most it is pleas'd?"[30]

Analogues may sharpen this image of an eye, but do they reveal anything wholly unexpected in this text? After all, we need no special confirmation that this is one dirty riddle. In fact, attention to this kind of evidence does open up at least one entirely new possibility for interpretation. What I have in mind is an alternative view of the riddle's penultimate event: the woman's dawning recognition of the nature of the object she has just received into her body: "Feleð sona / Mines gemotes se þe mec nearwað, / Wif wundenlocc" (Straightaway, she feels the full force of my contact, the one who confines me, a woman with braided hair). The significance of the *wif wundenlocc* 'woman with braided hair' has occasioned quite a bit of discussion, primarily because the epithet *wundenlocc* is used twice elsewhere to describe another head-robbing heroine, the title character of *Judith*.[31] It is also used to describe

26. Rulon-Miller, "Sexual Humor," 111.

27. Parsons, *Folk-lore of the Antilles,* 446.

28. Ralph Steele Boggs, "North Carolina White Folktales and Riddles," *Journal of American Folklore* 47 (1934), no. 14.

29. See, for example, Peachy, *Clareti Enigmata,* nos. 82 and 22, and the Holme Riddle cited in Williams, *Dictionary of Sexual Language,* s.v. "flap," which is solved "a woman wth a mote in her eye & the man licked it out wth his tonge." Taylor, *English Riddles from Oral Tradition,* nos. 1425–28, classifies such riddles under their own distinct category (though he does not acknowledge their erotic suggestion).

30. Cited in Williams, *Dictionary of Sexual Language,* s.v. "eye."

31. B. J. Timmer, ed., *Judith* (Exeter: University of Exeter Press, 1978), lines 77, 103. Indeed, the epithet appears in the very act of beheading Holofernes, lines 103b–106a: "Sloh ða wundenlocc / þone feondsceaðan fagum mece / heteþoncolne, þæt heo healfne forcearf / þone sweoran him" (The one with braided-hair slew the hostile ravager then with the bright sword, that hostile one, so that she cut through half his neck).

her kin, the Hebrew people, who are said to be *wlanc wundenlocc* 'proud with braided hair', an association that reminds us of the *modwlonc meowle* 'proud/haughty maid' of Riddle 25.[32] It is difficult to say what we are to make of these parallels. Some see evidence here of the underlying sexual aggression and power involved in Judith's decapitation of Holofernes, while others consider these coincidences as just that: flukes from which we may draw no firm conclusions.[33] Others focus on the significance of the hair itself: for example, are we to read *wundenlocc* as part of the heroic register, "noble-sounding language," or as a "racial marker" for the Hebrew people, of which Judith is the leader?[34] More to the point for a discussion of Riddle 25 is Peter Lucas's observation that "what is significant about the word applied to a woman is that the hair is described at all," since there were rigid church strictures against women exposing their hair.[35] Might mention of a woman's hair alone titillate an Anglo-Saxon audience? Susan Kim takes this observation to its logical conclusion when she writes of Riddle 25, "The connotation of *wundenlocc,* in the context of onion's shagginess 'underneath,' and in this highly sexual context, is clearly pubic hair."[36] Certainly Kim is right to see the erotic duplicity of these curly or braided locks, but the question remains, whose hair is being described here?

Attention to riddling traditions suggests a surprising answer. Archer Taylor's collection of oral riddles supplies us with innumerable examples of root vegetables described as "women with braided hair." According to Taylor, such riddles usually are solved as "an onion, a leek, a beet, a carrot, or a

32. Ibid., line 325a.

33. See especially John P. Hermann, *Allegories of War: Language and Violence in Old English Poetry* (Ann Arbor: University of Michigan Press, 1989), 190–95. Lori Ann Garner, for one, believes that "the sample for comparison is too small to read any connection into the fact," though she does find it suggestive that both Judith and the wanton lady of Riddle 25 are "very powerful figures" (at least from the onion's perspective). Garner, "The Art of Translation in the Old English *Judith,*" *Studia Neophilologica* 73 (2001): 181.

34. For the former, see Hugh Magennis, "Gender and Heroism in the Old English *Judith,*" in *Writing Gender and Genre in Medieval Literature,* ed. Elaine Treharne (Cambridge: D. S. Brewer, 2002), 14. For the latter, see Heide Estes, "Feasting with Holofernes: Digesting Judith in Anglo-Saxon England," *Exemplaria* 15 (2003): 325.

35. Peter J. Lucas, "*Judith* and the Woman Hero," *Yearbook of English Studies* 22 (1992): 19.

36. Susan Kim, "Bloody Signs: Circumcision and Pregnancy in the Old English *Judith,*" *Exemplaria* 11 (1999): 299. Howell Chickering notes that "in the obscene Riddle 25 'wundenlocc' (curly-haired) describes a woman's pubic hair." Chickering, "Poetic Exuberance in the Old English *Judith,*" *Studies in Philology* 106 (2009): 120.

radish," the same set of vegetables associated in the analogues cited above for the motif of "standing in the bed." Taylor cites more than thirty instances of this well-attested conceit, but a few examples will suffice to suggest the common pattern. A carrot riddle reads, "She stands in the earth and her braids show green on the earth." The vegetable's position buried in the earth is often compared to imprisonment, recalling the position of Riddle 25's speaker *on fæsten* 'in confinement'—for example, this beet riddle: "A red maiden, she sits in prison, but her braids hang out." Many such examples clearly betray an erotic edge: "Cock in the hole and the braids outside" describes a beet, while a related riddle on the same topic, "I have a thing with its beard downward and its leg up," comes close to the *neoþan ruh nathwær* 'down below there's hair (I know not where)' description of the creature of Riddle 25.[37] Such analogues strongly suggest that critics may have been too quick to identify the *wif wundenlocc* with the *modwlonc meowle* 'haughty maid' who plucks the onion. Is a double take needed for this riddle's duplicity?

And yet the text seems to say that the woman with braided hair feels the impact of her meeting with the speaker (*mec* in 10). Notice, however, the ambiguity of these lines: "Feleð sona / mines gemotes se þe mec nearwað, / wif wundenlocc" (Straightaway, [someone] feels my contact, the one who confines me, a woman with braided hair). *Wif,* a neuter noun, might be considered to be in apposition *either* with the subject, *se þe* (*mec nearwað*) 'the one who (confines me)', *or* with the accusative object *mec.*[38] And so the lines may quite reasonably be translated, "Straightaway, the one who confines me feels my contact, [me] a woman with braided hair." Note too that this line has often suffered unnecessary emendation: MS *se þe* is altered to *seo þe.* Tupper, Williamson, and most recently Muir all thus emend "so that there is agreement between the relative and its antecedent."[39] But no

37. All analogues cited here are from Taylor, *English Riddles from Oral Tradition,* 196. Others may be found in Sadovnikov, *Riddles of the Russian People,* nos. 765–66, 772a–772e. With respect to the weepy conclusion of Riddle 25, witness this Polish riddle cited in a separate article by Taylor: "A German woman came in red garments. When they stripped her, they wept over her." Taylor, "Varieties of Riddles," 4. In "The Riddle," as an example of a riddle "defeating the hearer with an innocent answer," Taylor cites the following onion riddle: "I have a little maiden, and when I undress her, I weep" (133).

38. Orchard admirably preserves this ambiguity in his translation: "she soon feels it, her encounter with me, the one who confines me, the curly-locked lady." "Enigma Variations," 297.

39. Muir, *Exeter Anthology,* 1:592. Noting the only occasional "triumph of natural over grammatical gender" in Old English, Bruce Mitchell, *Old English Syntax,* 2 vols. (Oxford:

such emendation is required if we understand this as a general statement of onion potency, such as we have in the creature's declaration not to harm anyone save his slayer: "[Anyone] who confines me will straightaway perceive my contact, [me] a woman with braided hair."

It is true that the apparent narrative momentum of the riddle argues against this reading. If we go here by our standard model of "double entendre," the woman with braided hair can only be read as the doughty daughter, but that is to treat the riddle as if it were something other than a riddle. There is no single referent for any of the eyes, hairs, or heads in the riddle. Nor is there any incongruity in calling a phallic vegetable a *wif*. As Senderovich points out, it is quite possible in traditional riddles for a female creature to be suggestive of a penis.[40] Reading Riddle 25 as a highly allusive poem with deep roots in tradition, this *wif wundenlocc* may take on a versatile role more akin to the "southern man" of Riddle 62 and the *wonfeax wale* 'dark-haired slave woman' of Riddle 12 and Riddle 52. If so, these Old English sex riddles would be heir to a venerable line of braided conceits.

And so the *wundenlocc* woman is not simply the onion, nor is she only the daughter, for even solved, these riddles resist clear-cut resolution. There is no sequence of real events behind these chains of riddling games and allusions, after all. A discrete riddle within a collection of riddles, Riddle 25 itself might be called a kind of riddling anthology, its themes drawn from disparate sources and layered together with care. Like so many of these so-called obscene texts, the onion's sufferings dramatize the body's proud potential to dominate the imagination. And while readers may have found various pleasures in unriddling its images, Riddle 25's most scrupulous solvers would surely have tolerated, even appreciated, its comic deflation of sexual pride and the mischief of old riddles serving a new master. An enigma wrapped in riddles, Riddle 25 is also a text that hangs together remarkably well, but not on account of a coherent backstory. Rather, its Symphosian core of an onion's caustic revenge shapes the poem from start to finish, so that, unlike many other suffering creatures of the Exeter Book, the speaker of Riddle 25 bites back and forces a tearful reaction from the eye of its tormenter. Such an ending may have struck an Anglo-Saxon

Oxford University Press, 1985), vol. 2, sec. 2356, calls the ASPR emendation of these lines "officious." Indeed, if my reading is accepted as plausible, this change goes beyond mere officiousness to destroy the riddling potential of the lines.

40. Senderovich, *Riddle of the Riddle*, 91.

reader as particularly appropriate, for in the context of Riddle 25's tale of tit for tat, this playful game of shifting eyes might easily evoke a phrase that had the force of proverb long before Anglo-Saxon England: the tooth for a tooth of Symphosius's bitten biter has become the Exeter Book's riddling eye for an eye.[41]

41. William Ian Miller points out that even Christ seems to think of the phrase as a proverbial distillation of the concept of *lex taliensis* when he quotes sacred scripture in the Sermon on the Mount: "quia dictum est oculum pro oculo et dentem pro dente" (therefore is it said "an eye for an eye and a tooth for a tooth"). Miller, *Eye for an Eye* (Cambridge: Cambridge University Press, 2006), 28.

AFTERWORD

A highly original response to very traditional materials and genres, the Exeter riddles are riddled with paradox. A varied collection, the riddles plunder the conceits of Latin literary *enigmata* and draw on traditional riddling modes and motifs. They redeploy riddling commonplaces in unlooked-for fashion, embedding innocent conceits (such as smoke as the sire of fire) within indecent propositions. They expand others (such as ice as the eternal, maternal daughter of water) into outlandish spectacles of familiar phenomena. At times they braid together well-worn riddling ideas (such as the various layers of onion enigmatics) in the creation of artfully allusive poems. They transform popular patterns of riddling (such as the transformation riddle) in the context of textual culture, and re-pose venerable riddling types (such as the riddle of the year) in the light of very precise forms of Anglo-Saxon learning. They provide new questions for ancient answers (such as Samson's lion), and rework old impossibilities (such as live chicks stripped of their skin) through the lens of fresh metaphors. They bring new complexity to obvious comparisons (such as the sun and the Son) and are quite capable of charging a few spare lines with both literal and figural significance. Above all, they challenge us to follow their tracks less by our own lights and more according to the dark wit of unfamiliar forms of riddling.

In this book I have argued that very precise metaphors play a larger role in Old English riddling than past solvers have guessed, and this argument implies paradoxes of its own. The Exeter riddles are not complete riddles, if we think of the genre as the problematic unity of a proposition and a solution (problematic in the sense of posing the implied solver a practical problem, yes, but also in the sense of the unstraightforward fit we must expect between the description and the answer). To read them as riddles, then, we must first solve them. And yet to solve them, we must place less stress on their solutions, for any coherent account of an Exeter riddle must do more than add up its literal clues. Unriddling the riddles requires interpreting other patterns behind their dark language. In fact, to read them as plainspoken descriptions is, in a sense, to "un-riddle" them—to interpret them as something unlike riddles. It is clear that we must account for their obscurity, though in the eclectic Exeter collection more than one strategy may be at play, even within a single text. Metaphor, however, is frequently the key. Unspoken metaphors often lend a shape and coherence to the dark language and imagery of these elegant poems, selecting, filtering, and distorting elements of their enigmatic descriptions. It seems to me that this has not usually been recognized or emphasized, in part because so many of these riddles have been deemed resolved through the evidence of one or two telltale clues, effectively obviating the need to understand their obfuscations. Knowing the solutions to the Exeter riddles, then, can prevent us from solving them in a broader sense. The bare solution does not solve an Old English riddle. The answer alone is not its interpretation.

That is not to say that all the riddles of the Exeter Book are best read as shaped by extended metaphors, but the approach I have pursued here may help explain aspects of the collection that have resisted an unforced reading or seemed to require a loose translation or a change in the text itself. If the sore side of a chicken, the warm limb of a bell, or the flight pattern of bright horses do not make literal sense, metaphors may help clarify such clues. At the same time, we may discover ways to reconcile readings that were previously considered in opposition, as mutually exclusive. Many of the readings I have proposed here suggest a share of insight for more than one past solver. Riddle 22 is not an enigma about *either* stars or passing time but a riddle about both. Riddle 29 resonates with Christian as well as natural significance. Riddle 4 may be an embattled *bord* in more than one sense. Riddle 57 is probably not a literal description of either black birds or dark written marks but a metaphor involving them both. The origins of ore in Riddle 83 may lie likewise both in the present and in the past. Riddling is an occasion for debate and dialogue, but good solutions have a way of reconciling opposing perspectives with a single solution. This, after all, is one thing that most makes riddles riddles.

But attempting to read the Old English riddles more like riddles also reveals them to be something more than riddles. Certainly readers have long wondered at their remarkable range. A collection so decked out with diversity—birds and books, bells and bookworms, beakers and barnacle geese, churns and chalices, coats of mail and layers of innuendo, fish in the river and ice in the water, the sun and the moon and the stars in the sky—is indeed a marvelous thing. As I have sought to show, though, the Exeter riddles glory not only in their variety of solutions but also in the intricacy of the links they reveal in the fabric of creation. The expansiveness of the collection is contained within the very mode of metaphorical riddling, its tendency to uncover elemental connections underlying the created world: airy letters in the sky, the living river of the soul, earthly violence buried in its origin. For such images alone, the Exeter riddles deserve a second look. It is easy, after all, to see how such texts would reward Anglo-Saxon solvers who once untangled the hidden similarities bound up in these texts, and it is no mystery why they would lavish such resources on mere riddles or why they prized these intricate poems.

The end of a riddle is marked as a challenge, a taunt, a tease, or perhaps even a crucial clue in its interpretation. The endings of the Exeter riddles are at times quite simple, demanding nothing more than *saga hwæt ic hatte* 'say what I am called'. Often, though, the riddles exchange for these formulas enigmatic codas that seem to suggest something more. The implied challenge might be, for instance, that a solver grasp a tantalizingly *þrindende þing* 'swelling thing', rising up in the mind and under the sheets. Others implicitly mock the riddlee as a clueless reader, a thoughtless *stælgiest* 'sneak thief', who is not "wihte þy gleawra þe he þam wordum swealg" (a whit the wittier for the words he has swallowed). Others suggest a weightier sense of the unknown, in keeping with the Exeter collection's expansive view of the enigmatic. Riddle 29, for instance, appears to pose a mystery of faith in its final lines—"Nænig siþþan / wera gewiste þære wihte sið" (No one afterwards knew the path of that being)—while the ending of Riddle 13 resonates with a reassuring promise that *hrægl bið geniwad* 'the garment will be renewed' for those who tread the earth. Other riddles conclude with no less haunting wonders of the written word. The last riddle in the book, the last text in the Exeter anthology, provides fitting final words:

Þeah nu ælda bearn,
londbuendra, lastas mine
swiþe secað, ic swaþe hwilum
mine bemiþe monna gehwylcum.

[Although now the children of men, of land dwellers, eagerly pursue my tracks, I nevertheless at times conceal my path from everyone.]

Here is an apt metaphor for the enduring allure and elusiveness of these enigmatic texts. The last page of a book is a good place to acknowledge the limitations of one's own wit, and I am at the end of mine. My best guess is that we will be pursuing these dark tracks for some time to come.

BIBLIOGRAPHY

Abbot, H. H., trans. *The Riddles of the Exeter Book.* Cambridge: Golden Head Press, 1968.

Abrahams, Roger D., and Alan Dundes. "Riddles." In *Folklore and Folklife: An Introduction,* ed. Richard M. Dorson, 129–43. Chicago: University of Chicago Press, 1972.

Adams, John F. "The Anglo-Saxon Riddle as Lyric Mode." *Criticism* 7 (1965): 335–48.

Ælfric. *Ælfric's Catholic Homilies: The Second Series.* Edited by Malcolm Godden. Early English Text Society SS 5. London: Oxford University Press, 1979.

———. *Ælfric's Colloquy.* Edited by G. N. Garmonsway. Exeter: University of Exeter Press, 1991.

———.*Ælfrics Grammatik und Glossar.* Edited by Julius Zupitza. Berlin: Weidmann, 1880.

———. *De temporibus anni.* Edited by Heinrich Henel. Early English Text Society 203. Oxford: Oxford University Press, 1942.

Afros, Elena. "Linguistic Ambiguities in Some Exeter Book *Riddles.*" *Notes and Queries,* n.s., 52 (2005): 431–37.

———. "Syntactic Variation in *Riddles 30a and 30b.*" *Notes and Queries,* n.s., 52 (2005): 2–5.

Aldhelm. *Prosa de virginitate.* Edited by Scott Gwara. Corpus Christianorum: Series Latina 124A. Turnhout: Brepols, 2001.

Alexander, Michael. *A History of Old English Literature.* Ontario: Broadview Press, 2002.

Anderson, Earl R. "The Uncarpentered World of Old English Poetry." *Anglo-Saxon England* 20 (1991): 65–80.

Anderson, James E. "Exeter Latin Riddle 90: A Liturgical Vision." *Viator* 23 (1992): 73–93.

———. Review of *Die altenglischen Rätsel des Exeterbuchs,* ed. and trans. Hans Pinsker and Waltraud Ziegler. *Speculum* 63, no. 4 (1988): 981.

———. *Two Literary Riddles in the Exeter Book.* Norman: University of Oklahoma Press, 1986.

———. "Two Spliced Riddles of the Exeter Book." *In Geardagum* 5 (1983): 57–75.

Anlezark, David, ed. and trans. *The Old English Dialogues of Solomon and Saturn.* Cambridge: D. S. Brewer, 2009.

Aristotle. *Poetics.* Translated by Ingram Bywater. New York: Random House, 1984.

Aristotle's legacy: or, his golden cabinet of secrets opened. London, 1699.

Artemiodorus. *Oneirocritica.* Translated by Robert J. White. Park Ridge, N.J.: Noyes Press, 1975.

Assmann, Bruno, ed. *Angelsächsische Homilien und Heiligenleben.* Kassel: Georg H. Wigand, 1889.

Athenaeus. *The Deipnosophists.* Translated by Charles Burton Gulick. London: Harvard University Press, 1957.

Bacon, A. M., and E. C. Parsons. "Folk-Lore from Elizabeth City County, Virginia." *Journal of American Folklore* 35 (1922): 250–327.

Bagwell, William. *Sphynx Thebanus, With his Oedipus: Or, Ingenious Riddles, With their Observations, Explications and Morals*. London, 1664.

Bammesberger, Alfred. "*Freo* 'Woman' in *Genesis,* Line 457a." *Notes and Queries,* n.s., 52 (2005): 282–84.

Barley, Nigel F. "Structural Aspects of the Anglo-Saxon Riddle." *Semiotica* 10 (1974): 143–75.

Basgöz, Ilhan, and Andreas Tietze, eds. *Bilmece: A Corpus of Turkish Riddles*. Folklore Studies 22. Berkeley and Los Angeles: University of California Press, 1973.

Baum, Paull F., trans. *Anglo-Saxon Riddles of the Exeter Book*. Durham: Duke University Press, 1963.

Bayless, Martha. "Alcuin's *Disputatio Pippini* and the Early Medieval Riddle Tradition." In *Humour, History, and Politics in Late Antiquity and the Early Middle Ages,* ed. Guy Halsall, 157–78. Cambridge: Cambridge University Press, 2001.

Bayless, Martha, and Michael Lapidge, eds. and trans. *Collectanea Pseudo-Bedae*. Scriptores Latini Hiberniae 14. Dublin: School of Celtic Studies, Dublin Institute of Advanced Studies, 1998.

Beckwith, Martha Warren. *Jamaica Anansi Stories*. New York: American Folk-Lore Society, 1924.

Bede. *De schematibus et tropis*. Edited by C. B. Kendall. In Bede, *De orthographia,* ed. Charles W. Jones. Corpus Christianorum: Series Latina 123A. Turnhout: Brepols, 1975.

———. *On Genesis*. Translated by Calvin B. Kendall. Liverpool: Liverpool University Press, 2008.

Ben-Amos, Dan. "Solutions to Riddles." *Journal of American Folklore* 89 (1976): 249–54.

Ben Johnson's last legacy to the sons of wit, mirth, and jollytry. London, 1756.

Bennett, J. A. W. *Poetry of the Passion*. Oxford: Clarendon Press, 1982.

Bevington, David, ed. *Medieval Drama*. Boston: Houghton Mifflin, 1975.

Bhattacharji, Santha. "An Approach to Christian Aspects of *The Wanderer* and *The Seafarer*." In *The Christian Tradition in Anglo-Saxon England,* ed. Paul Cavill, 153–61. Cambridge: D. S. Brewer, 2004.

Biblia sacra iuxta vulgatam versionem. 3d ed. Edited by Robert Weber. 2 vols., paginated consecutively. Stuttgart: Deutsche Bibelgesellschaft, 1983.

Bierbaumer, Peter, and Elke Wannagat. "Ein neuer Lösungsvorschlag für ein altenglisches Rätsel (Krapp-Dobbie 17)." *Anglia* 99 (1981): 379–82.

Bitterli, Dieter. "Exeter Book Riddle 15: Some Points for the Porcupine." *Anglia* 120 (2002): 461–87.

———. *Say What I Am Called: The Old English Riddles of the Exeter Book and the Anglo-Latin Riddle Tradition*. Toronto: University of Toronto Press, 2009.

———. "The Survival of the Dead Cuckoo: Exeter Book *Riddle* 9." In *Riddles, Knights, and Cross-Dressing Saints,* ed. Thomas Honegger, 95–114. Bern: Peter Lang, 2004.

Black, Max. *Models and Metaphors*. Ithaca: Cornell University Press, 1962.

Blackburn, F. A. "The *Husband's Message* and the Accompanying Riddles of the Exeter Book." *Journal of Germanic Philology* 3 (1901): 1–13.

Blakeley, L. "Riddles 22 and 58 of the Exeter Book." *Review of English Studies,* n.s., 9 (1958): 241–52.

Bland, Desmond, ed. *Gesta Grayorum*. Liverpool: Liverpool University Press, 1968.

Blauner, D. G. "The Early Literary Riddle." *Folklore* 78 (1967): 49–58.

Boggs, Ralph Steele. "North Carolina White Folktales and Riddles." *Journal of American Folklore* 47 (1934): 289–328.

Book of a Hundred Riddles. London: W. Rastell, [1530?].

The Booke of Meery Riddles. London, 1629.

Booke of Merrie Riddles. London, 1631.

Boryslawski, Rafal. "The Elements of Anglo-Saxon Wisdom Poetry in the *Exeter Book* Riddles." *Studia Anglica Posnaniensia* 38 (2002): 35–47.

Bosworth, Joseph, and T. Northcote Toller. *An Anglo-Saxon Dictionary*. Oxford: Oxford University Press, 1898.

Bradley, Henry. "Two Riddles of the Exeter Book." *Modern Language Review* 6 (1911): 433–40.

Bradley, James. "St. Joseph's Trade and Old English *smiþ*." *Leeds Studies in English* 22 (1991): 21–42.

Bremmer, Rolf H., Jr., and Kees Dekker. "Leiden, Universiteitsbibliotheek, Vossianus Lat. Q. 106." In *Anglo-Saxon Manuscripts in Microfiche Facsimile,* vol. 13, ed. A. N. Doane, 107–11. Tempe: Arizona Center for Medieval and Renaissance Studies, 2006.

Brett, Cyril. "Notes on Old and Middle English." *Modern Language Review* 22 (1927): 257–64.

Brewer, Elizabeth. *Sir Gawain and the Green Knight: Sources and Analogues*. Cambridge: D. S. Brewer, 1992.

Brooke, Stopford A. *English Literature: From the Beginning to the Norman Conquest*. New York: Macmillan, 1898.

———. *The History of Early English Literature*. New York: Macmillan, 1892.

Brown, George H. "The Psalms as the Foundation of Anglo-Saxon Learning." In *The Place of the Psalms in the Intellectual Culture of the Middle Ages,* ed. Nancy van Deusen, 1–24. Albany: State University of New York Press, 1999.

Brown, Ray. "The Exeter Book's *Riddle 2:* A Better Solution." *English Language Notes* 29, no. 2 (1991): 1–3.

Bryant, Mark, ed. *Riddles: Ancient and Modern*. New York: Peter Bedrick Books, 1984.

Butler, Robert M. "Glastonbury and the Early History of the Exeter Book." In *Old English Literature in Its Manuscript Context,* ed. Joyce Tally Lionarons, 173–215. Medieval European Studies 5. Morgantown: West Virginia University Press, 2004.

Caillois, Roger. "Riddles and Images." *Yale French Studies* 41 (1968): 148–58.

Calder, Daniel G. "Histories and Surveys of Old English Literature: A Chronological Review." *Anglo-Saxon England* 10 (1982): 201–44.

Carroll, Lewis. *Alice in Wonderland*. Edited by Donald J. Gray. New York: W. W. Norton, 1971.

———. *The Annotated Alice*. With an introduction and notes by Martin Gardner. New York: Clarkson N. Potter, 1960.

Carruthers, Mary. *The Book of Memory: A Study of Memory in Medieval Culture*. Cambridge: Cambridge University Press, 1990.

Cassidorus. *An Introduction to Divine and Human Readings*. Translated and edited by Leslie Webber Jones. New York: Columbia University Press, 1946.

Chappell, L. W. "Riddle Me, Riddle Me, Riddle Me Ree." In *Folk-Say: A Regional Miscellany,* ed. B. A. Botkin, 227–38. Norman: University of Oklahoma Press, 1930.

Chaucer. *The Riverside Chaucer*. Edited by Larry D. Benson. Boston: Houghton Mifflin, 1987.

Chickering, Howell. "Poetic Exuberance in the Old English *Judith*." *Studies in Philology* 106 (2009): 119–36.

Cicero. *Les aratea*. Edited by Victor Buescu. Hildesheim: Georg Olms, 1966.

Cochran, Shannon Ferri. "The Plough's the Thing: A New Solution to Old English Riddle 4 of the Exeter Book." *Journal of English and Germanic Philology* 108 (2009): 301–9.

Cockayne, Oswald, ed. *Leechdoms, Wortcunning, and Starcraft of Early England*. 3 vols. London: Longman, Green, Longman, Roberts, and Green, 1864–66.

Coleman, Julie. "Sexual Euphemism in Old English." *Neuphilologische Mitteilungen* 93 (1992): 93–98.

Conlee, John Wayne. "Artistry in the Riddles of the *Exeter Book*." PhD diss., University of Illinois, 1968.

Conner, Patrick W. *Anglo-Saxon Exeter: A Tenth-Century Cultural History*. Studies in Anglo-Saxon History 4. Woodbridge, Suffolk, UK: Boydell Press, 1993.

Considine, John. "Two Riddles by Sir Philip Sidney and Their Solutions." *English Language Notes* 41, no. 2 (2003): 32–36.

Conybeare, John Josias. *Illustrations of Anglo-Saxon Poetry*. London: Harding and Lepard, 1826.

Cook, Albert S. "Recent Opinion Concerning the Riddles of the Exeter Book." *Modern Language Notes* 7 (1892): 20–21.

Cook, Eleanor. *Enigmas and Riddles in Literature*. Cambridge: Cambridge University Press, 2006.

———. "Riddles of Procreation." *Connotations* 8 (1998–99): 269–82.

Crawford, S. J., ed. *The Old English Version of the Heptateuch, Ælfric's Treatise on the Old and New Testament, and His Preface to Genesis*. Early English Text Society, o.s., 160. London: Oxford University Press, 1922.

Cray, Ed. *The Erotic Muse*. Urbana: University of Illinois Press, 1992.

Cross, James E., ed. *Two Old English Apocrypha and Their Manuscript Source: The Gospel of Nichodemus and the Avenging of the Saviour*. Cambridge: Cambridge University Press, 1996.

Cross, James E., and Thomas D. Hill, eds. *The Prose Solomon and Saturn and Adrian and Ritheus*. Toronto: University of Toronto Press, 1982.

Crossley-Holland, Kevin, trans. *The Exeter Book Riddles*. London: Penguin Books, 1993.

———, trans. *Storm*. New York: Farrar, Straus and Giroux, 1970.

Crossley-Holland, Kevin, and Lawrence Sail, eds. *The New Exeter Book of Riddles*. London: Enitharmon Press, 1999.

Daly, Lloyd William, and Walther Suchier, eds. *Altercatio Hadriani Augusti et Epicteti philosophi*. Illinois Studies in Language and Literature 24. Urbana: University of Illinois Press, 1939.

Davidson, H. R. Ellis. *The Sword in Anglo-Saxon England*. Oxford: Clarendon Press, 1962.

Davis, Glenn. "The Exeter Book Riddles and the Place of Sexual Idiom in Old English Literature." In *Medieval Obscenities*, ed. Nicola McDonald, 39–54. York: York Medieval Press, 2006.

Delights for young Men and Maids. London, 1725.

Dendle, Peter. *Satan Unbound: The Devil in Old English Narrative Literature*. Toronto: University of Toronto Press, 2001.

Dewa, Roberta J. "The Runic Riddles of the Exeter Book: Language Games and Anglo-Saxon Scholarship." *Nottingham Medieval Studies* 39 (1995): 26–36.

Dictionary of Old English: A–G on CD-ROM. Edited by Angus Cameron, Ashley Crandell Amos, Antonette de Paolo Healey, et al. Toronto: Pontifical Institute of Mediaeval Studies, for the Dictionary of Old English Project, 2008.

Dietrich, Franz. "Die Räthsel des Exeterbuchs: Verfasser, weitere Lösungen." *Zeitschrift für Deutsches Alterthum* 12 (1865): 232–52.

———. "Die Räthsel des Exeterbuchs: Würdigung, Lösung, und Herstellung." *Zeitschrift für Deutsches Alterthum* 11 (1859): 448–90.

DiNapoli, Robert. "In the Kingdom of the Blind, the One-Eyed Man Is a Seller of Garlic: Depth-Perception and the Poet's Perspective in the Exeter Book Riddles." *English Studies* 81 (2000): 422–55.

Doane, A. N., ed. *Genesis A: A New Edition.* Madison: University of Wisconsin Press, 1978.

———. "The Other Anglo-Saxons." *Queen's Quarterly* 86 (1979): 302–13.

———. "Spacing, Placing, and Effacing: Scribal Textuality and Exeter Riddle 30 a/b." In *New Approaches to Editing Old English Verse,* ed. Sarah Larratt Keefer and Katherine O'Brien O'Keeffe, 45–65. Cambridge: D. S. Brewer, 1998.

———. "Three Old English Implement Riddles: Reconsiderations of Numbers 4, 49, and 73." *Modern Philology* 84 (1987): 243–57.

Dobbie, Elliott van Kirk. *The Anglo-Saxon Minor Poems.* Anglo-Saxon Poetic Records 6. New York: Columbia University Press, 1942.

Donatus. *Ars grammatica.* Edited by Heinrich Keil. *Grammatici Latini,* vol. 4. Leipzig: Teubner, 1864.

Donoghue, Daniel. "An *Anser* for Exeter Book Riddle 74." In *Words and Works: Studies in Medieval English Language and Literature in Honour of Fred C. Robinson,* ed. Peter S. Baker and Nicholas Howe, 45–58. Toronto: University of Toronto Press, 1998.

———. *Old English Literature: A Short Introduction.* Oxford: Blackwell, 2004.

Dorst, John D. "Neck-Riddle as a Dialogue of Genres: Applying Bakhtin's Genre Theory." *Journal of American Folklore* 96 (1983): 413–33.

Edwards, Carol L. Review of *A Feast of Creatures: Anglo-Saxon Riddle-Songs,* trans. Craig Williamson. *Western Folklore* 43, no. 2 (1984): 144–46.

Ehwald, Rudolf. *Aldhelmi opera.* Monumenta Germaniae Historica: Auctores Antiquisimi 15. Berlin: Weidmann, 1919.

Eliason, Norman E. "Riddle 68 of the Exeter Book." In *Philologica: The Malone Anniversary Studies,* ed. Thomas A. Kirby and Henry Bosley Woolf, 18–19. Baltimore: Johns Hopkins University Press, 1949.

Eliot, Kamilla. *Rethinking the Novel/Film Debate.* Cambridge: Cambridge University Press, 2003.

Erhardt-Siebold, Erika von. "An Archaeological Find in a Latin Riddle of the Anglo-Saxons." *Speculum* 7 (1932): 252–56.

———. The Old English Hunt Riddles." *PMLA* 63 (1948): 3–6.

———. "The Old English Loom Riddles." *Philologica: The Malone Anniversary Studies,* ed. Thomas A. Kirby and Henry Bosley Woolf, 9–17. Baltimore: Johns Hopkins University Press, 1949.

———. "Old English Riddle 13." *Modern Language Notes* 65 (1950): 97–100.

———. "Old English Riddle No. 57: OE *Cā 'Jackdaw.'" *PMLA* 42 (1947): 1–8.

———. "Old English Riddle 95." *Modern Language Notes* 62 (1947): 558–59.

Estes, Heide. "Feasting with Holofernes: Digesting Judith in Anglo-Saxon England." *Exemplaria* 15 (2003): 325–50.

Eugenio, Damiana L. *Philippine Folk Literature: The Riddles*. Diliman, Quezon City: University of the Philippines Press, 1994.

Fanger, Claire. "A Suggestion for a Solution to Exeter Book Riddle 55." *Scintilla* 2–3 (1985): 19–28.

Finch, Chauncey E. "The Bern Riddles in Codex Vat. Reg. Lat. 1553." *Transactions and Proceedings of the American Philological Association* 92 (1961): 145–55.

Foley, John Miles. "How Genres Leak in Traditional Verse." In *Unlocking the Wordhord: Anglo- Saxon Studies in Memory of Edward B. Irving, Jr.*, ed. Mark C. Amodio and Katherine O'Brien O'Keeffe, 76–108. Toronto: University of Toronto Press, 2003.

———. *Immanent Art*. Bloomington: Indiana University Press, 1991.

———. "Riddles 53, 54, and 55: An Archetypal Symphony in Three Movements." *Studies in Medieval Culture* 10 (1977): 25–31.

Förster, Max. "Ein altenglisches Prosa-Rätsel." *Archive für das Studium der Neueren Sprachen und Literaturen* 115 (1905): 392–93.

———. "Das älteste mittellateinische Gesprächbüchlein." *Romanische Forschungen* 27 (1910): 343–48.

———. "The Donations of Leofric to Exeter." In *The Exeter Book of Old English*, 10–32. London: Percy Lund, Humphries, 1933.

———. "General Description of the Manuscript." In *The Exeter Book of Old English*, 55–67. London: Percy Lund, Humphries, 1933.

Fowler, Alastair. *Kinds of Literature*. Oxford: Oxford University Press, 1982.

Frank, Roberta. "Sex in the *Dictionary of Old English*." In *Unlocking the Wordhord: Anglo-Saxon Studies in Memory of Edward B. Irving, Jr.*, ed. Mark C. Amodio and Katherine O'Brien O'Keeffe, 302–12. Toronto: University of Toronto Press, 2003.

———. "Some Uses of Paronomasia in Old English Scriptural Verse." *Speculum* 47 (1972): 207–26.

Fraser, H. Malcolm. *Beekeeping in Antiquity*. London: University of London Press, 1931.

Friedman, John Block. *The Monstrous Races in Medieval Art and Thought*. Cambridge: Harvard University Press, 1981.

Frow, John. *Genre*. New York: Routledge, 2006.

Fry, Donald K. "Exeter Book Riddle Solutions." *Old English Newsletter* 15, no. 1 (1981): 22–33.

Frye, Northrop. *Spiritus Mundi: Essays on Literature, Myth, and Society*. Bloomington: Indiana University Press, 1976.

Gameson, Richard. "The Origin of the Exeter Book of Old English Poetry." *Anglo-Saxon England* 25 (1996): 135–85.

Garde, Judith N. *Old English Poetry in Medieval Christian Perspective: A Doctrinal Approach*. Cambridge: D. S. Brewer, 1991.

Garner, Lori Ann. "The Art of Translation in the Old English *Judith*." *Studia Neophilologica* 73 (2001): 171–83.

Georges, Robert A., and Alan Dundes. "Toward a Structural Definition of the Riddle." *Journal of American Folklore* 76 (1963): 111–18.

Girsch, Elizabeth Stevens."Metaphorical Usage, Sexual Exploitation, and Divergence in the Old English Terminology for Male and Female Slaves." In *The Work of Work: Servitude, Slavery, and Labor in Medieval England*, ed. Allen J. Frantzen and Douglas Moffat, 30–54. Glasgow: Cruithne Press, 1994.

Glorie, Frans, ed., *Variae collectiones aenigmatum Merovingicae aetatis*. 2 vols., paginated consecutively. Corpus Christianorum: Series Latina 133 and 133a. Turnhout: Brepols, 1968.

Göbel, Helga. *Studien zu den altenglischen Schriftwesenrätseln*. Würzburg: Königshausen und Neumann, 1980.

Goldstein, Kenneth S. "Riddling Traditions in Northeastern Scotland." *Journal of American Folklore* 76 (1963): 330–36.

Green, Thomas A., and W. J. Pepicello. "Wit in Riddling: A Linguistic Perspective." *Genre* 11 (1978): 1–13.

Greenfield, Stanley B. *The Interpretation of Old English Poems*. London: Routledge and Kegan Paul, 1972.

———. "Old English Riddle 39 Clear and Visible." *Anglia* 98 (1980): 95–100.

Griffith, Mark. "Exeter Book Riddle 74 *Ac* 'Oak' and *Bat* 'Boat'." *Notes and Queries* 55 (2008): 393–96.

———. "Riddle 19 of the Exeter Book: SNAC, an Old English Acronym." *Notes and Queries,* n.s., 237 (1992): 15–16.

Gwara, Scott, and Barbara L. Bolt. "A 'Double Solution' for Exeter Book Riddle 51, 'Pen and Three Fingers.'" *Notes and Queries,* n.s., 54 (2007): 16–19.

Haist, Margaret. "The Lion, Bloodline, and Kingship." In *The Mark of the Beast: The Medieval Bestiary in Art, Life, and Literature,* ed. Debra Hassig, 3–22. New York: Garland, 1999.

Halsall, Maureen. *The Old English Rune Poem: A Critical Edition*. Toronto: University of Toronto Press, 1981.

Hamnett, Ian. "Ambiguity, Classification, and Change: The Function of Riddles." *Man,* n.s., 2 (1967): 379–92.

Hansen, Elaine Tuttle. *The Solomon Complex: Reading Wisdom in Old English Poetry*. Toronto: University of Toronto Press, 1988.

Harbus, Antonina. "*Exeter Book Riddle 39* Reconsidered." *Studia Neophilologica* 70 (1998): 139–48.

Hayes, Mary. "The Talking Dead: Resounding Voices in Old English Riddles." *Exemplaria* 20 (2008): 123–42.

Hermann, John P. *Allegories of War: Language and Violence in Old English Poetry*. Ann Arbor: University of Michigan Press, 1989.

Heyworth, Melanie. "The Devil's in the Detail: A New Solution to Exeter Book Riddle 4." *Neophilologus* 91 (2007): 175–96.

———. "Perceptions of Marriage in *Exeter Book Riddles 20 and 61*." *Studia Neophilologica* 79 (2007): 171–84.

Hieatt, Constance B. "The Harrowing of Mermedonia: Typological Patterns in the Old English 'Andreas.'" *Neuphilologische Mitteilungen* 77 (1976): 49–62.

Higley, Sarah L. "The Wanton Hand: Reading and Reaching into Grammars and Bodies in Old English Riddle 12." In *Naked Before God: Uncovering the Body in Anglo-Saxon England,* ed. Benjamin C. Withers and Jonathan Wilcox, 29–59. Morgantown: West Virginia University Press, 2003.

Hill, David. "Anglo-Saxon Mechanics. 1. blæstbel(i)g—The Bellows." *Medieval Life* 13 (2000): 9–13.

———. "Cyrn: The Anglo-Saxon Butter Churn." *Medieval Life* 15 (2001): 19–20.

Hill, Thomas D. "The Old English Dough Riddle and the Power of Women's Magic: The Traditional Context of Exeter Book Riddle 45." In *Via Crucis: Essays on*

Early Medieval Sources and Ideas in Memory of J. E. Cross, ed. Thomas N. Hall, 50–60. Morgantown: West Virginia University Press, 2002.

———. "A Riddle on the Three Orders in the *Collectanea Pseudo-Bedae?*" *Philological Quarterly* 80 (2001): 205–12.

———. "Saturn's Time Riddle: An Insular Latin Analogue for *Solomon and Saturn II,* Lines 282–91." *Review of English Studies,* n.s., 39 (1988): 273–76.

Hoffman, David, and Sharon Hoffman. "Enigma, Paradox, Parable." *Parabola* 25, no. 2 (2000): 14–21.

Holthausen, F. "Ein altenglisches Rätsel." *Germanisch-Romanische Monatsschrift* 15 (1927): 453–54.

Hough, Carole. "Place-Name Evidence for Anglo-Saxon Plant-Names." In *From Earth to Art: The Many Aspects of the Plant-World in Anglo-Saxon England,* ed. C. P. Biggam, 47–78. Costerus, n.s., 148. Amsterdam: Rodopi, 2003.

Howard, Elizabeth. "Modes of Being in Anglo-Saxon Riddles." *In Geardagum* 25 (2005): 61–77.

Howe, Nicholas. "Aldhelm's *Enigmata* and Isidorian Etymology." *Anglo-Saxon England* 14 (1985): 37–59.

Hudson, Arthur Palmer. "Some Folk Riddles from the South." *South Atlantic Quarterly* 42 (1943): 78–93.

Hull, Vernam E., and Archer Taylor. *A Collection of Irish Riddles.* Folklore Studies 6. Berkeley and Los Angeles: University of California Press, 1955.

———. *A Collection of Welsh Riddles.* University of California Publications in Modern Philology 26. Berkeley and Los Angeles: University of California Press, 1942.

Hyatt, Harry Middleton. *Folk-Lore from Adams County, Illinois.* New York: Memoirs of the Alma Egan Hyatt Foundation, 1935.

Hyginus. *De astronomia.* Edited by Ghislaine Viré. Leipzig: Teubner, 1992.

Igarashi, Michelle. "Riddles." In *A Companion to Old and Middle English Literature,* ed. Laura Cooner Lambdin and Robert Thomas Lambdin, 336–51. Westport, Conn.: Greenwood Press, 2002.

Irvine, Martin. *The Making of Textual Culture: "Grammatica" and Literary Theory (350–1100).* Cambridge: Cambridge University Press, 1994.

Irving, Edward B., Jr. "Heroic Experience in the Old English Riddles." In *Old English Shorter Poems: Basic Readings,* ed. Katherine O'Brien O'Keeffe, 199–212. New York: Garland, 1994.

Isidore. *De natura rerum.* Edited by G. Becker. Berlin: C. Schutzii, 1857. Reprint, Amsterdam: A. M. Hakkert, 1967.

———. *The Etymologies of Isidore of Seville.* Translated by Stephen A. Barney, W. J. Lewis, J. A. Beach, and Oliver Berghof. Cambridge: Cambridge University Press, 2006.

———. *Opera omnia.* Edited by Faustino Arevalo. Patrologi;ae Cursus Completus: Series Latina 83. Paris: J.-P. Migne, 1850.

Jacobs, Nicholas. "The Old English 'Book-Moth' Riddle Reconsidered." *Notes and Queries* 35 (1988): 290–92.

Jember, Gregory K. "A Generative Method for the Study of Anglo-Saxon Riddles." *Studies in Medieval Culture* 11 (1977): 33–39.

———. "An Interpretive Translation of the Exeter Riddles." PhD diss., University of Denver, 1975.

———. *The Old English Riddles.* Denver: Society for New Language Study, 1976.

———. "Riddle 57: A New Proposal." *In Geardagum* 2 (1977): 68–71.

Jerome. *Opera omnia*. Edited by Jacques-Paul Migne. Patrologi;ae Cursus Completus: Series Latina 25. Petit-Montrouge [Paris]: J.-P. Migne, 1845.

Johnson, David F. "Riddles, Old English." In *Medieval England: An Encyclopedia,* ed. Paul E. Szarmach, M. Teresa Tavormina, and Joel T. Rosenthal, 642–43. New York: Garland, 1998.

Jonassen, Frederick B. "The Pater Noster Letters in the Poetic *Solomon and Saturn*." *Modern Language Review* 83 (1988): 1–9.

Jordan, Louis. "Demonic Elements in Anglo-Saxon Iconography." In *Sources of Anglo-Saxon Culture,* ed. Paul E. Szarmach, with Virginia Darrow Oggins, 283–317. Studies in Medieval Culture 20. Kalamazoo: Medieval Institute Publications, 1986.

Joyce, John J. "Natural Process in *Exeter Book* Riddle #29: 'Sun and Moon.'" *Annuale Mediaevale* 14 (1974): 5–8.

Kaske, Robert E. "A Poem of the Cross in the Exeter Book: 'Riddle 60' and 'The Husband's Message.'" *Traditio* 23 (1967): 41–71.

Kay, Donald. "Riddle 20: A Revaluation." *Tennessee Studies in Literature* 13 (1968): 133–39.

Kiernan, K. S. "*Cwene:* The Old Profession of Exeter Riddle 95." *Modern Philology* 72 (1975): 97–99.

———. "The Mysteries of the Sea-Eagle in Exeter Riddle 74." *Philological Quarterly* 54 (1975): 518–22.

Kim, Susan. "Bloody Signs: Circumcision and Pregnancy in the Old English *Judith*." *Exemplaria* 11 (1999): 285–308.

Klaeber, Frederick, ed. *Beowulf and the Fight at Finnsburg*. 3d ed. Lexington, Mass.: D. C. Heath, 1950.

Klein, Thomas. "The Old English Translation of Aldhelm's Riddle *Lorica*." *Review of English Studies,* n.s., 48 (1997): 345–49.

Klinck, Anne. L. *The Old English Elegies: A Critical Edition and Genre Study*. Montreal: McGill-Queen's University Press, 1992.

Knortz, Karl. *Streifzüge auf dem Gebiete amerikanischer Volkskunde*. Leipzig: E. Wartigs Verlag E. Hoppe, 1902.

Korhammer, Michael. "The Last of the Exeter Book Riddles." In *Bookmarks from the Past: Studies in Early English Language and Literature in Honour of Helmut Gneuss,* ed. Lucia Kornexl and Ursula Lenker, 69–80. Oxford: Peter Lang, 2003.

Krapp, George Philip, ed. *The Junius Manuscript*. Anglo-Saxon Poetic Records 1. New York: Columbia University Press, 1931.

———, ed. *The Vercelli Book*. Anglo-Saxon Poetic Records 2. New York: Columbia University Press, 1932.

Krapp, George Philip, and Elliott van Kirk Dobbie, eds. *The Exeter Book*. Anglo-Saxon Poetic Records 3. New York: Columbia University Press, 1936.

Kries, Susanne. "*Fela í rúnum eða í skáldskap:* Anglo-Saxon and Scandinavian Approaches to Riddles and Poetic Disguises." In *Riddles, Knights, and Cross-Dressing Saints,* ed. Thomas Honegger, 139–64. Bern: Peter Lang, 2004.

Kristensen, Evald Tang. *Danske Folkegaader*. Struer, Denmark: M. Christensens Bogtrykkeri, 1913.

Krouse, Michael F. *Milton's Samson and the Christian Tradition*. Princeton: Princeton University Press, 1949.

Kuhn, Sherman M. *The Vespasian Psalter.* Ann Arbor: University of Michigan Press, 1965.

Kurath, Hans, and Sherman M. Kuhn, eds. *Middle English Dictionary.* Ann Arbor: University of Michigan Press, 1952.

Lapidge, Michael. *The Anglo-Saxon Library.* Oxford: Oxford University Press, 2006.

———. "Stoic Cosmology and the Source of the First Old English Riddle." *Anglia* 112 (1994): 1–25.

Lapidge, Michael, and James L. Rosier, trans. *Aldhelm: The Poetic Works.* Cambridge: D. S. Brewer, 1985.

Law, Vivien. *Grammar and Grammarians in the Early Middle Ages.* London: Longman, 1997.

Le Goff, Jacques. *Medieval Civilization, 400–1500.* Translated by Julia Barrow. Oxford: Basil Blackwell, 1988.

Lendinara, Patrizia. "E se B Stesse per *Bana?* Una nuova interpretazione dell'enigma n. 17 del Codice Exoniense." *Annali Sezione Germanica* 18 (1975): 161–81.

Lepschy, Giulio. "History of the Italian Language." In *Encyclopedia of Italian Literary Studies,* vol. 1, ed. Gaetana Marrone, 967–70. New York: Routledge, 2007.

Lerer, Seth. "The Riddle and the Book: Exeter Book Riddle 42 in Its Contexts." *Papers on Language and Literature* 25 (1989): 3–18.

Lester, G. A. "*Sindrum Begrunden* in Exeter Book Riddle No. 26." *Notes and Queries,* n.s., 38 (1991): 13–15.

Lieber, Michael D. "Riddles, Cultural Categories, and World View." *Journal of American Folklore* 89 (1976): 255–65.

Liebermann, Felix. "Das angelsächsische Rätsel 56: 'Galgen' als Waffenständer." *Archiv für das Studium der neuren Sprachen und Literaturen* 114 (1905): 163–64.

Liuzza, Roy Michael. "The Texts of the Old English *Riddle 30.*" *Journal of English and Germanic Philology* 87 (1988): 1–15.

Lucas, Peter J. "*Judith* and the Woman Hero." *Yearbook of English Studies* 22 (1992): 17–27.

Machan, Tim William, and Robyn G. Peterson. "The Crux of Riddle 53." *English Language Notes* 24, no. 3 (1987): 7–14.

Mackie, W. S., ed. and trans. *The Exeter Book.* 2 vols. Early English Text Society, o.s., 194. Oxford: Oxford University Press, 1934.

Macrobius. *Commentary on the Dream of Scipio.* Translated by William Harris Stahl. New York: Columbia University Press, 1966.

———. *Macrobius: The Saturnalia.* Translated by Percival Vaughan Davies. New York: Columbia University Press, 1969.

Magennis, Hugh. "Gender and Heroism in the Old English *Judith.*" In *Writing Gender and Genre in Medieval Literature,* ed. Elaine Treharne, 5–18. Cambridge: D. S. Brewer, 2002.

Maranda, Elli Köngäs. "Riddles and Riddling: An Introduction." *Journal of American Folklore* 89 (1976): 127–37.

Marckwardt, Albert H., and James L. Rosier. *Old English Language and Literature.* New York: W. W. Norton, 1972.

Marino, Matthew. "The Literariness of the *Exeter Book* Riddles." *Neuphilologische Mitteilungen* 79 (1978): 258–65.

Marsden, Richard. "'Ask What I Am Called': The Anglo-Saxons and Their Bibles." In *The Bible as Book: The Manuscript Tradition,* ed. John L. Sharpe III and Kimberly van Kampen, 145–76. London: British Library, 1998.

Martianus Capella. *Martianus Capella and the Seven Liberal Arts.* Vol. 2, *The Marriage of Philology and Mercury.* Translated by William Harris Stahl and Richard Johnson, with E. L. Burge. New York: Columbia University Press, 1977.

Maximus of Turin. *Maximi episcopi Taurinensis sermones.* Edited by Almut Mutzenbecher. Corpus Christianorum: Series Latina 23. Turnhout: Brepols, 1962.

McCarthy, Marcella. "A Solution to Riddle 72 in the Exeter Book." *Review of English Studies,* n.s., 44 (1993): 204–10.

McCluskey, Stephen C. *Astronomies and Cultures in Early Medieval Europe.* Cambridge: Cambridge University Press, 1998.

Meaney, Audrey L. "Birds on the Stream of Consciousness: Riddles 7 to 10 of the Exeter Book." *Archaeological Review from Cambridge* 18 (2002): 119–52.

———. "Exeter Book Riddle 57 (55)—a Double Solution?" *Anglo-Saxon England* 25 (1996): 187–200.

The Merry Fellow: A Collection of the Best Modern Jests, Comic Tales, Poems, Fables, Epigrams, Epitaphs, and Riddles. London, 1754.

Miller, William Ian. *Eye for an Eye.* Cambridge: Cambridge University Press, 2006.

Mish, Charles C., ed. *Restoration Prose Fiction: 1666–1700.* Lincoln: University of Nebraska Press, 1970.

Mitchell, Bruce. *Old English Syntax.* 2 vols. Oxford: Oxford University Press, 1985.

Muir, Bernard J., ed. *The Exeter Anthology of Old English Poetry.* Vols. 1–2. Exeter: University of Exeter Press, 2000.

Müller, L. C. *Collectanea Anglo-Saxonica.* Copenhagen: Libraria Wahliana, 1835.

Murray, Hilda M. R., ed. *The Middle English Poem, Erthe upon Erthe.* Early English Text Society, o.s., 141. London: Oxford University Press, 1911.

Musgrave, Elaine K. "Cithara as the Solution to Riddle 31 of the Exeter Book." *Pacific Coast Philology* 37 (2002): 69–84.

Nelson, Marie. "The Paradox of Silent Speech in the Exeter Book Riddles." *Neophilologus* 62 (1978): 609–15.

———. "Plus Animate: Two Possible Transformations of Riddles by Symphosius." *Germanic Notes* 18, nos. 3–4 (1987): 46–48.

———. "The Rhetoric of the Exeter Book Riddles." *Speculum* 49 (1974): 421–40.

———. "Social Functions of the Exeter Book Riddles." *Neophilologus* 75 (1991): 445–50.

———. "Time in the Exeter Book Riddles." *Philological Quarterly* 54 (1975): 511–18.

———. "Tolkien's 'Orthanc' and Exeter Book Riddle 83: An Ecological Connection." *Germanic Notes and Reviews* 31, no. 1 (2000): 18–24.

A New Booke of Merry Riddles. London, 1665.

Nicol, Alexander. *Nature without art: Or, Nature's progress in poetry. Being a collection of miscellaney poems.* Edinburgh, 1739.

Niles, John D. *Old English Enigmatic Poems and the Play of the Texts.* Turnhout: Brepols, 2006.

Norton, F. J. "The Prisoner Who Saved His Neck with a Riddle." *Folk-Lore* 53 (1942): 27–57.

Noyes, Dorothy. "Riddle." In *Encyclopedia of Folklore and Literature,* ed. Mary Ellen Brown and Bruce A. Rosenberg, 550–53. Santa Barbara: ABC-CLIO, 1998.

———. "Riddle Joke." In *Folklore: An Encyclopedia of Beliefs, Customs, Tales, Music, and Art,* ed. Thomas A. Green, 730–32. Santa Barbara: ABC-CLIO, 1997.

O'Brien O'Keeffe, Katherine. "The Text of Aldhelm's *Enigma* no. c in Oxford, Bodleian Library, Rawlinson C. 697 and Exeter Riddle 40." *Anglo-Saxon England* 14 (1985): 61–73.

———. *Visible Song: Transitional Literacy in Old English Verse.* Cambridge: Cambridge University Press, 1990.

Obrist, Barbara. "Wind Diagrams and Medieval Cosmology." *Speculum* 72 (1997): 33–84.

Ohl, Raymond Theodore, ed. and trans. *The Enigmas of Symphosius.* PhD diss., University of Pennsylvania, 1928.

Ohlgren, Thomas H. "Five New Drawings in the *MS Junius 11:* Their Iconography and Thematic Significance." *Speculum* 47 (1972): 227–33.

Okasha, Elisabeth. "Old English *hring* in Riddles 48 and 59." *Medium Ævum* 62 (1993): 61–69.

O'Neill, Patrick P. *King Alfred's Old English Prose Translation of the First Fifty Psalms.* Cambridge, Mass.: Medieval Academy of America, 2001.

Orchard, Andy. "Enigma Variations: The Anglo-Saxon Riddle-Tradition." In *Latin Learning and English Lore: Studies in Anglo-Saxon Literature for Michael Lapidge,* ed. Katherine O'Brien O'Keeffe and Andy Orchard, 2 vols., 1:284–304. Toronto: University of Toronto Press, 2005.

———. *The Poetic Art of Aldhelm.* Cambridge Studies in Anglo-Saxon England 8. Cambridge: Cambridge University Press, 1994.

———. *Pride and Prodigies: Studies in the Monsters of the Beowulf-Manuscript.* Cambridge: D. S. Brewer, 1995.

Orton, Peter. "The Technique of Object-Personification in *The Dream of the Rood* and a Comparison with the Old English *Riddles.*" *Leeds Studies in English,* n.s., 11 (1980): 1–15.

Osborn, Marijane. "Anglo-Saxon Tame Bees: Some Evidence for Bee-Keeping from Riddles and Charms." *Neuphilologische Mitteilungen* 107 (2006): 271–83.

———. "Old English Ing and His Wain." *Neuphilologische Mitteilungen* 81 (1980): 388–89.

———. "'Skep' (*Beinenkorb, *beoleap*) as a Culture-Specific Solution to *Exeter Book* Riddle 17." *ANQ* 18, no. 1 (2005): 7–18.

Parkes, M. B. "The Manuscript of the Leiden Riddle." *Anglo-Saxon England* 1 (1972): 207–17.

Parsons, Elsie Clews. *Folk-lore of the Antilles, French and English.* Memoirs of the American Folk-lore Society 26. New York: American Folk-Lore Society, 1943.

———. *Folk-lore of the Sea Islands, South Carolina.* Chicago: Afro-Am Press, 1969.

Pavlovskis, Zoja. "The Riddler's Microcosm: From Symphosius to St. Boniface." *Classica et Mediaevalia* 39 (1988): 219–51.

Peachy, Frederic, ed. and trans. *Clareti Enigmata: The Latin Riddles of Claret.* Folklore Studies 7. Berkeley and Los Angeles: University of California Press, 1957.

Pearsall, Derek A. "Rhetorical 'Descriptio' in 'Sir Gawain and the Green Knight.'" *Modern Language Review* 50 (1955): 129–34.

Peden, Alison M. "Macrobius and Mediaeval Dream Literature." *Medium Ævum* 14 (1985): 59–73.

Perrello, Tony. "An Undiscovered Riddle in Brussels, Bibliothèque Royale MS 1828–1830." *English Language Notes* 43, no. 2 (2005): 8–14.

Petsch, Robert. "Fifty Welsh-Gypsy Folk-Riddles." *Journal of the Gypsy Lore Society,* n.s., 5 (1911–12): 241–54.

Pinsker, Hans. "Neue Deutungen für zwei altenglische Rätsel (Krapp-Dobbie 17 und 30)." *Anglia* 91 (1973): 11–17.

Pinsker, Hans, and Waltraud Ziegler. *Die altenglischen Rätsel des Exeterbuchs*. Heidelberg: Carl Winter, 1985.

Pliny. *Natural History*. Edited by H. Rackham. Cambridge: Harvard University Press, 1956.

Pope, John C. "A Supposed Crux: Old English *apolwarum* in *Maxims I*." *Modern Philology* 93 (1995): 204–13.

———. "An Unsuspected Lacuna in the Exeter Book: Divorce Proceedings for an Ill-Matched Couple in the Old English Riddles." *Speculum* 49 (1974): 615–22.

Porter, David W. "Aethelwold's Bowl and the *Chronicle of Abingdon*." *Neuphilologische Mitteilungen* 97 (1996): 163–67.

———. "A Double Solution to the Latin Riddle in MS. Antwerp, Plantin-Moretus Museum M16.2." *American Notes and Queries* 9, no. 2 (1996): 3–9.

———, ed. *Excerptiones de Prisciano: The Source for Ælfric's Latin–Old English Grammar*. Anglo-Saxon Texts 4. Cambridge: D. S. Brewer, 2002.

Porter, John. *Anglo-Saxon Riddles*. Hockwold-cum-Wilton, Norfolk, UK: Anglo-Saxon Books, 1995.

Pound, Ezra. *Pisan Cantos*. New York: New Directions, 1948.

Powers, Luke. "Tests for True Wit: Jonathan Swift's Pen and Ink Riddles." *South Central Review* 7, no. 4 (1990): 40–52.

Praeger, S. Rosamond. "Rimes and Riddles from County Down." *Béaloideas: The Journal of the Folklore of Ireland Society* 8 (1938): 167–71.

Priscian. *Institutiones grammaticae*. Edited by Heinrich Keil. Grammatici Latini, vols. 2–3. Leipzig: Teubner, 1855.

Prudentius. *Dittochæum*. Edited by Jacques-Paul Migne. Patrologi;ae Cursus Completus: Series Latina 40. Petit-Montrouge [Paris]: J.-P. Migne, 1847.

Pulsiano, Phillip. *Old English Glossed Psalters: Psalms 1–50*. Toronto: University of Toronto Press, 2001.

Pulsiano, Phillip, and Kirsten Wolf. "*Exeter Book* Riddle 57: Those Damned Souls, Again." *Germanic Notes* 22, nos. 1–2 (1991): 2–5.

Puttenham, George. *The Arte of English Poesie* (1589). Edited by Gladys Doidge Willcock and Alice Walker. Cambridge: Cambridge University Press, 1936.

Raffel, Burton. "Six Anglo-Saxon Riddles." *Antioch Review* 20, no. 1 (1960): 52–54.

Rahner, Hugo. *Greek Myths and Christian Mystery*. London: Burns and Oates, 1963.

Randolph, Vance. *Pissing in the Snow and Other Ozark Folktales*. Urbana: University of Illinois Press, 1976.

Raw, Barbara C. *Anglo-Saxon Crucifixion Iconography*. Cambridge: Cambridge University Press, 1990.

Richards, I. A. *The Philosophy of Rhetoric*. New York: Oxford University Press, 1936.

Riché, Pierre. *Education and Culture in the Barbarian West*. Translated by John J. Contreni. Columbia: University of South Carolina Press, 1976.

Ridpath, Ian. *Star Tales*. New York: Walker, 1988.

Riedinger, Anita R. "The Formulaic Style in Old English *Riddles*." *Studia Neophilologica* 76 (2004): 30–43.

Riffaterre, Michael. *Semiotics of Poetry*. Bloomington: Indiana University Press, 1978.

Rigg, A. G., and G. R. Wieland. "A Canterbury Classbook of the Mid-Eleventh Century (the 'Cambridge Songs' Manuscript)." *Anglo-Saxon England* 4 (1975): 113–30.

Risden, Edward L. "Script-Based Semantic Theory of Humor and the Old English Riddles." *Publications of the Medieval Association of the Midwest* 8 (2001): 61–70.

Rissanen, Matti. "*Nathwæt* in the *Exeter Book Riddles.*" *American Notes and Queries* 24, nos. 7–8 (1986): 116–19.

Robbins, Rossell Hope, ed. *Secular Lyrics of the Fourteenth and Fifteenth Centuries.* Oxford: Clarendon Press, 1952.

Robinson, Fred C. "Artful Ambiguities in the Old English 'Book-Moth' Riddle." In *Anglo-Saxon Poetry: Essays in Appreciation for John C. McGalliard,* ed. Lewis E. Nicholson and Dolores Warwick Frese, 355–62. Notre Dame: University of Notre Dame Press, 1975.

Robson, Peter. "'Feorran Broht': Exeter Book Riddle 12 and the Commodification of the Exotic." In *Authority and Subjugation in Writing of Medieval Wales,* ed. Ruth Kennedy and Simon Meecham-Jones, 71–84. New York: Palgrave Macmillan, 2008.

Rolland, Eugéne. *Devinettes ou énigmes populaires de la France.* With a preface by Gaston Paris. Paris: F. Vieweg, 1877.

Rositzke, Harry August, ed. *The C-Text of the Old English Chronicles.* Beiträge zur Englischen Philologie 34. 1940. Reprint, New York: Johnson Reprint Corporation, 1967.

Rulon-Miller, Nina. "Sexual Humor and Fettered Desire in Exeter Book Riddle 12." In *Humour in Anglo-Saxon Literature,* ed. Jonathan Wilcox, 99–126. Cambridge: D. S. Brewer, 2000.

Russell, Jeffrey Burton. *Lucifer: The Devil in the Middle Ages.* Ithaca: Cornell University Press, 1984.

Ryan, William M. "Let the Riddles Be Your Key." *New Letters* 45 (1978): 107–12.

Sadovnikov, D. *Riddles of the Russian People.* Translated by Ann C. Bigelow. Ann Arbor: Ardis, 1986.

Salvador Bello, Mercedes. "Direct and Indirect Clues: Exeter Riddle No. 74 Reconsidered." *Neuphilologische Mitteilungen* 99 (1998): 17–29.

———. "The Evening Singer of Riddle 8 (K-D)." *SELIM: Journal of the Spanish Society for Medieval English Language and Literature* 9 (1999): 57–68.

———. "The Key to the Body: Unlocking Riddles 42–46." In *Naked Before God: Uncovering the Body in Anglo-Saxon England,* ed. Benjamin C. Withers and Jonathan Wilcox, 60–96. Morgantown: West Virginia University Press, 2003.

———. "*Nemnað hy sylfe:* A Crux in Exeter Riddle 57." *Old English Newsletter* 27, no. 3 (1994): A-21.

———. "The Oyster and the Crab: A Riddle Duo (nos. 77 and 78) in the *Exeter Book.*" *Modern Philology* 101 (2004): 400–419.

Sayers, William. "Exeter Book Riddle No. 5: Whetstone?" *Neuphilologische Mitteilungen* 97 (1996): 387–92.

Scattergood, John. "Eating the Book: *Riddle 47* and Memory." In *Text and Gloss: Studies in Insular Learning and Literature Presented to Joseph Donovan Pheifer,* ed. Helen Conrad O'Briain, Anne Marie D'Arcy, and John Scattergood, 119–27. Dublin: Four Courts Press, 1999.

Schlauch, Margaret. "The 'Dream of the Rood' as Prosopopoeia." In *Essays and Studies in Honour of Carleton Brown,* ed. P. W. Long, 23–34. New York: New York University Press, 1940.

Scott, Charles T. "On Defining the Riddle: The Problem of a Structural Unit." *Genre* 2 (1969): 129–42.

———. *Persian and Arabic Riddles: A Language-Centered Approach to Genre Definition.* Indiana University Research Center in Anthropology, Folklore, and Linguistics 39. Bloomington: Indiana University Press, 1965.

———. "Some Approaches to the Study of the Riddle." In *Studies in Language, Literature, and Culture of the Middle Ages and Later,* ed. E. Bagby Atwood and Archibald A. Hill, 111–27. Austin: University of Texas Press, 1969.

Scragg, Donald., ed. *The Battle of Maldon, AD 991.* Oxford: Basil Blackwell, 1991.

———. "A Late Old English Harrowing of Hell Homily from Worcester and Blickling Homily VII." In *Latin Learning and English Lore: Studies in Anglo-Saxon Literature for Michael Lapidge,* ed. Katherine O'Brien O'Keeffe and Andy Orchard, 2 vols., 2:197–211. Toronto: University of Toronto Press, 2005.

———, ed. *The Vercelli Homilies and Related Texts.* Early English Text Society, o.s., 300. Oxford: Oxford University Press, 1992.

The Second part of Merry drollery. London, 1661.

Senderovich, Savely. *The Riddle of the Riddle: A Study of the Folk Riddle's Figurative Nature.* London: Kegan Paul, 2005.

Seneca. *Physical Science in the Time of Nero: Being a Translation of the Quaestiones naturales of Seneca.* Translated by John Clarke. London: Macmillan, 1910.

Shippey, T. A. "'Grim Wordplay': Folly and Wisdom in Anglo-Saxon Humor." In *Humour in Anglo-Saxon Literature,* ed. Jonathan Wilcox, 33–48. Cambridge: D. S. Brewer, 2000.

Shook, Laurence K. "Old English Riddle No. 20: *Heoruswealwe.*" In *Franciplegius: Medieval and Linguistic Studies in Honor of Francis Peabody Magoun, Jr.,* ed. Jess B. Bessinger Jr. and Robert P. Creed, 194–204. New York: New York University Press, 1965.

———. "Riddles Relating to the Anglo-Saxon Scriptorium." In *Essays in Honour of Anton Charles Pegis,* ed. J. Reginald O'Donnell, 215–29. Toronto: Pontifical Institute of Mediaeval Studies, 1974.

Sievers, Eduard. "Zu Cynewulf." *Anglia* 13 (1891): 1–25.

Sims-Williams, Patrick. "Riddling Treatment of the 'Watchman Device' in *Branwen* and *Togail Bruidne Da Derga.*" *Studia Celtica* 12–13 (1977–78): 83–117.

Skeat, Walter W. *The Gospel According to Saint Matthew, in Anglo-Saxon, Northumbrian, and Old Mercian Versions.* Cambridge: Cambridge University Press, 1887.

Smith, D. K. "Humor in Hiding: Laughter Between the Sheets in the Exeter Book Riddles." In *Humour in Anglo-Saxon Literature,* ed. Jonathan Wilcox, 79–98. Cambridge: D. S. Brewer, 2000.

Smith, John. *Mystery of Rhetoric Unveiled.* London, 1657.

Sorrell, Paul. "Alcuin's 'Comb' Riddle." *Neophilologus* 80 (1996): 311–18.

———. "A Bee in My Bonnet: Solving Riddle 17 of the Exeter Book." In *New Windows on a Woman's World: Essays for Jocelyn Harris,* ed. Colin Gibson and Lisa Marr, 544–53. Dunedin, New Zealand: University of Otago Press, 2005.

———."Oaks, Ships, Riddles, and the Old English *Rune Poem.*" *Anglo-Saxon England* 19 (1990): 103–16.

Staal, Julius D. W. *Patterns in the Sky.* London: Hodder and Stoughton, 1961.

Stanley, Eric Gerald. "Heroic Aspects of the Exeter Book Riddles." In *Prosody and Poetics in the Early Middle Ages: Essays in Honour of C. B. Hieatt,* ed. M. J. Toswell, 197–218. Toronto: University of Toronto Press, 1995.

———. "Playing upon Words, II." *Neuphilologische Mitteilungen* 102 (2001): 451–68.

———. "Stanley B. Greenfield's Solution of *Riddle* (ASPR) 39: 'Dream.'" *Notes and Queries* 38 (1991): 148–49.

Stévanovitch, Colette. "Exeter Book Riddle 70a: Nose?" *Notes and Queries,* n.s., 42 (1995): 8–10.

Stevens, Wesley M. "Astronomy." In *The Blackwell Encyclopaedia of Anglo-Saxon England,* ed. Michael Lapidge et al., 50–52. Oxford: Blackwell, 2001.

Stewart, Ann Harleman. "The Diachronic Study of Communicative Competence." In *Current Topics in English Historical Linguistics,* ed. Michael Davenport, Eric Hansen, and Hans Frede Nielsen, 123–36. Odense, Denmark: Odense University Press, 1983.

———. "Double Entendre in the Old English Riddles." *Lore and Language* 3 (1983): 39–52.

———. "Kenning and Riddle in Old English." *Papers on Language and Literature* 15 (1979): 115–36.

———. "Old English Riddle 47 as Stylistic Parody." *Papers on Language and Literature* 11 (1975): 227–41.

———. "The Solution to Old English Riddle 4." *Studies in Philology* 78 (1981): 52–61.

Stork, Nancy Porter, ed. *Through a Gloss Darkly: Aldhelm's Riddles in the British Library MS Royal 12.C.xxiii.* Toronto: Pontifical Institute of Mediaeval Studies, 1990.

Swift, Jonathan. *Miscellanies.* London, 1753.

Tanke, John W. "The Bachelor-Warrior of Exeter Book Riddle 20." *Philological Quarterly* 79 (2000): 409–27.

———. "*Wonfeax wale:* Ideology and Figuration in the Sexual Riddles of the Exeter Book." In *Class and Gender in Early English Literature: Intersections,* ed. Britton J. Harwood and Gillian R. Overing, 21–42. Bloomington: Indiana University Press, 1994.

Tarlton, Richard. *Tarlton's newes out of purgatorie.* London, 1590.

Taylor, Archer. "Biblical Conundrums in the *Golden Era.*" *California Folklore Quarterly* 5 (1946): 273–76.

———. "A Bibliography of Riddles." *FF Communications* 53, no. 126 (1939): 5–32.

———. *English Riddles from Oral Tradition.* Berkeley and Los Angeles: University of California Press, 1951.

———. *The Literary Riddle Before 1600.* Berkeley and Los Angeles: University of California Press, 1948.

———. "The Riddle." *California Folklore Quarterly* 2 (1943): 129–47.

———. "A Riddle for the Sun, Sky, and Stars." *California Folklore Quarterly* 3 (1944): 222–31.

———. "The Varieties of Riddles." In *Philologica: The Malone Anniversary Studies,* ed. Thomas A. Kirby and Henry Bosley Woolf, 1–8. Baltimore: Johns Hopkins University Press, 1949.

Taylor, Keith P. "Mazers, Mead, and the Wolf's-Head Tree: A Reconsideration of Old English *Riddle* 55." *Journal of English and Germanic Philology* 94 (1995): 497–512.

Teale, Edwin Way. *The Strange Lives of Familiar Insects.* New York: Dodd, Mead, 1964.

Thorpe, Benjamin, ed. *Codex Exoniensis.* London: William Pickering, 1842.

Thrupp, John. *Anglo-Saxon Home: A History of the Domestic Institutions and Customs of England.* London: Longman, Green, Longman, and Roberts, 1862.

Tigges, Wim. "Signs and Solutions: A Semiotic Approach to the Exeter Book Riddles." In *This Noble Craft: Proceedings of the Tenth Research Symposium of the Dutch and*

Belgian University Teachers of Old and Middle English and Historical Linguistics, ed. Erik Kooper, 59–82. Costerus, n.s., 80. Amsterdam: Rodopi, 1991.

———. "Snakes and Ladders: Ambiguity and Coherence in the Exeter Book Riddles and Maxims." In *Companion to Old English Poetry,* ed. Henk Aertsen and Rolf H. Bremmer Jr., 95–118. Amsterdam: VU University Press, 1994.

Timmer, B. J., ed. *Judith.* Exeter: University of Exeter Press, 1978.

Toelken, Barre. "'Riddles Wisely Expounded': Poetic Ambiguity in the Riddle Songs." Chapter 6 in *Morning Dew and Roses.* Urbana: University of Illinois Press, 1995.

Tolkien, Christopher, ed. and trans. *The Saga of King Heidrek the Wise.* New York: Thomas Nelson and Sons, 1960.

Tolkien, J. R. R. "Beowulf: The Monsters and the Critics." In *Interpretations of Beowulf: A Critical Anthology,* ed. R. D. Fulk, 14–44. Bloomington: Indiana University Press, 1991.

Tolkien, J. R. R., and E. V. Gordon, eds. *Sir Gawain and the Green Knight.* 2d ed. Oxford: Oxford University Press, 1967.

Trahern, Joseph B., Jr. "The *Ioca Monachorum* and the Old English *Pharaoh.*" *English Language Notes* 7, no. 3 (1970): 165–68.

Trautmann, Moritz. "Alte und neue Antworten auf altenglische Rätsel." *Bonner Beiträge zur Anglistik* 19 (1905): 167–218.

———. "Die Auflösungen der altenglischen Rätsel." *Beiblatt zur Anglia* 5 (1894): 46–51.

———. "Cynewulf und die Rätsel." *Anglia Anzieger* 6 (1883): 158–69.

Treharne, Elaine, ed. *Old and Middle English: An Anthology.* Oxford: Blackwell, 2000.

Tristram, Hildegard L. C. "In Support of Tupper's Solution of the Exeter Book Riddle (Krapp-Dobbie) 55." In *Germanic Dialects: Linguistic and Philological Investigations,* ed. Bela Brogyanyi and Thomas Krömmelbein, 585–98. Amsterdam: John Benjamins, 1986.

Tucker, Susie I. "'Sixty' as an Indefinite Number in Middle English." *Review of English Studies* 25 (1949): 152–53.

Tully, Chris, trans. *Old English Poems and Riddles.* Manchester, UK: Carcanet Press, 2008.

Tupper, Frederick, Jr., ed. "The Holme Riddles (MS. Harl. 1960)." *PMLA* 18 (1903): 211–72.

———. "Originals and Analogues of the *Exeter Book Riddles.*" *Modern Language Notes* 18 (1903): 97–106.

———. "Riddles of the Bede Tradition: The 'Flores' of Pseudo-Bede." *Modern Philology* 2 (1904): 561–72.

———, ed. *The Riddles of the Exeter Book.* Boston: Ginn and Co., 1910.

Virtanen, Leea. "The Function of Riddles." In *Nordic Folklore: Recent Studies,* ed. Reimund Kvideland and Henning K. Sehmsdorf, 221–31. Bloomington: Indiana University Press, 1989.

Wagman, Morton. *Lost Stars.* Blacksburg, Va.: McDonald and Woodward, 2003.

Walker, Greg, ed. *Medieval Drama: An Anthology.* Oxford: Blackwell, 2000.

Walker-Pelkey, Faye. "'Frige hwæt ic hatte': 'The Wife's Lament' as Riddle." *Papers on Language and Literature* 28 (1992): 242–66.

Walter, Frank. "Language Structure and the Meanings of the *Exeter Book* Riddles." *Ball State University Forum* 19 (1978): 42–55.

Walz, John A. "Notes on the Anglo-Saxon Riddles." *Philology and Literature* 5 (1896): 261–68.

Wehlau, Ruth. *"The Riddle of Creation": Metaphor Structures in Old English Poetry.* New York: Peter Lang, 1997.

Wells, Richard. "The Old English Riddles and Their Ornithological Content." *Lore and Language* 2 (1978): 57–66.

Welsh, Andrew. "Riddle." In *Medieval Folklore: An Encyclopedia of Myths, Legends, Tales, Beliefs, and Customs,* vol. 2, ed. Carl Lindahl, John McNamara, and John Lindow, 824–32. Santa Barbara: ABC-CLIO, 2000.

———. *The Roots of Lyric.* Princeton: Princeton University Press, 1977.

———. "Swallows Name Themselves: Exeter Book Riddle 55." *ANQ* 3 (1990): 90–93.

Whitman, F. H. "Aenigmata Tatwini." *Neuphilologische Mitteilungen* 88 (1987): 8–17.

———. "The Christian Background to Two Riddle Motifs." *Studia Neophilologica* 41 (1969): 93–98.

———. "The Influence of the Latin and the Popular Riddle Traditions of the Old English Riddles of the Exeter Book." PhD diss., University of Wisconsin, 1968.

———. "Medieval Riddling: Factors Underlying Its Development." *Neuphilologische Mitteilungen* 71 (1970): 177–85.

———. "OE Riddle 74." *English Language Notes* 6, no. 1 (1968): 1–5.

———. "Riddle 60 and Its Source." *Philological Quarterly* 50 (1971): 108–15.

Wilbur, Richard. "The Persistence of Riddles." *Yale Review* 78 (1989): 333–51.

Wilcox, Jonathan. "Masters and Slaves: Servants of Desire in the Old English Riddles." Paper presented at the Thirty-fifth International Congress on Medieval Studies, Kalamazoo, May 2000. http://www2.kenyon.edu/AngloSaxonRiddles/Wilcox-.htm (accessed February 26, 2006).

———. "Mock-Riddles in Old English: Exeter Riddles 86 and 19." *Studies in Philology* 93 (1996): 180–87.

———. "New Solutions to Old English Riddles: Riddles 17 and 53." *Philological Quarterly* 69 (1990): 393–408.

———. " 'Tell me what I am': The Old English Riddles." In *Readings in Medieval Texts: Interpreting Old and Middle English Literature,* ed. David F. Johnson and Elaine Treharne, 46–59. Oxford: Oxford University Press, 2005.

Williams, David. *Cain and Beowulf: A Study in Secular Allegory.* Toronto: University of Toronto Press, 1982.

Williams, Edith Whitehurst. "Sacred and Profane: A Metaphysical Conceit upon a Cup." *In Geardagum* 13 (1992): 19–30.

———. "What's So New About the Sexual Revolution? Some Comments on Anglo-Saxon Attitudes Toward Sexuality in Women Based on Four Exeter Book Riddles." *Texas Quarterly* 18, no. 2 (1975): 46–55.

Williams, Gordon. *A Dictionary of Sexual Language and Imagery in Shakespearean and Stuart Literature.* London: Athlone Press, 1994.

Williamson, Craig, trans. *A Feast of Creatures: Anglo-Saxon Riddle-Songs.* Philadelphia: University of Pennsylvania Press, 1982.

———, ed. *The Old English Riddles of the Exeter Book.* Chapel Hill: University of North Carolina Press, 1977.

Willis, Jacob, ed. *Saturnalia.* Leipzig: Teubner, 1994.

Worde, Wynkyn de. *Demandes Joyous.* London, 1511.

Wossidlo, Richard. *Mecklenburgische Volksüberlieferungen.* Wismar: Hinstorff'sche Hofbuchhandlung Verlagsconto, 1897.

Wright, Charles D. "The Blood of Abel and the Branches of Sin: *Genesis A, Maxims I,* and Aldhelm's *Carmen de uirginitate.*" *Anglo-Saxon England* 25 (1996): 7–19.

———."The Persecuted Church and the *Mysterium Lunae.*" In *Latin Learning and English Lore: Studies in Anglo-Saxon Literature for Michael Lapidge,* ed. Katherine

O'Brien O'Keeffe and Andy Orchard, 2 vols., 2:293–314. Toronto: University of Toronto Press, 2005.

Wright, Thomas. *Biographia Britannica Literaria*. London: John W. Parker, 1842.

Wulfstan. *The Homilies of Wulfstan*. Edited by Dorothy Bethurum. Oxford: Clarendon Press, 1957.

Wyatt, A. J., ed. *Old English Riddles*. Boston: D. C. Heath, 1912.

Young, Jean I. "Riddle 15 of the Exeter Book." *Review of English Studies* 20 (1944): 304–6.

Youth's treasury; or, A store-house of wit and mirth. London, 1688.

Ziolkowski, Jan M. *Talking Animals: Medieval Latin Beast Poetry, 750–1150*. Philadelphia: University of Pennsylvania Press, 1993.

INDEX